Praise for *Getting to the Heart of Your Cha*

'An immensely valuable new book... [A] stimulating, exciting, life enhancing guide to the heart of astrology... Frank reminds us of the joy, excitement and awe of entering into dialogue with individuals and their chart.'
– Margaret Gray, *The International Astrologer*

'A book that many in the astrological community have been waiting for – it gives a unique insight into how a professional pulls together the many threads of a natal chart. There is just no other book on the market like it... The wealth of information in this book is simply breathtaking.'
– *The Astrological Journal*

'*Getting to the Heart of Your Chart* is an excellent textbook that offers a creative (and sometimes funny) approach to understanding the essence of a birth chart. Clifford states his intention to make "horoscope delineation straightforward and systematic". He does that with a very engaging voice and a real depth of experience in client work and research... This is a book I could only have dreamed about in the long-ago past when I began studying astrology and stumbled my way forward... His insights are so informed that even well-experienced astrologers will enjoy and learn from this book.'
– Mary Plumb, *The Mountain Astrologer*

'This book is absolutely jam-packed with ideas and information, including many original concepts that will come in particularly handy for those of you who teach... In addition to all this information, there are over 150 charts here – all discussed with enough depth to convince you that Clifford's approach to astrology works... Clifford is not only a good astrologer and data collector; he also writes very well. His brief biographies and case studies are very readable and not without humour.'
– Donna Van Toen, *NCGR Memberletter*

'This is the best modern teaching manual in person-centred astrology that I have come across. Condensing over 20 years of experience and learning into its 250 pages, replete with over 150 chart examples which dazzle the reader with their concision, wit and considerable educational value, Frank Clifford's aim of achieving an important contribution to astrological education has scored a direct hit... [The book is a] complete curriculum of tour de force astrology demonstrating to the reader exactly how to 'see' and think like an astrologer... [It contains] clarity, efficient articulation of thought, skilful writing, humour and freshness... Clifford has an almost addictive need to find the most apt phrase, precise epithet or description to capture the essence of an astrological placement... His wide teaching experience, relentless research and passion for astrology is here for all to share.'
– Astrologer Richard Swatton

'The text is underpinned by the principle of keeping things simple coupled with a delightful curiosity. It challenges you to really think about the core tenets you bring to your own astrology, offering you the opportunity to review and sharpen up some of the assumptions you might have made along the way... One reason that I enjoy Frank's work so much is his focus on understanding charts through people, whether through clients or biographies, and letting people "speak their charts"... I hugely enjoyed this book. It is peppered with so much astrological wisdom that you cannot read it without improving both your astrological knowledge and your astrological vocabulary... The astrology is simple, profound and devoid of complex technicalities.'
– Kathy Rogers, *Conjunction*

By the same author:

Birth Charts (due 2018)
The Frank Guide to Palm Reading (2017, revised edition of *Palm Reading*, Hamlyn, 2004)
Dialogues: Tools for the Working Astrologer with Mark Jones (mini-book, 2016)
The Midheaven: Spotlight on Success by Frank C. Clifford (mini-book, 2016)
Humour in the Horoscope: The Astrology of Comedy (mini-book, 2015)
The Astrology of Love, Sex and Attraction with Fiona Graham (mini-book, 2015,
     revised ed. of the *Venus* and *Mars* mini-books)
Solar Arc Directions (mini-book, 2011)
Palmistry 4 Today (2010, revised, expanded edition of the 2003 book published by Rider)
The Astrologer's Book of Charts (2009)
Palm Reading (2004)
Palmistry 4 Today (2002)
Venus: Your Key to Love (mini-book, 2000)
Mars: Your Burning Desires (mini-book, 2000)
The Essentials of Hand Analysis (mini-book, 1999)
British Entertainers: The Astrological Profiles (1997, 2003)
The Clifford Data Compendium (Solar Fire program, 1997, revised 2000)

Published by Flare Publications & The London School of Astrology:

The Horary Process by Richard Swatton (due 2018)
Vocational Astrology: Finding the Right Career Direction by Faye Blake (2017, revised ed. of
    Using Astrology to Create a Vocational Profile by Faye Cossar)
The Draconic Chart by Reverend Pamela Crane (1st ed., 2000; 2nd ed., 2013)
Astrology The New Generation: Essays from 14 Rising Stars of Astrology by various contributors (2012)
From Symbol to Substance: Training the Astrological Intuition by Richard Swatton (2012)
Kim Farley's Astro Mind Maps by Kim Farley (2010)
Jane Struthers' 101 Astrology Questions for the Student Astrologer by Jane Struthers (2010)
The Twelve Houses by Howard Sasportas (2007)
The Contemporary Astrologer's Handbook by Sue Tompkins (2006)
Jupiter and Mercury: An A to Z by Paul Wright (2006)
Astrology in the Year Zero by Garry Phillipson (2000)
The Sun Sign Reader by Joan Revill (2000)
Shorthand of the Soul: The Quotable Horoscope by David Hayward (1999)

All titles are available online and through the following websites:
www.frankclifford.co.uk
www.flareuk.com
www.londonschoolofastrology.co.uk

Getting to the Heart of Your Chart
Playing Astrological Detective

Frank C. Clifford

Flare Publications
The London School of Astrology

Small sections in this book were first published in edited form in
The Mountain Astrologer and *The Astrological Journal*.

Second edition published in 2017 by Flare Publications
in conjunction with the London School of Astrology
BCM Planets, London WC1N 3XX, England, UK

www.flareuk.com and www.londonschoolofastrology.co.uk
email: admin@londonschoolofastrology.co.uk

A CIP catalogue record for this book is available from the British Library

ISBN: 978-1-903353-10-3 (softcover)
978-1-903353-35-6 (ebook)

To contact the author, please email him at info@flareuk.com
www.flareuk.com

Cover: Tamara Stamenkovic
Text editing: Jane Struthers, Nan Geary, Sy Scholfield
Data and worksheet editing: Sy Scholfield, www.syscholfield.com
Diagrams: Craig Knottenbelt
Charts: Solar Fire (Esoteric Technologies)
Additional images: www.shutterstock.com, Corbis Images
Layout: Craig Knottenbelt and Frank Clifford

To Mario Trevino and Sue Harriet Smith

– with my love always

With the Sun conjunct my 11th House Venus in Aries and both opposite Uranus,
I have been extremely fortunate, during my twenty years or so as an astrologer,
to have come into contact with, and learned from, a number of highly intelligent,
dynamic, creative and inspirational women.

I dedicate this book to the following women – all astrologers I have been privileged
to learn from, and many of whom have become friends:

Lynne Beale, Lynn Bell, Faye Blake, Grazia Bordoni, Bernadette Brady, Linda Kubota Byrd,
Caroline Casey, Darby Costello, Pamela Crane, Sue Dibnah, Kim Farley, Fiona Graham,
Liz Greene, Jenni Harte, Dana Holliday, Deborah Houlding, Mavis Klein, Jessica Murray,
Dietrech Pessin, Melanie Reinhart, Lois Rodden, Wendy Stacey, Jane Struthers,
Erin Sullivan, Kira Sutherland and Sue Tompkins.

And my sincere thanks to those who supported me in creating and updating this book:
Mario Trevino, Nan Geary, Jane Struthers, Sy Scholfield, Tamara Stamenkovic, Albert Buga,
Michael Nile, Barry Street of The Astrology Shop in Covent Garden, and Craig Knottenbelt.
Finally, thanks to Paul Wright who, through his book *Astrology in Action*, helped open my
eyes as a novice astrologer to spotting themes and overtones in horoscopes.

Charts have been drawn in Equal houses (see the Introduction) and include the major aspects only (unless noted in the text) to the planets, ASC and MC. On occasion, to highlight a pertinent area of the chart, only aspect lines showing a specific configuration or aspect have been included.

Abbreviations:
ASC – Ascendant
DSC – Descendant
EQHS – Equal house
IC – Imum Coeli
MC – Midheaven
SA – Solar Arc
TR – transiting

CONTENTS

When looking at a birth chart, where do you start? How do you assess the most important areas and themes? How do you spot overtones and repetitive patterns in the horoscope?

It's easy – even for the astrologer with years of experience – to get lost in the detail and attempt to integrate so many areas of the horoscope that the major themes become obscured. This book is designed to help beginners, students and professional astrologers pinpoint the essential components, signatures and storylines of *any* horoscope.

Getting to the Heart of Your Chart focuses on the overtones, key aspects, imbalances and focal planets – the areas being underscored by repetition. It is not my intention to reduce the horoscope to a handful of key factors and miss the more subtle aspects of the chart (and its owner). Rather, I wish to show that once we've *prioritized* matters by locating the primary players of the horoscope, we discover that the major dynamics in the life story become clear. It makes our job as astrologers simpler and more effective.

This book is not a cookbook of interpretations or a guide to mix-and-matching planets in signs, houses and aspects. There are wonderful books around that do this (I've listed some in the Recommended Reading on page 234). It is a book about locating what's significant and then introducing examples to show 'astrology in action'.

In the upcoming chapters, I shall show you simple ways 'in' to the chart, methods to help you assess the important players in the drama, as well as the planets that work effectively.

You'll learn how to streamline the information but then, rather than employing a reductionist approach throughout, you'll be encouraged to flesh out the key material and shown how to interpret it.

Getting to the Heart of Your Chart has been designed to help readers learn to identify, prioritize and then synthesize the details found in any horoscope. Here are details of each of the six sections.

1. **Introducing the Tools**: the essential components found in every birth chart (the elements, modes, zodiac, planets, the four angles and twelve houses, the aspects). In this section, there are quick guides to understanding rulers and dispositors, retrogradation, and to interpreting the sequence of planets.

2. **Initial Considerations**: learning to spot the major planetary players in any horoscope, and gauging their influence and specific ways of functioning.

3. **Major Assessments**: a methodical 'way in' to assess the key areas of any birth chart. With the aid of numerous thumbnail biographies, you'll learn to:

   • Identify key planets or areas from the distribution of planets around the houses

   • Gauge the orientation of the 'compass' by considering the signs on the cusps of the four angles

   • Recognize the differences between (and dynamics of) the Sun, Moon and Ascendant (the 'Big Three')

   • Calculate the elemental and modal imbalances

   • Zoom in on the major aspects (the conjunction, square and opposition) in a horoscope

   • Analyse aspect configurations such as the T-square, Grand Cross and Grand Trine

   • Spot a chart's main overtones

4. **The Five Chart Themes**: with biographical sketches, you'll see how the chart themes (from modal imbalances to planetary overtones and configurations) manifest in the lives of well known people.

5. **Speaking Your Chart**: exploring biographies to build planetary profiles, playing detective with particular aspects, and having fun with astrological correspondences found in TV, music, books, crime and political speeches.

6. **Putting it All Together**: presenting five extended profiles and worksheets, and using biography to identify and synthesize key areas of each chart.

The Mercury Method

There are numerous ways to approach chart synthesis and interpretation. With my own chart being strongly Mercurial (Gemini Rising, Moon in Virgo in the 3rd, Mercury in the 10th), my approach and this book undoubtedly reflect this. Some astrologers start with the Sun, others with the Ascendant and then move on to the Chart Ruler. Some first weigh up the elements and modes, while others zoom in to a stellium or reach out intuitively to whatever 'speaks' to them. All of these are, in my opinion, valuable and there is no right or wrong way. (Saying that, I do advise students not to go straight to the Moon complex, because touching immediately on this highly sensitive area in consultation can do much harm.) Many astrologers don't work with clients, which is a matter for discussion in itself! Of course, there is no single, definitive way of reading a horoscope. With a good vocabulary, an effective technique and a thorough understanding of the main building blocks of the chart, all roads can lead to Rome.

Before any analysis begins, it's essential to know these major components – the signs, planets, houses, aspects – and to have a good idea of what constitutes a strongly positioned planet and an influential one. These form the first two sections of the book (Introducing the Tools, from page 16, and Initial Considerations, from page 46). Then, before analysing a chart, I like to see what stands out (such as singletons and elemental lacks) and which planetary themes repeat (from looking at the Sun–Moon–Ascendant trio to considering major aspect configurations). These form the basis of the Major Assessments section, which starts on page 50.

As working astrologers, it could be argued that we need be a little less of the social and outer planets. Please excuse the slight exaggeration that follows.

- A little less Uranus – where we become principals of the School for One True Astrology, where only the enlightened may enrol and there's an ironic contempt for different approaches.

- A little less Neptune – where any woolly statement can apply to anything and everything; where there is a lack of discrimination when judging the chart; and where consultations are given in order to save/rescue the client (and are done so over a five-hour marathon reading).

- A little less Jupiter – where we play the judgemental guru who holds all the answers and is keen to be seen as a great seer or prognosticator.

- A little less Saturn – with us as the astrologer who bleats and repeats doctrine to the point of being blind to new discoveries, progress or hundreds of years of new research; where we mechanically apply rigid rules based upon restrictive strictures, missing (or failing to have compassion for) the real person behind the chart; where judging the nativity becomes an excuse for judging the native or pigeonholing them into black-and-white categories.

- A little less Pluto – where we scare clients into thinking they don't have a hope in hell of changing their situation or avoiding their horrendous 'fate' or karma; where clients leave the consultation viewing the chart as an excuse for staying in a victim-based situation, giving power over to the heavens or the astrologer, and having heard the word 'abuse' once too often.

In my opinion, planet-wise, those of us wishing to use a person-centred astrology could benefit from looking closer to Earth and employing a little more Mercury. As consultant astrologers, we have a Mercurial job to do. In effect, this means we need to develop a good vocabulary, learn key phrases for planetary positions, and draw from a variety of examples from clients, friends and family.

By considering the lives and experiences of people we know, we witness how a Moon in Capricorn *reacts* or how Saturn on the IC *manifests* in a *variety* of ways across a *range* of people. Without numerous case studies, we end up reinforcing other astrologers' ideas and imposing stereotypes onto clients. Only by building up an arsenal of our own observations can we avoid plastering clients with planetary presumptions and astrological assumptions! By studying the charts of those who share similar life experiences, events or traits, we can look for common denominators in their charts.

We need to know *what means what* in the horoscope, and to be the go-between, the agent, the interpreter of symbols *with* the client. Most importantly, we need to ask for *context*. 'The truth is out there' – not simply in the birth chart, but in the person in front of us. It may be important to have phrases that we can use in consultation that begin to explain an aspect or planetary placement, but we need to listen to our clients and their stories. Rather than imposing a set of interpretations (based on chart factors) onto a person, we gain much more from a *dialogue* and listening to how clients use a particular aspect or placement. Only they can truly bring the chart to life, because without context we have a series of (nevertheless remarkable) symbols that have a spectrum of possible interpretations. The more clients we see and the more stories we hear from them, the more able we are to articulate certain placements (and their variations) when we next see a client who shares them. (For more on this Mercurial process, see Speaking Your Chart on page 114.)

And let's not forget the other inner planets, too. We need a little bit of Venus so we smell nice, appear reasonably groomed and don't look as if we've walked in from a field. And we need a little bit of the Moon so we can empathize, open our heart, imagine what it's like to live day to day with our client's chart, and remember that respect and compassion should override the desire to prognosticate, give advice or 'get it right'.

Well, He Would Say That, Wouldn't He?
This book has been written to offer one way – my particular method – of making horoscope delineation straightforward and systematic. My method comes from many years spent researching horoscopes and over twenty years of reading birth charts for clients. Astrologers have their own way of doing things and this reveals the type of person they are (and the chart they have). My way is expressive of the person I am and the astrologer I have become. I hope this method is useful but I also hope it helps you to find or develop your own style as an astrologer.

When interpreting a chart, we cannot ignore how our own charts, experiences and blind spots impact the way we see the world, as well as our general level of awareness and ability to view and live these symbols ourselves. On page 70, I have published my chart. There is little point in writing a book offering one's approach without showing the

astrological significators that lie behind it. Mine is a chart that has Mars and Mercury overtones and these two planets are concerned with making quick connections. My Mercury–Pluto opposition loves to dig deep, follow trails and play detective, and Saturn rising in Gemini and the Moon in Virgo are good significators for my love of researching biographies, collecting accurate data, and my desire to get to the heart – the very essence – of the chart so that it can be of use to clients.

No Chart is Difficult to Read!
The KISS Principle
Many years ago, when I was in my early twenties, I was invited to a masterclass in Los Angeles run by a well known astrologer. Those who attended were astrologers who had many years of experience. The workshop leader presented the chart of Hermann Hesse and someone immediately piped up, 'Oh, this is a difficult chart to understand'. The rest agreed and gave up trying to read it! This was an eye-opener for me: watching professionals struggle without a method of chart delineation and becoming quite defeatist in the process. Hesse's chart had some very key, simple themes that (even then, at age 23) I could see. Three planets were in Pisces and Jupiter was conjunct the Ascendant in Sagittarius, giving a Jupiterian overtone to the chart. Thinking that I couldn't possibly know as much as anyone else in the room and would just embarrass myself by speaking up, I kept quiet. I have regretted it ever since!

Nowadays, I don't think any chart is difficult to read. With a method, all charts can be taken apart, understood and then synthesized. It is important, particularly when starting the process of reading charts as a professional astrologer, to employ the KISS principle: keep it simple, sweetheart! In my opinion, the work of many astrologers can suffer from a proliferation of techniques and chart points. But when an *expert* astrologer is using quadriwheels or many extra chart points, they are usually doing so with tight orbs and a focus on specific areas that line up in the chart (the experienced astrologer Pamela Crane comes to mind). But many others, however, appear inundated with too many reference points so that *anything means anything*. Inevitably this creates chaos and delivers diminishing returns for clients.

I don't use the recently discovered bodies much yet or the asteroids, but I hope to spend more time researching them at some point. Over the years,

Pamela Crane has demonstrated some wonderfully clever links between asteroid names and the names of important people/places/things in our lives, so this intrigues me. Maybe soon the 'roids will be all the rage again, and many will accept that they don't detract from the essentials or dilute the chart, but rather they add *specific information*.

And here's something that really rankles: blind adherence to 'a system'. The more charts we read, the more we realize that set astrological significators written many years ago about what makes an eminent professional, a successful actor or an era-defining painter, for instance, no longer stand up to scrutiny. Perhaps part of this originates from a different understanding of what the birth chart can actually describe and the various external factors that must be taken into consideration. I sat aghast when one visiting tutor to my school dismissed a series of timed birth charts of presidents and prime ministers as incorrect because their charts didn't have the requisite positions for a world leader (according to the doctrine she followed). I was tempted to say, 'If these (accurately sourced) charts don't back up your presumptions, don't query the chart – simply find better tools.' Another rare lip-biting moment.

With the help of our winged messenger Mercury, we can look for patterns, make links and reveal connections. We can isolate essential themes and maintain, as the American astrologer Steven Forrest says, 'order, clarity and perspective'. (Steven has Saturn on a Virgo MC.) We need to study hundreds of charts to sharpen our tools. We need to organize our chart preparation and employ a reliable method of playing detective before we attempt to extract meaning from the horoscope. A tried and tested method is necessary but we need one that is open to some revision, as every new chart and biography will teach us something new and enrich our understanding of astrology in action. We'll have our own experiences of life and people to draw from, but we must begin with a method. As one astrologer wrote, 'Astrology makes the conversation between the heavens and earth audible.' Reading charts is a process of discovery *with* the client, weaving an on-going story with an unfolding narrative from the chart. And we are there to read the chart, not rewrite it!

House Systems
I have chosen to present charts in the Equal system of house division because over the years

I've found it superior when forecasting and interpreting, and it also gives me two additional tools: the nonagesimal and nadir, points at 90° to the Ascendant that begin the Equal 10th and 4th Houses respectively. Each of the twelve Equal house cusps aspect the Ascendant, making the natural/appropriate aspect with the signs involved (e.g. a chart with a Taurus Ascendant will have squares from the 10th and 4th House cusps in Aquarius and Leo respectively, signs that naturally square Taurus). In my observation, the most clearly noticeable planet-in-house interpretations come from when a planet is very close to an Equal house cusp, regardless of which of the two houses it occupies; it carries a powerful message of that planet-in-house interpretation and has an appropriate aspect back to the Ascendant.

But all techniques and ideas in this book can be used regardless of the house system – please use the one that works best for you! There is no right way, no 'only way'. In classes, I ask my students to test many charts in various house systems before choosing one they feel comfortable with, and to avoid simply opting for a system that appears, on the surface, to put their planets in 'better' houses.

I have stayed away from an emphasis on house interpretations, focusing instead on the four angles, planet–sign dynamics, and the aspectual dialogue between the planets. Major chart themes repeat in a number of ways, regardless of the house system chosen. For more on the houses, see pages 31–2.

Some Further Thoughts
An astrological chart is not a fait accompli, a set of irreversible characteristics and events. We are called upon to write our own biographies, to be the author of our lives. From the moment of birth, the chart may be 'fated' to receive transits, progressions and directions at fixed, predictable times, but the journey and numerous choices appear to be far from non-negotiable – we have available to us various routes around a particular terrain. Arguably, the horoscope reveals a *number* of treks across a particular landscape and many possible destinations. Dane Rudhyar referred to the chart as being 'a set of instructions' to enable us to use our basic energies to our best advantage. Each chart has the same tools (the signs, planets and houses) – indicating there is nothing in the human make-up that is foreign to us – but we have different options, territory and signposts. Astrologer Richard Swatton, considering the

various levels of correspondence in *From Symbol to Substance* (Flare, 2012), reminds us that these can be read on numerous levels: as objects, principles, feelings, emotions, attitudes, places, actions, professions and people.

Here's one of my few 'beliefs' about astrology. We are all born with a set of planets in specific signs, houses and in aspect to one another that reveals our drives and life scripts – a range of possible events, situations and encounters. We then meet life through people and circumstances that *bring out these drives and scripts*, encouraging us in many ways to become more of *who we were born to be*. Put another way, from birth, we encounter our horoscope's themes (our 'contract') in people and events in order for us to 'practise' ways of relating/living with our chart (see the final sections of each sign on pages 20–5). So, the man with Libra strong in his chart will encounter conflict early in life (e.g. a brother in dispute with the father, or the mother divorcing the father and asking the Libran boy to choose between them). This encourages him to put his birth chart to *use* and *fulfil his purpose* in life by resolving disputes, to flex his muscles as an arbitrator, to experience the importance of justice and making the right

decision from seemingly impossible choices. Ironically, for a sign that doesn't like discord, without dispute and division, Libra would not be engaging in a major part of his life purpose! An acceptance of our life challenges and meaning (as seen in the horoscope) is a major part of our journey, as is using our horoscope themes positively. (Noel Tyl puts it differently: planets are needs that require fulfilment.) We are drawn to life stories that express natal themes and these play out at specific times in our life (depending on transits or directions). With conscious awareness of our chart's themes, we end recurring patterns that no longer benefit us (i.e. we stop acting out unhelpful scripts) and start to experience/choose different ways of using these planetary placements.

We often gravitate towards others who have similar scripts, and they can play a part in helping us to pursue positive aspects of our chart and/or tear up negative scripts. Have a quick look at the chart of **Ted Kennedy** (below). On page 97, I write that his chart is strongly Neptune-themed (Sun in Pisces opposite a Moon–Neptune conjunction in Virgo). It comes as no surprise that his first wife, **Joan Kennedy** (chart pictured on the opposite page), has a Sun–Neptune–Venus conjunction rising in Virgo. Her Sun–Ascendant in Virgo opposes Saturn at 6° Pisces on the Descendant, tying in with Ted's Virgo–Pisces polarity (at 6° Virgo and 2° Pisces) and his own Saturn subtone (Capricorn Rising, Saturn in Capricorn in the 1st House).

The Neptune influence is key to Joan's biography: born to alcoholic parents (one of whom was an advertising executive), she became a model and musician. She married Ted Kennedy on 29 November 1958 (the day of her Jupiter Return and when the TR Sun had reached the couple's Sun midpoint of 6° Sagittarius). True to Neptune, they both battled alcohol addiction, suffered much heartache with calamities that befell their children, and when Ted damaged his back in a plane crash while on the campaign trail, Joan soldiered on (Saturn–Descendant in Pisces) and fulfilled his campaign-appearance schedule and met all the

Ted Kennedy

obligations. It was her Saturn Return. TR Saturn had stationed at 5° Pisces on her Descendant and opposed TR Uranus at 6° Virgo. Ted's flight from the Chappaquiddick drowning accident brought scandal and a third miscarriage for Joan. Sadly, after their divorce, she continued to battle chronic alcoholism, suffered alcohol-related injuries and was arrested for repeated drunk-driving incidents.

Context and Other Factors
There is much debate over what can be 'seen' in the horoscope; the chart is simply *a moment of time* – it could be a chart for anything (our chart does not belong to us, we belong to it, that moment of time). The astrologer must have *context* in order to read the chart appropriately – and even then, it contains numerous symbolic interpretations that could play out in all manner of ways.

Joan Kennedy

It helps to remember that there are many external, educational, cultural and social factors that affect how well someone expresses the potential inherent in their horoscope. (These external factors can to some extent be read from the chart or mundane/generational cycles around birth and through the lifetime.) Regardless of one's understanding of (or belief in) the pre- or afterlife, we could say that each of us 'chooses' a set of life experiences 'because' of our chart – 'My horoscope shows how I view life, and how I view life affects what I encounter' – but these choices are also affected by external conditions.

We can go further and say that, for instance, someone with a strongly placed Uranus may 'find' herself in an environment (appropriate to its placement) that she perceives as unjust and in need of shattering or waking up (functions of Uranus). She is, on a number of levels, seeking somewhere in which she can utilize her compulsion to speak out and be a catalyst for some sort of progressive action and change. It's the same under Uranus transits: there must be some stifling of self or restriction of circumstance to warrant a Uranus transit! Using this planet once again as an example, homosexuality is often associated with Uranus, in

part because of the planet's connection to differentness, deviancy and people 'on the outside'. As a simple correspondence, there is a good argument for this being the case – but only in a culture or society where same-sex love is considered different and deviant and homosexuals *are* on the outside. In the individual charts of gay men and women, I would argue that Uranus is strong only when the person finds themselves shattering expectations, perceptions and 'the norm' in their environment (e.g. a woman with Moon–Uranus who stirs up her small hometown by rejecting the conventions of marriage, family and domesticity and setting up home with her female lover).

But external factors so often dominate and shape our opportunities. What of a Uranian chart that suggests a highly revolutionary character/life for someone born into famine, where starvation and survival take precedence over 'speaking up' and standing up against injustice? This person may never experience much of what we consider to be Uranian, but with opportunity and longevity the chart will seek expression through its owner in some form that reflects this dominant planet.

Before we go any further, I'd like to share some information about the importance of using accurate data and obtaining full data sources when learning key concepts in astrology and presenting observations and research.

In the 1970s, there was a move by a few astrologers to publish large collections of birth data for the astrological community. These collections listed the sources of their information (for example, 'data from birth certificate'). Prior to this, astrologers rarely questioned the reliability of birth data in print, and so few verified data of public figures were available that collections were often indiscriminate compilations of speculative, rectified and unsourced information.

To this day, some books and articles list birth data *without* a source or fail to mention that the data are speculative or have been rectified. The reader has no idea whether the information is correct, so may naively trust and reuse inaccurate charts. Worse still, some may latch on to a chart because it 'fits' assumptions of what such a person should 'look like' in horoscope form.

Nowadays, there are accurate collections offering tens of thousands of data, and astrologers can perform number-crunching analyses to look for correlations and distinguish the repeatable from the coincidental. Using a computer, researchers wishing to consider astrology in quantitative terms can instantly select a few hundred horoscopes that have a key personality trait or event in common and put astrological theories to the test. In doing so, we have the potential to demolish and 'clean up' a number of assertions found in astrological 'cookbooks'.

Luckily for us, we have some die-hard, committed collectors in our community who still gather, source, rate and publish data. But it all began with one astrologer on a mission...

Modern Data Collecting

I was privileged to work with Lois Rodden for ten years, and also on her final book (a revised edition of *Profiles of Women*) and her regular newsletter *Data News*. Lois dedicated her working life to raising professional standards. Her own (rectified) chart has Saturn (as the handle of her bucket chart) on the MC in Sagittarius and her work acted as a benchmark for professionalism and accountability.

Lois's complaint was not with the use of rectified or speculative charts, if they were presented as such (although basing theories on inaccurate charts was cause for concern). The issue was (and remains) the lack of referencing of source data in astrological literature and presentations.

In her first data volume, *Profiles of Women* (AFA, 1979), she wrote:

> I implore astrologers everywhere to record the data source on every chart... Accuracy of data is essential to sound research, as well as to skilful delineation... Speculation and rectification are valid techniques in our business and, used skilfully, may constitute brilliant displays of astrological expertise. However, presentation of rectified data that are not designated as such is careless or presumptive and is an insult to the intelligence of our community.

Rodden was always a collector, beginning with index cards and files that read 'family', 'politicians', 'movie stars', and so on. Following the publication of her first data book, *Profiles of Women*, she became the central source for collectors to send in their contributions and exchange data, and for astrologers to retrieve data. Recognizing that data are volatile and subject to correction (even birth certificates can be error-prone), her newsletter, *Data News*, became a means to present new finds, bring information up to date and for her to connect with astrologers in 24 countries. With tenacity and diplomacy, Rodden was able to set standards of excellence in data collecting, and encourage writers and publications to adopt professional levels of reporting and data etiquette.

The Rodden Rating System
Her campaign to cite sources led many magazines (such as *The Mountain Astrologer*) to accept articles that were based only on accurate, sourced data. In addition to incorporating the work of many collectors

into her files, by 1980 Lois had also created and developed a simple system to rate the integrity of data. Her classification system would become data collecting's most significant and enduring contribution to astrological practice today. The ratings given below are now instantly recognized and widely used to indicate a 'shorthand' of data accuracy, as well as a writer's awareness of data etiquette and willingness to meet the professional standards set by Rodden.

AA Data from birth certificate, hospital, church or governmental birth record; notes from the Vital Statistic Registry Offices; notations in a family Bible, baby book or family written record. Although birth times may be rounded off or, on occasion, information may be in error, this is the best evidence of data accuracy.

A Data from the person, family member, friend or associate. Also included are newspaper birth announcements, as well as birth times given within a 'window of time' of sixty minutes (e.g. 'between 3.30 p.m. and 4.00 p.m.') from any of these sources.

B Data from biographies, autobiographies and personal websites, where no other source is given.

C Caution, data not validated. No source; vague, rectified/speculative data; 'personal' ambiguous sources; approximate birth times (e.g. 'early morning', 'around lunchtime').

DD Dirty Data. Two or more unsubstantiated quotes of time, place or date; unverified data contradicted by another source.

The thousands of data now available to astrologers were accumulated by a worldwide community of astrologers who have, for many years, found ingenious ways of tracking down and double-checking correct birth information, and have sniffed out rare data finds by writing to celebrities and Vital Records offices, wading through excerpts from interviews, sidestepping 'resumé' ages, and examining numerous badly handwritten birth records. David Fisher spent twelve years compiling and updating the British AA's data collection card index (some 5742 data), while fastidious researchers Tom and Thelma Wilson, Frances McEvoy, Stephen Przybylowski, Grazia Bordoni, the late Edwin Steinbrecher, and Sy Scholfield have tapped

remarkable veins of hard-to-get data for astrologers worldwide. Bordoni gathered an eclectic series of verified natal and mundane data, published in over twenty volumes. Steinbrecher wrote to birth registries in the US and Europe to collect thousands of additional newsworthy data (from celebrities to war criminals) and published his collection on the Pathfinder program. Today's most active collector, Sy Scholfield, has accumulated data on various websites (see http://astrodatablog.blogspot.co.uk) and created a new collection for Solar Fire. Dana Holliday amassed hundreds of serial killer and crime data by corresponding incognito with inmates, while media/celebrity astrologers Lynne Palmer, Fredrick Davies and Shelley Ackerman opened their files to share rare data. Doris Chase Doane and Nicholas Campion collected enormous amounts of mundane data while, in Edinburgh, Caroline Gerard and Paul Wright provided direct access to timed birth records in Scotland and created monumental works. For the launch of Astro-Databank and its *Data Collector's Handbook*, I called every state's principal Vital Records office in the US to determine the years that birth times appeared on birth certificates. We 'data freaks', as Rodden labelled us, have enjoyed this unpaid astrological labour of love for many years.*

Most importantly, the last sixty years of data collecting, storage and sharing have given student and working astrologers access to accurate, verified information. With this, we can build our astrological vocabulary, test our own theories and avoid falling into a derivative pattern of regurgitating the work of other astrologers or reinforcing stereotypes from past generations without question or update. Such data collections have also given lecturers and writers the opportunity to present observations and findings from accountable, verified sources – the lifetime wish and goal of many collectors worldwide. At the UAC before Rodden's death in 2003, Mark McDonough, her partner in Astro-Databank software, said, 'We as a community are blessed that Lois Rodden's life's passion has given us a cornerstone for rebuilding the respect that astrology so richly deserves.' It is up to us, as a community, to take advantage of this gift and build upon it.

* Due credit must go to the generous contributions of T. Pat Davis, Victoria Shaw, Eugene Moore, Tashi Grady, Janice Mackay, Robert Paige and Linda Clark of the US, and international colleagues André Barbault, Didier Geslain and Patrice Petitalot of France, Jany Bessiere, Luc De Marre, Michael Mandl and Geirtje Versavel of Belgium, Marcello Borges of Brazil, Peter Niehenke and Hans-Hinrich Taeger of Germany, and Ivan Nilsson of Sweden.

Although this is not a book on how to interpret each of the fundamental components (or 'building blocks') of the horoscope, the following section is a brief introduction to these. There are many excellent books on these areas of astrology, and some of my favourites are listed in the Recommended Reading section on page 234.

The Zodiac and the Planets
The signs are archetypes of human experience and expression; the types of energy; the adjectives describing how the planets act through them. The planets are the energy, the players/actors, the nouns.

The Four Angles and Twelve Houses
The angles show our particular orientation to the world around us, and the houses show where the planets act out their 'scripts'.

Rulerships and Dispositors
Rulerships link the planet to a particular house, while dispositors show how planets are linked to each other though their sign placement.

Retrograde Planets
Planets that appear to be moving backwards reveal parts of ourselves that are triggered early, are then put on hold and eventually given a 'second chance'.

The Aspects
Planets in combination (aspect) describe the storylines, while the specific aspect says much about the particular dynamic – the type of flow and relationship – between the planets.

Interpreting the Sequence of Planets
Recognizing the order of planets in conjunction shows the order in which these planets/energies act and how they react to one another.

The Zodiac and the Planets

Signs: The Four Elements

A reliable method with which to begin understanding the signs of the zodiac is to consider the element and the mode under which each sign is classified. Every zodiac sign is a unique combination of one element and one mode. Later on we will explore weighting these in an individual birth chart (see the section on pages 72–3), and will look at why this is *the* ultimate psychological balancing act. For now, let's meet the four elements and three modes. They provide an excellent starting point towards our goal of getting to the 'heart of the chart'.

Fire	Aries, Leo, Sagittarius
Earth	Taurus, Virgo, Capricorn
Air	Gemini, Libra, Aquarius
Water	Cancer, Scorpio, Pisces

The Fire and Air signs are considered masculine/ yang energy, bestowing an extroverted, externalized, conscious and active coloration. The Earth and Water signs are feminine/yin energy – personifying the qualities of introversion, internalization, the subconscious and passivity.

The most pronounced element in the horoscope provides the first vital clue to understanding our particular *type* of energy – what *motivates* and *drives* us.

When Fire dominates, we:
- Are ignited by challenge, competition, excitement and risk.

- Seek glory, greatness ('the spark of divinity') and some recognition of our individuality, largely eschewing the pursuit of money and rank.

- Need to believe in a positive outcome and to retain an array of future scintillating possibilities, some doubtlessly unrealistic and impractical.

- Tend to actively court attention, and get noticed, elevated and even awarded more easily than others.

- Are fuelled by a desire to enthuse others with the passion and optimism that courses through our own veins.

- Are compulsive about our pursuits and obsessed with causes, for fire consumes without satiation and needs to be contained.

- Have a strong intuition and express it forcefully.

- Are childlike, playful and effervescently spirited.

- Can descend to being hustlers, (self-) promoters, evangelists with feet of clay or self-serving Svengalis, or we can rise to being visionaries, inspirational teachers or extraordinary leaders.

When Earth dominates, we:
- Are motivated by expediency and tangible results, and seek to leave the world a better place than we found it.

- Incline towards routine, safety and a steady income – we are security-conscious and stay with what is familiar.

- Enjoy releasing our emotions through physical activity and seek to indulge our sensual side.

- Can be hardwired to the material world and unwilling to look beyond it.

- Work to keep both feet on the ground, are aware of limitations, and gain pleasure from a job well done.

- Are more likely to be slow, deliberate, persistent and constructive.

- Prove ourselves as reliable providers, dependable 'rocks' and productive, purposeful 'realists'.

- Excel as craftspeople and builders (from homes to empires), supportive colleagues, sensualists who work with our bodies (sports, physical work), and lovers of the countryside.

When Air dominates, we:
- Are propelled by exchange, dialogue and debate.

- Seek interaction, variety and travel.

- Want to learn more, read more, question more and communicate more.

- Are interested in theory, concept, abstraction, formulas and patterns, and strive to analyse, deduce and reason.

- Gather information to gain perspective, satisfied only when we are able to make considered, fair, rational observations and judgements.

- Are civilized, tolerant and abidingly interested in people.

- Express ideas in words – rationalizing and talking about emotions rather than engaging with them directly.

- Are prone to living in our heads and overlooking the needs of the body.

- Avoid emotional closeness and feelings of confinement, for we need space in all aspects of our life.

- Are communicators, salespeople, persuaders and advocates who live on our wits.

When Water dominates, we:
- Are swept towards making an emotional connection.

- Focus on human values – seeking to help others, to care for them and to be of service to the human condition.

- Perceive that which has not been verbalized and engage with that which cannot be articulated.

- Are empathetic and sympathetic, with psychic antennae that absorb the slightest nuance.

- Find fulfilment through an uncanny affinity with the whole spectrum of human emotions.

- Embrace feelings and gut instincts, which usually emerge as being spot-on judgements.

- Seek harmony and flow, and we should avoid competitive environments.

- Can be hypersensitive, touchy, reactive; we can be emotionally manipulative and indulge our feelings.

- Draw others into our emotional crises, while also being prone to over-attachment, dependency and even symbiosis.

- Have a deep sense of the dramatic, and can attract 'psychic vampires' who bleed us dry; at times we need to pull away and detox.

- Are survivors, with our strength often residing in our very non-resistance.

- Are carers, counsellors, therapists, intuitives.

In *Love and War Between the Signs* (Three Rivers, 1996), astrologer Amy Keehn describes Earth and Air as 'thinkers' who avoid emotionality and focus on practicality. In palmistry, these types share a square palm, revealing a pragmatic and orderly approach to life. Keehn labels Fire and Water signs 'feelers' who live for emotional interaction (from the enthusiasm of the Fire trio to the empathy of the Water signs). In palmistry, Fire and Water types are those with rectangular palms, suggesting an intuitive approach.

Elemental Lacks
Whenever we find an element that dominates, we know there will be a lack elsewhere. Identifying a lack of an element is just as crucial to the assessment of the chart (and the person's psychology) as locating an emphasis – perhaps more so. When a chart lacks a particular element, this element assumes greater significance to the person. They often seek to find this element outside themselves: perhaps by working in a related field or marrying someone who epitomizes that element.

This lack can operate from an unconscious or unsophisticated worldview (e.g. a person/subject without an Earth element may look to find ostentatious ways of appearing wealthy) or there may be a need to overcompensate (e.g. someone with little or no Air might enrol on numerous courses, buy a multitude of books and take every exam possible so as to appear to be actively 'gaining knowledge'). Someone with little or no Water, for example, may seek to rationalize their emotions by discussing feelings, but may not be able to engage with the actual emotion. Their partner could be pleading for some recognition of their feelings and receive a blank, detached response from the person with no Water. Yet, put on a song or film that touches them and they'll be off – crying all the way through it! With any lack, there's the motivation to *access* that element in a less sophisticated way, which paradoxically may manifest in a very obvious manner.

There might also be great sensitivity about the lack, a dismissal of those qualities, or a fear of not being seen as possessing those characteristics. I remember a student who, after being told she had a lack of Water, got overly emotional and seemed hell-bent on making me realize just how sensitive she was – even when all I was saying was that people who lack planets in Water may worry that others don't think they're sensitive!

Signs: The Three Modes

Cardinal	Aries, Cancer, Libra, Capricorn
Fixed	Taurus, Leo, Scorpio, Aquarius
Mutable	Gemini, Virgo, Sagittarius, Pisces

The modes are our modus operandi, our personal style, manner of approach and way of negotiating, and they influence how we adapt to situations and handle conflict. Reading about the modes in some books can lead us to believe that they are personified by the first sign in their group (Aries, Taurus, Gemini respectively), but these descriptions may not fit the rest of the signs. Cardinal signs are not all head-on – only Aries, the first, has a purely forceful directness about it. All fixed signs come off sounding like that most fixed of signs, the earthy Taurus (fixed Earth), while mutable signs are depicted as being flighty, like butterfly Gemini (mutable Air) – but these, I think, are due to the element–mode combination rather than the mode itself. Nevertheless, each set of signs within a mode group does have certain styles in common.

When cardinality dominates, we:
- Seek challenge, activity and swiftness.
- Create change; really make things happen.
- Initiate, instigate, lead, take the first step and stick our neck out; we put ourselves on the line and are prepared to negotiate the major conflicts of life.
- Have a directed, motivated, pulsating energy.
- Are concerned with the 'big issues'.
- Can be pushy, misdirected, conflict-creators.

When fixity dominates, we:
- Seek to establish, sustain and 'own' in a literal sense; we accumulate power or position.
- Are durable, loyal, grounded, principled and have concentrated reserves of energy.

- Are stubborn and predictable, and can be powerfully entrenched in our opinions and sense of rightness; we will listen to our stance being questioned and reply with, 'I am what I am – like it or lump it'.
- Should be mindful of stagnating, for we resist any change that's not on our terms or in our own time.

When mutability dominates, we:
- Are flexible, changeable, adaptable and variable.
- Are a perpetual work in progress.
- Copiously question and learn; we are drawn to joining, meeting and referencing from a variety of sources; we insist on re-enactment and repetition.
- Boast an ingenious array of skills with which to solve problems.
- Sometimes have dissipated energy and can feel paralysed by numerous possibilities or pressure.
- Are plagued by issues relating to avoidance – of conflict, responsibility, commitment or blame – and often use apology to sidestep confrontation.

Modal Lacks

The lack of a mode is simpler to understand than an elemental lack – usually there is less need to overcompensate. The lack is simply inherent in the subject's *style*. For example, having no planets in cardinal signs often indicates a lack of get-up-and-go – someone who avoids conflict and whose energy is either too stuck/constant (fixed) or too dispersed/diverse (mutable).

The Essence of the Signs and Planets

What follows are short pieces on the essence of each sign, followed by notes on some of the principles of the ten 'modern planets' (from the Sun to Pluto). These are intended to introduce some key concepts rather than provide a complete overview.

Each zodiac sign profile comprises: the sign's stage in human development; its birthright; the sign at its polar worst; and the sorts of scenarios expected when that sign is dominant in a horoscope.

THE ESSENCE OF ARIES

Following the cold, dark, symbolic hibernation of Pisces, we encounter Aries, who marks the zodiacal start to the year, and the unlocking and awakening of a new day. He brings with him the boundless energy, unbridled enthusiasm and innocence of a newborn. Full of hope and expectation, Aries is impetuous, spontaneous, uncomplicated and in possession of a dynamic, adventurous spirit.

Aries is born to develop a self-determining individuality and to sprint ahead of the pack. Aries must learn courage, dare to break new ground, fight for a cause or the underdog, and put himself first without apology. By focusing on himself, Aries reminds us of the importance of attending to one's own happiness before we attempt to help others. He must learn to act and lead independently – as a pacesetter or warrior – rather than to crave or depend on the reassurance of a following.

But when he disengages from his birthright, Aries settles into a place of immature laziness where he expects others to provide maintenance. Staying in someone else's shadow or acting as a perpetual supporting player, he refuses to blaze his own trail. When he is afraid of going it alone or engaging in healthy conflict, he turns into a lazy lamb or an apologetic sheep desperate to please and appease.

Aries-dominated Horoscopes
There is an instinct to make an impact on his surroundings, to fight, conquer and be seen as a winner. Perfectionism is a theme – not the diligence, precision or craft of Virgo, but a goal to be #1 and a refusal to accept any less than what he is truly capable of. Aries will meet situations in life where he's overlooked or challenged to assert his individuality and will. He will encounter conflict, violence, unfairness or solitude that will force him to face his fears of disapproval, to recognize his own needs, and stand up and be counted. But he must learn that life is about balance: the moment of victory is too short to live for that alone, and workaholism is no match for a life spent sharing adventures with another.

THE ESSENCE OF TAURUS

After the impetuosity of Aries, Taurus instinctively knows that a slower, pragmatic pace can result in more productivity – and it ensures still being in the race at the finish line. In this stage of human development, Taurus is aware of her physicality, her basic everyday needs of food and succour, and she desires a state of blissful indolence. A natural collector, Taurus holds dear the simple, familiar possessions in life that she works to accumulate.

Taurus is born to be the 'rock', the practical stalwart upon which others can rely. Her job is to build, preserve, maintain; to demonstrate faithfulness, to stay for the long haul. Being a principled character, she must learn to apply stubborn determination and to hold on to what she believes in. A sensualist and connoisseur, Taurus enjoys and revels in the pleasures of life. She builds foundations designed to last and amasses something of material value that will weather any storm.

At worst, there's a covetous attachment to what's not hers and a fanatical obsession with sexual or emotional situations, particularly with people she can't control. Recognizing her innate power and the dependency of others on her, she takes advantage by holding loved ones to ransom. Gluttonous, greedy, a monument to self-indulgence and a slave to the senses, Taurus can wallow in laziness or remain in outgrown or detrimental conditions.

Taurus-dominated Horoscopes
There is often a marked dependency on the material world and on the tangible, tried and tested. The gathering of trusted friends or the investment in property is often highlighted, as is a reluctance to try new experiences or waver from a fixed, secure path. Taurus will encounter people pushing her or attempting to impose their will; others will bring unexpected crisis and change to her environment. She will also have experiences in which loved ones attempt to take possession of what she values. These encounters will encourage her to dig her heels in, define her boundaries, remain faithful to who she is and loyal to what she desires.

GEMINI

CANCER

After the stoical firmness and perseverance of taciturn Taurus, Gemini longs to get out and about, to engage and exchange with others. At this stage in development, Gemini learns a vocabulary that expands his knowledge on a variety of topics that presently amuse him. He yearns to be seen as intelligent and works to remain forever young.

Born to spot patterns, to connect people and ideas, Gemini seeks to communicate, understand and articulate. An agile wit, persuasive salesman and agent, he learns to excel in debate, to trade and to clinch the deal. He doubts, asks questions, makes links and offers alternative viewpoints for consideration. A magpie, he 'borrows' ideas and melds aspects of numerous philosophies to create his own eclectic system of thought. Easily bored and distracted, Gemini longs for a busy life, free of responsibility or stale routine.

At worst, Gemini becomes a proselytizer, a fundamentalist who has discovered 'The Truth'. Moving from being an objective information-gatherer, he revels in superstition rather than facts, or becomes a know-it-all with a condescending attitude or moral arrogance – claiming God, education or the righteous path for his own. In an attempt to avoid conflict or liability, he engages in deceit – but transparently so, adding insult to injury.

Gemini-dominated Horoscopes
A life of change and movement is to be expected, as is an encyclopaedic knowledge of facts and a talent for language. A history of short-term projects and juggling commitments is common, too. Never content to settle, Gemini searches for new people to interest him and likes to keep his options open. Gemini will meet people he cannot communicate with, people who (sometimes literally) speak a very different language, offer mixed messages or misunderstand his motives. This further fuels his desire to be in dialogue and be understood. His innate duality is evident externally whenever he is presented with a choice, and is experienced internally when he struggles to make decisions.

Following commitment-shy Gemini, Cancer emerges keen to develop a sense of belonging and a connection to her roots. Whereas Gemini roams freely, Cancer feels bound sentimentally to the past and her instinct is to retreat to the familiar and safe. In this stage of human development, Cancer is aware that we all share a family unit, blood ties and emotional bondage with loved ones. She understands that our history shapes our emotional nature and the family we later create.

Cancer is a romantic, wistful and poetic sign, born to help others reconnect to their heritage and treasure their past – ideally without becoming a slave to it. She is the tenacious, devoted protector and midwife, guiding people through life's emotional conflicts and rites of passage. With psychic empathy, Cancer weeps for the misery in the world; she yearns and seeks to recapture a yesteryear of magical, forgotten melodies.

At worst, Cancer uses moods and emotional blackmail to preserve situations – or to advance causes close to her heart, which can harden with ruthless ambition. Believing that blood is not thicker than water, she reinvents her past – or disconnects from it, striving to attain rank and position. She can get toxic: seething in resentment over others' achievements, bitter at her early struggles and past sacrifices or her perceived exclusion from 'the system'.

Cancer-dominated Horoscopes
There's a shrewd approach to life, an intuitive knack for predicting the public mood, and a talent for gauging the emotional climate of those around her. There is often an overpowering need to understand her relationship with her mother. Cancer may encounter emotional desertion or isolation – or in adulthood she may have to cut an umbilical cord of family dependency and release a legacy of long-held, buried emotion. Eventually, Cancer discovers that she can choose like-minded friends with which to create her own family of choice – without paying such a high price.

LEO

VIRGO

After the ancestral ties of Cancer and her desire to re-create the familiar, Leo emerges as a separate entity with an *identity*. At this stage in the zodiac, Leo is the teenager who makes a self-discovery of potency, separates from the influence of the family, and is compelled to announce this by making a personal statement of self-expression.

With 'enlightened self-interest', Leo is born to tap into the power of his individuality and stand apart from familial or overbearing patriarchal influences. His journey is to realize his creative vision and to explore the divine, golden child within. (The challenge is to do so before he becomes a parent and expects his child to act this out for him.) Full of 'heart', warmth, courage and parental counsel, Leo is at his most radiant when inspiring others to realize their greatness. Majestic and dramatic, Leo adores recognition for his magnanimous efforts.

At worst, Leo turns to an audience to provide the approbation he craves. With a sense of entitlement, he uses others without giving due credit, and he begrudges them their time in the sun – secretly worried that there will not be enough praise left for him. Afraid of not being respected or invited into the elite's circle, proud Leo joins the cliques of intellectual snobbery and slavishly follows science, theory or ideology – anything that's been 'proven' or cannot be derided – rather than pursuing his heart's pathways to art and passion.

Leo-dominated Horoscopes
When Leo is strong in the chart, the individual has usually embarked upon a personal journey to understand why he has been born and how he can play a major part in the world around him. There are often bullies to face up to, dictators to dethrone or, if the father has been a personal hero, there are big shoes to fill before assuming a position of authority. Leo's own relationship with children is complex. In work, there is often publicity or hype – for people are attracted to his personal charisma and dignity – but, inside, Leo doubts that he is good enough and fears being 'found out'.

After Leo's search for identity, along comes understated, industrious Virgo. More complex than the fussy, fault-finding image we have of her, Virgo keeps quiet about her true nature and downplays her vital role. Virgo's stage in the cycle is the young adult working as an apprentice, perfecting a skill and becoming a small but integral cog in the wheel that keeps the machine running efficiently.

Virgo is born to be the craftswoman, specialist and the scrupulous selector. A natural harvester, she separates the wheat from the chaff, and her interest lies in getting to the heart of the matter and of being of service to the greater whole. Relishing the discovery of any detail that is useful and essential, Virgo analyses to create systematic order and make the world a better place. The most controlling and idiosyncratic of the signs, she follows the pomp and ceremony of Leo by putting things back into sequence and ensuring they function economically – all without creating a noticeable fuss. Her gifts of precision and restoration are indispensable.

When unproductive, Virgo wallows in chaos, confusion and wastefulness. Running from her mundane duties, she adopts a fatalistic worldview, acts indiscriminately and wanders aimlessly. She becomes a martyr and blames others for feeling victimized. A narrow-minded and illogical tyrant, she dictates the agenda in others' lives through subtle undermining and relentless criticism.

Virgo-dominated Horoscopes
Intelligence and discrimination are marked traits, and there is a studious, frugal lifestyle and a desire to be alone. Virgo is presented with many mix-ups and shambles to unravel and put back in order. A work-dominated, treadmill existence or a lack of recognition can manifest as unusual health issues or allergies. Her challenges are to discover through *experience* rather than through questions, and to integrate mind, body and spirit by developing a relationship with her own physical pleasure – rather than disrespecting her body or treating it solely as a temple of exercise and health regimes.

LIBRA

SCORPIO

Following the processing of Virgo and its relentless pursuit of perfection, Libra arrives with an uncanny knack of establishing order and making this look effortless! After the cloistered existence of Virgo the craftswoman, Libra the charmer turns his hand to meeting, negotiating, comparing and relating with 'the other'.

Libra is born to be the strategist, the peacemaker and agreeable mediator. He learns to bring a balanced objectivity to situations and is interested primarily in justice and the restoration of harmony. Forever the bridge-builder, Libra is less emotionally involved than people think. He irons out disputes in a diplomatic, fair and civilized way: decisions are based on reason, unhampered by emotion. A 'polite Aries', Libra uses persuasive charm to have his own needs met and agreed upon – less 'I'm happy if you're happy' and more 'I'm looking for you to agree with what I propose'.

At his worst, Libra loses his cool and creates conflict – often simply in order to resolve it. When anxious and insecure, Libra separates people, keeping them to himself in order to maintain his position as top dog. Thus Libra turns into a biased, intolerant, disruptive or divisive troublemaker who relishes rudeness and lives to provoke. Cunning, manipulative, lazy and vain, Libra lives for admiration and for the endorsement of his tastes.

Libra-dominated Horoscopes
Early in his life, Libra is faced with crippling, seemingly impossible decisions that need to be made or discord that must be mediated. Whether this division is inside or outside the family, the Libran learns to correct injustice and help others resolve conflict. Relationships are paramount, but addressing the *imbalance* of power (particularly in partnership) is the key theme in the life of Libra. Yet, the expert in other people's personal lives has difficulty in making and accepting a final decision in his own. Eventually, a healthy measure of self-worth enables him to choose someone worthy of him and capable of meeting him halfway.

Libra's superficial air of civility is shattered when intense, all-or-nothing Scorpio enters the fray and the gloves come off. This is the point where relationships become intimate and encounter dangerous, emotional, volatile and vulnerable terrain: 'we complement each other' becomes 'you're a part of me and I'll never let you go'.

Scorpio is born to become the alchemist, the potent healer and the unflinching investigator of life's mysteries. A character of extremes, she lives to explore the deeper meaning of existence, the dialectics of nature, the taboo and the forbidden. She must find intimacy and trust, and her immense strength lies in an ability to shed her skin, regenerate and emerge tougher. A natural detective and riddle-solver, she probes others' motives, honing her sixth sense to anticipate any emotional change on the horizon. Her challenge is to shed light on her darker side and soar to a higher level of consciousness.

But Scorpio cannot see that the biggest mystery is, in fact, herself. She avoids self-analysis, refusing pathologically to question her underlying motives. Instead, she stays in a comfort zone – free of risk and imagination – and focuses on the physical and sexual, acquires possessions and accumulates wealth. Afraid of her own co-dependency and the impulses that lurk beneath the surface, vampiric Scorpio is scornful of anyone else's weaknesses and uses subtle intimidation to control others.

Scorpio-dominated Horoscopes
Scorpios provoke extreme reactions from others. There is often an early exposure to the sordid side of life, which results in a loss of innocence and a 'knowingness' of the power games people play. There is usually a dramatic metamorphosis in her life – the death of a pivotal figure or the personal rebirth of an attitude or lifestyle. Scorpio becomes someone who learns self-mastery and courage in the face of crisis. A need to control and anticipate crisis dominates her life to the extent that it is, ironically, what could ultimately control her.

THE ESSENCE OF SAGITTARIUS

THE ESSENCE OF CAPRICORN

From the psychological depth of private, suspicious Scorpio, we emerge into the open space of the great outdoors and encounter the philosophical *breadth* of sociable Sagittarius. This is the stage where the obsessions and compulsions with one's own nature evolve into a quest for the meaning of life and the purpose of one's existence.

Sagittarius is born to aim high, search for meaning, ask the big questions and explore the possibilities *beyond* the facts. Born with a voracious appetite for knowledge, he welcomes all philosophies and, as a natural front-of-house greeter, he is able to tear down barriers of race or rank. An evangelist, he ignites other people's interest with his vision, optimism, enthusiasm and a desire to live a full, rich life. His secret to living is to enjoy the journey rather than to focus on the arrival. He welcomes luck to his front door by expecting life to deliver as much as he orders.

At worst, Sagittarius indulges in gossip or the superficial, and becomes careless or overly logical, reporting the evidence but missing the significance within. He loses any hard-won integrity by turning into the morally arrogant hypocrite, the name-dropper or the silver-tongued confidence trickster who promises too much, lives on his wits and good name, and takes any advantage he can.

Sagittarius-dominated Horoscopes
An infectious *joie de vivre* is apparent, as is an endless desire to explore, meet people and learn about life in other places. Often there is a major move of country or an immersion into a different culture. Sometimes there are marked periods of depression – melancholy not born from pessimism but as a result of being disheartened and disappointed that life has not delivered what was expected and people have not committed as fully as he has. There is usually a situation of injustice in early life where Sagittarius speaks up but isn't believed – and this prompts a lifelong desire to tell *his* truth and shoot down pretence, highlight hypocrisy or blow apart corruption.

After the adventures of Sagittarius, the eternal student and explorer, we meet Capricorn, the professor and master determined to *arrive*, make her mark and achieve tangible results. At this stage in human development, Capricorn is focused on using the knowledge and experience she's gained in order to create a worthwhile legacy and a reputation of distinction. On this path towards mastery over her environment, she is challenged to work within a rigid hierarchy, guard her principles and retain a moral code that is beyond reproach.

A wise, serious soul, Capricorn is born to rise above initial hardship, endure a long apprenticeship and deny her personal needs in order to receive rank, acclaim and prestige from the outside world. She is a monument to self-discipline, long-term ambition and individual achievement. Whereas Sagittarius reached out, broke down barriers but over-extended himself, worldly-wise Capricorn's duty is to shoulder responsibility during the recession and get matters back on schedule, delivering on time what has been promised.

She loses the grip on all she has worked for when she is driven by an underlying, repressed emotional fanaticism – or when her credo becomes 'the end justifies the means'. She fails when she cannot work within the 'system', and when she clings to outdated systems or structures, loses track of goals, fears success or retreats to wallow in self-pity.

Capricorn-dominated Horoscopes
Early in the life, there appears to be much adversity – a handicap, tyrannical figure or a *lack* of some kind that delays her progress or closes the door on opportunities frequently offered to others. Not only does this act as a spur to achieve great things, but it also instils patience and a belief that application, unswerving dedication and hard work eventually win out. Although there's often an early rebelliousness, she later becomes a respected member of the community or an elder stateswoman of the establishment. The irony is that Capricorn often becomes what she once rebelled against.

We move from the red tape, committee-laden sign of Capricorn to the independent and contrary sign of Aquarius. Aquarius tears up the rulebook and works to topple the rigid hierarchies, stereotypes, traditions and values laid down by his predecessor – to build a society where all are special *and* equal.

Aquarius is born to provide a clear, original perspective on social issues of justice and responsibility (the true, unadulterated spirit of *liberté, égalité, fraternité*). An outsider, Aquarius shifts from trying to please everyone (in order to gain their acceptance and be included) to recognizing the value of his own unique take on the world. This journey leads to independence, an uncompromising stance and a certainty in his own rightness. A catalyst for others, he is resistant to personal change unless on his own terms.

At worst, Aquarius operates from an egocentric, autocratic standpoint where 'some are more equal than others'. He fights for the group but secretly feels above them and despises 'commonness'. Yet, desperate to be adored and singled out as special, he employs prejudice, favouritism and preferential treatment. He considers himself ahead of his time and intellectually superior; these traits result in an unwillingness to learn from others. He knows *all* about human nature but doesn't know how to relate to people on an intimate level; he adores the concept of fellowship and humanity but can't tolerate individual members of the human race.

Aquarius-dominated Horoscopes
Early life events confirm the inner feeling that he doesn't fit in and that his 'road less travelled' approach is alien to family and acquaintances. An early lack of emotional warmth from others can result in Aquarius struggling to feel comfortable in his own skin or let rip his untamed, less civilized side. As with Leo, the father is often absent physically or emotionally, leaving Aquarius without a role model of leadership. This encourages him to seek others to fill this role or, ideally, to think for himself and define his own rules.

After the social idealism, cliques and aloofness of Aquarius, Pisces ends the zodiac cycle with an awareness of the need for love, unity and wholeness. Pisces looks beyond the brotherhood of man – she knows no boundaries and sees that *all* life and creation are interconnected and interdependent, and in need of redemption.

The Good Samaritan, Pisces is born to offer service, empathy, altruism and compassion – without prejudice, ego investment or agenda. An artist, composer and prophet, she conveys the universal joys and sufferings of the human condition. She is the choreographer of humanity's dance with its higher self, providing a glimpse into the state of nirvana. Pisces devotes herself to the emotional needs of others while recognizing their transient nature: she understands that everything has consequence but is ultimately inconsequential.

When not following a spiritual journey, she becomes critical and destructive, attacking others' faiths and pouring scorn on their attempts to understand life's mysteries. Pisces the piranha's self-sacrificing nature turns to self-sabotage and, with the power of the guilt-inducing martyr, she attempts to seduce and then sink everyone around her. When she feels undervalued, she fusses over hygiene, becomes addicted to rituals or pointlessly 'sweats the small stuff'. She creates mess, retreats to a sloppy comfort zone of miserable self-pity and blames others for putting her there.

Pisces-dominated Horoscopes
An emphasis on Pisces will often be seen in a fatalistic or over-accepting philosophy and a life mixed with transcendent 'highs' and desperate, dependent 'lows'. Usually, if a worldly path has been followed, Pisces ends up renouncing her youthful strivings for renown and conquering addictions and allergies to embark upon a more spiritual course instead. There are often Svengali-type figures in her life until Pisces forms a strong identity and recognizes her talent for acceptance and forgiveness – and her ability to survive.

- Our core identity, essence, individuality and inner philosophy/creed.
- Our journey/path of self-discovery; what is most important to us; our major life statements and purpose – who we were born to become.
- Our image and experience of our father and subsequent authorities in our life.
- Following the Sun's path and engaging in its message brings recognition; we should avoid wallowing in the worst of the sign's polar opposite.

A solar overtone: a creative and self-expressive life and personality; a personal, self-involved quest to embody the Sun sign and discover ourselves; vain, selfish, narcissistically self-entitled with an 'enlightened self-interest'; being popular, on display and under the glare of the spotlight; a life that experiences failure or the squandering of early promise – where courage is then needed to assume personal control over the individual destiny.

- Our emotional temperament, habitual 'gut' responses, instincts, feelings, moods and behaviour; how we express our feelings; who we truly are 'behind closed doors'; many right-brain functions.
- What we're attached to; what we need to feel safe, secure, rooted and to belong; eating/dietary habits; our attitude towards spending money on the essentials.
- Our tender, vulnerable and immature side; our reactions when feeling insecure and threatened; the emotions we create out of our feelings.
- Our image and experience of our mother and subsequent nurturing figures in our life; how we care for/mother other people to receive comfort and succour in return.
- Our memories of our past and home; our current home environment.

A lunar overtone: an intuitive, responsive, malleable, moody and instinctive nature; a fluid expressiveness; aware of the rhythms, cycles and necessities of life; a talent for having a finger on the pulse of fashion, public taste and opinion; an inconstant life of ebb and flow, being moved by currents; a life of much movement and travel in search of a home/family that resonates with our soul and emotional centre.

- Our urge to communicate, name, connect, link, negotiate and analyse; many left-brain functions.
- Our capacity to reason and assimilate; our thought processes, opinions and academic interests; how we learn, form opinions and express ourselves; our logical mind and rational voice; how we speak and what stimulates the 'little grey cells'.
- Our perception and experience of siblings.

A Mercurial overtone: a storyteller, messenger, neutral go-between, agent and deal-maker playing both sides; curious, inquisitive and analytical; obsessed with youth; a voyeur preferring to observe or interview instead of directly *experiencing*; the ingenious and supple trickster; a life of questioning and sharing opinions; a life of variety and juggling numerous endeavours, sorting and sifting through superficial interests (Gemini) or working on developing a craft and a specialism (Virgo).

- Our urge to form relationships, exchange, co-operate and find common ground.
- How we need to be found attractive; our 'windowbox': how we adorn ourselves to attract others and be popular and desirable.
- Our self-worth and values – our wish to have others reflect these; the urge to compare; how a woman sees herself – her first point of reference.
- Our personal style and tastes; our pleasure principle; how we pleasure and entertain ourselves; how/where we spend money in the pursuit of leisure and pleasure.

A Venusian overtone: agreeable, entertaining, charming, attractive, lazy and vain; a need to be liked and validated; a life in pursuit of equal exchange in relationship; an expert in negotiation, persuasion, diplomacy and bridge-building; a life of restoring harmony to areas of conflict, and enjoying the finer things and sensual side of existence.

- Our urge to *take* what we desire; our type of energy, action, driving force and spirit.
- How we compete, hunt and fight; how we deal with conflict and express anger.
- What arouses us; our primal and sexual nature – the chase, conquest and penetration; how we express passion and our instinctual desires; how a man sees himself – his first point of reference.
- Our ability to stand up for what we believe in and to assert ourselves; our instinct to survive, compete, win, attack, defend and put ourselves first; our type of courage.

A Martian overtone: dynamic, powerful, spirited, self-motivated and quarrelsome; the pugnacious, competitive or ambitious upstart looking for contests to win; a life of clearly defined battles between good and evil, and where we must discover the various sides of our potency; a life of facing conflict that triggers our independent and entrepreneurial spirit, challenging us to meet life with energy and daring.

- The urge to find meaning, explore, learn and broaden our horizons; where we invest belief and our personal idea of faith and views of providence.
- Our belief in the future and in the overall pattern/scheme of life.
- Where our confidence lies; where we're blessed in abundance to teach and give freely of our talent; our insight and wisdom; where we feel invincible, able to 'get away with murder' or take advantage; where we must seek integrity and follow the 'straight path' to avoid our ethics or morality being questioned.
- The areas in life that provide opportunity, growth and luck – where we get something for nothing and where we expect plenty; the side of us that is greedy, excessive, inflated, 'too much' and invites parody.

A Jupiterian overtone: a philosopher or eternal student/teacher; hypocritical and haughty – a 'diva' temperament; the flamboyant promoter; a philanthropist, charismatic evangelist, guru or con artist, star-maker or Svengali; a desire for recognition, fame, authority, influence and acclaim; a life of lucky breaks, fortunate contacts, good reputation (which may be challenged) and being in the right place at the right time; a jovial, hopeful, questing and future-orientated nature; a life of exploration, learning and teaching; an embodiment of the power of positive thought.

- The psychological opposite of *every* planet.
- Where and how we feel constraint and are aware of limitations and boundaries.
- Where our doubts, fears, guilt and lack of confidence lie; where and how we feel inadequate, clumsy or fear failure and how these make us feel vulnerable; what our inner voice of disapproval says to us.
- How and where we face reality; where we experience delays and frustrations and 'where we might not get what we paid for, but where we pay for everything we get'.
- Our biggest life lessons and tasks carried out over a lifetime; how and where our fears become our greatest strengths over time, when we eventually bear fruit, reap what we sow; in which areas we can eventually become an authority.
- Our conscience and moral compass; where we stick to the rules; where and how we have been disciplined or must cultivate discipline.

A Saturnian overtone: a long apprenticeship with an eventual mastery of our surroundings and condition; a self-contained, conscientious, inhibited or responsible person – 'adult' and wise beyond our years; a disability/burden that weighs heavily that we must overcome, adapt to or turn into a strength; a spartan life of work, sacrifice or penance; the cynic, the miser, the balloon-popper; a morally upstanding citizen and stalwart anchor and time-keeper for others.

- How and where we wish to be different, radical or extreme; where we must speak out, break the mould, shatter existing ideas of conformity, tear up the rulebook or overthrow the status quo.
- Where we seek out change; how and where our lives are subject to sudden reversals, disruptions, break-ups, breakdowns or breakthroughs.

- Our image of perfection; our particular intellectual ideas of 'the one truth' – ones that are detached from emotion; how and where we 'think outside the box'.
- Where we feel different, separate or singled out from our peer group; where we are cast out or blacklisted; how and where we experience things differently from our peers; our deviant, perverse streak.

A Uranian overtone: a radical, unemotional stance marching to a different drummer; strong political or social ideologies that dominate all else; a catalyst who shocks or wakes up others, and who receives flashes of insight or inspiration; a life of the outsider – not 'born of our time'; a life encountered as restrictive or suffocating which forces us to break away and liberate ourselves; an original, erratic, highly-strung free spirit who follows 'the road less travelled'; a life impacted by sudden changes, quantum leaps and startling severances.

- Where we yearn to experience Nirvana or the sensation of ecstasy, how we seek to touch/connect to the divine and experience our full set of senses; who and what we seek in order to project our image of perfection and the divine; how and why we seek to escape the mundane or harsh existence of life; how we attain some sort of spiritual connection with the universe or transcend to a higher realm of creative expression; where we seek to redeem ourselves.
- The area of our life and personality that is nebulous, impressionable, oversensitive, without structure or boundary; where we can lose touch with reality; where we wish to be rescued or to save others.
- How and where we are confused, disillusioned or deceive ourselves; where we eventually wake up to a situation and discover that it is less than ideal or has been dissolved; the areas of our lives where boundaries have been blurred or where we seek the unattainable.
- Where we meet and how we deal with disorder; where we can let chaos reign; where we may be subject to others' influence and manipulation, gossip, scandal and speculation; the areas in which we must learn to 'let go'.

A Neptunian overtone: a magical life of eclectic or nebulous experiences; a poet, artist, chameleon/shape-shifter, musician, music-lover, image-maker, visionary, dreamer or guru; a life pursuing a path of enlightenment or escape; a perennial victim, addict, martyr or drop-out with a hard-luck story who cannot function in life, earn a living or organize their everyday existence; a life free from earthly attachments, a connection to unconscious realms or one where we are in tune with the rhythms of life or have heightened emotions or extrasensory perceptions.

- The hidden and buried aspects of our personality; the profound, seismic experiences we have swept under the carpet; our personal, family and ancestral taboos; secrets and skeletons in the closet; the source of our compulsions to control and to avoid having the fears revealed that secretly control us.
- Where we experience crisis and how we cope with trauma, paranoia and inner demons; where and why we have been stripped away and humbled.
- Where and how we have been (or fear being) violated, impotent, victimized, persecuted or abused; areas of psychological demolition or domination; where we have lacked control; where and how we must purge ourselves and cleanse our past.
- Where and how we can reclaim a sense of personal power over our lives; the buried treasures and reserves of underlying power and energy; the areas that dominate us until we 'air' and release them and wrest control; our place in the group and political dynamic; where and how we can exercise power and influence others.

A Plutonic overtone: a life of extremes, intense experiences and life-death survival issues; a life of influence and/or powerlessness, where we have been at the mercy of someone else or where a taboo or circumstance beyond our control has overshadowed our life; a power player influencing their generation; a life of extreme wipeouts, purgings, overhauls or personal transformations; a life of reinvention and metamorphosis – rising from the ashes.

The Four Angles and the Twelve Houses

The horoscope's four angles – the Ascendant (ASC), Midheaven (MC), Descendant (DSC) and Imum Coeli (IC) – are the most *personal* areas of the birth chart and are very much dependent on the actual birth time and place. Whereas the planets do not move a great deal through the zodiac each day (only the Moon will make much headway – from 11° to 15° a day), *every sign* (indeed, each degree of every sign) will rise (over the Ascendant), culminate (at the MC), set (over the Descendant) and anti-culminate (at the IC) during a 24-hour period. To put it another way, the Sun will move through approximately one degree of the zodiac in a day, so everyone born on that day will have the Sun within a degree of each other. But throughout that day, it is possible for people to have any one of the 360 degrees of the zodiac on their Ascendant (and each of the other angles).

The four angles are the most powerful places in the horoscope for a planet to be positioned. They act like a highly personal compass: they reveal our orientation to our environment; and they are also 'receivers', showing what we pick up from our surroundings and how we interact with the world around us. They are two-way windows on our world, representing our personal, relationship, family and social lenses (me, you, us and them).

The four angles are like labels or badges. The Ascendant is an identity badge – our meet-and-greet personality. The Midheaven is the social or professional badge we wear that says 'doctor' or 'counsellor' – how we and others may sum up our CV in shorthand. The Descendant is our partner badge – who we're looking for, as well as the areas of ourselves we project onto others. The IC badge is our family coat of arms – a collective history and summation of what went before.

The angles are not planets but astronomical reference points – they are the celestial patterns of the planets brought down to Earth, manifested as two axes forming a cross of matter. (The houses – whichever system of division employed – take their cues from all or some of these reference points; the houses describe *where* the activity of the planets in signs takes place.) The four angles are our own personal reference points – our views of (and perspectives on) our inner, personal landscape and professional, ⟨...⟩ impact, impressions and project⟨...⟩

The Sun's relationship to the angles gives us an immediate idea as to the time of day we were born. The Sun is on the Ascendant at dawn, on the MC around midday (or 1 p.m. summer time), on the Descendant at sunset, and on the IC around midnight (or 1 a.m. summer time). Our day is shaped by this celestial timer and we can use these associations to better understand each angle:

- The ASC is in the east where the Sun rises at dawn – a spectacular launch we cannot miss; this point is the birth of a new day, we 'arrive', appear and are 'born into a body'. It symbolizes the *emergence* of the self.

- The MC is where the planets and the Sun (the hero) are at their highest and most glorious, in full view, shining above us; an example to look up to; the *externalization* of the self.

- The DSC is where the Sun descends and merges with/disappears into the horizon; the *merging* of the self.

- The IC is where the Sun reaches its low point and plants the seed for a new day as it crosses over; the *internalization* of the self.

The Sun (or any planet) is at its most *impressive* at three of these points – the Sun becomes visible at the ASC, glides through its high peak at the MC, and then sets at the DSC. Of the four stages, it is only invisible to us at the IC, which in itself is significant. The impression it makes at the IC is one that is not as obvious or as easy to spotlight, but it is a deeply internal impression that marks (and stays with) us.

Axes are oppositions (the ASC is exactly opposite the DSC; the MC is opposite the IC). Oppositions make us more aware – conscious of both inseparable and interlinked sides/ends, and how an emphasis on one can affect the other. We cannot define ourselves (ASC) without the other (DSC); we cannot understand where we're going (MC) unless we understand from where we've come (IC). Later, we'll look for links between the four angles, e.g. are all the signs on the angles fixed? Perhaps they're a combination of Air and Fire?

Ascendant–Descendant Axis

Picture the ASC–DSC axis as a see-saw. The challenge is the balancing act of 'I' and 'you' – negotiating and compromising with others to achieve equilibrium. Too much weight on one end of the axis puts the whole see-saw out of kilter. This axis is our horizon, our surroundings and immediate environment.

The direction is left and right/east and west: what we see naturally looking around us, what grabs our attention. It is the axis of *encounters* – what we attract into our life. It reveals how we invite others into our world, our impact on them and their impact on us. Here, we are forced to understand who is doing what to whom! It's where our personality and notion of who we are (ASC) – our very survival – is challenged by another (DSC).

The Ascendant

• Our one-to-one personality.

• Our vehicle for interaction; our personal interface; the 'skin', stereotype or mask we slip on in order to approach and connect with others; our approach to life.

• Our appearance and how we expect our environment and people to 'appear' when we walk out of our front door; first impressions made and received.

• Our opening position; our take on reality; our expected route, open agenda, personal stance and mottos for survival/interaction.

• Early messages about behaviour; early childhood experiences; our birth experience.

The Descendant

• What we look for in others; our 'other' half; that which threatens our survival.

• Others involved in our search for discovery; those we seek out to help us define/refine who we are.

• What we are attracting, projecting and advertising for.

• What we receive from others; their reactions to, and perceptions of, us.

The MC–IC Axis

Imagine the MC-IC axis as being like a vertical pillar or tree. We are able to grow up and branch out, to rise above and soar, but we must be aware of what's below – the roots and foundation. The challenge of this axis is the balancing act of growing and becoming our own construct (creating our own name/reputation) without putting the past (the family 'name') completely in the shade.

The direction is above and below: what we need to stretch out to see, to look up towards (the middle of) heaven – out of ourselves and towards the future. It is also what we see when we look down and inwards – and back to the past – when we contemplate the steadiness of our foundation. What is inherited or instilled early on (IC) is called upon to be manifested in the world (MC). This axis reveals the messages we receive from parental figures that relate to personal, deep-rooted principles (IC) and the work/social philosophies that affect our place in the world (MC); it shows what was stressed as being important by our parents (consciously or unconsciously) – and their expectations and deep-rooted motivations. It speaks of the early signals we picked up from them about achievement, aspirations, social roles and 'the big world out there'.

The Midheaven (MC)

• How we actualize potential and 'become ourselves' (self-actualization) in society;

our reputation, social persona and social shorthand.

- What we wanted to be growing up; how we wish to be remembered.

- The social or public arena in which we can express our vocation (the Sun) and fulfil our promise; the best pathway to social recognition; the conduct we need in order to succeed; our definition of success and the people we admire and aspire to emulate.

The Imum Coeli (IC)
- Our foundation, roots; what we're born into.

- Inner messages and drive; subconscious motivations to achieve in the outside world.

- Our kind of 'soil' to develop roots (IC) and foliage (MC); our seed, source, heritage.

- How we are in private; our cellar.

- The area of life we ignore at our peril; our secret fears that can unconsciously steer our direction (MC).

A planet on one angle will affect both sides of the axis but will make its presence felt most on the angle with which it is conjunct. It can act as a support or a millstone, or both.

For more on the four angles, see my book, *The Midheaven: Spotlight on Success* (Flare, 2016).

A Quick Guide to the Twelve Houses
I prefer to see the houses as mundane *areas of life*, rather than overemphasizing their psychological interpretations, which tend to be extensions of the signs. Although each house and its corresponding sign (e.g. the 1st House and the first sign of Aries) have matters in common, the houses show the 'where' – the areas of life *where* the planetary energy and key principles are expressed in a particular manner (depending on their sign position). Each house describes an environment. I also see the four angles as being different to the houses that they begin (in most house systems, e.g. the 1st House and the Ascendant) – the angles are influential points on our personal compass showing our psychological orientation in the world.

Over the years, I have worked with most house systems but returned to Equal house because of clarity and better forecasting results. Many astrologers dismiss this system because of its simplicity and sole reliance on the ascending degree as the starting and defining point in the horoscope. (Some astrologers prefer a quadrant system – where the four angles begin the four angular houses – and some adopt the Whole Sign house system, in which the 1st House begins at 0° of the ascending sign, regardless of the Ascendant's actual degree.) I'd recommend being open to various systems of house division while studying – don't just pick a system simply because it places your planets in what looks like a 'better light'! In truth, there's no escaping key chart patterns. A major theme of the horoscope will be written in at least three different ways, regardless of the chosen method of house division. And we can endeavour, for instance, to move the Sun into the 11th or 1st House to keep it away from the 'dreaded' 12th, but the Sun may still rule the 12th or be conjunct a planet that does so. You can run but you can't hide – avoiding a planetary placement or restructuring the chart to 'keep it pretty' only serves to underline the importance of the meaning of that position!

If the choice of house system determines one's viewpoint of the horoscope and its

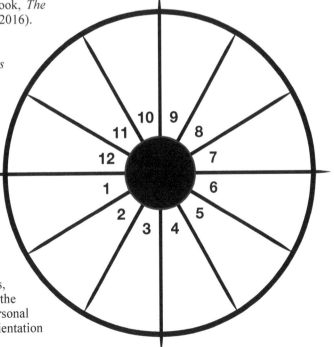

construction, using Equal houses (where each house is in exact aspect to the all-important 1st House starting position) would link every consequent house directly to the viewpoints, attitudes and 'reality' of the personal lens of the 1st House ('my appearance', 'my approach', 'my expectations'). Taking the 1st House/the cusp of the ASC as the starting point of the chart, the 2nd House becomes 'my money', the 3rd House is 'my siblings' or 'my schooling', and so on – they all relate back to the Ascendant and its sign. And when using Equal (or Whole Sign) houses, the MC and IC – rather than being the starting points for the 10th and 4th Houses, respectively – will 'float' and may be positioned in other houses.

The houses reveal our *experiences* in particular areas of life, but these can also be personified by the people we *encounter* in those areas (e.g. Saturn in the 10th may be a fear of authority figures at work, but we may often meet various embodiments of the Saturn-type boss at work, too).

1st House
The immediate, personal area of life: our appearance, complexion and presentation; what we wear; our physicality.

2nd House
Our money, income, wealth, assets and possessions; values and valuables; resources, cash flow and earning power; the physical relationship with our body; what sustains us, food and the experience of comfort.

3rd House
Our early experiences and contacts with friends, neighbours and siblings; short journeys and mobility; schooling, the classroom, brief communications, books and information to hand.

4th House
Our home environment, our sanctuary and place of retreat when in need of privacy and replenishment; land, immovable possessions, property and other fixed wealth; our ancestry, roots and forebears.

5th House
Recreation, play, theatre, creativity, romance, sex; our dealings with our children; speculation; our general audience and 'following'.

6th House
Our daily routines, rituals and systems; diet, exercise and health regimes; factors that affect our health; the workplace, office life and co-workers; labour, unequal relationships, in service and servitude; pets and small animals.

7th House
Our relationship, marriage or committed partnership; open enemies, adversaries and those in conflict with us; equitable relationships; projections of the 'not' self.

8th House
Our encounters with other people's money and possessions; joint resources; credit and financial power; crises, secrets, legacies, inheritances and wills; regeneration and renewal; our experiences of digging deep into mysteries, taboos and the occult/hidden.

9th House
Our experiences of long-distance journeys; higher education and ethics; travel, foreign countries and cultures; religion, our belief systems and our image of God; publishing, marketing, advertising and publicity.

10th House
Our career (long-term work perspective); people in authority and our experiences of bosses; our social position, rank and standing; public life; the measure of our acclaim, distinction and honour.

11th House
Our teams, unions, focus groups, movements, brotherhoods and comradeship – a specific audience of like-minded colleagues working with us towards a common purpose; our community and social circle; social causes; our idealized aspirations; advisors, brokers and counsellors (rather than the 9th House).

12th House
Our experiences of seclusion, withdrawal, isolation and down time; our clandestine affairs, phobias, hidden weaknesses, unconscious patterns and self-undoing (actions against our best interests); encounters with the mystic realms. (Any planet here has just risen above the horizon – come into view, emerged into the light. The planet has just been 'born', and its energy is perhaps unconscious to us, expressing itself in a raw manner. The planet in the 12th House will be most noticeable to others but we may be unaware of its burgeoning power in this influential but premature position.)

Rulers and Dispositors

Here's a quick guide to how planets and houses can be linked/in dialogue in the horoscope, in order of importance:

1. A planet in a house – this is the most effective and obvious manifestation.

2. A planet aspecting another planet in a house (e.g. Mars in the 2nd square Jupiter in the 5th, linking the planets and houses).

3. A planet ruling the sign on the cusp of a house (or, in the case of intercepted signs in unequal house systems, a sign that lies within the house).

4. A planet positioned on the cusp of a house (from a 'doorway' position able to access both houses).

5. A planet in its natural house (e.g. Jupiter in the 9th or 12th, Mars in the 1st or 8th).

A house may be 'empty' (using the ten 'planets' – Sun to Pluto – will always mean there will be at least a couple of untenanted houses in our horoscope). But there are no inactive houses because (as listed above) there's always some link by rulership. The sign on the cusp of each house has an influence on the affairs of that house, but the planet ruling the sign on the cusp of that house will give more information – its position and aspects will reveal the true motives and expression behind the general set of characteristics associated with the sign on the cusp of the house. Rulerships link the affairs of one house (and a planet) with another. The cusp of a house makes 'a general statement, while the position of its ruler always gives more factual information and shows the direction in which the story goes.' (*The Contemporary Astrologer's Handbook*). For instance, if Cancer is on the 2nd House cusp, this will say much about our general attitude to money, income and assets, as well as our earning potential. But the sign and house position (and aspects) of the 2nd House ruler (in this case, the Moon) will show how the potential can manifest specifically in the temperament, situations encountered and life choices made. It will show *where* you can earn your money – the best environments and circumstances in which to generate 2nd House activities such as income. One

student with the 2nd House ruler placed in Virgo in the 4th was rather downcast when she realized that this link described the way she was earning a living: cleaning (Virgo) homes (4th). (Planets in mundane Virgo sometimes have a way of leaving us feeling underwhelmed until we recognize the gifts inherent in the art of the craft.)

When looking at rulerships, always consider:

The sign on the cusp
For example, Cancer on the 2nd House cusp – a shrewd, considered attitude to money with an instinctive way of investing or accruing funds; the importance of saving or having enough money to remain secure and comfortable in one's home.

The planet that rules the sign on the cusp
For example, the Moon – an inconstant, fluctuating energy linked to our fundamental needs and protective instincts; wages/finances can wax and wane; our spending depends on our mood; money is linked to security, the home and activities of the past.

The position of that planet
For example, the Moon (ruling the 2nd) in Sagittarius in the 7th: making money (2nd) by caring, facilitating or assisting (Moon) others (7th) such as foreign people, or in the areas of teaching, direct advertising or the law (Sagittarius); our ways of making money (2nd) expand (Sagittarius) by working with the public (Moon); learning to separate financial needs (Moon/2nd) from dreams and big plans (Sagittarius). Also... taking risks or benefiting from lucky financial breaks from important contacts; partners who are either generous or high maintenance; high expectations of others to take care of us; money comes from partnership, such as finding a Sagittarian type who keeps us positive and secure – or someone who gambles our/their money away!

Much practical information can be garnered by linking the planets to the houses. For example, if the ruler of the 7th House is in the 9th, our partners may be from overseas or linked to education, the law or some other 9th House activity. The sign on the cusp of the 7th will say much about the type of qualities we attract, but the ruler of the 7th 'becomes' the 'other person' (7th) and will often be highly descriptive of the types of people we attract and with whom we get involved.

One of the benefits of an Equal or Whole Sign house system (where the MC–IC axis floats) is the useful consistency seen in all charts with shared Ascendants. For instance, all those with Leo Rising will have Venus-ruled signs on the cusp of the 10th House (Taurus) and 3rd House (Libra). Their career or measure of acclaim (10th) will always be tied in with 3rd House activities such as education and informing others. They will want to have a career that brings security and a steady income (Taurus on the 10th) and be attracted to diplomatic, romantic or charming ways of expressing themselves in everyday life (Libra on the 3rd). They will value (Venus) their career and professional development (10th) and recognize the need for information, courses and books (3rd) to enhance these areas of their life; their work (10th) may involve much short-term travel (3rd), and so on. The natal position of Venus will describe an area in which these houses can best be manifested and the strivings and energy involved in their pursuit. As always, the planet is the prime mover – the energy – whereas the sign is the style, attitude and *colour* with which that energy is expressed.

I look mainly at traditional rulers when considering the effects on a house. So, for the house with Scorpio on the cusp, look to Mars rather than Pluto. Do the same for Aquarius by interpreting Saturn's position, and for Pisces by looking to Jupiter. Cusps 'ruled' by the outer planets (Uranus, Neptune and Pluto) reveal how a particular house is tied to the larger issues that affect our lives and to the zeitgeist (the 'spirit of the times').

As we shall be doing elsewhere, look for repetition/ enforcement with rulerships. A placement may be backed up and underlined elsewhere. Perhaps the ruler of the 4th is the Moon (a repetitive statement in itself) or the ruler of the 4th is in the 4th House. Someone with an Aries Ascendant will find that many (if not all – particularly if an early degree of Aries is rising) planets are 'double whammys' by house and sign position: e.g. Venus in Scorpio in the 8th (the natural house of Scorpio). This is because Aries is the start of the natural zodiac. If there's a late Aries Ascendant (as in the example opposite), the planets may not do this, unless they're in a later degree than that of the Ascendant.

Dispositors and Mutual Reception

If the Sun and Mercury, for example, are in Taurus, then both planets are said to be disposited by Venus, the ruler of Taurus. It's another way of saying that anything in Taurus is Venusian in character and so these planets are ultimately governed by Venus and its natal position. If that Venus is in Aries, then Mars is the dispositor of Venus. We would then look at the sign position of Mars to see which planet is the dispositor of Mars, and so on. Astrologers (particularly Mercury-ruled ones!) love these trails and chains and working out the chart's 'final dispositor'. Personally, I'm not convinced that most of this is useful. Looking at the chart of Barbra Streisand (see page 53), four planets in Taurus ensure that Venus plays an important role in her horoscope, and Venus is in Pisces in the 12th, the natural house of Pisces. Her Venus is strongly linked to Pisces, but I don't think there would be more pertinent information available to me if I continued the trail by looking at either Jupiter or Neptune, the rulers of Pisces.

If Mercury were in Taurus and Venus in Gemini, there would be a 'mutual reception': Venus in Mercury's sign and vice versa. A mutual reception is considered influential by some astrologers, particularly those using horary. In natal astrology, it underscores a link between the planets, but in my experience not so strongly as to consider it as powerful as when planets are in aspect.

Chart (Ascendant) Ruler

The Chart Ruler is the planet that rules the sign on the Ascendant. For example, with Aries on the Ascendant, Mars becomes the Chart Ruler. It could be in any one of the twelve signs so, in effect and without taking into consideration additional facets, there are twelve types of Aries Rising. Each of the twelve will show a specific path and areas where the person can express their personality and reinforce their self-image (Ascendant). Astrologer Steven Forrest calls the Chart Ruler 'the Ascendant's ambassador, transported to another part of the birth chart, but still serving the same end.' He adds that it 'plays a pivotal role in establishing the individual's sense of personal distinction and identity.'

The Chart Ruler is an important player in the drama. In consultation charts (cast for the start of an astrology reading), the Ascendant describes the circumstances surrounding the client, while the Chart Ruler is the client themselves, revealing how they are positioned and where they are going. The ruler of the Ascendant is the hidden directive, *the motivation behind* both our approach to life and our interactive, face-to-face way of dealing with the world.

The Ascendant represents our personal style. Aries Rising needs stimulation; it goes out to conquer, to be seen as a winner, ground-breaker or pioneer. That's the way it meets the world. It expects competition, conflict and 'if you want something done, you have to do it yourself'. If the Chart Ruler Mars is in Virgo in the 6th House, the Aries directness will be channelled into areas of health, routine, work or service (6th House) and carried out in a precise, discriminating manner and with an attention to detail (Virgo). In *The Twelve Houses* (Flare, 2007), Howard Sasportas described the house position of the Chart Ruler as 'the area of life where important experiences which directly influence growth and self-discovery [the Ascendant] are met.' With Mars in Virgo, the competitive, confrontational nature and pioneering spirit of Aries could be directed towards being the best craftsperson in their field, a pioneering nurse or a union representative. We could expect someone who pours their energy into health matters or fighting to improve working conditions, or who works independently to keep the machines (internal and external) well oiled and functioning well. (The Chart Ruler will usually be in aspect to other planets, sometimes reinforcing the original statement, other times throwing another spin onto the interpretation.)

In the chart above, Aries is rising and the Chart Ruler Mars is in Virgo in the 6th House. It is the horoscope of writer **Barbara Cartland**, famous for her historical romance novels (her Sun–Mercury conjunction is in Cancer in the 3rd House). Cartland was a long-standing society figure and colourful, snobby and outspoken media personality (Saturn joins Jupiter to crown the MC in Capricorn). Early experiences (the Ascendant and Moon) in her life included watching her enterprising mother launch a dress shop in London to make ends meet (note the Aries

Barbara Cartland

influence and the industrious Mars in Virgo). In 1923, Cartland published her first novel, which was considered racy and risqué. But as society changed, Cartland's innocent, virginal heroines went from being chased to chaste – her writings of a pure, idealized love began to be seen as outdated and tame. Nevertheless, her output was remarkable. She wrote 723 books, maintained an enviable work ethic (Mars in Virgo) into her late nineties, and left 160 unpublished manuscripts when she died in 2000. Cartland was an embodiment of the power of positive thinking, and was known for her promotion of vitamins, her stance against the removal of prayer in schools, and a health-conscious, energetic lifestyle (Virgo).

We find Aries on the Ascendant and ruler Mars in Sagittarius in the 9th – a righteous placement that suggests reaching out to the masses, calling for freedom, and fighting for one's fundamental rights and beliefs – in the horoscope of the influential preacher–crusader and high-profile evangelist Billy Graham (whose Mars conjuncts his Moon in Sagittarius). The same combination of Ascendant and Chart Ruler occurs in the chart of protest singer Joan Baez, who has long been a campaigner for social change, justice and peace.

Retrograde Planets

Retrogrades (℞) are an interesting phenomenon – not just in their apparent backwards motion but also in how astrologers perceive and interpret this optical illusion, as seen from the Earth. Much has been written on retrograde cycles (most famously, the Mercury retrograde) and on the importance of retrogrades in horary and electional astrology. Yet relatively little has been written about how they function in the natal horoscope. This is surprising if we consider how much of our art – from the diurnal (daily) cycle to the eternal dance of the Sun, Moon and Earth – stems from observing the heavens from our own viewpoint.

But first things first. When a planet appears to move backwards, we have a celestial 'second chance' to revisit old ground and retrace our steps (as the planet does) and to put things back on track. Observing Mercury's retrograde cycle (for three weeks every 3–4 months, 3–4 times in a twelve-month stretch) teaches us that Mercurial areas of life (and those associated with our own Mercury placement) encounter delays, derailments and detours – often in order to help us rethink our options. We learn to value and practise the prefix 're-': to research, rethink, reconfirm, reorganize and review. It is a time to notice slip-ups, correct mistakes and, where possible, to maintain a healthy distance from 'conveyer belt' situations. But, ideally, we should stop short of making firm decisions for the future or taking new action – unless we wish to revise or renegotiate these later. It's not as though all communications *go wrong* under the retrograde, it's more that further information is often revealed during this time that shows a situation in a new light.

During Mercury's retrograde in May 2009, for instance, the UK press revealed the gross misuse of allowances and expense claims by Parliamentary ministers. At that time (see diagram top right), Mercury had crept into Gemini, stationing at 1° (both planet and sign delight in 'getting away with things'), only to traverse back into Taurus (being 'called to account' on monetary matters) and squaring the Jupiter–Neptune conjunction (large-scale scandal/deception) in Aquarius (elected representatives of the people). The news reports resulted in a number of resignations, firings and impromptu retirements from the political scene.

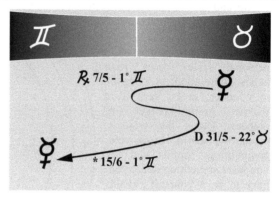

Here's a quick guide to handling Mercury retrograde, the most notorious and regular optical illusion:

• Rest/reflect/recharge batteries, enjoy mental down time/time out, retreat from urban life and get some space from the professional conveyer belt; stop and smell the roses; avoid buying Mercury-type products.

• Revise opinions, readjust priorities, check and reconfirm, and read the fine print (but sign on the dotted line later!) – make the decisions that you've been putting off.

• Check, rearrange, re-explore, reorganize material. Retrograde means 'second chance'.

• Research, investigate, gather information, re-evaluate, rethink recent decisions and perhaps return to an approach that worked in the past; avoid long-term decisions; review/edit/sharpen work and spot mistakes made.

• Clean up, carry out maintenance/repair work, catch up on filing/emails/writing and reconnect with friends and restore old friendships.

• If you do get thrown for a loop, take a step back and look at the problem objectively (Mercury's function) and work with it or go with the flow – 'this too shall pass'.

After Mercury moves direct, matters don't really progress until the planet reaches the degree in the zodiac at which it first went retrograde, and this is usually two to three weeks after it has gone direct (see * on the diagram above).

What is often written about retrograde planets in the natal chart (frequently derived or skewed from horary and electional astrology) can have a deleterious effect on the student astrologer. For example, those born with Mercury retrograde are sometimes labelled as slow learners or even 'mentally backward'. In historical texts, words such as 'deception' and 'dishonesty' crop up. My students who have natal Mercury retrograde seem to learn best when approaching a problem from a different angle, accessing and reworking the information visually or laterally. Interestingly, in doing so, they've taught me to adapt and teach them in a different way (Mercury).

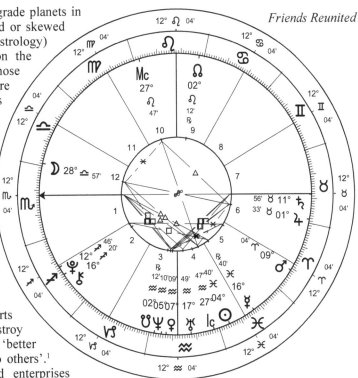

Friends Reunited

Astrologer Robert Hand asserts that retrogradation does not destroy a planet's influence but makes it 'better suited to some situations than to others'.[1] I've found that companies and enterprises born under Mercury retrograde can thrive if they *actively engage* in work linked to the process of retrogradation, and I'm reminded of the chart for the (now-defunct) social networking website, **Friends Reunited** (chart pictured above). Mercury (ruler of the 11th House of social connections) is retrograde in Pisces: the purpose of the site is to get back in touch (Mercury retrograde) with lost (Pisces) friends (11th), exchange information, and, as the website proclaims, 'never lose touch with your past'.

The more natal charts we study, the more we realize that words such as 'backward' don't assist the client, nor do they do justice to such a placement. The chart of the late Steve Jobs of Apple reminds us of what a retrograde, (almost) unaspected Mercury can accomplish. Mercury is his Chart Ruler and in a very wide square to the 'malefic' planet Saturn (reflecting his poor early education rather than any lack of intelligence). With Apple, Jobs created his own 'language' and used his Mercury (and other planets) to great effect *in his own, roundabout and particular way*.

Others see natal retrograde planets as areas where the promise is not fully materialized, or potential is withheld until later. Linda Reid writes that retrogrades 'remain dormant or grow ready for release at some future time'.[2]

In my experience, a natal retrograde planet (less so for the outer planets) can be fully engaged early in life – perhaps too early, before the maturity or self-awareness needed to handle it is present – only for this early promise to be put 'on hold' while we catch up on other levels. Later, we are given a *second chance* to explore and benefit from the planet's potential, but on a more secure and grounded basis. The planet pauses, gestates (is subjugated, even) until we are ready to manifest it and work with it in a way that serves us best. In fact, the planet fully blossoms later rather than sooner, perhaps once we've recognized our true purpose (the Sun).[3] And indeed, astronomically, retrogradation is dependent upon a planet's relationship to the Sun, as seen from Earth. One of the modern astrologers to have written extensively on the subject of retrogrades in natal charts is acclaimed astrologer Erin Sullivan.[4]

Venus retrograde in the natal chart would suggest some kind of early experience of Venusian principles (e.g. getting married early) but then returning to this theme later in life in a more structured and mature way (e.g. a second chance in love). Saturn is retrograde for 36.5% of its cycle, but, when retrograde and prominent in a chart, it can suggest that we take on burdens or parental responsibilities early in life and must wait to realize our personal ambitions later. Astrologer Noel Tyl writes of a legacy of feelings of inferiority due to the lack of an authority figure in early childhood – or the presence of a tyrannical one – and 'a pause built into development for some very hard lessons to be learned'.[5]

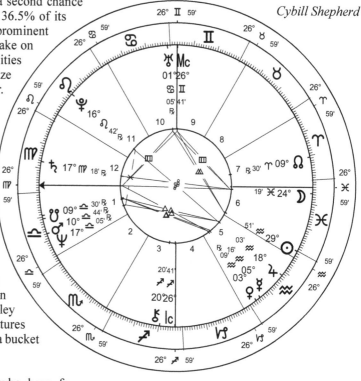

Cybill Shepherd

A retrograde planet takes on greater importance when placed in a key position, for instance, on an angle or as a singleton or a 'handle'. This is the case in the horoscope of child star Shirley Temple (see page 113), which features Saturn retrograde as the handle of a bucket chart.

I've often worked with clients who have four or more retrograde planets. According to Neil Michelsen's *Tables of Planetary Phenomena* (ACS, 1993), roughly 14 per cent of people born in the 20th century have four retrograde planets; 5 per cent have five; and 1 per cent have six. My clients often say they feel that much of their life has seemed to be 'on hold' or that they've cast aside initial aims or talents and settled for 'real life'. Yet the promise inherent in these placements is a second chance to explore and establish early ambitions later in life.

It would be convenient to have an idea of when this second chance takes place (e.g. under a particular transit or when a planet changes direction by progressed), but there doesn't seem to be a predictable trigger or age at which it occurs.

A high number of celebrities with four or more retrograde planets have had initial, sometimes prodigious, periods of success, only to face a long 'pause' before developing a more solid career basis and firmer trajectory. (A surprising number, including Princess Diana, Karen Carpenter and James Dean, have died young – their lives cut short before being able to take advantage of a second, more stable period. But please do not infer that

having many natal retrogrades suggests an early death!)

Consider the story of comeback queen **Cybill Shepherd** (chart above), who began as a model, became an overnight Hollywood sensation at age 21 and then went back home to Memphis at age 28, married, had a child and dropped out of the movie business. She re-emerged in her mid-30s with her greatest successes on TV: firstly *Moonlighting* and later as star–executive producer of her own comedy show, *Cybill*. Shepherd has six planets (Venus, Mars, Saturn, Uranus, Neptune and Pluto) retrograde (and a Void Moon). A pause followed by a second, more solid chance also took place in her singing career: Cybill recorded a few albums but hung up her microphone when critics savaged her. Later, she returned a better, more confident jazz singer and resumed her recording career.

The Aspects

Aspects are the all-important angular relationships between any two planets or points (i.e. a specific number of degrees between two parts of a chart). They link these two planets/points and form a *dialogue* – an interaction, a flow of energy. That two planets are in conversation is the most important consideration, regardless of the actual aspect involved (e.g. a square). It is the combination of planetary energies that is paramount to chart interpretation.

A Few Considerations
There is a hierarchy to keep in mind: the outermost planet of the two in aspect will most influence the inner planet. For example, in a Mercury–Saturn aspect it is Mercury that is feeling the full range of Saturn's influence, instilling a disciplined or serious (Saturn) type of mind, voice or other means of expression (Mercury). But it does work the other way round, too, albeit less so: there will be intellectual interest in and discussion about (Mercury) all things Saturnian, from science, the laws of cause and effect, to organized religion, etc.

I haven't found there to be much difference in natal astrology between applying aspects (where the aspect hasn't yet perfected) and separating aspects (where the faster moving planet has moved on from an exact aspect but is still within orb).

Some astrologers may not use them, but dissociate (i.e. out of sign) aspects work perfectly well. However, the symbolism and interpretation may be more complex because the aspect involved – e.g. a conjunction of one planet at the end of Taurus to another at the start of Gemini – does not match the natural zodiacal relationship between the signs.

An important consideration is the *signs involved* in the aspect: much can be gleaned from analysing what they have in common and how they differ. They also offer important clues to the aspect itself. Unless they happen to be dissociate (out of sign) aspects, all oppositions involve polarities (Aries–Libra, Taurus–Scorpio, and so on) – signs that are strongly linked but have very different priorities. Squares link signs of the same mode but different elements (e.g. cardinal Cancer, a Water sign concerned with emotional connection, is square to both cardinal Libra, belonging to the detached,

rational element of Air, and cardinal Aries, the gung-ho Fire sign). These signs have difficulty in understanding the other's motivation (element) and butt heads because they have similar tactics (mode): the cardinal signs want to move things to a new level but they clash when trying to establish who is boss; the fixed signs want to sustain, maintain and keep a steady pace but disagreement can result in a stubborn stand-off; while the mutable signs are born to communicate, teach and disperse information, but their energy can dissipate and conflict arises from their need to 'pass the buck' – to avoid accountability.

Aspects from planets to the angles should be considered when analysing a chart, but these are not dynamic exchanges between planetary 'energies'. Rather, they say much about how we make our mark on our environment and our orientation to – and personal interactions with – the world around us. A planet that is aspecting an angle shows the ways in which we can manifest that planet in our personal and social surroundings (see pages 29–31).

Orbs
An orb is the distance in degrees (°) by which an aspect can deviate from being exact yet still be considered influential. As a general rule, allow 8° for the conjunction, opposition, square and trine, and 4° for a sextile. In practice, I would not look at a trine or sextile with an orb of more than 2° or 3°, but I would allow up to 10° when considering conjunctions. Tight aspects between planets (i.e. close orbs) will always be felt strongly in our life patterns and stories, but just as many examples of relevant life events, themes and character traits are found in those who have aspects with wider orbs. As with any wide orb, *listen* to how (or if) the aspect is being expressed by the client. An orb of 9° for a conjunction may seem too wide but, when using Solar Arc directions, the aspect will have become exact around the age of nine. At that age, the client will have experienced the fusion of these planets, so the aspect may represent a defining time in the client's life and be a recurring theme later on. I would be generous with the orbs of conjunctions to the angles because, as shown in the work of the Gauquelins (see page 49), the crossing over of any of these angles is a gradual yet important process.

The Aspects (major aspects are in bold)

0°	**Conjunction**
30°	Semi-sextile
45°	Semi-square
60°	**Sextile**
72°	Quintile
90°	**Square**
120°	**Trine**
135°	Sesquiquadrate (Sesquisquare)
150°	Quincunx (Inconjunct)
180°	**Opposition**

The conjunction is termed a 'neutral' aspect but is an unequal collaboration between two planets. The 'soft' aspects (the sextile and trine) create self-perpetuating behavioural patterns and 'comfortable' situations that can trap us, while 'hard' aspects (the square, opposition, semi-square and sesquiquadrate) symbolize the stages when friction erupts – they demand awareness or activity and offer a release of tension.

The Major Aspects
The Conjunction (0°)
The conjunction is an intensified, potent and focal point in the horoscope. The planets/energies join forces and are inextricably linked, never acting alone. There may be a lack of objectivity in the areas linked to the planets conjunct (unless they receive an opposition from another planet). Conjunctions are usually very familiar parts of our personality that were formed early in life – areas we're used to working with ('It's just who I am') and a facet of ourselves that others see vividly. Tip: always consider the zodiacal sequence of planets when interpreting a conjunction (see pages 42–5).

When outer planets form a conjunction, this heralds a new age for societies. But unless this conjunction is aspecting a personal planet or angle, it won't say much about us individually. Neptune–Pluto came together in Gemini towards the end of the 19th century (the conjunction was exact three times: August 1891 and November 1891 at 8°, and in April 1892 at 7°), heralding the super-fast, information-driven nature of the 20th century, while Uranus–Pluto in Virgo (exact in 1965–6) began technological and sexual revolutions that brought about industrial changes from the silicon chip to the contraceptive pill (Virgo) – in fact, developments that affect almost every system that we use to run our lives today. (For more, see *Uranus Square Pluto* [Mayo Press,

2012] by Wendy Stacey.) In *Astro Mind Maps* (Flare, 2010), Kim Farley writes that the signs of the outer planets show the 'backdrop of the times we are born into… the major headlines of that era… [and reflect] a seed that is planted within us which flowers only when we start making an impact on our wider world.'

The Opposition (180°)
The conjunction is the beginning of a cycle between two planets, whereas the opposition is the culmination, the climax, the fruition point in that journey. Picture the Full Moon – the Sun in opposition to the Moon – when the Moon has reached its furthest distance from the Sun and receives *maximum* light from the Sun. All matters linked to the planets in opposition are 'out in the open' and fully realized through our interactions with others.

We learn about the opposition aspect through relationship – oppositions in our horoscopes reveal the issues, needs and areas of our personality that we explore when in some sort of exchange with another; we cannot avoid acting these out in relationship and feel *compelled to balance* this astrological see-saw and planetary showdown. Oppositions are often the parts of ourselves that we find easier to blame others for or project onto others (usually the more 'difficult' of the two planets involved), yet it is the role of the opposition to make us *fully aware* of the areas we find most difficult to integrate *in ourselves*. Descriptive of our relationship patterns, oppositions reveal the problem areas for which we enter therapy. The conflict of opposites always brings about change, so this is a dynamic axis in any horoscope. This planetary face-off is a key spotlight in our life, and constantly demands attention, balance and resolution. Tip: when interpreting a non-dissociate opposition, consider the differences and similarities of the polar signs involved.

The Square (90°)
An 'edgy' aspect, the square is associated with the crisis, make-or-break stage in the cycle – where a difficulty emerges requiring action in order for a situation to progress. Yet, rather than being an aspect to dread, research shows that our greatest accomplishments (the areas in life where we can have an impact and manifest things in concrete terms) can be defined by the planets involved in this aspect. This is because we are sent repeatedly challenging situations or obstacles of the nature

of the planets in square until we master these and use them to their fullest. The nature of the square forces us to prove that *we can* master this aspect and deliver the riches promised.[6] Yet, there are times when a square can feel like the weakest link in our chart – our hard luck sob story or perpetual, self-defeating actions – if we fail to see these on-going situations as lessons for growth. With squares, there's no gain without pain, and we're reminded of the phrase 'no guts, no glory'. Courage is needed to focus, apply, strive and take action in these areas – being thrown a lemon and making lemonade! Tip: keep squares well 'oiled'; accept the on-going challenges thrown across our path and look to ways of using these planets dynamically in our life.

The Trine (120°)

An 'easy' aspect, the trine represents a natural flow of energy between two planets – 'being' rather than 'doing'. A trine in the chart shows the types of things we do well, quickly and with ease; talents that we have and enjoy but rarely practise. With trines, we usually accept situations the way they are and always have been. Unless the trine is linked to a square or opposition, it can be an area of least resistance or a place of stagnation. Associated with luck and opportunity, planets linked by trine are the areas of life where things flow without much effort (e.g. being in the right place at the right time), where the obstacles have been removed; these areas have the potential for unlimited growth but we need to make some effort to hone these natural gifts.

The Sextile (60°)

Another 'easy' aspect, the sextile offers fewer direct opportunities than a trine and requires more work to manifest its promise. Astrologer Lois Rodden saw this aspect as offering a bridge of opportunity – but one that we often turn down and later regret. The door of opportunity may open at regular intervals but only for short periods of time. Both the trine and sextile are sometimes too easy or not valued enough, and we pass up the chance to turn them into great strengths.

Some 'Minor' Aspects

For the charts in the book, I have only included the five major aspects. The minor aspects usually have an orb of 2° and, in my experience, they have a *specific function* and can be seen in precise storylines played out and repeated at various times (more akin to the subplots in our life).

Here are some keywords and ideas associated with three of the most important minors.

The Semi-square (45°)

An agitating area of indecision or friction, or a situation that requires on-the-job training or learning by trial and error.

The Sesquiquadrate/Sesquisquare (135°)

Unexpected, disruptive situations that break up and reform; quantum leap 'detours' that take us off-course; they are prominent in the charts of adventurers and others who travel uncharted waters or blaze new trails.

The Quincunx (150°)

Incomplete, out of kilter situations (a feeling of discomfort or dis-ease) where adjustment or adaptation is required; or areas in life where a situation that has been ignored or kept under wraps urgently needs addressing. Tip: when interpreting the quincunx, always consider the signs involved – their similarities and differences. Because they are of different elements and modes, signs in natural quincunx to each other contrast sharply in motivation (element), method and style (mode), but upon further investigation often have planets in common: Venus's signs (Taurus and Libra) are in quincunx, as are Mars's (Aries and Scorpio). More interestingly, there are major differences of approach and style *around a similar theme*. For example, Gemini the fact-finder, curious gossip and information-disperser is quincunx both secretive Scorpio and cagey Capricorn, both signs that crave respect and privacy and have an innate understanding of political dynamics and undercurrents. Sagittarius, the eternal student and traveller who lives to experience the journey, is in quincunx to Taurus and Cancer – the two signs associated with home, hearth, gardens and a contentment with one's lot (or allotment!). Cancer, the homebody attached to the past, is quincunx Sagittarius and Aquarius, the two most future-orientated signs that reach out to the world. Leo wants the best quality, as does Capricorn, the sign it quincunxes, but Leo is flashy and shiny and Capricorn is classy and understated. In synastry, the all-important Sun, Moon and Ascendant are often in signs that quincunx each other, whether by exact degree or not. There appears to be a fascination with what we don't have! With the quincunx, the shared theme but sharp contrast of method and attitude create an irresistible temptation and 'pull' to form a relationship.

Interpreting the Sequence of Planets

When learning to interpret planetary conjunctions, a useful tool to play with is the sequence of the planets involved: looking at how the grouped planets line up in the order of their zodiac signs and degrees. I started considering this after listening to clients' stories of how events tended to develop and repeat in their lives. One client with Saturn (27° Taurus) conjunct Uranus (29° Taurus) in her 7th House became pregnant and made a commitment to a very solid provider who was a builder (represented by Saturn in Taurus), but she spent many years in the marriage feeling hemmed in and was forever wanting to leave or shake up the union irrevocably (Uranus). In fact, she would play a part in triggering arguments that would prompt her husband to pack his bags. Another client, with the same conjunction in her 7th, but with Uranus a few degrees earlier than Saturn, would meet someone, fall in love suddenly, only to find that what was once exciting was now restrictive and too familiar (Saturn can be experienced as the anchor or the millstone). Both women experienced the themes of Saturn–Uranus in their 7th House but in a different sequence.

The *planetary combination* is always the key factor. Regardless of the aspect or sequence, Saturn–Uranus will always have the same basic qualities: 'change meets resistance', 'radical ideas become accepted' and 'growing rebellious with age' are just three ideas. But the order in which the two planets appear in the zodiac says a great deal about how this pattern arises and unfolds. This can be applied to combinations with other aspects, but it is seen more vividly with the conjunction.

For example, some expressions of Mars–Uranus, based on keywords and planetary principles, are:

- Original, pioneering action; a new order.

- Instigating/receiving a dramatic wake-up call.

- Activity that is sudden, sporadic, spasmodic, shocking or boundary-shattering.

- Daring to fight for human rights and freedom – to overturn the established order (often only to then be censored or shut out).

- Provoking outrage and flouting convention.

- Dramatic accidents or sudden attacks.

- Sexual revolution, excitement, or danger; changing what is considered masculine.

The well known people listed below embody many of these expressions. But it is not surprising that we find Mars preceding Uranus by conjunction in the charts of those whose actions or sexuality (Mars) have led to shocking results, rebellion or a change of conditions (Uranus): gender-bender Boy George, and Marjoe Gortner, the child prodigy (Mars) and evangelist who turned people on to social change before exposing his own money racket, breaking away from the church (Uranus) and pursuing his film star aspirations. Victim of police brutality Rodney King and unpredictable, self-destructive actor Robert Downey, Jr. have the conjunction ending with the planet Pluto, while dancer–spy Mata Hari and Christine Keeler (whose sexual affairs with political figures brought down the British government in the 1960s) have this sequence along with other planets.

Uranus leads Mars in the charts of those whose controversial stance breaks up an existing order and then invokes the Mars principle or evokes Mars-like repercussions (e.g. conflict, sex, embarking on a 'mission'): homophobic activist Anita Bryant, sci-fi writer and religion founder L Ron Hubbard, talk-show-host-cum-ringmaster Jerry Springer, Jim Morrison and Neale Donald Walsch, whose automatic writing led to his calling as a messenger with his *Conversations with God* (Gemini/10th).

Another with Uranus followed by Mars is sex therapist **Dr Ruth Westheimer** (chart opposite page, top), who became an iconic sex educator and pioneer in 'sexual literacy' (the Uranus–Mars and Gemini influence) in the 1980s. Her dramatic life-story is as shocking as her Uranus–Mars conjunction in Aries, and speaks volumes about the sequence of her Saturn–Moon in Sagittarius, too (suggestive of restrictive ideologies that led to her moving country on numerous occasions). Born Karola Ruth Siegel, she was sent to Switzerland on 5 January 1939 to escape the Nazis. It was the last time she saw any member of her family, who would later perish in the Holocaust. Her childhood and teenage years were spent in an orphanage and in servitude. Later, while living in Palestine and training to be a teacher, a sudden outbreak (Uranus) of guerilla warfare (Mars) led to her joining the Jewish underground army and being trained, she says, as a 'ruthless sniper' (Mars) and messenger (Gemini) – until her legs were almost ripped off by a bomb, causing serious damage to her feet. While studying psychology at the Sorbonne, Ruth received compensation from the West German government, left her studies and took off for a trip to the US in 1956. There, she won a scholarship, relocated, graduated and began training educators to teach sex education. Her forthright style and ability to discuss explicit sexual matters with frankness, common sense and enthusiasm led to *Sexually Speaking*, the first of many radio shows, in May 1980.

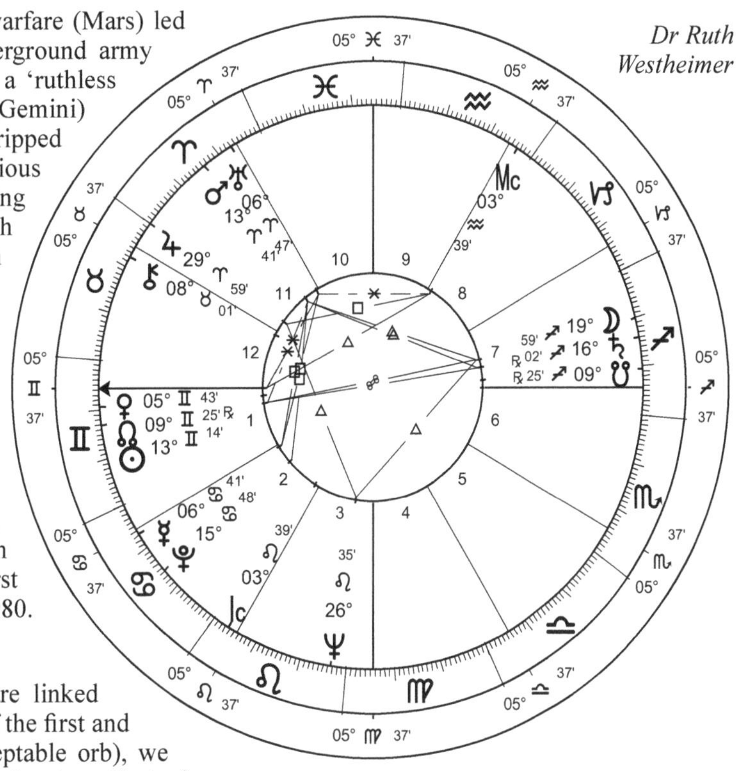

Dr Ruth Westheimer

Threesomes

When three or more planets are linked together by conjunction (even if the first and final planets are out of an acceptable orb), we can see a life pattern at work, a domino effect of developments.

Bill Clinton's chart (left) has Mars–Neptune–Venus in Libra, which is suggestive of personal charm, insatiability and serial adultery. But looking at the sequence, Mars' arousal instigates the pattern. It is followed by Neptune (scandal) and ends with Venus (the likeability factor, the charm offensive, not being taken seriously, the Teflon syndrome – nothing sticks).

Originally a copywriter who created some memorable one-liners for advertising agencies (Gemini), author **Salman Rushdie** (chart over the page) has Uranus–Moon–Sun conjunct in Gemini. Born to upper middle class privilege in Bombay, Rushdie grew up feeling an outsider, alienated by being an Indian with an old-guard, colonial upper-crust British accent (Sun–Moon–Uranus in Gemini). But this would pale in comparison to the reaction his fourth novel provoked. *The Satanic Verses*

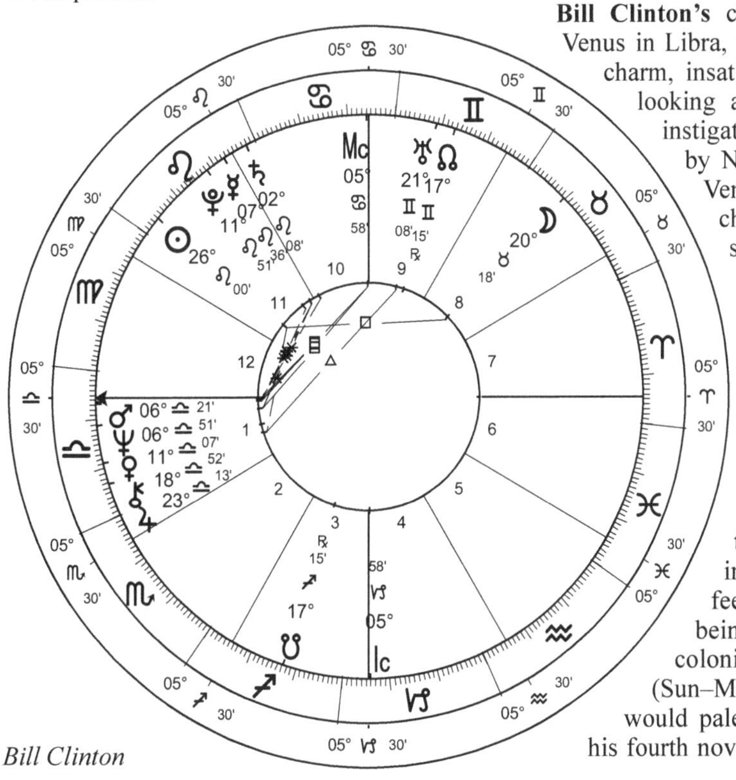

Bill Clinton

was published on 28 September 1988, just three weeks before Saturn conjunct Uranus in the sky at 27° Sagittarius – opposite his natal Sun and Moon. The book caused a furore in the Muslim world, which considered it highly *blasphemous* (TR Uranus in Sagittarius opposite the Gemini planets) and, on 14 February 1989, his provocative writing suddenly (Uranus) found him issued with a *fatwa* and condemned to death by Iran's Ayatollah Khomeini (Rushdie's natal Jupiter is in Scorpio in the 7th opposite Mars in the 1st). Rushdie went into hiding and was given police protection (the Moon is linked to seclusion, withdrawal, safety), only to emerge socializing as a guest celebrity at various literary events (Sun in Gemini)! When Pluto reached 27° Sagittarius in June 2007, Rushdie was knighted, provoking further protests and threats.

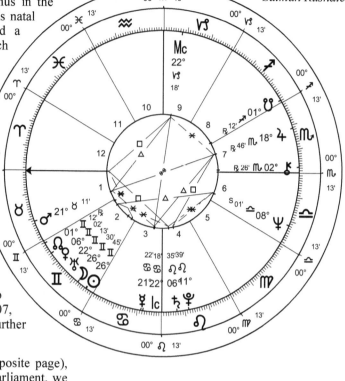

Salman Rushdie

In the chart of **Jeffrey Archer** (opposite page), a novelist and former Member of Parliament, we note a Bowl-shaped chart contained by the 'rim' of a Mercury–Neptune opposition. Archer is a great storyteller, in both senses of the word. His novels have soap opera-style twists and turns, intrigue, suspense and deception, while his personal life and political reputation – replete with lies, lurid cover-ups and perjury – resemble the dirty waters of a Neptune-polluted Mercury.

Much of the chart consists of conjunctions tying up the four angles (often a sign of worldly success or a strong impact on one's environment). His Chart Ruler, the Moon, conjoins Pluto on the Ascendant: sales of more than 100 million copies of his novels have made Archer one of the most widely read authors of all time. The Midheaven ruler, Mars in Gemini, conjoins Venus: his most popular book is *Kane and Abel*, the story of male Aries time-twins (Gemini) who lock horns and carry on a bitter lifelong feud in their struggle to each build an empire. At the top of his chart is Jupiter conjunct Sun in Aries, followed by the Sun's wide (and dissociate) conjunction with Saturn in early Taurus. If read in this sequence, it reveals Archer's go-getting philosophy (Jupiter in Aries), his personal ambition to be Number One (Sun in Aries) and his

need to amass wealth to combat fears of poverty (Saturn in Taurus).

Consider the sequence of Jupiter–Sun–Saturn in the pattern of his life. With 'a certainty that he could command success', Archer was a runner at school and bristled with ambition (Jupiter in Aries). He sprinted into Parliament at age 29 (on 4 December 1969, his Saturn Return), with plans to be Prime Minister, and started to forge an identity as an enterprising young politician (Sun in Aries). Five years later on 23 August 1974, he resigned after being swindled in a dodgy financial scheme (natal Saturn in Taurus). With transiting Pluto on the IC and transiting Uranus opposite the Sun, Archer downsized and began writing novels to pay his creditors. His first book was a #1 publishing sensation (Jupiter in Aries) and brought him new celebrity (Sun) and financial security (Saturn in Taurus). *Not a Penny More, Not a Penny Less* (published in April 1976, when TR Jupiter hit natal Saturn) was based upon his quest to retrieve lost monies and avoid bankruptcy.

One Jupiter return after his resignation, Archer had climbed back on top as a successful, international novelist (Jupiter) and a popular media personality. He had been given a position (Sun) in Margaret Thatcher's Conservative Party. But, elevated and seemingly untouchable as Thatcher's golden boy, he then found himself accused of philandering and paying off a prostitute (late October 1986, following a lunar eclipse at 24° Aries, close to his Sun–Jupiter conjunction). It was Saturn's turn: once again he resigned from his political position, but sued for libel and won substantial damages in the July 1987 trial (TR Jupiter conjunct natal Sun).

The legal win reinstated his reputation (in part) and began the Jupiter–Sun–Saturn cycle again. Twelve years later, Jupiter and the Sun had been activated once more: Archer was now a Lord and the candidate favoured to become the first (Aries) modern Mayor of London. But on 21 November 1999 (with TR Jupiter conjunct his Sun), it was revealed that he had asked a friend for a false alibi and had perjured himself to win the 1987 libel suit. Expelled from the Conservative Party, Archer was found guilty of perjury in July 2001 and served two years in prison (Saturn).

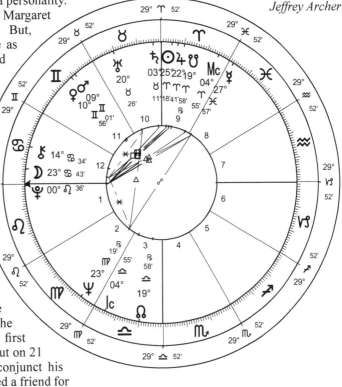

Jeffrey Archer

On each of these occasions, Archer's desire to be prominent and seen as a self-made man and success story (Jupiter in Aries) led quickly (note the close orb) to an established reputation and identity (Sun). But since Saturn in Taurus ends the sequence (albeit taking its time – 8° away), it was vital that he settled accounts before being *forced* to pay the bill. (The zealous enterprises of Aries must move into Taurus with substance and grounding.)

With Sun–Jupiter in Aries, Archer was reckless, brazen and felt untouchable. Exploiting and cashing in on opportunities offered, cutting corners, overextending one's reputation and taking opportunistic gambles are various ways of playing the Sun–Jupiter 'confidence trick'. But with Saturn in the mix, reality can bite, integrity is put to the test, and reputations based on 'a house of cards' fall apart. (The square of these planets to the rising Moon and Pluto also suggests financial wipeout and resurgence, issues of betrayal, and haunting secrets from the past.)

Archer's unofficial biographer, Michael Crick, wrote: '[His] life is a carnival of risk, bluff and naked ambition, all twisted by, in the words of his wife Mary, Archer's "gift for inaccurate précis".'[7] Crick has been described as Archer's nemesis, and it was Crick's dogged investigations that led to Archer's final disgrace, trial and imprisonment. Crick was born on 21 May 1958; his Jupiter at 22° Libra exactly opposes Archer's, and his Mercury at 5° Taurus conjoins Archer's Saturn.

Yet, with Sun–Jupiter (and an Aries MC), Archer is viewed by the British public as a charming rascal, a resilient, schoolboyish opportunist. Down but not out, Archer made good use of his time served behind bars (Saturn) by publishing a series of books about prison life (Jupiter, thus restarting the sequence again). The Sun–Jupiter in Aries, as noted in the charts of Joseph Campbell and Maya Angelou (see pages 122 and 123), can be 'seen' in many titles of his books (*First Among Equals*, *A Matter of Honour*, *Sons of Fortune*, *Paths of Glory*) and in this very apt description of Archer:

The greatest Archer quality: resilience, the determination to bounce back, a refusal to be defeated.

In this concise section, I'll be examining some initial areas to keep in mind before we start looking for 'ways in' to explore the horoscope. In particular, I'll be considering how vital it is to know the differences between the various parts of the astrological alphabet – to know that signs are different from planets and both are quite different from houses.

Having clear ideas of what the Sun (for instance) means in *any* birth chart (and having a good vocabulary to describe the planet) helps to break the chart down into manageable pieces. Once the main alphabet (the signs, planets, houses and aspects) has been learned, the next stage is to keep in mind the fact that planets, signs and houses have distinct, discrete meanings. Each part of the astrological jigsaw is unique.

Occasionally, astrology books have 'cookbook' headings for interpretations that group a sign and house together (for instance, 'Sun in Taurus *or* Sun in the Second House'), as though they were interchangeable. The Sun in the Second House may have some similar themes to the sign of Taurus (value, worth and money) but the house is an *area* of life, while the sign is the *way* in which a planet *expresses* itself.

In this section, I have also laid out my ideas about what makes a planet influential. I think most astrologers have their own take on how they 'weight' information in the chart, but I've presented my own ideas of what constitutes an influential planet. I also wanted to make the point that there is a difference between a planet that functions effectively (according to its core nature) and one that plays an influential, dynamic role in a horoscope.

Know the Differences

Firstly, consider how planets in combination differ. For instance, a Sun–Uranus aspect is very different from a Moon–Uranus one. Uranus contacting either the Sun or Moon (by major aspect) would make it an important player in the chart regardless, but our job is to discover how, why and where Uranus differs between its aspect to the Sun and to the Moon. The next step is to consider the specific astrological aspect (such as the conjunction, square and opposition) and what it might bring to the dialogue.

With the Sun in aspect to Uranus, there is an innate feeling of being on a different path – or of life 'conspiring' to put us on one. It is the signature of the catalyst, the outsider, the radical. Our journey and essential philosophy (Sun) is concerned with waking up other people and speaking *our* truth, but it is always a journey that contains twists of fate or unforeseen deviations in the road ahead.

When these planets are conjunct, this theme is a fundamental part of our life story, and it may be difficult for us to recognize objectively the power to change (or disrupt) that lies within us. When in square, there is a tension that brings change to the fore – obstacles appear to kick-start the revolutionary aspect of our nature. When in opposition, our purpose (Sun) is to act as a catalyst for others, and in return we are changed profoundly while in relationship. When there is a close trine, we find ways to express our differentness naturally without the compulsion to provoke. (The signs involved say much about our attitude to breaking the rules: Earth signs, Leo and Libra are conventional, while the fixed signs want change only on their own terms and in their own time.)

If the aspect is Moon–Uranus, then the change is likely to manifest as drama or instability in the home or working life. There may be emotional independence, a daily need for excitement or an instinct to shake up stagnant situations. Early shock or emotional breaks could lead to self-containment and self-reliance, a sensitivity to rejection, or a safety valve that helps us to detach or cut off when there's too much pressure. The Uranian need for perfection is directed towards eating habits, the body and emotional needs.

A final point: when looking to understand a specific area of life (e.g. children, work, money), start with the planets associated with these areas before looking for links between appropriate houses and rulers.

Planetary Effectiveness vs. Influence

There is an important difference between a planet's 'condition' (its ability to carry out the job it is *designed to do* effectively) and its 'weight' in the horoscope (where it is set apart, worthy of notice and therefore playing a major role in the chart).

Rather than using the term 'planetary strength', perhaps we could start by distinguishing between the words 'effective' and 'influential':

Effective: successful in producing a desired, intended/expected result; creating a deep, vivid impression or strong response; getting the right things done; productive

Influential: of considerable importance; having or exercising power; an astrological term meaning 'emanation from the stars that acts upon one's character and destiny'; a 'flowing in'

A planet can be deemed 'strong' and 'powerful' under both of these classifications, of course, but it is more useful to see it in terms of effectiveness and influence. It can accomplish *effectively* what is set out in its nature to do (when planet and sign are in accord), and/or it can be *influential* by being placed in a 'remarkable' position in the chart where it dominates, receives singular recognition or is set apart from other planets.

Influential (Weighty) Planets

An influential planet is one that is placed around a key area of the horoscope (e.g. the four angles), in a standout position (such as being the handle of a Bucket chart), and/or in heavy dialogue with other parts of the chart (i.e. it aspects many other points, or it stands alone in no dialogue with any other planet – i.e. it is unaspected). A full list can be found on page 49.

An influential planet is a guiding force, a leader in the chart, and it manifests as such in the life. This planet is a dominating force in that person's life stories, traits and experiences. The exact *quality* of that impact, however, is seen by the planet's sign position and the planets it aspects.

Effective Planets: Quality and Affinity

An effective planet is one found in a sign that resembles its key principles and themes (Mars in Aries and Scorpio, Venus in Taurus and Libra). It manifests, clearly and certainly, those 'textbook' planetary themes in a person's life, character and events. Its 'condition' is free from impediment, obstruction or hindrance – and unplagued by doubt or confusion. *The planet does what it says on the tin!* It takes care of business. The planet and sign are in tune and speaking a similar language – they have an *affinity* – so the job of the planet is accomplished with greater ease and simplicity. This is also true for a planet in its associated house (for instance, Saturn in the 10th).

Planets in signs that have less (or seemingly nothing) in common with each other carry out their jobs differently – but this is not to be feared, because they have *different* jobs to do! The jobs are no less important. Here, the planet has a particular way of operating and a different agenda. For instance, Mercury (ruler of Gemini and Virgo) may be out of its depth in the Water signs because its natural function is a mix of Airy Gemini's rationality and perspective and Earthy Virgo's order and analysis. But, at best, Mercury in Water connects to a fluid expression of itself in a realm that is initially unfamiliar. For instance, it may learn to express (Mercury) empathy (Water), make emotional (Water) connections (Mercury), speak a language (Mercury) of the soul (Water).

In natal astrology, I prefer to avoid traditional words like 'exaltation', and 'detriment' or 'fall'. Although the latter are ways of classifying a planet's lack of familiarity to, and correspondence with, a particular sign, what might result is a failure to recognize the potential and talent inherent in a 'foreign' placement. For instance, Mars is traditionally in 'detriment' in the signs Taurus and Libra, which are ruled by its psychological and planetary opposite, Venus. Yet when placed in the Venusian sign of Libra, we discover Mars to be an effective player of the game, where energy (Mars) is put into negotiation, discussion and issues of fairness (Libra). Not everyday Mars interests, but an important alternative to warlike, selfish and pugnacious Mars activities (which have their place, too, of course!). The art of negotiation and some forethought, grace and energy directed towards peace are necessities (think Nelson Mandela, the Dalai Lama and peace protestor John Lennon, all of whom were born with Mars in Libra). Mars in the Venusian sign of Libra puts energy into finding a way forward, *beyond* conflict. It is the lover (Venus) of argument (Mars in Air), although Libra would prefer the word 'discussion'. In times of immense Mars-type strife, what's needed is strategy and a cool Libran head (unhampered by the hotheadedness of Mars in Aries or the volatile, emotional attachment of Scorpio). Mars in Libra has a proven track record of dynamic leadership. Winston Churchill and Margaret Thatcher were both born with Mars in Libra (in aspect to Jupiter). Churchill (with Mercury opposite Pluto) understood that 'rhetorical power is neither wholly bestowed nor wholly acquired, but *cultivated*'. He coined two phrases that epitomize Mars in Libra: 'the sinews of peace' and 'the special relationship'.

This placement, and any other of its kind, is not dysfunctional, ineffectual or weak. It is Mars out of his comfort zone – not doing a traditionally *effective* job – and he is forced to express his key functions and desires in a foreign voice.

Combinations
A planet that is both effective and influential will demonstrate *powerfully* the planet's *innate message*. A planet that is influential but not effective will still dominate but the message will differ from the by-the-book interpretation. A planet that is effective but not influential will be expressed simply but not as a leading player in the person's life. And, finally, a planet that is neither effective nor influential may fade into the background, or seek some way to compensate (for instance, getting involved with those who are embodiments of that planet).

When looking for examples, consider the highly influential (but not effective) Mercury in the chart of Richard Nixon (page 58) and Jupiter in the chart of John DeLorean (page 104). Then take a look at the effective but not influential Mars in the horoscope of Paul Newman (page 100). Here, Mars is in Aries but away from an angle and making few aspects to other planets. Paul Newman had a passion for speed racing; it was a simple, direct way of expressing his competitive spirit (Mars in Aries) but it was contained in one separate corner of his life. And, as a final example, consider Saturn in the horoscope and biography of Jim Jones (page 106). It is effectively placed

(in Saturn's sign of Capricorn) and strongly influential (the Chart Ruler and part of a major six-planet cardinal T-square).

Yet...
The more charts we read, the more we realize that people accomplish extraordinary things with 'debilitated' positions, while others choose paths where 'pristine' placements languish, stagnate or fall by the wayside. The most 'exalted' and 'pure' or 'diminished' and 'detrimental' placements can produce varying results depending on a number of personal choices and external factors. Benefics (Venus and Jupiter) can be 'too much of a good thing' or get away with murder (ask your local con artist), while malefics (Mars and Saturn) can provide the backbone necessary for success.

There is much to admire in astrology's history: techniques, tools and tips from master astrologers that can be of benefit to us today. But we need to avoid sticking too rigidly to techniques that, simply put, *no longer stand up to scrutiny* or are formed from a narrow set of assumptions. (At one conference, I heard an inexperienced astrologer recall discouraging a client from following a cherished dream because her chart didn't show that she would achieve eminence in that field. Heck! How about just encouraging a client to pursue something they enjoy?)

All aspects, planets and signs have a *range* of expression and possibilities (and I have no qualms about identifying problem areas in the chart), but to reduce these to simple equations (soft aspects = good, hard aspects = bad) more than misses the point. And it offers little to the client. Nor should we attempt to throw endless (sometimes unrealistic) possibilities at a client or put a Pollyanna spin on every catastrophe and see everything as a 'lesson for growth' (although, pursuing *meaning* can affect their perception, responses and processing of such misfortune).

In *Astrology for the Light Side of the Brain*, Kim Rogers-Gallagher quotes David Pond, who said that he'd 'never seen a "bad" aspect that someone hadn't done a great job with'. The charts of successful people (and I use the term broadly) throw up *every* type of configuration. Success and fulfilment are combinations of energy, talent, practice and timing (opportunity) – and external factors, too. The human spirit makes choices that transcend simple astrological categories and assumptions.

Influential Planets – Some Observations

An influential planet is one that is:

1. **Involved in much of the chart's action**:

   - Heavily aspected by other planets (in particular, many conjunctions, squares or oppositions)

   - The dispositor of a stellium, or the Chart Ruler, particularly when influential in other ways according to points 1, 2 or 3
   (see: Venus – Barbra Streisand)

   - The focal planet ('apex') in a major configuration
   (see: Pluto – Brigitte Bardot, and pages 80–1 for more information)

2. And/or **placed in a significant area**:

   - Conjunct one of the chart's four angles (especially the Ascendant or Midheaven) up to 10°
   (see pages 29–31 on the angles)

   - In a Gauquelin Plus Zone*

   - A planet positioned at 0° or 29° of a sign*

3. And/or **standing apart from other planets**:

   - The handle of a Bucket chart
   (see: Moon – Alexander Graham Bell, and pages 54–5)

   - A singleton planet (or conjunction) by hemisphere
   (see: Moon–Neptune – Amy Winehouse)

   - An unaspected* planet (not receiving a conjunction, opposition, square, trine or sextile) from any other planet

   - A stationary (S) planet

   - A personal planet (Mercury, Venus or Mars) that is retrograde (℞)
   (see pages 36–8)

* These points have not been written about elsewhere in the book, so here is some information:

Research carried out by French statisticians Michel and Françoise Gauquelin demonstrated the importance of planets in key positions during their diurnal (daily) cycle. Using a rough-and-ready Placidus-type system of house division, the Gauquelins showed that much hinges on the angles – but, to the dismay of many astrologers, it was the cadent houses (3, 6, 9, 12, see diagram above) that proved character-defining areas, rather than the anticipated, neighbouring angular houses of 1, 4, 7, 10. A planet in a Gauquelin Sector (or G–Zone) has a powerful bearing on the individual's most fundamental, innate and compelling drives. Their research found only five planetary bodies (the Moon, Venus, Mars, Jupiter and Saturn) to be statistically significant (perhaps the Sun and Mercury's closeness in the sky obscured any noticeable patterns for each of them) but, towards the end of her life, Françoise was finding strong results with Uranus. Although most of their work examined the links between eminent professionals and associated planets (e.g. top scientists had Saturn in a G–Zone more often than expected), their greatest legacy to astrologers is their keyword research, which offers a broad classification system that describes planetary types (e.g. the Saturn type is 'solemn', 'reserved', 'precise', 'methodical', 'dignified' and 'careful').

Planets at 0° of a sign exhibit obvious, raw traits associated with that sign. Extreme aspects of a sign's nature form the backdrop of any planet at the final, thirtieth degree (29°) of a sign. (For more info, see my book *Horoscope Snapshots*.) Unaspected planets are said to function autonomously and in an all-or-nothing manner.

In the worksheets presented in Part Six, I list any social or outer planets in aspect to one another ('generational aspects' such as Saturn–Pluto or Uranus–Neptune). These suggest specific generational challenges for that group to grapple with throughout their lives. In addition, I have listed where a planet or angle is found very close to the discovery degree of an outer planet (e.g. Uranus was discovered when it was at 24° Gemini; Neptune at 25° Aquarius). Here, the planet or angle carries an *essence* of that outer planet's meaning. For example, astrologer Mike Harding noted that the Moon and Saturn were at 18° Cancer at the time of the biggest explosion of World War I and once again at the time of the atom bomb over Hiroshima. When Pluto was discovered, its exact position was 17°46' Cancer.

We've looked at each of the main components of the horoscope (the signs, planets, houses and aspects). It's essential to know the meanings and importance of each of these and to develop a good astrological vocabulary. But where do we go from here? It's easy to feel overwhelmed when first looking at a horoscope, so I've found it useful to have guidelines on the areas to consider first. This chapter offers a methodical 'way in'. Once you've considered the points herein, you'll be well on your way to getting to the heart of any chart. Here's what's coming up:

1. The Distribution of Planets
Learning to spot groups of planets or empty spaces in the wheel in order to reveal emphases or lacks.

2. Links between the Four Angles
Recognizing the set of signs – and any possible similarities – on the four angles to reveal our *orientation*. By noting any joint rulerships, we can ascertain planets that play key roles in the horoscope.

3. The Sun–Moon–Ascendant Trio
Looking for links between the 'Big Three' to provide valuable insights as to our inner desires, daily emotional needs and personal interactions.

4. The Elemental and Modal Balances
Making a quick calculation to reveal the driving and underlying motivations and personal style.

5. Major Aspects
Learning to highlight the key aspects to see the major personality drives, life themes and challenges.

6. Major Aspect Configurations
Beginning to piece together the configurations that reveal the life stories and scripts.

7. Spotting Overtones
Looking for repetitive patterns to isolate the key themes of the chart.

1. The Distribution of Planets

Before dissecting the horoscope and examining the major placements, aspects and rulership trails, it is useful to look at the horoscope *as a whole* – to see what jumps out first – to gain an overview and avoid being distracted by too much detail.

By noticing the distribution of planets around the zodiac wheel, we can ascertain if there's an *emphasis* on a particular hemisphere, quadrant, sign or house. We'll also have our first clue as to where there are *lacks* in a horoscope, for wherever there's an emphasis, there will be a corresponding lack elsewhere.

Looking at where the planets are placed in relation to each other, we might notice a concentration bundled into one area, or a planet positioned away from the rest (such as a singleton in its own hemisphere or simply away from the other planets). In some cases, the planets may be more dispersed, appearing randomly around the wheel, or they might form more subtle clusters. The more scattered the planets, the less focus there is on one specific area of life or the personality; it also reveals that this particular distribution of planets will not be a major factor in the analysis of the chart.

Wherever there's an emphasis, this will show where the planetary energies are focused. As we've seen in the previous section, Initial Considerations, anything that stands out will be an important area and a fundamental part of our assessment of the horoscope.

Chart Shapes
There are a number of ways in which to spot an emphasis (e.g. on a sign, house or hemisphere), but one of the most well known is to look at the sequential pattern (or geometric form) that the planets create around the wheel. Marc Edmund Jones, in his 1941 book *The Guide to Horoscope Interpretation*, classified seven basic types of chart shape: the Splash, the Bowl, the Bucket, the Locomotive, the See-Saw, the Bundle and the Splay. Later, astrologer Robert Carl Jansky renamed some and added an eighth type, the Fan.

In their book *The Only Way to ... Learn Astrology, vol. II* (ACS, 1981), Marion March and Joan McEvers stated that the basic patterns 'seem to pull the entire chart or the entire individual into a definite direction'. Noting that certain horoscopes do not fall into any of the eight patterns, they added, 'That is exactly what makes the pattern reading valuable – not every chart has an overall motivation, and only those that truly do should be interpreted as having a set pattern.'

I don't think Jones's seven types show personality types per se, but I've found that there are three patterns (the Bundle, Bowl and Bucket) that play a role in disclosing where the main action and focus will take place. In my opinion, the other types don't say much in particular.

The Bundle is a chart shape where all the planets are contained within a third of the wheel (120°), while the Bowl has planets filling up to half of the circle (180°). Both, particularly the Bundle, can indicate obsession, focus and the chart of a specialist. (Taking another look at Archer's Bowl horoscope on page 45, you'll notice that all of his planets are 'contained' within a semi-circle bowl. The 'rims' of the bowl are Mercury and Neptune, and they are also in opposition to each other, making them important players.) The Bucket (180° plus a planet or conjunction of planets on the opposite side of the horoscope) emphasizes the importance of that singleton planet *out there on its own* (see pages 54–5).

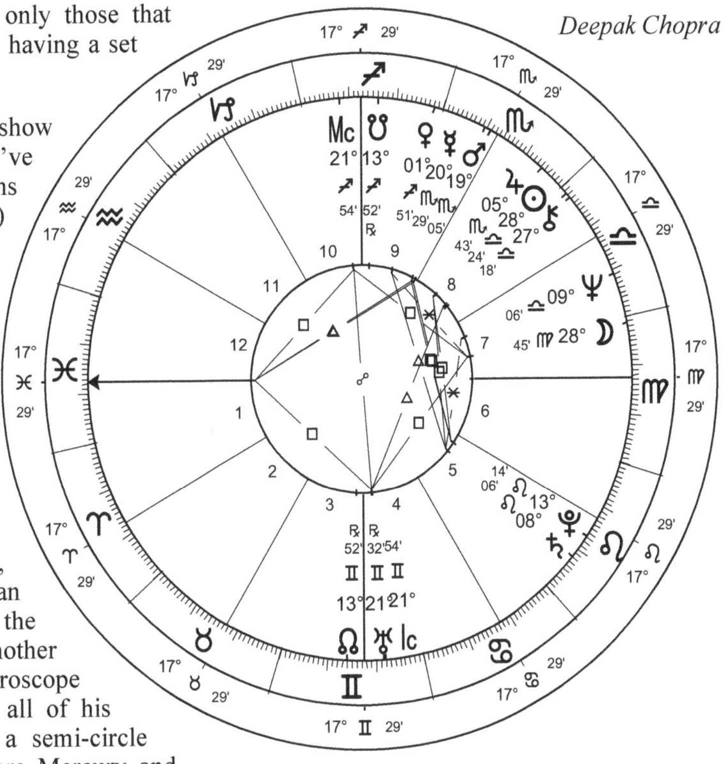

Zooming In
Let's look at a chart and spot where the emphasis lies. In the horoscope of writer **Deepak Chopra** (chart above), all the planets are contained within an opposition (180°). They fall in the signs from Gemini to Sagittarius and from the 4th to 9th Houses. The main grouping of seven planets (including all the personal planets) falls in the 7th, 8th and 9th Houses, with an emphasis on Libra (two planets) and Scorpio (three planets). This sign emphasis is underscored by the Sun and Moon (plus two other planets) falling in the 7th and 8th Houses, which are naturally associated with the signs of Libra and Scorpio, respectively. Although the meanings of the signs and houses are not interchangeable, it is useful to observe situations in which a focus on a particular house *emphasizes* a cluster of planets in a sign (e.g. four planets in Taurus in the 2nd House), or where there's a combination of an unrelated sign and house (e.g. a

Deepak Chopra

collection of planets in Scorpio in the 9th would suggest an in-depth exploration – Scorpio – of 9th House matters such as education and travel).

Before we go any further, I want to comment on two areas of interpretation that are often presented in books in chart interpretation: quadrants and hemispheres, and the leading planet.

Quadrants and Hemispheres
The chart is often divided up into quadrants. They start at an angle (Quadrant I starts at the Ascendant, Quadrant II at the IC, and so forth in an anti-clockwise order) and contain three houses apiece, which are numbered in the order that they rise to reach the Ascendant. Quadrants can best be seen in a quadrant-based system of house division such as Placidus, where the four angles mark the start of each angular house. Those who write about the quadrants often do so by linking them (and the houses) with key stages of human development. Although I would argue that these stages are best seen in the *signs* rather than the houses, it is interesting to consider the houses as stages in our life. In *The Twelve Houses* (Flare, 2007), Howard Sasportas describes these quadrants succinctly:

• Quadrant I (from the Ascendant to the IC: Houses 1, 2, 3) is 'where the individual begins to take shape as a distinct entity' – self-development.

• Quadrant II (from the IC to the Descendant: Houses 4, 5, 6) is where 'growth involves the further expression and refinement of the differentiated self' – self-expression.

• Quadrant III (from the Descendant to the MC: Houses 7, 8, 9) is where 'the individual expands awareness through relationship with other people' – self-expansion.

• Quadrant IV (from the MC to the Ascendant: Houses 10, 11, 12) focuses on 'the expanding or transcending of the boundaries of the self to include not just one other but many others' – self-transcendence.

There are also four hemispheres, the beginning of each is marked by one of the four angles. The hemispheres comprise the upper (Houses 7–12), lower (Houses 1–6), eastern (Houses 10–12 and 1–3) and western (Houses 4–9). Some astrologers believe that an emphasis on the western hemisphere (in quadrant systems, houses 4 to 9) depicts someone who is receptive, other-orientated and must take into account the needs of others (no doubt because the centre of that hemisphere is the relationship angle, the Descendant – even if there are no planets on this angle or in the 7th House). An emphasis on the eastern hemisphere (Houses 10 to 12 and 1 to 3 – the symbolic midpoint being the Ascendant) is said to indicate a more action-orientated, self-motivated individual (once again, regardless of whether there are planets around the person-centred Ascendant). An emphasis on the upper hemisphere (Houses 7–12) is said to depict someone who focuses on outside events, while many planets in the lower hemisphere (Houses 1–6) is said to indicate a private, subjective person. But *unless there is a collection of planets around the appropriate angle*, I have not found any of these assessments to hold much weight in overall chart and character delineation.

In Chopra's chart, most of the planets fall into the third quadrant and the western hemisphere (Uranus is, by minutes, in the eastern half of the chart). Although I do look at these initially to see where the emphasis is, I haven't found a concentration on a single quadrant or hemisphere to be a determining factor in a person's life themes

or personality drives – it doesn't really say much about the person. Such an emphasis reveals *where* the main action will take place, but the planets, signs, houses and aspects give the details.

There are two exceptions – of sorts – to this and they both involve a lack, rather than a concentration, of planets. Firstly, where a planet is the only one positioned above or below the Ascendant–Descendant (horizon) axis (see 'The Morning Star', below). This says much about what is seen (the visible planet above the horizon) or what is hidden from view (a planet below). Secondly, when a planet (or conjunction) is set apart from the rest of the planets by at least 60° (ideally more) – even when in the same quadrant or hemisphere – it becomes a 'handle' and hive of much activity and a driving, dynamic force in the person's life. It *stands out in isolation*, its position becomes significant and makes the planet, sign and house involved important.

The Leading Planet
Another factor that some astrologers consider, but which I don't find hugely influential, is the leading planet. Where there is much unoccupied space (at least a trine – 120° – between planets), the leading planet is the one that rises first in the sequence. Working out the 'leading' planet sometimes confuses students but is pretty simple: it is the first by zodiac degree in the sequence of planets. This is often considered the driver or engine of a chart.

In Chopra's chart, the first planet to rise would be Uranus (looking in zodiac order, Uranus in Gemini comes before Saturn in Leo, Pluto in Leo and so on). In Jeffrey Archer's horoscope on page 45, you'll notice that the first planet in zodiac order is Mercury in Pisces (Pisces directly precedes Aries), followed by Jupiter, then the Sun.

Far more interesting to note is the sequence of planets in conjunctions. See pages 42–5.

The Morning Star
Now take a look at the chart on the opposite page and notice how once again all ten planets are placed in half of the circle (actually, 10° more than a semi-circle). Again, a Bowl chart suggests the obsessional focus of a specialist, but an additional point to note is that all the planets are below the horizon (in houses 1 to 6) except Venus, which has just risen into the 12th House ahead of the Sun (in this position, it is known as the morning

star). This makes it the only *visible* planet in the horoscope (i.e. above the horizon and able to be seen at that moment by the observer). It is also the 'leading' planet (the earliest of the planets in zodiac sequence) and the dispositor of the four planets in Taurus (i.e. Venus naturally 'rules'/disposits all the planets found in its sign of Taurus – and Libra).

This horoscope gives us insight into how both the Ascendant and the planets that have risen into the 12th House say much about *the impact made* (Ascendant) and *what is visible to others* (above the horizon). Rather than believe the 12th House is 'hidden', we might wish to consider that it shows that which has *just emerged into the light*, revealing a fresh, undeveloped or unsophisticated side to the character.

Looking at Venus in Pisces – along with a very different-natured Ascendant in Aries – we can see what is apparent (having just risen) and thrust forward (the energy of the sign on the Ascendant). Such a contradictory combination describes the nature of chanteuse, composer, actress and pioneering director **Barbra Streisand** (chart below). Private, wilful, bullying, demanding, nervy, self-conscious and notorious for having

the *audacity* to take control and do things her way, Streisand is aware of the mythology surrounding her: 'I've been called many names like perfectionist, difficult and obsessive. I think it takes obsession, takes searching for the details for any artist to be good.' She describes herself as 'simple, complex, generous, selfish, unattractive, beautiful, lazy and driven.'

Venus in Pisces is soft, melodic, compassionate and devotional, while Aries Rising is in-your-face, urgent, confrontational and self-obsessed. Both signs are selfish, painfully thin-skinned – with a sympathy for the underdog and its related causes (knowing too well the fear of being overlooked or persecuted). They also have a range of personal insecurities drawn from a mix of damn-you independence and impudence (Aries) and don't-leave-me neediness and vulnerability (Pisces). Together, they symbolize the breathing of life into one's dreams and turning them into form, plus the drive to make one's longings *happen*. This creative Aries–Pisces combination is one of the features of the horoscope of another perfectionist, Martina Navratilova (see her profile starting on page 200).

Streisand's individuality (Aries) has always defined her creativity (Pisces). In her voice, we hear the impact, power and full-on, unsubtle attack of Aries (the sheer force of personality when Aries rises) and the lyrical, emotional delicateness and femininity of Pisces. The songstress has demonstrated a Piscean ability to cross over and then transcend all genres. In this Fire–Water mix, we meet the quirky, screwball comedian adept at cinema farce (Aries) and the glamorous torch singer able to transport an audience to distant places (Pisces).

Venus in Pisces conjures up images of Cinderella longing to escape the banality of her existence, put on her glass slippers and fall in love with her prince. But with Aries in the mix, Cinderella is an edgy diva and soon loses her cool when the footman takes too long to attend to her needs. She tells him how to do his job, then stomps on his hand with her delicate glass slipper as she emerges from the carriage.

Barbra Streisand

Getting a Handle

With the Bucket, we have a Bowl with a 'handle' on it. The handle (a single planet or conjunction) is on the other side of the horoscope, ideally opposite the 'midpoint' of the planets in the Bowl. The handle should, at the very least, be 60° away from one rim of the Bowl.

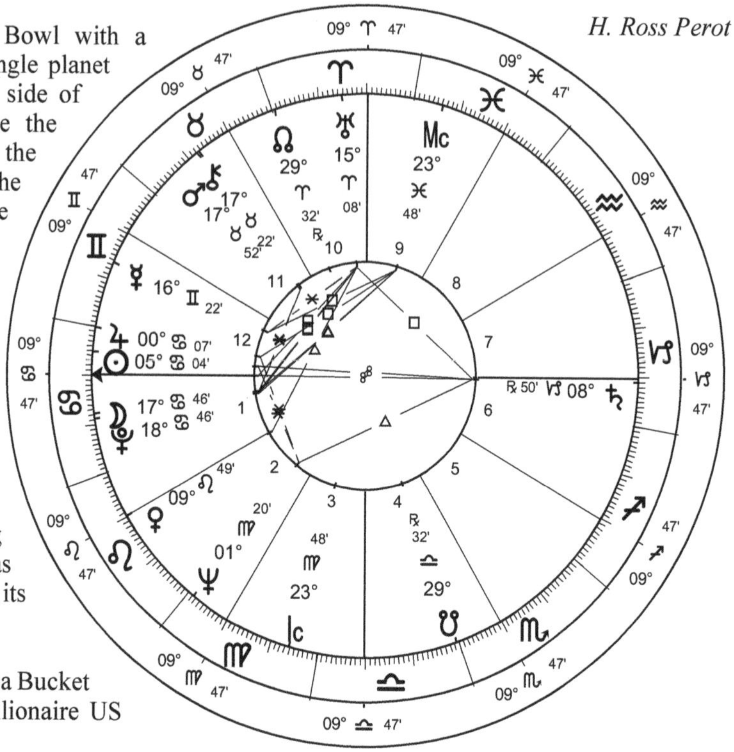

Although the Bucket is considered the second most common pattern, its handle is a very important point to notice when first looking at a horoscope. The planet that is the 'handle' is a significant player; its position by sign and house is a major key to grasping the essence of a horoscope, as well as the focus and fixations of its owner.

The chart above is an example of a Bucket horoscope. It is the chart of billionaire US entrepreneur **H. Ross Perot**.

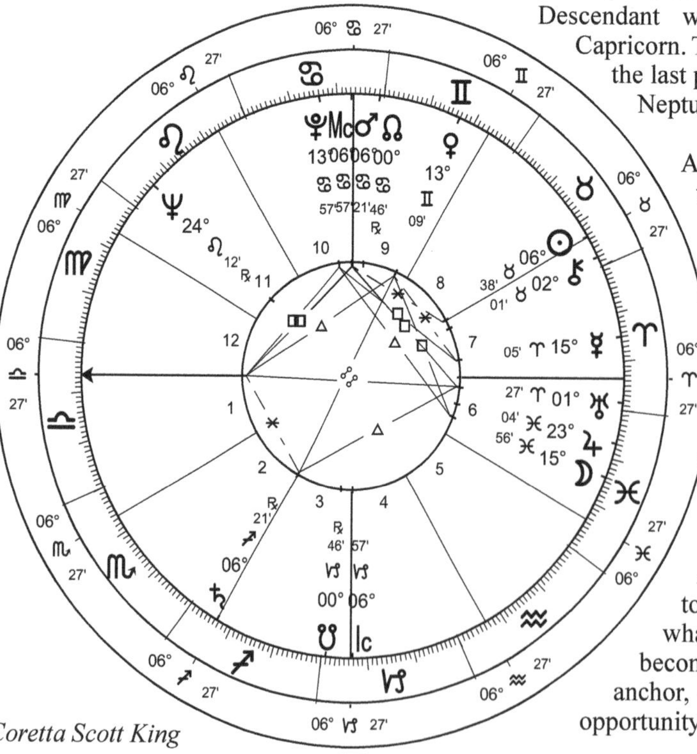

H. Ross Perot

Coretta Scott King

Above, there's a focus on Cancer, but on the Descendant we find the handle: Saturn in Capricorn. The rest of the chart, from the first to the last planet in sequence (from Uranus to Neptune), will work through this funnel.

A Bucket's handle assumes tremendous importance in the life. The planet in question (plus its sign and house position) says much about our general *raison d'être*. We 'hold on' to this handle and feel compelled to act out the drives and motivations that lie at its heart. It becomes the outlet, willingly or not, for the energies and potentials seen in the rest of the horoscope (on the far side of the chart).

At times, we may become too focused or obsessed with what the handle represents. It can become an 'excuse', obsession or an anchor, depending on our awareness and opportunity to express this all-important planet. It may guide us towards achieving something extraordinary or act as a millstone, stopping us from exploring and developing the rest of the horoscope's potential. If this planet is in opposition to a planet in the Bowl area, certainly relationship matters (the opposition) are the focus of the handle, and much of the life will be centred on experiencing and resolving issues pertinent to the planets involved.

When the remaining planets are in a tighter, Bundle shape (within 120°), it is known as a Fan. This is a term coined by Robert Jansky, who believed that where the Bucket person too often focuses solely on the handle to the detriment of the rest of the chart, the Fan's handle/singleton creates momentum and directs the Bundle to greater achievement.

Gillian McKeith

The chart pictured on the opposite page (below) is another example of a Bucket chart. Here, the handle is Saturn in Sagittarius on the cusp of the 3rd House. The Bowl part of the chart begins with the Moon in Pisces and ends with Neptune in Leo. It is the horoscope of **Coretta Scott King**, who took up the weighty mantle of expectation (Saturn) and faith (Sagittarius) to lead the fight for racial equality after the assassination of husband Martin Luther King, Jr. on 4 April 1968.

Some Tips on Chart Shapings
- Use only the planets, not the four angles. I haven't experimented with Chiron, the Centaurs or other bodies.

- Don't become fixated on making the chart fit a category exactly, e.g. if a Bowl shape is slightly more than 180°, allow it! Jones himself was less technical about having exact criteria for patterns and relied more on the chart's overall visual. Jansky, however, looked for planetary aspects (e.g. the Bowl needs an opposition between the planets at its 'rim') before he classified charts as true types.

- Charts don't always fit into one clear type, and some fall into two categories. With chart shapes, if it's not obvious, it's not important!

Many charts don't have an immediate eye-catching cluster of planets. *It is more important to spot what clearly stands out rather than attempt to categorize everything.* If not much is conspicuous in the distribution of planets, move on to the next 'ways in' to getting to the heart of the chart.

Focal Points in the Chart
Above, we have an example of a horoscope that has all its planets contained in just over the space of a trine (120°) – from the Moon at 17° Leo to Saturn at 0° Capricorn. It also has three pockets of conjunctions. The horoscope belongs to *You Are What You Eat* holistic nutritionist, author and bossy (Mercury–Mars) TV presenter **Gillian McKeith**, who is obsessed with the elimination of waste (Pluto) from people's sugar-driven, daily diets (Venus in Virgo). Her books and TV shows changed people's daily habits (Moon–Uranus).

In the chart over the page, we can see an interesting pattern – all but one of the planets are in two clusters: the Gemini–Cancer/12th–1st Houses and the Capricorn–Aquarius/7th–8th Houses. If it weren't for the position of Neptune, these clusters would create a See-Saw pattern (as classified by

Marc Edmund Jones) – one that could be described as a delicate cosmic balancing act! Neptune around the midpoint of the Moon–Mercury opposition makes this unusual chart a pseudo-Bucket (!) with Neptune as its handle. Adding importance to this planet is its involvement in a Grand Trine in Air with Jupiter and Pluto and its role as the apex of a T-square. We'll look at Grand Trines and especially at T-squares soon, and see how the apex acts as the focal point and a means of resolution.

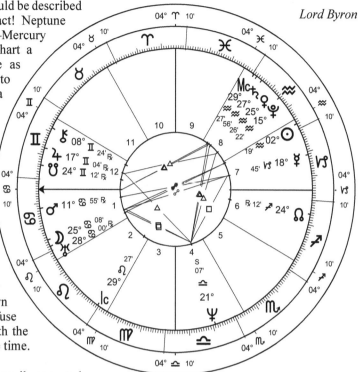

Lord Byron

The outer planets (Uranus, Neptune and Pluto) always speak of the broader, generational picture and, when tied to personal planets, they become drawn into our own personal drama. In turn, they infuse our life story and experiences with the associated collective energy of the time.

Focusing on this chart's pivotal, heavily aspected 'handle', we could speculate that this individual was somehow tied into his Neptune in Libra generation and its longings for an ideal (Neptune) relationship (Libra). Due to Neptune's involvement with his personal planets, he may have had the chance to embody or resonate to Neptunian themes such as romanticism or compassion. He may have been subjected to scandal, celebrity (Neptune has links to fame, infamy, 'mania') or scapegoating. Or he may have used Neptune to create and express himself in an inspired or transcendental way through areas such as art, painting or poetry.

This is the horoscope of the charismatic heart-throb of his age, **Lord Byron**, one of the great Romantic poets also infamous for his outrageous, scandalous sex life. He was an icon, winning the sort of celebrity that's hungered for nowadays. His wife called his fame 'Byromania'.

His self-promoted myth as the spirit of the Romantic age is best seen in the Byronic hero, which features in much of his work (including his epic poem *Don Juan*): an idealized, flawed character with a secret past who lacks respect for rank and society. Thwarted in love, he leads himself down a destructive path.

Byron's Moon–Uranus conjunction is clearly demonstrated in the well-known summation of his reputation ('mad, bad and dangerous to know'), his unconventional lifestyle, as well as the scandal and accusations of sodomy and cruelty that led to his self-imposed exile (the year his Sun directed into Pisces). This flight was a reaction to the censure of British society over his questionable morality (Venus–Saturn on his MC).

Later, in Speaking Your Chart, we'll look at how people's words reveal the major components of their charts. Consider how the following quotes from Byron resonate to his strong Neptune and the provocative, perverse Moon conjunct Uranus:

I have a great mind to believe in Christianity for the mere pleasure of fancying I may be damned.

The great art of life is sensation, to feel that we exist, even in pain.

The best of life is but intoxication.

Opinions are made to be changed – or how is truth to be got at?

Absence – that common cure of love.

Here are two final examples of how the distribution of planets can play an important first step in interpretation.

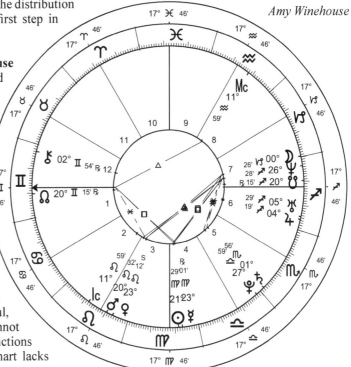

Amy Winehouse

In the chart of **Amy Winehouse** (right), all the planets are contained in just over a trine (120°), so it would fit roughly into the Bundle classification. The signs range from Leo to Capricorn and from the 3rd to the 7th House. The leading planet is Mars in Leo and the final planet in the sequence is the Moon, found at the very first (0°) and powerful degree of Capricorn. What's unusual about this chart? Have you noticed that it contains five sets of conjunctions? Each planet pairs up with another. It's not something I recall having seen before, but it suggests a powerful, intense set of planetary pairs that cannot work independently. Many conjunctions imply that the owner of such a chart lacks objectivity and perspective.

Another feature is the Moon–Neptune conjunction as the only pair above the horizon. This is what has been *visible* to us: a soap opera saga of her symbiotic relationship with her ex-husband, and the addictions that bound them (7th House).

A final example of visible planets can be found in Princess Margaret's chart (see page 65). Saturn and Venus are the only planets above the horizon: what the public saw was her struggle between duty and love.

To the left is the Bowl chart of **Jimi Hendrix** – the 'rim' is a powerful aspect of Mercury–Sun–Venus (in that order) opposite Uranus–Saturn. Uranus in Gemini is the leading planet, while Mars assumes importance being in its own sign (suggesting clear expression of its purpose) and being virtually unaspected. The 12th and 8th Houses are the most 'tenanted'. Sagittarius is the dominant sign in this chart.

Jimi Hendrix

2. The Set of Signs on the Four Angles

Our second assessment is to note the set of signs on the four angles. Are they of a particular mode? Are all four elements found on the angles? Does a pair have a planetary ruler in common? This assessment is important when considering our relationship with our immediate and broader environments, and it may also introduce a key theme that will become apparent in later stages of interpretation.

The angles reveal our *orientation* and the type of *interaction* we have with the world around us. Is our stance seemingly rock-like or permanent, or even stuck or immovable (fixed signs on the angles)? Is it focused on initiating matters and engaging with life's conflicts (cardinal)? Or do we pursue freedom and versatility, and have less of a grip on our environment, but are more able to mutate into new surroundings with ease (mutable)?

Once we've looked for links between the four signs on the angles, what about their rulers? Are they connected in any way? Perhaps the rulers are in aspect to one another, making that aspect a pivotal one in the horoscope. In addition, look out for planets that rule more than one angle, e.g. when Virgo is on the Ascendant and Gemini on the MC, Mercury automatically becomes doubly important (as does Jupiter, which co-rules the Descendant and rules the IC). It would be noteworthy then if Mercury and Jupiter were in major aspect to one other, suggesting that a dialogue/bridge is built between all four angles.

And finally, how does our particular compass (four angles) sit with the elements and modes of our inner planets (especially the Sun and Moon)? If we have a fixed compass/orientation, this might prove frustrating to those of us with a mutable Sun and Moon, for example. Or if used well, the fixed angles might stabilize us (and make others see us as secure and grounded) and provide necessary support and steadiness (fixed signs) to go off and enjoy the freedom and flexibility of personal pursuits (the energy of mutable planets).

Richard Nixon's chart (below) has four mutable angles. These are ruled by Mercury and Jupiter, which are found conjunct in Capricorn in the 4th House. Astrologer Richard Swatton (who has studied Nixon's horoscope and psychology for years) told me of traits central to Nixon's character that epitomize this pivotal Mercury–Jupiter in Capricorn: young Nixon was brought up in a Quaker household, was celebrated for winning a number of debating competitions as a child, and by age fourteen had written a theological argument on the existence of God. Books and his imagination brought freedom from the appalling conditions of his home life. He dreamed of being someone of importance – a 'great man' – perhaps to make up for the unlived ambitions of his father. Nixon's own ambitions were grandiose and matched his exaggerated sense of purpose (Jupiter).[8]

Richard Nixon

The Mercury–Jupiter conjunction also conjuncts Mars and it opposes Pluto in Gemini in the 10th House of career. The following quotes reveal these aspects:

Several warring personalities struggled for preeminence in the same individual. One was idealistic, thoughtful, generous; another was vindictive, petty, emotional.

His decisions were courageous… often taken in loneliness against all expert advice.

The thoughtful analytical side of Nixon was most in evidence during crises, while periods of calm seemed to unleash the darker passions of his nature… Calm periods seemed to drive him to disequilibrium as if he could find his own balance only in tension.

Nixon's reputation is inextricably linked to Mercury–Pluto: the controlling, conniving, suspicious, tunnel-visioned 'Tricky Dicky' obsessed with power and information. The runner-up who underwent psychotherapy for many years, eventually achieved his ambition to be president (Saturn disposits six planets), and whose clandestine, dirty tricks and Watergate cover-up were unearthed, brought him disgrace, forced his resignation and fueled his paranoia.

A Master of the Deal

Donald Trump's chart (above) has a set of fixed signs on the angles, with the two angles governing one's social persona (the ASC and MC) in Leo and Taurus, respectively. The Leo–Taurus combination can be seen in his confident persona and the flaunting of his glitzy, golden, ostentatious brand of wealth and luxury. The combo is evident in Trump the figurehead, in the energy behind his real estate empire (Mars rises in Leo), and in his drive to become president. He is one of the few celebrity (Leo) businessmen (Taurus) in America.

Leo Rising *appears* to be unplagued by self-doubt. Growing up, Donald took great pride in his appearance and was known as 'The Great I Am'. He never respected authority at school until he began a five-year stint in Military Academy. The Leo–Taurus combination embodies *certainty* – others follow and believe (Leo/Fire) in Trump and see him as a solid investment (Taurus/Earth). His famous name (Leo) brings value (Taurus).

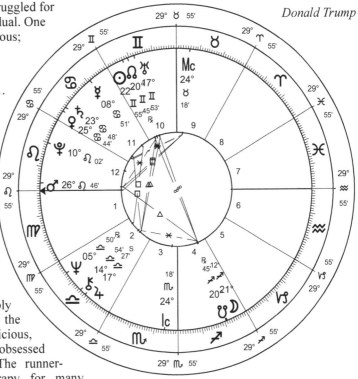

Donald Trump

The rulers of the four angles are:
• Sun (Ascendant ruler)
• Saturn and Uranus (Descendant rulers)
• Venus (MC ruler)
• Mars and Pluto (IC rulers)

If any of these rulers are connected by aspect in the natal chart, they immediately link and tie up the affairs of one angle with the affairs of another. The Sun conjuncts Uranus (i.e. the Ascendant ruler is conjunct the Descendant ruler, making it a particularly important conjunction and significator of his relationships). The second link is the conjunction of the MC ruler with the traditional ruler of the Descendant (Venus conjuncts Saturn in the 11th in Cancer). When the MC ruler aspects the Descendant ruler, partnerships are vital to one's reputation, success and advancement. Not only have Trump's relationships (DSC) been high-profile news (MC) and each wife (DSC) instrumental in his success and public image (MC), they have also been financial assets and, when divorcing, financially costly (Venus–Saturn). Trump learned the hard way (Saturn) and his second wife signed a prenuptial agreement (Venus–Saturn). The importance of Trump's other relationships – those with his financial backers – is also indicated here, as is his interest and expertise in real estate (a legacy from his father – parental messages are seen in the MC–IC axis), and how precariously close he has come to personally declaring bankruptcy.

Much of Trump's real estate bears his name (with Leo Rising the person *is* the product, the star of his own business). These buildings are permanent (fixed angles) fixtures around America. Yet, this man is essentially mutable and not overly materialistic by nature: he was born at a mutable Full Moon with the Sun in Gemini opposite the Moon in Sagittarius. For him, it is about *making the deal* (Gemini–Sagittarius) and *being seen as winning* (Mars rising in Leo). As he says, 'Negotiation is an art, and I have a flair for it.' Trump is a PR great, a born salesman keen to wheel and deal. He enjoys selling (Gemini) his grandiose visions (Sagittarius) with a persuasive charm that he himself describes succinctly as 'truthful hyperbole'. The etymology of his surname suggests two meanings, one Gemini, one Leo/Sagittarius: to fabricate, deceive, or cheat (as in 'trumped up'); and 'triumph', to surpass or beat, a playing card that ranks above the others (as in 'to trump an ace').

His father – a self-made real estate developer – gave Donald some simple but fittingly mutable advice: 'Know everything you can about what you're doing.' Donald grew up watching his father, a tough negotiator and businessman, on the construction site. Trump Senior benefited from the Baby Boom of 1945–6 and the demand for housing that followed (Donald's MC ruler is Venus, which conjuncts Saturn in Cancer – a *lack* of *homes*). He learned practical skills (Taurus MC) from his father and a need to maintain control (Scorpio IC). The secret to success and key motivating factors are often found at the IC. For tycoon Trump, he's been able to build and accumulate (Taurus) because of the *control* he has by privately owning his empire. This enables his finances to be kept secret and for him to remain free of the demands of shareholders (Scorpio IC).

After obtaining air rights on Fifth Avenue to build an extravagant sixty-eight storey building (Trump Tower, 1983), he later moved into the gambling business (Sagittarius) and bought and opened Trump's Castle (Leo) in 1985. With Uranus aspecting the mutable Sun and Moon, there's an electric charisma but also an added unpredictability to the already most unsteady of modes. His fortunes have fluctuated wildly over the years, but he has proven to be a 'comeback kid'.

Internally Yours
The chart of infamous intern **Monica Lewinsky** (below) has all four angles in cardinal signs plus a cardinal T-square, suggesting that her 'orientation' is one of conflict and confrontation, and a need to assert herself in her environment. Her parents' acrimonious divorce when she was fourteen was an early sign of the cardinal cross in action.

The rulers of the four angles are:
• Venus (Ascendant ruler)
• Mars (Descendant ruler)
• Moon (MC ruler)
• Saturn (IC ruler)

Are they connected in any way? Venus is closely sextile Saturn, and two of the four ruling planets

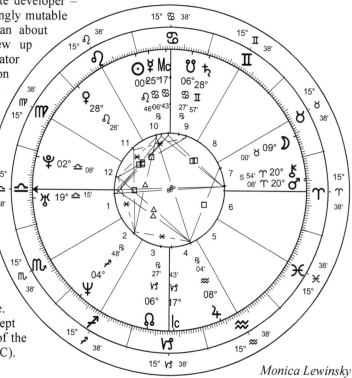

Monica Lewinsky

are in a house linked to Venus – the 7th – but neither observation uncovers a major statement in the horoscope. There is one emphasis, however. The Descendant ruler (Mars) is conjunct the Descendant and in its own sign (Aries), suggesting that this angle is the one to look out for. Mars in Aries on the Descendant would indicate that much energy is poured into passionate relationships or engaging in conflict (from impetuous, impulsive sexual pursuits to full-scale war). It's a good placement, too, for a personal trainer, motivator or life coach ('You can do it, Bill'). It could also suggest the 'throwing away' (Descendant) of her fighting spirit (Mars) or having others act this out for her (by taking charge or attacking her).

With Libra Rising and the Sun in Leo, her eagerness to please resulted in two on-going relationships with married men: one in college, and the other in the White House. (Note that her 'celebrity' came from an association with a famous, charismatic Leo leader – Sun at 0° Leo in the 10th House.)

What dominates her chart is a cardinal T-square that conjuncts three of the four angles. (We'll be looking at T-squares in detail later.) It is very descriptive of her most famous exploits with then-President Clinton: Uranus rises in Libra and opposes Mars in Aries, suggestive of the explosive relationship that shook Clinton's second term of office. Both planets square Mercury in Cancer on the MC – the 'improper' relationship was the *talk* of America for well over a year. (Monica's pivotal Mercury is a degree away from the Mercury in the US's 4 July chart.) The T-square describes the news (Mercury) of the shocking truth (Uranus) of her sexual relations (Mars) and her compatibility with a randy president (the pair share the exact Sun–Moon–Ascendant combo). For a long time, she was the punchline of jokes broadcast into American homes (Mercury in Cancer on the MC).

Its mid-cardinal degrees link the horoscopes of the principal players in the scandal. Clinton has Venus at 11° Libra conjunct Chiron at 18°. Linda Tripp, who secretly taped conversations with Lewinsky about the affair for Kenneth Starr, has Neptune at 16° Libra square to Venus at 19° Capricorn. Starr, who led the salacious witch hunt, has Chiron at 16° Libra, Jupiter at 19° Libra, and an Ascendant at 13° Capricorn. When Lewinsky was intimidated by the FBI on 16 January 1998 and the scandal broke nationally five days later, TR Saturn was at 14° Aries, fast approaching her Descendant.

Here's a guide to the 38 angle combinations, listed in Ascendant sign order, starting with MC/IC possibilities for Aries Rising. Some are rare – they occur at extreme latitudes or for a short time. I've omitted combinations that only occur above 60° North or below 40° South.

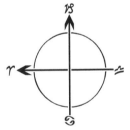

All Cardinal
All four elements
'Natural Zodiac'

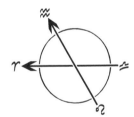

Cardinal and Fixed
Fire and Air

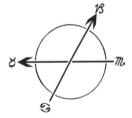

Cardinal and Fixed
Earth and Water

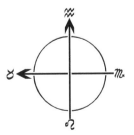

All Fixed
All four elements

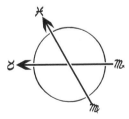

Fixed and Mutable
Earth and Water

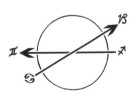

Cardinal and Mutable
All four elements

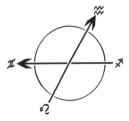

Fixed and Mutable
Fire and Air

All Mutable
All four elements
Rulers: Mercury, Jupiter

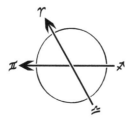

Cardinal and Mutable
Fire and Air

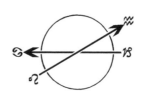

Cardinal and Fixed
All four elements

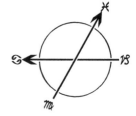

Cardinal and Mutable
Earth and Water

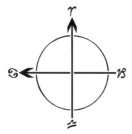

All Cardinal
All four elements

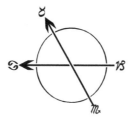

Cardinal and Fixed
Earth and Water

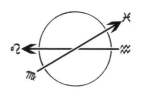

Fixed and Mutable
All four elements

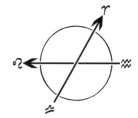

Cardinal and Fixed
Fire and Air

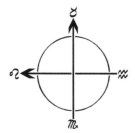

All Fixed
All four elements

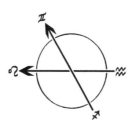

Fixed and Mutable
Fire and Air

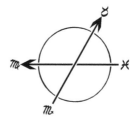

Fixed and Mutable
Earth and Water

All Mutable
All four elements
Rulers: Mercury, Jupiter

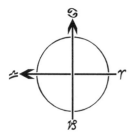

All Cardinal
All four elements

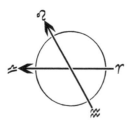

Cardinal and Fixed
Fire and Air

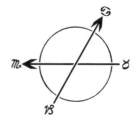

Cardinal and Fixed
Earth and Water

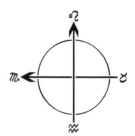

All Fixed
All four elements

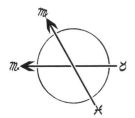

Fixed and Mutable
Earth and Water

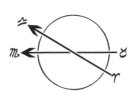

Cardinal and Fixed
All four elements
Rulers: Venus, Mars

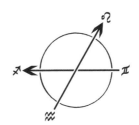

Fixed and Mutable
Fire and Air

All Mutable
All four elements
Rulers: Mercury, Jupiter

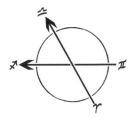

Cardinal and Mutable
Fire and Air

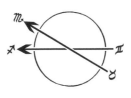

Fixed and Mutable
All four elements

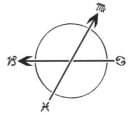

Cardinal and Mutable
Earth and Water

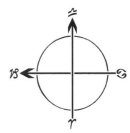

All Cardinal
All four elements

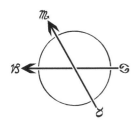

Cardinal and Fixed
Earth and Water

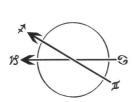

Cardinal and Mutable
All four elements

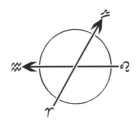

Cardinal and Fixed
Fire and Air

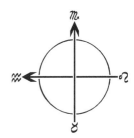

All Fixed
All four elements

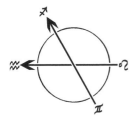

Fixed and Mutable
Fire and Air

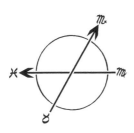

Fixed and Mutable
Earth and Water

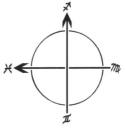

All Mutable
All four elements
Rulers: Mercury, Jupiter

For an in-depth look at the angles, various ASC-MC combos, and interpretations of the signs and planets on the MC–IC axis, please see my mini-book *The Midheaven: Spotlight on Success* (Flare, 2016), which can also be found in the ebook entitled *The Astrology Quartet.*

3. The Sun–Moon–Ascendant Trio

Ability is what you're capable of doing.
Motivation determines what you do.
Attitude determines how well you do it.

We can provide horoscope 'readings' that are pertinent, informative and insightful simply by describing the signs of the Sun, Moon and Ascendant. Such an interpretation is perfect for a quick assessment or as an introduction to astrology beyond Sun signs. But the Sun, Moon and Ascendant are more than that. The Big Three in the horoscope describe:

• Our inner identity, life purpose, essence; our ultimate inner mission that we are *born* to pursue, personify and manifest – the Sun.

• Our needs, habitual behaviour, temperament, innate responses, gut reactions; our fundamental *relationship* needs, drives and expectations (personally and professionally) – the Moon.

• Our everyday personality we rely on to socialize and meet and greet; our approach to life and expectations – the Ascendant.

In addition, when introducing a chart to a client, I often include the Midheaven. In fact, I start with the MC, as this says much about the image others have of us before they meet us (Ascendant), or understand our temperament and emotional needs (Moon), or 'what we are in essence' (the Sun).

The main object of isolating the Big Three is to pinpoint what each of the trio means and how these blend and can work with each other. For example, a **male client** of mine has the Sun in Capricorn, the Moon in Scorpio and a Sagittarius Ascendant (below). We might first see his happy-go-lucky, accessible, friendly public face that attempts to meet the world with enthusiasm (Sagittarius Ascendant). That face is also desperate not to be disappointed in people. Hiding behind this public face, we could say that his inner life is intensely and privately felt. Emotional security is cultivated when there's trust, depth and intimacy, and emotional crises and betrayal are anticipated or self-fulfilled (Scorpio Moon). This would be a man who seeks someone who can look beyond his sunny disposition and understand the complexities and depths of his emotions underneath. Finally, looking at his essence (the Sun), he is on a mission to 'be someone' in the eyes of the world, to gain status, authority and respect, and to build and achieve something while working within a structure or establishment (Sun in Capricorn).

If two or more of the Big Three have a planetary link in common, e.g. Sagittarius Ascendant with the Moon conjunct Jupiter, it can sometimes be tricky to differentiate them and see how each appears in the life or character. But when that occurs, we know there is an overtone to the chart, which will make the planet's message stronger. We'll look at this later.

The next step is to look for links between the Big Three. Are they all mutable signs? Is there a majority of Fire signs? For example, if there's a Gemini Moon and a Virgo Ascendant, then there is the beginning of a Mercury overtone. This would be a Mercury-based person at home

Male Client

and work (Moon) and in outlook/interaction (Ascendant). Both Moon and Ascendant are significators for our relationships: the Moon shows the deep needs we have to nurture and be cared for, and what makes us feel safe, while the Ascendant (being part of an axis) says much about who comes into our lives through interaction, expectation and attraction. In **Princess Margaret's** chart (below), we have an almost 'natural chart': with early Aries Rising, most of the planets in their signs will also be in the appropriate natural house (e.g. the Moon in Cancer in the 4th House, the house of Cancer).

Behaviour, Character and Personality

The Sun is the centre of the chart and of who we are – the very heart of what we're working towards. But to understand someone's personality and behavioural traits, we must look at their Ascendant and Moon signs (and any planets conjunct or, to a lesser extent, opposite or square). These two are of greater importance than the Sun when considering how people behave, react and interact in life.

The Moon: Behaviour

Astrologically, we could define *behaviour* as a collection of instincts formed to create a complex pattern – an interconnected web of habitual responses, particularly with the aim of remaining safe and being looked after. Behaviour is how we *conduct* ('to bring together') ourselves to create a range of responses. This is seen most clearly by the Moon (e.g. the Moon in Virgo learns to be polite and of service in order to be – and feel – needed). Another word that is descriptive of the Moon astrologically is *temperament*, which is often linked to the four elements (the four 'humours' that make up our disposition). But the Moon is a mix of elements of the emotional realm – our emotional *nature*.

The Sun: Character

We often hear of the *development of one's character*, perhaps an accumulation of traits, responses and behavioural patterns that becomes the central direction, focus and set of *beliefs* in a person's life. Character permeates our life and our actions. In a way, this is symbolic of our journey towards the true meaning of why we were born – a concept inherent in the message of the Sun. Its message

is not one of adjectives and traits but of *essence* – the Sun in the horoscope embodies a message and an archetype, and by bringing that principle to the fore we can participate in life and start to fulfil some of our potential. It is, perhaps, the embracing of character that leads to a healthy self-esteem and a path of integrity and wholeness. Like grasping the sometimes elusive concept of the Sun, character is more difficult to ascertain in others, too, and it takes time for us to uncover it, and time for it to reveal itself.

The Sun describes how we picture our individual role in life's drama – and how we pursue it – and the ways in which we ascribe meaning to life, e.g. Sun in Sagittarius or Sun–Jupiter: 'Life is a journey to explore'. Our character is a collection of fundamental, integral philosophies that we have gathered over time. The Sun's position shows one's main life purpose and vocation, such as being an 'innovator', 'radical', 'interpreter', rather than a set of personality traits. (Traits, such as stubbornness, flexibility or arrogance, are described by the sign or planet on the Ascendant. The way we deal with life is seen in the modes. What drives our actions and the patterns of our life events is seen in our chart's conjunctions, squares and oppositions.)

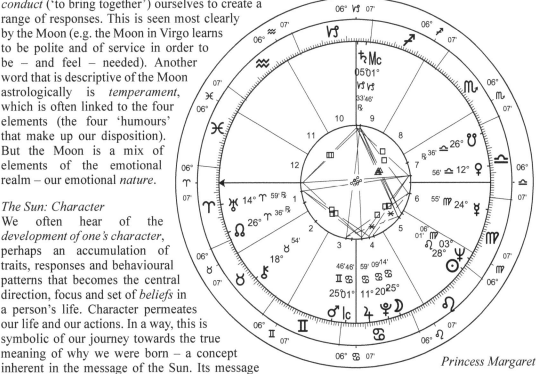

Princess Margaret

The Ascendant: Personality

The *personality* (as seen by the Ascendant complex – most importantly the sign on it and major planetary aspects to it) is the variable means by which we negotiate our needs (Moon) with others and formulate or build something we can identify as character (Sun). There is an energy here – an attitude, humour, engagement and interaction – that is different from the accumulation of early (lunar) behaviours or the formation of a (solar) character. Personality is easy to pick up on, quick to read and decipher – usually upon meeting someone (Ascendant). It often shows up in personal mottos (e.g. 'If you want it done, you have to do it yourself,' says the Aries Ascendant, and 'no pain, no gain,' says the Scorpio Ascendant). Personality traits may have little to do with our true character, but they are what we show to others (our appearance, in many ways) and the means by which we get through life. Astrologically, the Ascendant is often seen as the vehicle by which we reach the Sun's destination/ our life goal. It is also often a route to getting our needs (Moon) met in relationship. (The Gauquelins considered that the planets in the key Gauquelin Zones were markers of character, but they appear to be powerful expressions of *motivation* that trigger *personality* traits that others notice.)

Putting the Trio Together

Once we have a good grasp of each of the Big Three, we can start to get a feel for what they could all mean together. It's very useful to look at the signs in pairs and then in threes, and consider what they have in common and how they differ. For example, in a **client**'s chart (right), the Sun is in Capricorn, the Moon in Taurus and Leo Rises.

Leo and Capricorn may not seem to have much in common and have no immediate links by element or mode (although their respective rulers – the Sun and Saturn – are symbolic opposites). But both signs value status and authority. They are signs that wish to preserve a status quo of sorts (usually with themselves at the helm): Leo doesn't want a revolution in the kingdom that it rules, while Capricorn may dethrone a despot to assume control and

restore the social order it had before things soured. Both are also signs linked to quality and high value. A chart with a Leo–Capricorn combination may love designer labels or goods of distinction that immediately tell others of their social status, class and 'taste'. (Both signs have different tastes – Leo tends to veer towards the flashy, shiny and bling, while Capricorn appreciates the traditional, classier look and those things that have aged well.) Both may exhibit hubris (in the modern sense) and suffer as a consequence of it: Leo has the cocky, arrogant front of a teenager; Capricorn may forget humility while empire-building or lose track of its original goals when it dwells on the letters it has earned after its name.

What if we add Taurus to the mix? It has links with Leo (both are fixed signs, a mode that is concerned with attachment and principles) and with Capricorn (both are Earth signs, an element that values steadiness, expediency and the material world). All three signs are traditional, steadfast and are preservers of some kind.

Taking into account which of the Big Three is linked to which sign, we could say that the owner of the horoscope is at heart (Sun) someone who was born to make a contribution to a larger

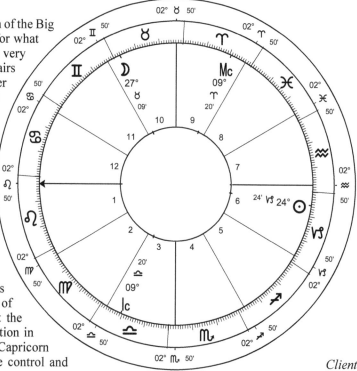

Client

whole, hierarchy or system (Capricorn). Whatever successes may come early, he will attain this desire *in a meaningful way* only after a long, strategic and, in some ways, lonely apprenticeship (Capricorn and the Sun's 6th House placement suggest this). There is an inner striving (Sun) for respect and authority, to achieve and be recognized for that achievement. The law of cause and effect warns of cutting corners and failing to maintain a strict moral code, either of which would obstruct the Capricornian journey of mastery/distinction (see John DeLorean's chart, page 104).

Francis Ford Coppola

With the Moon in Taurus, the emotional nature is one that dislikes change, seeks steadiness, security and calm at work, and desires the quiet life, the good life and sensuality at home. Its owner feels comfortable in the here and now, bides his time and may not seize chances quickly – thereby lagging behind faster folk when opportunities arise. But he shows loyalty to those around him and is a supportive, stolid 'constant'.

If encouraged to blossom, with Leo Rising, he may appear confident, superior, self-assured and dignified – the perfect mask to hide any fears of ridicule or rejection. Again, loyalty is valued and displayed. He would have a way of commanding attention, giving advice, displaying creativity and even a certain flair or élan in his appearance.

In short, the Sun–Moon–Ascendant trio offers a quick way in to the major traits of a person – their character, behaviour and personality. Sometimes there are common denominators; at all times there are links to be found. At this stage in the book, it is important to know the general meanings of each of the trio, delve deep to understand what they mean, and to recognize any links and follow trails to explore how they interact with each other and other parts of the horoscope.

Saturn and Mars: It's Business *and* Personal

The chart of **Francis Ford Coppola** (above) is a fascinating example of a repetitive statement in a horoscope. With an Aries Sun and Scorpio Moon, the chart has the makings of a Mars overtone.

We'll be looking at overtones later in this section, but in essence they are *repetitive statements* between signs, planets and houses. In Coppola's chart, the overtone is made stronger by Mars conjunct the Ascendant in the 1st House, Mars square to the Sun in Aries, and Mars ruling the Scorpio Midheaven. Mars, Mars, Mars!

Following the trio's trails, we can also see that the chart contains another overtone: Saturn. The Ascendant is in Capricorn (with the dispositor of the Sun and Moon – Mars – in Capricorn, too). The Chart Ruler is Saturn, which is in Aries and is in a key position by being conjunct the Sun.

So, we have Mars and Saturn overtones written in a number of ways. Coppola emerged from his sickly, bedridden, polio-afflicted childhood (Saturn) to become a master film-maker, triumphing against all odds and without the belief/backing of others (Saturn). He went from ambitious young upstart (Mars) to recognized authority (Saturn) who opened doors for a generation of directors. Though never part of the boys' club (Mars is always individual), young Coppola was a gambler with unrelenting gusto, intent on doing battle (Mars) with the Hollywood establishment (Saturn).

His most famous film collection, *The Godfather* trilogy, is considered by most critics to be a masterpiece (Saturn). The trilogy is most clearly in evidence through his Moon and MC in Mars-ruled Scorpio, but also has links to the Mars–Saturn theme in his horoscope. The films examined the loyalties, betrayals and violent realities of a mobster clan of 'businessmen'. Issues of respect, fear, ruthlessness, honour, corruption, loyalty, criminality, hierarchy, revenge and the exchange of favours were all high on the Mafia agenda. But ultimately, Saturn triumphs over Mars: 'It's business, not personal.' The first film premiered with much fanfare in mid-March 1972, with TR (transit) Jupiter close to Coppola's Ascendant, TR Uranus opposite his Sun in Aries, and TR Neptune conjunct his SA (Solar Arc) MC.

The Mother of Attention

Check out the chart of **Jacqueline Stallone**, who is one tough, scary mother (of Sylvester). In her chart (below), the Sun–Moon–Ascendant trio is strongly interlinked. Born a day after a New Moon, Stallone has the Sun and Moon in Sagittarius and her Ascendant in Libra. Her Chart Ruler is Venus in Scorpio (conjunct Mercury). Here we have a focus on three consecutive signs (where a total of seven planets plus the Ascendant are positioned). To add to this, there is a conjunction of Mars and Jupiter (rulers of Scorpio and Sagittarius, respectively) on the Ascendant in the sign of Libra. The majority of her planets are in Scorpio–Sagittarius but, as the planetary rulers of these signs are together in Libra on the Ascendant, the power of Mars–Scorpio and Jupiter–Sagittarius is projected through this part of her horoscope.

These repetitive statements in the horoscope create the sort of character that cannot be anything other than what it was born to be! Successful people (those who are truly doing what they feel they were born to do) are often actively engaging in key themes in their horoscopes and finding ways to live these out. This is usually seen by the Sun–Moon–Ascendant trio having strong links to one another. (Often, to be recognized in our field or in society, we must have links to the MC.)

We can see the Mars–Jupiter theme clearly in Jackie Stallone's life. She is a tough, raucous and flamboyant businesswoman and astrologer. With the conjunction on a Libra Ascendant, there's little of Libra's famous façade of diplomacy – there's too much for her to be getting on with. Famously self-promoting and name-dropping, Jackie can hog the limelight like no one else. Her opinions on her famous son's love life made headlines, and her blunt outspokenness made her a riveting guest on interview shows at the height of her fame in the 1980s. Tact and discretion are traits best left to other, less dynamic Libra Rising complexes.

Following Mars–Jupiter from the very start, as a teen she ran off and joined the circus. Later, she ran a women's weightlifting gym and promoted her own team of models-turned-wrestlers. So much of what she has done is promoted in an outlandish, wild way. Jupiter *knows all about* spectacle and hyperbole – it's no surprise that many Jupiterians are painted as figures of fun and set up for ridicule. It's hard enough to be taken seriously as a businesswoman without the added over-the-top, larger-than-life antics of Jupiter (see the profile of Tammy Faye Bakker starting on page 182).

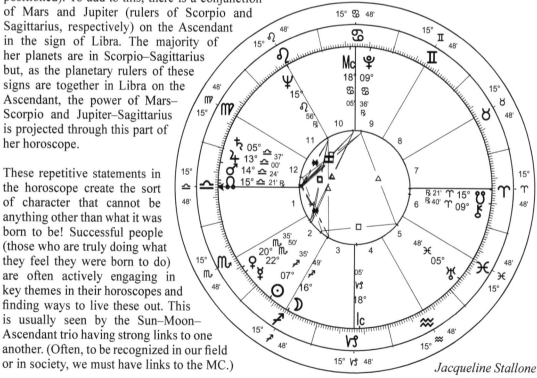

Jacqueline Stallone

An Aside: On One's Laurels

I used to wonder why so many Sagittarians (Sun or Ascendant) would wear a sneer or look of scorn on their face. Jackie Stallone has the sneer, which I think reveals the very superior disposition of Sagittarius – a noble sign that can mock or scorn and enjoy looking down on the rest of us mere mortals. And then there's Jackie's love of headbands. Why do Sagittarians have a penchant for headbands (and not just in the 1970s/early 1980s when Neptune – the planet of fashion trends – moved through Sagittarius!)? These are things astrologers wonder about in cinemas when others are just watching the film! And, anyway, weren't headbands supposedly for Aries, the sign that rules the head?

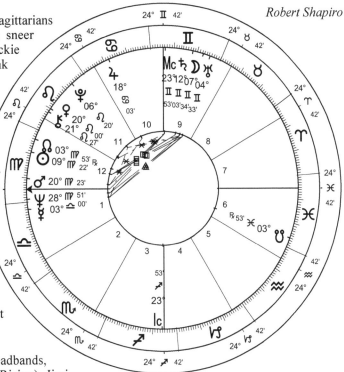

Robert Shapiro

Stallone was famous for wearing headbands, as was Brigitte Bardot (Sagittarius Rising), Jimi Hendrix – actually, a bandana (Sun and Ascendant in Sagittarius), and country singer Janie Fricke (Sun in Sagittarius, Jupiter rising in Sagittarius), who once said it was a sad day when the fashion had passed and she had to put her headbands away in the closet!

Why Sagittarius? The Greeks and Romans wore laurel wreaths (in honour of the son of Zeus/Jupiter) as a sign of their achievements, rank, status and education (we are warned not to 'rest on our laurels'). They were woven into a horseshoe (Sagittarius) shape. Caesar proclaimed the laurel wreath to be a 'symbol of the supreme ruler'. They were later used to crown victors at the Olympic Games. I associate Sagittarius with the Olympics – the international event, the sporting excellence, the spirit of competition, and the torchbearer carrying the Olympic Flame.

Celebrity Lawyer

In the Bundle chart of defence lawyer **Robert Shapiro** (above), there's a focus on the Mercury signs. The Sun and Ascendant are in Virgo, while the Moon is in Gemini. In fact, eight of the twelve points (ten planets and two angles) are either in Gemini or Virgo. Both are mutable signs concerned with gathering information but,

interestingly, in Shapiro's chart, their ruler Mercury is in Libra. Gemini is adept at separating itself (Air) from the data it collects, but Virgo finds itself easily immersed in its research. Virgo's findings eventually become embedded (Earth) in its own philosophy, influencing the way it operates and moulding its agenda (in both senses of the word). Virgo is also a planner and strategist but can get overwhelmed by policy. Originally, the word 'strategy' had links to 'the deployment of troops', and Mars in Virgo in Shapiro's chart makes for an excellent strategist – one with a *plan* (Virgo) of *action* (Mars) – as does Mercury in Libra, which anticipates well the other side's approach and *sensibility*.

Shapiro is known for his meticulous approach to his legal work and for developing a close personal relationship with his celebrity clients. Most famously, Shapiro was on the 'dream team' that worked to have O.J. Simpson acquitted. Simpson's Moon in Pisces squares Uranus in Gemini and they conjunct Shapiro's Descendant and MC, respectively. Simpson's Mars is conjunct Shapiro's Moon in Gemini (an advocate protecting the glove-wearing perpetrator of a double murder?) and, apt for a winning partnership, Simpson's

Sun is conjunct Shapiro's Jupiter. Interestingly, Shapiro's synastry with his convicted client Christian Brando contains difficult oppositions: Brando's Saturn opposite Shapiro's MC, and a Moon–Mars conjunction opposite Shapiro's Sun.

Following Trails
Trying to stay somewhat objective, I usually resist using my chart as 'evidence' of anything. But, as I wrote in the introduction, this book presents my own personal method of chart synthesis, so it is important to show how my own horoscope reflects my approach to the subject. The following observation took some time to notice – it was so simple, it escaped me for years!

I have the Sun in Aries, Moon in Virgo and the Ascendant in Gemini. Mars rules Aries (so it disposits my Sun) while Mercury (natural ruler of Virgo and Gemini) disposits/rules the other two parts of the trio (the Moon and Ascendant).

In effect, my trio is Mercury–Mars themed, and that would be a good place to start to understand my vocation and where my heart is (the Sun), my needs and temperament (Moon), and my approach to life and day-to-day personality (the Ascendant). In addition, Mercury and Mars are in semi-square

aspect to each other (suggesting an irritability or an impatience for information). But if we look a little deeper, we can see more connections that show the *type* of Mercury–Mars that runs through my particular chart.

The planets linked to Mars in my chart have an Aquarian or Uranian theme:

• My Sun is in Aries and opposite Uranus.

• Venus, also in Aries, is opposite Uranus as well.

• In most house systems, Sun–Venus are in the 11th House (linked to Aquarius and Uranus).

• Mars itself is in the sign of Aquarius and widely trine to Uranus and to Saturn (both associated with the sign Aquarius).

What would an Aquarian/Uranian–flavoured Mars indicate? It might describe a very fast, on-off type of energy, or fighting (Mars) to liberate a group (Uranus/Aquarius) and pushing people (Mars) into waking up (Uranus) and acting (Mars) independently (Uranus/Aquarius). On an intimate level, it could suggest someone who desires space and much personal freedom.

We can see that both the Moon and Ascendant have their own planetary overtone, too.

• The Moon in Virgo has one major aspect: a square from Neptune (in the 6th House: this underlines the message from the Virgo Moon – so please don't ask me about my daily work patterns and my refusal to have a regular, routine 9-to-5 job).

• The ruler of my Ascendant (the Chart Ruler) is Mercury and it is found in the sign of Pisces; Mercury is also closely square to the Ascendant it rules.

A Mercury that is tinged with a Pisces/Neptune coating could suggest intuition or perception, a storyteller (in both senses), a colourful imagination, or an empathic, over-sensitive or fluid approach to communication.

Frank Clifford

In summary, the trails from my Big Three show Mars and Mercury to be important; further investigation reveals that Mars has an Aquarian/Uranian flavour, while my Mercury has a Piscean/Neptunian feel.

Superhypermost

With an unaspected Jupiter and Mars and the MC in gypsy, hippy Sagittarius, **Janis Joplin**'s philosophy ('I'd rather have ten years of superhypermost than live to be seventy sitting in some goddamn chair watching TV') is encapsulated in her songs, including 'Get It While You Can' and 'Me and Bobby McGee'. Both were from the album *Pearl*, released on 1 February 1971, the day Jupiter conjunct Neptune in Sagittarius and a few months after she had died of a *drugs overdose* (Jupiter–Neptune).

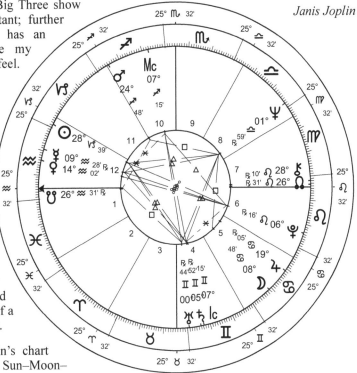

Janis Joplin

But if we look closely at Joplin's chart (above), and in particular her Sun–Moon–Ascendant trio, we can see two conflicting themes emerge. She was born with the Sun in Capricorn, the Moon in Cancer and the Ascendant in Aquarius. Cancer and Capricorn 'understand' each other, being polar opposites concerned with the preservation of the familiar and the status quo (either at work or home), but detached Aquarius is truly the odd one out in this trio – it is left out in the cold. Aquarius knows little of the clinginess and emotional safety blankets craved by Cancer, nor can it bear to be bound by the political handcuffs worn by status-aware Capricorn.

One side of Joplin was needy, self-conscious and desperate to fit in (her inner nature – Cancer and Capricorn), yet her appearance and shyness made her an outsider at high school, so she chose to rebel and stand out from the crowd (her persona – the Aquarius–Sagittarius angles). She would later become an emblem of the free-loving, unrestrained and hedonistic hippie generation (Sagittarius MC).

The inner conflicts of her nature and life are given additional weight by the conjunction of her Sun and Ascendant rulers – Saturn and Uranus – on the IC. When such a conflicting conjunction is personalized in a horoscope (by aspecting an angle or personal planet), there is the potential to shatter existing structures, to tear down barriers, to break free or deviate from what's expected (Uranus to Saturn) – or a potential to fear true freedom, or to pay for breaking the mould and rebelling against the social code of conformity (Saturn to Uranus).

Joplin lived these contradictions: a workaholic who managed her time expertly (Saturn), she nevertheless descended into heavy drugs. (Uranus relates to the excitement and buzz of drugs – 'speed freaks'; while Moon square Neptune can create a daily dependency – her favourite drink was aptly named Southern *Comfort*.) She was one of the first women to break into the all-boys' club of rock 'n' roll. And she was a middle-class white woman who sang her soulful, bluesy heart out on stage without restraint. She summed up the dichotomy of electrifying her audience but feeling profoundly separate from them: 'On stage I make love to 25,000 people – and then I go home alone.'

Ultimately, Saturn wins out (especially when it follows Uranus in sequence). Uranus joins the firm and ceases to be cutting-edge, or Saturn cuts it down to size, or over time it turns rebellion into cranky eccentricity. But, used effectively, the pair can help us affect social change without losing sight of our own limits and expendability.

4. *The Elemental and Modal Balances*

In this brief section, we'll look at how to make a list and a quick assessment of the elemental and modal balances. I used to reject this 'way in' as being a little too 'old school', but I rediscovered it and now see it as an essential, initial stage in analysis.

There are various ways to 'weight' the elements and the modes. Some experienced teachers, like Kim Farley of the LSA, assign points: the most points are given to the Sun and Moon, while fewer are awarded to personal planets and even fewer to the outers. Using this system, signatures and anti-signatures are created. For example, if mutability and Fire gain the most points, then the mutable Fire sign Sagittarius is the chart's signature; if fixity and Earth receive the lowest respective scores, then the fixed Earth sign Taurus is the anti-signature.

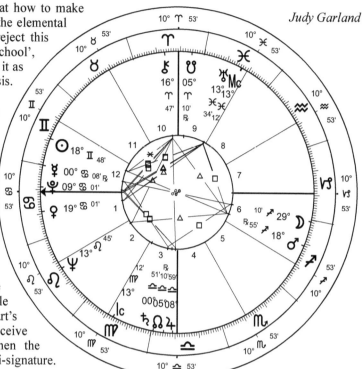

Judy Garland

(Kim has found that the anti-signature is usually the sign next to or in quincunx to the signature's sign.) Despite my Virgo Moon and its love of creating lists and rankings, I don't use a points system. I prefer to place the planets and angles (Sun to Saturn, plus the ASC and MC – nine positions in total) into a simple grid and look for emphases or lacks. This way, I can see each element or mode and spot 'lacks' and singletons quickly by looking down the rows or across the columns. Essentially, when assessing the elements and modes, our job is to ignore the average. Remember:

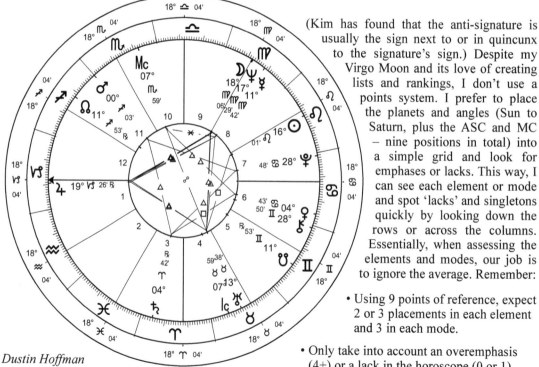

Dustin Hoffman

• Using 9 points of reference, expect 2 or 3 placements in each element and 3 in each mode.

• Only take into account an overemphasis (4+) or a lack in the horoscope (0 or 1).

• Give more weight to an element or mode that contains 2 or all 3 of the Big Three (Sun, Moon and Ascendant).

Elements/modes are interdependent – one that's prominent or missing affects the others. Sometimes all are reasonably in balance. Other times there's one imbalance or – especially with the elements – there may be two dominant elements and two weak ones.

One final note: Saturn can often feel like a 'lack', a minus in the scoring system or assessment. If it's the only planet in a particular element or mode, that element or mode may require attention or may feel undervalued. As with other lacks, Saturn's elemental or modal position assumes greater importance, as we often overcompensate and work for many years to fulfil the delayed promise of Saturn.

Brooke Shields

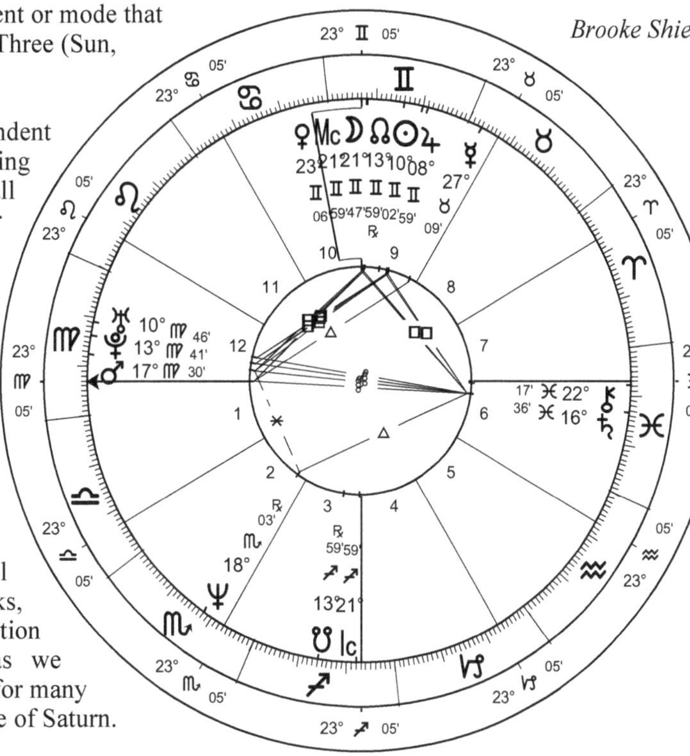

	Cardinal	Fixed	Mutable
Fire			☽♂
Earth			
Air	♃♄		☉
Water	☿♀ASC		MC

	Cardinal	Fixed	Mutable
Fire	♄	☉	♂
Earth	♃ASC		☽☿
Air			
Water	♀	MC	

	Cardinal	Fixed	Mutable
Fire			
Earth		☿	♂ASC
Air			☉☽♀♃MC
Water			♄

In **Judy Garland's** chart (opposite, top), the first of three performers, Water has four placements, followed by Air (three) and Fire (two). There's no Earth. Mutability and cardinality dominate the mode column and there's a lack of fixity. Without Earth *and* fixity, the chart lacks (and seeks) 'grounding' and anchorage. The challenge here may be to manage finances and develop staying power.

In **Dustin Hoffman's** chart (opposite, below), Earth dominates, followed by Fire, Water – and Air, which has no placements. The modes are reasonably balanced, with the fixed signs being slightly under-represented.

In **Brooke Shields's** chart (above), we see a predominance of Air, then Earth, a lack of Water and no Fire. With the modes, mutability dominates in eight of a possible nine placements, with a lack of fixity, and cardinality missing altogether. (Note that the major dispositor Mercury is in Earth, is a fixed singleton and in no aspect to any other planet.)

5. Major Aspects

Aspects show a dialogue and flow of energy between planets. The most important and dynamic interactions occur with the conjunction (a neutral aspect) and the square and opposition (two of the hard aspects). As a general rule, use 8° orbs for these. At this stage, I recommend ignoring all other aspects (except for trines under 3°) because these three take priority. They manifest clearly as factors that contribute to our personality traits and, accordingly, to our relationship patterns, life events and experiences. I don't include aspects between the outer planets, although these assume importance when personalized by contact with an angle or personal planet. Here's a recap of the main three to highlight, consider and interpret:

Russ Meyer – hard aspects

- Conjunction – subjective, powerful and focal areas in the chart and in the life.

- Opposition – areas that demand resolution and balance; relationship patterns, themes and projections; anchors or millstones.

- Square – areas that require action, effort, striving, stretching; life/personality challenges that arise; events and situations that manifest in concrete ways to spur on achievement and reward, or 'failures' that 'build character'.

The Subtlety of Aries
Above is the chart of the irreverent, independent, cult film-maker **Russ Meyer,** with only the squares and oppositions marked in (conjunction aspects are not shown in the centre of chart wheels). What do these aspects reveal about him?

Meyer made his name in low-budget sexploitation films. An amateur film-maker from age 14, he became a US Army combat cameraman before turning his attention to glamour models for *Playboy* shoots in the mid-1950s. When he graduated to film in 1959, the comedy *The Immortal Mr Teas* saw him labelled 'the King of the Nudies'. Meyer moved into writing, directing, editing and distributing (note the Gemini Ascendant) a series of satirical, surreal, campy films with Amazonian pneumatic starlets (Venus in Aries opposite Jupiter, and Mars conjunct a Sagittarius Descendant). His films revealed a personal obsession with violence (Aries) and an unabashed fixation on gargantuan, gravity-defying breasts (the Moon is squared by Jupiter) in 'cult classics' such as *Faster, Pussycat! Kill! Kill!* (1965) and *Vixen!* (1968), proving that there is little that's understated or refined in a Sun in Aries man (particularly at its first degree).

Proclaimed by some as an inadvertent feminist film-maker (his females were powerful, dominating forces of nature), with his Sun in Aries opposed by Saturn in Libra, Russ Meyer gained a reputation for mocking moral stereotypes, lampooning conservative values and (with an ample helping of Venus in Aries with Pluto in Cancer as the apex of a T-square) using sex to satirize American society. His autobiography was entitled *A Clean Breast*. Known for his quick wit, he was once confronted by a woman who accused him of being 'nothing but a breast man'. He responded, 'That's only the half of it.'

Perfect Illusion: 'It's a Good Thing'
In the horoscope of billionaire tycoon **Martha Stewart** (right, with one aspect drawn in), there are only eight major aspects:

- Sun conjunct Pluto
- Sun square ASC
- Sun conjunct MC
- Moon square Neptune
- Venus square Jupiter
- (Mars trine MC)
- Saturn conjunct Uranus
- Pluto square ASC

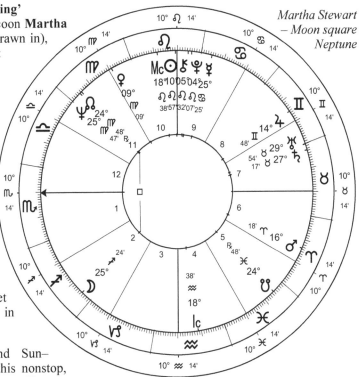

Martha Stewart – Moon square Neptune

Most of the aspects are quite wide but one that stands out is Moon square Neptune – an extremely close aspect with an orb of under one degree. The Moon is important because it is the handle of Stewart's Bucket chart. It is placed in Sagittarius in the 2nd House.

Although the Leo–Scorpio and Sun–Pluto combinations are key to this nonstop, compulsive and notoriously controlling over-achiever – a force of nature with a passion (Scorpio) for entertaining (Leo) – the Moon square Neptune describes the high-flying perfectionist and 'perfect housewife' image she projected personally for some years (which sadly was shown to be an illusion when her husband walked out after a Saturn Return of marriage). It also shows the catering business (presenting food as art) which led to a 'lifestyle' business born from her 'perfect home' philosophy (Moon in Sagittarius square Neptune).

Stewart's expertise has been in bringing back the lost art of housekeeping (an apt expression of Moon–Neptune), selling a glamorized lifestyle of gracious living and making it accessible to all. This has made her a fortune, as she has been able to reach American homes by permeating (Neptune) every aspect of the market and dreaming up an ideal way of life that her devoted following could re-create (Moon–Neptune).

Her enormous estate and huge income, generated from multi-media avenues (books, TV shows, and home products courtesy of Martha Stewart Living Omnimedia), are also suggested by the Moon's dispositor, Jupiter, in Gemini in the 8th House (widely sextile to, and the midpoint of, the

Sun –MC). With Sun–Pluto in Leo, she controls her business and, like so many Leo businesspeople, it is her name and image that form the brand itself.

Arguably, like many Sun–Pluto women featured in this book (three Cancerians – Nancy Reagan, Imelda Marcos and Leona Helmsley – spring to mind), Stewart has been persecuted for being a wealthy woman in a position of power and influence. (Interestingly, she is the only one of these four women who made her name and fortune without marrying a powerful man.)

One manifestation of the Moon in the 2nd square Neptune in the 11th proved to be a temporary glitch in the Martha Stewart phenomenon. A scandal erupted in early 2002 (as TR Neptune opposed her Sun) when she was involved in a questionable deal on the stock exchange (selling stock before shares plummeted). Stewart was charged with fraud and obstructing justice and was sentenced to prison for five months (October 2004 to March 2005). Interestingly, the assistant stockbroker for Stewart and a key witness against her in the trial was Douglas Faneuil, who was born with Mercury at 26° Virgo (on Martha's Neptune) and the Moon at 14° Taurus (near her Descendant).

Piano Man

The next chart (right) is the horoscope of entertainer **Liberace**. Here is the list of his conjunctions, squares and oppositions:

- Sun conjunct Mars
- Sun square Saturn
- Sun square Uranus
- Mercury square Neptune
- Mercury conjunct IC
- Venus conjunct Pluto
- Venus conjunct DSC
- Mars square Saturn
- Jupiter conjunct DSC*
- (Uranus trine MC)
- Neptune square MC
- Pluto conjunct DSC

* I allow wider orbs for conjunctions to the four angles. You may wish to include Jupiter in a conjunction to Venus and Pluto.

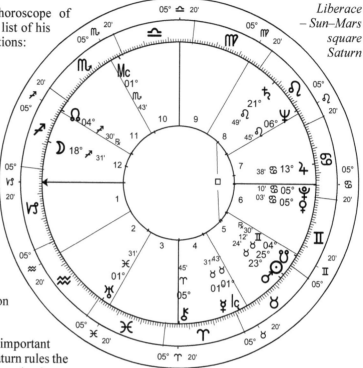

Liberace – Sun–Mars square Saturn

The Mars square Saturn aspect is important because Mars rules the MC and Saturn rules the Ascendant. The Venus–Pluto conjunction is strong because it is placed very close to the Descendant and Venus disposits the Sun, while Pluto co-rules the MC. These two sets of aspects are, in my opinion, major dynamics in Liberace's horoscope and keys to his life story and character.

His father was a hard taskmaster (Sun square Saturn in Leo) who introduced Liberace to the piano at age four (when the Sun-Saturn aspect perfected by Solar Arc). Rejecting sports, the young boy focused on cooking and piano practice – much to the teasing of schoolmates. He soon became interested in fashion (Mercury in Taurus is square to Neptune in Leo).

Arguably, with Sun–Mars square Saturn, Liberace built a wall of defence around himself to ward off taunts of his softness (and later his 'fruit-flavoured' mincing, as it was termed by the newspapers he successfully sued). He rejected masculine pursuits and he over-compensated (Saturn) by creating a bejewelled and fur-swamped showman persona (Leo). This creation earned him a reputation for flamboyance, won him millions of female fans, and brought wealth and an opulent, lavish lifestyle (the square is from Taurus to Leo). For many years, Liberace was the highest-paid entertainer in the world (Venus–Pluto). He famously shrugged

off criticism and 'cried all the way to the bank' (the conjunction is in Cancer!). Intensely private, his homosexuality was an issue he sued over and denied vehemently to his dying day.

'I Put a Spell on You'

The horoscope of singer **Nina Simone** (opposite, top) has the following major aspects, including a number of conjunctions and oppositions:

- Sun opposite Neptune
- Sun square MC
- (Moon trine Jupiter)
- Moon square Uranus
- Moon opposite Pluto
- Mercury opposite Mars
- Mercury opposite Jupiter
- Mercury opposite Neptune
- Venus conjunct Saturn
- Venus conjunct ASC
- Mars conjunct Jupiter
- Mars conjunct Neptune
- Saturn conjunct ASC

There is also a tight square involving the outer planets Uranus and Pluto; this square is personalized only because both are involved in a T-square with the Moon, and both planets are modern 'rulers' of the Ascendant and MC, respectively. This would make Nina Simone personally receptive to this aspect as well as future transiting aspects in the sky between the pair.

When there are many aspects to consider, invariably a pattern of some kind emerges. We'll be learning to spot overtones soon, but one that stands out from the list of major aspects above is a Mercury–Neptune theme to the horoscope.

Aside from the mutual reception of Mercury and Neptune (Mercury is in Neptune's sign, while Neptune is in Mercury's), Mercury makes three oppositions to planets in Virgo, a sign Mercury rules. Neptune opposes both the Sun and Mercury in the sign of Pisces, which is ruled by Neptune. There is also a Saturn-type overtone with the Moon in Capricorn and Saturn rising in the Saturn-ruled sign of Aquarius.

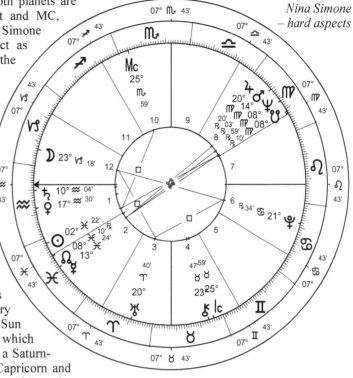

Nina Simone – hard aspects

The Invisible Man
In the chart below, the major aspects are:

- Sun conjunct Mars
- (Sun trine Jupiter)
- Sun conjunct ASC
- Moon square Mercury
- Moon square Neptune
- Moon conjunct MC
- Mercury conjunct Neptune
- Mercury square MC
- Venus square Jupiter
- Venus square Pluto
- Mars opposite Uranus
- Mars conjunct ASC
- Jupiter opposite Pluto

I would argue that the Mercury–Neptune conjunction in the 12th House is the key aspect in this horoscope because of Mercury and Neptune's rulership of three of the four angles (and Mercury being the Sun sign ruler/dispositor) and their square to the all-important Moon. It's an apt aspect for self-confessed chameleon, **Peter Sellers**, who battled to establish a concrete

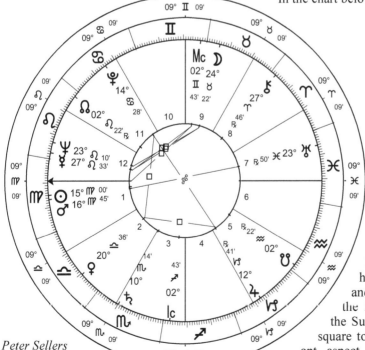

Peter Sellers – hard aspects

self-image off-screen and waited for a screen or TV role to bring him back to life. He once said, 'If you ask me to play myself, I will not know what to do… There used to be a me behind the mask, but I had it surgically removed.'

Interestingly, with Mercury–Neptune square Moon, it is believed that he continued to make contact with his mother long after her death, through ritual and séance. His perfectionism, volatility and raging temper (particularly in relationships) are seen by the Sun–Mars conjunction in the 1st, as perhaps are the eight heart attacks he suffered, too.

In an October 1962 interview for *Playboy*, the Mercurial Sellers described how he prepared for acting:

> I start with the voice. I find out how the character sounds. It's through the way he speaks that I find out the rest about him. I suppose that approach comes from having worked in radio for so long. After the voice comes the looks of the man… After that I establish how the character walks. Very important, the walk. And then, suddenly, something strange happens. The person takes over. The man you play begins to exist. I sink myself completely into every character I play, because he has begun to live in me. I suddenly seem to know what sort of life that man has had and how he would react to a given situation.

How I Live… Without You
The Bucket chart of **Diane Warren** (right) has the following major aspects:

- Sun opposite Mars
- Sun conjunct Jupiter
- Moon square Venus
- Moon conjunct Neptune
- Mercury conjunct ASC
- Mercury square MC
- (Venus trine Saturn)
- Venus conjunct Uranus
- Venus square Neptune
- Mars opposite Jupiter
- Saturn square Pluto

Again, without rushing ahead, three features stand out:

1. The Sun is in Virgo and Mercury is conjunct the Ascendant.

2. There's a Moon–Neptune conjunction, and the Sun–Jupiter conjunction in the 12th opposes Mars in Pisces (the chart's handle).

3. Venus–Libra is prominent: Venus makes two major aspects to outer planets, rules the Ascendant and three planets are in Libra.

What do these three features say about her? Warren is an acclaimed, award-winning composer of modern pop standards such as 'How Do I Live' and 'Un-break My Heart'. With a cloistered Moon–Neptune conjunction, Warren keeps her private life sacrosanct; she prefers the singers to take the spotlight. She has placed over 100 songs on the US charts – across various genres: pop, country, adult contemporary and R&B – and now earns up to $20 million annually in royalties ('in a good year,' she quips).

Warren says she has 'tapped this universality of message' in her songwriting and created pop ballads that are 'genre-transcendent'. This is the function of Neptune, which dominates her horoscope: it is conjunct her Moon (the MC ruler) and square Chart Ruler Venus. It also hints as to why so many of her hit songs have been written for motion pictures.

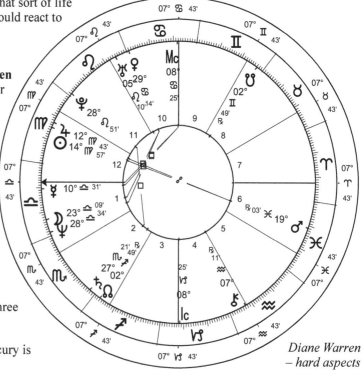

Diane Warren – hard aspects

Record producer David Foster says of Warren (whose Sun in Virgo opposes Mars), 'Without a doubt, she's the hardest working songwriter I've ever known… She just sits there, day after day. She's truly an island, and somehow she taps into the masses. The fact that she can do it by herself is extra special. She doesn't seem to need to rely on anybody else.' Warren describes her Sunset Boulevard office as a 'cave': 'It's very dirty, so I'm probably immune to every disease. I thrive on squalor [Virgo].' A Sun–Jupiter conjunction benefits from associating with 'important people', such as the pop divas hungry to snatch up her latest compositions, while the opposition to Mars in Pisces points to a productive and creative conveyor belt of contemporary, dramatic ballads. Yet, the self-confessed eccentric (Virgo) and 'bruised romantic' (Libra–Pisces), who shares her home with a cat and a parrot, admitted to *The Guardian* (UK) that she had never been in love. 'I have a good imagination. Look, I know what it feels like to have a broken heart… I'm just too weird to be in a relationship.'

Personal Power

Self-help guru **Anthony Robbins** (chart below) has been hugely influential over the past thirty years in bringing his own brand of Neuro-Linguistic Programming to public awareness. The keys to his chart are the MC ruler Moon in Aries in the 7th (the fire-walking, 'peak performance' coach aiming to help his audience achieve changes at record speed) and a strong Neptunian overtone, including the strategically placed Sun in Pisces opposite Pluto (his books include *Awaken the Giant Within*, *Unleash the Power Within* and *Unlimited Power*) and Mercury in Pisces contacting both its dispositors (a square to Jupiter in Sagittarius in the 3rd – the power of positive, inspirational thought – and a sesquisquare to Neptune). His products and seminars focus on Aries self-determination – taking action and making decisions. And he often speaks his Aries/Neptune themes:

A real decision is measured by the fact you've taken a new action. If there's no action, you haven't truly decided.

In life you either need inspiration or desperation.

Using the power of decision gives you the capacity to get past any excuse to change any and every part of your life in an instant.

A giant himself (standing at 6 feet 7 inches), Robbins has a Sun–Neptune–MC Grand Trine on the cusps of the Earth houses. This speaks of his highly lucrative businesses that have infiltrated American consciousness through infomercials, audio programs and motivational seminars, and have also brought him his own brand of celebrity.

The major aspects of his horoscope are:

- (Sun trine Neptune)
- Sun opposite Pluto
- (Sun trine MC)
- Moon square Saturn
- Mercury square Jupiter
- Venus conjunct Mars
- Venus opposite Uranus
- Venus square Neptune
- (Venus trine ASC)
- Mars square Neptune
- Saturn square ASC
- Saturn conjunct IC

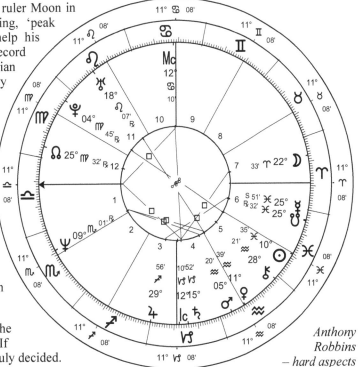

Anthony Robbins – hard aspects

6. Major Aspect Configurations

The aspect configurations show the life stories and key character dynamics. Their importance in a horoscope is due, in part, to the fact that they involve at least three planets that tie up numerous houses by tenancy or rulership – their influence will be felt in a major way. In addition, the aspects involved (particularly the main three: the conjunction, square and opposition) create a very powerful pattern that operates as an *interlinked system* and usually dominates a horoscope.

The three we are going to look at here, albeit briefly, are the T-square, the Grand Cross and the Grand Trine. There are others, such as the stellium (four or more planets conjunct, implying a centralized nucleus in the horoscope); the Yod (two planets in sextile both quincunx a third, bestowed with either mystical or medical connotations by various astrologers); the Kite (a Grand Trine with one opposition that sextiles the other two points of the configuration, implying dynamic talent); and the Grand Sextile (six planets spread around the chart, each approximately 60° from the last, suggesting opportunity and talent). There are also some fascinating configurations introduced by the astrologers Bruno and Louise Huber.

When interpreting an aspect configuration, the planets are the first consideration. Then, the particular aspects (such as the square or trine) involved in the configuration shed light on the *dialogue* between the planets. For example, a Grand Trine contains three harmonious, flowing trine aspects, while a Grand Cross comprises two sets of oppositions which are square (90°) – and at loggerheads – with each other.

Configurations with dissociate aspects (e.g. where two legs of a T-square are in one mode but the third leg is in another) are still important, but the statement is not underlined to the same extent as a regular configuration where the planets fall in the expected signs, element or mode (e.g. a Grand Trine with all three planets in Air signs).

Pulling apart the various legs of a T-square or other configuration is the easiest way of grasping what it means as a whole, so start with each individual planet. There are also a couple of useful points to remember when delineating an aspect pattern:

• Look for common links between the planets, signs, elements, modes or houses involved. For instance, it might be a T-square in fixed signs – the life issues around the configuration will be more rigid, wilful, determined, stuck. Or it might be a mutable T-square, which concerns itself more with the distribution and processing of information and a flexible, (over)adaptable approach to situations or issues. Or one planet might rule the signs in two of the three legs, creating a dominant theme to the configuration, e.g. Mercury opposite Jupiter in Gemini, both square Mars in Virgo – creating a Mercury theme in the T-square. These 'double whammies' (repetitive statements) are often the basis of an overtone in the chart.

• Look for a 'release' aspect – one that's foreign to the configuration (e.g. a square or opposition from one planet in a Grand Trine, or a trine from the apex of a T-square). This will show a constructive 'way out' – room to breathe – that can help to motivate us to explore the positive sides to the configuration without getting too tunnel-visioned or immersed in the 'set' configuration itself.

The T-square
T-squares are formed when two (or more) planets in opposition both square a third planet (the apex) located at right angles. *All* three 'legs' should be within an acceptable orb of the others (usually 8°).

In *The Contemporary Astrologer's Handbook* (Flare, 2006), Sue Tompkins writes: 'This energizing configuration can dominate the life and the chart. A T-square usually describes the most pressing problems in the life; by dealing with them, an individual stretches themselves and often makes noteworthy contributions to the world. So while indicative of obstacles and lessons to be learned, a T-square offers huge potential for personal growth.'

T-squares are like pressure cookers. Underneath, there's a huge amount of tension needing to be released – stress from parts of ourselves that are at odds with each other. T-squares are usually the source of much energy and edginess, and they demand resolution, action and discharge.

There's sometimes a state of paralysis because we are aware of the importance and fearful of the influence of these matters in our life. The most outstanding and memorable aspects of our character and life stories are found here, as too are the self-defeating, frustrating 'blocks' that can accumulate if we don't understand (or perhaps if we overemphasize) this configuration of enormous potential and transformation.

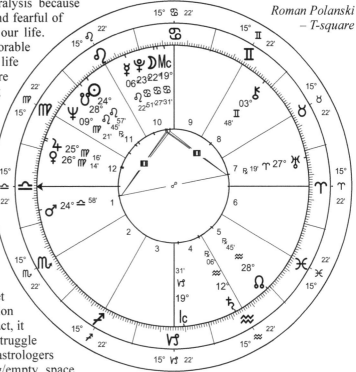

Roman Polanski – T-square

The most compelling part of the T-square (seen in both the chart and the person) is the apex itself – the planet that squares both ends of the opposition. It's a point of release. Understanding the apex (focal point) of a T-square – the planet involved, its sign and house position and other aspects – is the key. In fact, it is the *solution* to what drives the struggle inherent in the opposition. Some astrologers pay attention to the missing leg/empty space (opposite the apex), but I would focus on the areas of the chart directly involved in the configuration.

In some examples in this book, there are two focal planets receiving squares from the opposition. These are not always conjunct, but the actual exact degree of the apex is significant in terms of synastry with other charts and very sensitive to transits, directions and progressions (see Margaret Thatcher's chart on page 108).

I would also include the angles in a T-square, but only as *one* substitute leg, never as two. Where an angle is the apex, it acts as an active point of release for the opposition to work through, but it does not have the same energy that a planet has when it is the focal point of a such a configuration.

Plunging Emotional Depths
The first example belongs to director **Roman Polanksi** (above). Polanski's T-square suggests dynamic achievement through crisis, conflict and challenge (cardinal signs). Mars in Libra in the 1st opposite Uranus in Aries in the 7th speaks of wilful independence, disagreement and a need for space vs. fighting for freedom, rights and justice. A sudden act of violence and controversial (Uranus) sex (Mars) are two further manifestations.

The opposition is square to the Moon conjunct Pluto in Cancer on the Midheaven. This apex/focal point demands resolution by achieving recognition (MC) and creating a powerful, intense emotional impact or response (Moon–Pluto in Cancer) by exploring buried feelings, trauma or obsession (Moon–Pluto in Cancer) in the outside world (MC). It also suggests some powerful, seemingly non-negotiable (Pluto) experiences around his mother or wife. In *Aspects in Astrology*, Sue Tompkins suggests the aspect has much to do with 'primal feelings' and 'plunging and diving deeply into… feelings and relationships'.

As a film-maker he has demonstrated a bizarre interplay between the plots of his films and events in his own life, and as astrologers we can see this most vividly in his T-square. His films have often contained dark, violent, sexual conflicts, and his life has had its share of horror, murder and sex scandal. Obsessed with horror movies and sharp edges and razors (Mars), his first few films had claustrophobic settings (Moon–Pluto square Uranus) and were known as the 'apartment trilogy'. *Knife in the Water* is about a love triangle, *Repulsion* centres around a woman driven to murder and insanity, and in *Rosemary's Baby* a woman is betrayed and manipulated into carrying and birthing the spawn of the Devil (Moon–Pluto in Cancer). Polanski went on to repeat the Moon–Pluto theme in *Macbeth* (Lady Macbeth must truly be one of the oldest literary embodiments of Moon–Pluto) and in *Chinatown*, in which a private eye plunges into a complex web of deceit and murder, incest and corruption all related to the city's water supply.

Together, Moon–Pluto in Cancer and Mars opposite Uranus are themes that have appeared most dramatically in his private life. His mother perished in Auschwitz and young Roman fled to Poland to start a new life. Many years later, his wife Sharon Tate was eight months into carrying their child when she was murdered savagely by the Manson followers – one member plunged a knife into her sixteen times. (Tate's Ascendant is at 21° Cancer and Jupiter nearby at 18°, tying in with the apex of Polanski's T-square.) And on 10 March 1977 (with TR Pluto near his Ascendant), a sexual incident with a thirteen-year-old girl (Samantha Gailey, later Geimer, born 31 March 1963) led to six counts of drugging and raping a minor. Pleading guilty, Polanski fled to Europe on 1 February 1978 (one day before sentencing) and remained a fugitive until he was arrested at the request of the US authorities on 26 September 2009 in Switzerland. He was later released and declared a 'free man' by the Swiss on 12 July 2010, one day after a Solar Eclipse at 19° Cancer, exactly conjunct his MC.

The Call to Invention

What do you make of the chart on the right? I'm drawn to the tight grouping of planets (seven within less than 60° and mostly in Pisces) around the Ascendant but also to the handle of the chart: the Moon in Virgo in the 7th. This would suggest the importance of the Moon in being a funnel to direct the 'energies' of the planets in the 12th and 1st Houses. The grouping in Pisces and the handle in Virgo emphasize the Virgo–Pisces polarity of service, dedication and care. In particular, the exact opposition from the sensory Moon to aural Mercury (and their mutual square to the MC in Sagittarius) seems a pivotal player in

this chart. This is the T-square that I'll be focusing on. The chart belongs to **Alexander Graham Bell**, who shaped the future (MC in Sagittarius as the apex) by inventing the telephone. A practical way for people to connect with each other (Moon in the Mercury-ruled sign of Virgo in the 7th), his invention and vision gave a voice to millions (Mercury in Pisces).

An educator, Bell paved the way in X-ray, iron lungs and aerodynamics, but his greatest passion was in the mainstreaming and integrating (Sagittarius MC and its ruler Jupiter in Gemini) of deaf people and children into schools and society. He felt that sign language only marginalized and isolated deaf people. His pioneering work in harmonics and *voice transmission* is a true expression of the mutable T-square and the planets involved. And one function of the Mercury–Jupiter signs (the mutables) is to find a way to link, connect and bring understanding between people. One of Bell's pupils, Helen Keller, would later say that Bell dedicated his life to the penetration of that 'inhuman silence which separates and estranges'.

Education, teaching and an interest in reaching out to people are all suggested by his MC in

Alexander Graham Bell – T-square

Sagittarius, as is his family background (MC in Sagittarius and IC in Gemini). Bell was brought up by his overbearing father – who was well known for his passion for the spoken word, his work on 'visible speech' to enable the deaf to speak, and a crusade to solve stammering – and his musical mother, who despite being almost deaf played the piano and educated the young boy at home. Curious, intelligent and headstrong, Bell was also a loner and sought solace from his domineering father in quiet Piscean retreats.

Always fascinated by the art of communication and the construction of speech, young Bell was a natural problem-solver and invented his first machine at age nine. In the summer of 1870 (as TR Saturn crossed his MC), his brother died and Bell caved in to parental pressure to set sail with them on 21 July 1870 to start a new life in Canada. He became a tutor for deaf children (his lifelong cause), and Bell's initial work on a 'harmonic telegraph' would lead to inventing the telephone on 2 July 1874 (with TR Jupiter on his Moon at 24° Virgo). The telephone was first used on 2 June 1875 and the first transmission made on 10 March 1876, around the time of Bell's Saturn Return.

In spite of his famous invention, Bell saw himself primarily as a teacher of the deaf. Virgo–Pisces must create order/precision (Virgo) out of chaos/randomness (Pisces), or art (Pisces) from craft (Virgo). Inherent in Bell's passion for teaching children lay an understanding that young people possess an uncluttered mind (perhaps a response from the Virgo Moon to Mercury in Pisces) and could be educated and helped to rise above any handicap. Interestingly, and reflective of the Virgo–Pisces polarity (one that needs solitude in order to be productive), Bell refused to have a telephone in his own study, considering it an unnecessary intrusion into his science work.

We could say that, with the Moon in Virgo as the all-important handle in the 7th, Bell was inspired to create a device (Mercury in Pisces) because of the practical needs and everyday difficulties of those around him (Moon in Virgo in the 7th). Bell became highly sensitive to his mother's (Moon) gradual deafness, and this further shaped his interest in harmonics. His mother's deafness began when he was 12 (the year the Solar Arc Sun conjoined his Mercury at 24° Pisces and opposed the Moon, spotlighting this all-important opposition). No doubt, this had a role to play in

his desire to invent and to educate people about sound. Again, pertinent to this 7th House placement, Bell would later fall in love with and marry a woman named Mabel, who had been rendered deaf at age five from scarlet fever and was one of the first children to learn to lip-read and speak. His dedication to her being able to hear again is said to have inspired his famous invention.

When casting for the actor to play Bell on screen, a Hollywood studio chose Don Ameche, born with the MC at 25° Virgo (on Bell's Moon) and the Sun at 10° Gemini (close to Bell's Jupiter). The film, *The Story of Alexander Graham Bell*, prompted a generation to use the word 'Ameche' as slang for 'telephone' ('You're wanted on the Ameche').

A further expression of Bell's T-square is seen in the fact that many contested his patent design – it became the longest patent case in US history – and Bell was called to testify many times and to defend his reputation. (Sagittarius is so often elevated by others but, with MC ruler in versatile but magpie-like Gemini, there may be a question of ethics and originality.)

The Grand Trine
Just like the trine aspect, the Grand Trine – a circuit of three or more planets each a trine away from the other – can be a mixed blessing. On the one hand it can represent the areas in life where lucky, 'right place, right time' opportunities arise without much effort. Or there's a natural ability that is elevated and lauded which enables doors to be opened for us. The Grand Trine in the horoscope of Whitney Houston (see page 112) is one example. Houston's talent was nurtured by her environment of female relatives, who were celebrated pop, soul or gospel singers (Moon–Jupiter trine Sun–Venus trine MC in Sagittarius). Trines to (or Grand Trines involving) the MC often indicate early accolades in a particular endeavour, but the hard-won successes that *really mean something* to us are described by the T-squares and challenging aspects in our chart.

Because of its geometry and meaning, the Grand Trine has also been called a 'closed system' that maintains a particular status quo in our life. Noel Tyl sees this pattern as a defence mechanism and a 'self-contained perfection' where we retreat into a closed circuit of self-sufficiency. With an Air Grand Trine, the retreat is into our own company or thoughts, a defence against not being appreciated, while a Water Grand Trine encourages emotional isolation from relationship. Tyl sees Earth Grand Trines as practical self-sufficiency – not needing others' help and being an independent 'fix-it' person – and Fire as motivational self-sufficiency against being ignored ('You can't tell me anything I don't know').

As stated earlier, a hard aspect to one of the planets in the Grand Trine can act as a 'way out' – an exit strategy to break free from repetitive and stagnant patterns. As in Houston's chart (with Saturn opposing and Neptune squaring Sun–Venus), the 'way out' can also be the path of a major life challenge that disrupts or threatens to take away what has been naturally endowed.

The Grand Cross
The Grand Cross is a rare formation in which two sets of oppositions are at right angles to each other. This can feel like a heavy 'cross to bear', a constant fight with opposition from all quarters, and an obstacle-ridden course. Like the T-square it can produce something quite remarkable, but it is a major cosmic challenge and juggling act. Again, when delineating this configuration, look for common links such as signs, rulerships and modes in common.

One gruesome example of a Grand Cross is in the chart of child beauty queen **JonBenét Ramsey** (right), who was brutally murdered in her own home on Christmas Day 1996 at age six. This is not an example chart intended to terrify you into thinking a Grand Cross equals savage murder, but instead a chance to look at a life and see how each set of oppositions is involved.

Firstly, the Sun in Leo on the IC opposes the Moon in Aquarius on the MC. JonBenét's life was a series of competitions (Mars is involved too) to be crowned queen (Sun in Leo) among her peer group (Aquarius). But this was a group of precocious pre-teens – Barbie doll toddlers with tiaras (Leo). These child beauty contestants are often aggressively marketed (Full Moon) by overzealous, ambitious parents (Sun/Moon–MC/IC) wanting their child to be special and in the spotlight – but claiming that the bizarre

spectacle helps their child's self-esteem and confidence (Leo Sun opposite Aquarius Moon). JonBenét's high-profile (the Full Moon) murder cast a dark shadow onto these contests and led to much investigation into the ethics and practice of these mini-princess pageants.

The other part of the Grand Cross is Mars in Taurus exactly opposite Pluto in Scorpio, which is square to the Sun–Moon opposition. Firstly, beauty pageants for youngsters have been criticized as being nothing more than 'kiddie porn', and the process of sexualizing contestants into seductive temptresses and objects of desire is descriptive of both Mars in Taurus and Pluto in Scorpio. Secondly, *some* manifestations of Mars–Pluto combinations can be seen in brute force, victimization through violence or intimidation, and sexual abuse. JonBenét's skull (Mars) was fractured by a blunt instrument and a garotte was tied around her neck (Taurus).

It is also interesting that both her parents (Sun and Moon) were considered suspects in the case and spent many years under public scrutiny. They were not exonerated by the police until July 2008 – tragically, this was two years after JonBenét's mother died of cancer. The case remains unsolved.

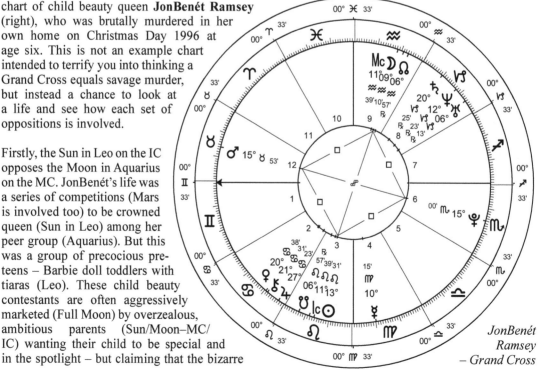

JonBenét Ramsey – Grand Cross

To the right is the horoscope of JonBenét's father, **John Bennett Ramsey**. Up until his daughter's death, Ramsey lived the American Dream. The wealthy, high-achieving president of a computer services company, he was named Entrepreneur of the Year by the Boulder Chamber of Commerce – Mars and Uranus flank the MC in Gemini. This conjunction and its opposition to his Sun can also be seen in the sudden reversal of fortune following his daughter's murder, an event that decimated his life and reputation. The focal point of the opposition is Chiron on a Virgo Ascendant, suggestive of the victimization and sorrow that followed. Chart Ruler Mercury is in Sagittarius square Neptune and opposite Saturn: police errors handicapped the investigation, and the Ramseys were victims of persecution and a national media witch-hunt that included unsubstantiated 'leaks', years of lies and trial-by-TV. Ramsey later sued several organizations for defamation.

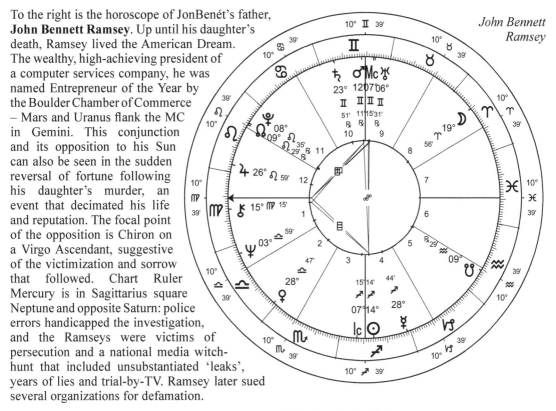

John Bennett Ramsey

Frank Sinatra – Thor's Hammer

Music and the Mob

To the left, we have a 'Thor's Hammer' (one square and two sesquisquares) with Neptune–MC as the apex. The configuration also includes the Sun and Mercury in Sagittarius and Jupiter in Pisces – a strong repetition of Jupiter, Neptune and their signs.

The chart belongs to legendary crooner and swing singer **Frank Sinatra**. The emphasis on Jupiter and Neptune (plus the 2nd, 5th and 10th Houses) is in line with his enormous success as an era-defining entertainer, his film acting, his excessive fame and wealth, and his shady reputation (thanks to alleged links to organized crime). The strong Jupiter overtone reveals not only how he was elevated by the public to iconic status, but also suggests his bouts of depression and his need to seek out excitement to avoid solitude at all costs. (For more on Sinatra and his town, Vegas, see pages 212–16.)

7. Spotting Overtones

The final consideration is to step back from the information we have amassed and consider the chart's key *overtones* – common themes, links and repetitions. We've already started to look at some of these in earlier sections. It's always said that, if a statement in the chart is strong, it will be written/expressed at least three times. For example, a chart may have a Capricorn Ascendant, and the Sun conjunct Saturn both opposite the Moon in the 10th House (a Saturn/Capricorn/10th signature). There may be several overtones in a chart, but there's often one dominant theme.

These overtones can be described as 'double-whammies' – for example, a Moon–Mercury conjunction in Pisces opposite Neptune in the 12th (note the Pisces/Neptune/12th House theme). You might spot a Venus overtone – but is that Venus–Taurus–2nd, or Venus–Libra–7th? Or perhaps both Venus signs are part of the overtone (e.g. Libra Rising, Sun conjunct Venus in Taurus in 7th).

Always pay particular attention to the Big Three: the Sun, Moon and Ascendant. An Aries Ascendant and Scorpio Moon create a Mars theme – but look to see whether this is reinforced by the position and strength of Mars (or any additional planets in Aries or Scorpio). Perhaps Mars is in its own sign or house and strongly aspected, or receiving few aspects and in a sign foreign to the Mars principle.

There's a simple, systematic way of spotting overtones. Start with the Sun and look to see if there are planets (or the Ascendant and MC) in Leo and the 5th House, or in aspect to the Sun; then look at the Moon/Cancer/4th, and so on, ending with Pluto. It's a bit laborious, but once you've done this a few times, you'll be spotting themes quickly without the need to do this step-by-step.

Let's try this with the chart on the opposite page. We're looking for an *emphasis* here – using all the things we've been examining in the first six points of this section on Major Assessments:

- A grouping of planets in a house (at least two personal planets or three to four including outer planets) or in a sign (at least two, especially personal planets, the MC or ASC).

- Making the Sun, Moon and Ascendant a priority.

- Planets strongly placed (e.g. on an angle) or heavily aspected or even unaspected.

Strongly placed/ heavily aspected	*Many/key planets in*	*Many/key planets in*
Sun* opp. Moon, Mars	**Leo** Pluto	**5th*** Moon, Mars
Moon* conj. Mars opp. Sun	**Cancer**	**4th**
Mercury sq. Pluto	**Gemini** Jupiter	**3rd**
	Virgo Neptune, MC	**6th**
Venus* conj. ASC opp. Sat, Ura	**Taurus** Saturn, Ura	**2nd**
	Libra Sun	**7th*** Jup, Sat, Ura
Mars* conj. Moon opp. Sun	**Aries*** Moon, Mars	**1st** Venus
	Scorpio* Merc, Venus, ASC	**8th**
Jupiter sq. Neptune	**Sagittarius**	**9th** Pluto
	Pisces	**12th** Mercury
Saturn* conj. Ura, DSC opp. Venus	**Capricorn**	**10th**
	Aquarius	**11th** Sun, Neptune
Uranus* conj. Sat, DSC opp. Venus	**Aquarius**	**11th** Sun, Neptune
Neptune sq. Jupiter	**Pisces**	**12th** Mercury
Pluto sq. Mercury	**Scorpio*** Merc, Venus, ASC	**8th**

I have added an asterisk * to the planets, signs and houses strongly placed above. I would also consider the following conjunctions, hard aspects and aspects to the angles:

- Sun opposite Moon
- Sun opposite Mars
- Moon conjunct Mars
- Mercury square Pluto
- Venus opposite Saturn
- Venus opposite Uranus
- Venus conjunct ASC
- Jupiter square Neptune
- Saturn conjunct DSC
- Uranus conjunct DSC

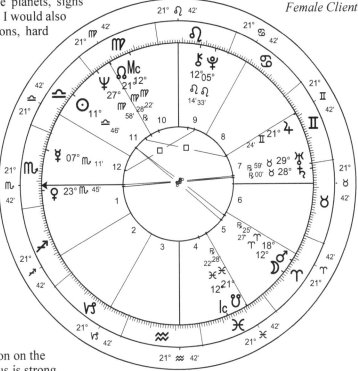

Female Client

So, looking at the table and asterisks, we notice:

- The 5th and 7th Houses are strongly tenanted.

- Venus is powerfully placed/ aspected.

- The Saturn–Uranus conjunction on the Descendant and opposite Venus is strong.

- The Sun and Moon have two major aspects but, unlike Venus, Saturn or Uranus, neither is on an angle.

- Mars is powerfully aspected and in its own sign of Aries.

- Aries and Scorpio are strongly featured.

Looking for planet, sign and house links, we notice that Venus and the 7th emerge strong, as does Mars and its two signs, Aries and Scorpio (but not their respective 1st or 8th Houses). Pluto makes a square to Mercury (this is important because Pluto co-rules the Ascendant and Mercury rules the MC), but it is not as involved in the action (the major dynamics of the chart) as Mars (being conjunct the Moon and opposite the Sun). So, I would consider this chart to have two major overtones:

Strongly placed/ heavily aspected	Many/key planets in	Many/key planets in
Venus	Libra	7th House
Mars	Aries, Scorpio	

Essentially, this horoscope is a combination of Venus and Mars. It is a Venus–7th overtone (relating and one-to-one exchange) rather than Venus–2nd (linked to money and values). And the Mars is both of the Aries (energy and motivation to fight for causes) and Scorpio (psychological exploration) kind. It is the chart of a therapist who also helped run a community centre (Sun in Libra in the 11th), organized the annual fireworks display and led various neighbourhood campaigns (Moon–Mars in Aries in the 5th).

Here are some further considerations:

- After this, we can look for confirmation of certain overtones that have come up. The Sun in Libra adds to the Venusian–7th House overtone, as does the Full Moon (Sun opposite Moon), which has a Libra–7th House feel. The simple fact that the Sun is in Libra opposite the Moon in Aries underscores the Venus–Mars theme, as does Venus Rising and Moon conjunct Mars.

- Later, we can begin looking for house rulership links/repetitions (e.g. the ruler of the 10th House placed in the 10th) – this is where areas of life are linked. Even though I now hesitate to use the outer planets as rulers of a particular house, I do think it is helpful to link these to get a feel for the major chart theme, and have listed these in the table.

- When there are a couple of overtones, consider these to be *a bit like* a planetary pair in aspect (e.g. Sun–Saturn). There may not be a dialogue/aspect between these two planets in the horoscope, but the main themes and thrust of the birth chart are *of the nature of both planets*. When those two planets happen to be in aspect with each other, the theme is strengthened.

- When listing combinations, it's usual to write the innermost planet first (e.g. Venus–Saturn instead of Saturn–Venus) but, in these and later examples, I've referred to the overtone combinations in the order of importance.

By spotting a planetary overtone, you'll be recognizing a key part of the life story/character – you can then assess the condition of that planet to pinpoint themes, life issues and needs. As I mentioned in the Introduction, it's not about reducing the chart and avoiding its complexities, it's a technique that can help you get to the very heart of what the chart and person are about – their driving forces, the engine of the person and their key life experiences. In The Five Chart Themes, we'll be looking at further examples.

Spotting Overtones – Further Examples

To the right is the horoscope of **Louise Woodward**, the British au pair convicted of the involuntary manslaughter of a child in her care while she was living in Massachusetts.

A Fish Out of Water
Woodward's chart has three personal planets in Pisces, the Moon in Virgo and Sagittarius on the Ascendant. Each of the Big Three is in a mutable sign. With Pisces and Sagittarius strong, we should be drawn to the planet they have in common, but Jupiter is not powerfully placed: it is in Gemini in the 7th, away from the Descendant and making a

few wide aspects. Despite being the Chart Ruler and dispositor of the Pisces places, it is not 'in conversation' with the major dynamics of this chart (this *does* say much about her not being able to utilize such an important planet and being at the mercy of other people's words, convictions or judgements – Jupiter in Gemini in the 7th). If we look at the other dispositor of her Pisces planets, Neptune, we find that it is in a far more dominant position. It is conjunct the Sagittarius Ascendant and is the apex of Woodward's mutable T-square that involves the Sun, Moon, Mercury and Venus. This is a chart with very powerful Neptune–Pisces and mutable messages.

Watching her sit quietly in court during the trial, one can imagine how much the nineteen-year-old – who couldn't have looked more Piscean – must have been scared, confused and alone, swept up in the media drama and chaos (Neptune) of her predicament. She found herself in a terrifying environment described by Saturn in the 9th and Neptune rising in Sagittarius: in prison, fighting a foreign judicial system for her freedom and up on a charge for a crime she said she didn't commit. After a jury found her guilty of second-degree murder (on 30 October 1997 at 21:39 EST, Cambridge, MA, when TR Neptune was conjunct

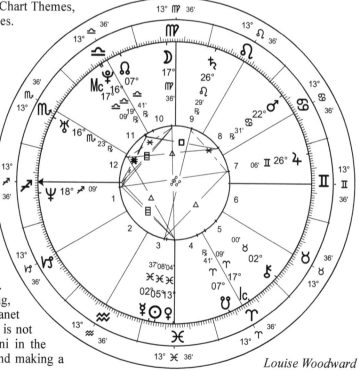

Louise Woodward

the verdict's Descendant), a judge reduced the conviction to involuntary manslaughter, stating: 'The circumstances in which the defendant acted were characterized by confusion, inexperience, frustration, immaturity and some anger, but not malice in the legal sense supporting a conviction for second-degree murder… I am morally certain that allowing this defendant on this evidence to remain convicted of second-degree murder would be a miscarriage of justice.'

Most of the activity in her horoscope is linked to the mutable T–square, but there are a few other key aspects that stand out:

- Pluto conjunct the MC in Libra and in square to Mars in Cancer in the 8th House. Pluto–MC can sometimes manifest as a 'non-negotiable' event that overshadows one's reputation. The square to Mars in *Cancer* in the 8th is suggestive of her being labelled a 'murderous nanny'. Interestingly, Mars (the ruler of Woodward's 5th House – children – and her 12th House) is conjunct the Ascendant of Matthew Eappen, the child she was convicted of injuring and killing (her Mars and his Ascendant are on Elwell's sadism axis, see page 145). The prosecution said that his death was a result of violent shaking and from his head – Mars – impacting a hard surface.

- Sun–Mercury widely opposite Saturn in the 9th. This is perhaps 'seen' in the weighty legal system and her incarceration while living abroad.

Woodward went on to study law but quit her training to pursue a Neptune–Pisces career as a ballroom and Latin dance teacher.

The Glamorous Mistress
A Neptune double-whammy can be seen in the chart of Kathleen DuRoss, who later became **Kathy Ford**, widow of Henry Ford II of the Ford Motor Company. In her horoscope (right), the Moon is conjunct Venus in Pisces and both planets are opposite Neptune. Three other key aspects stand out as important and repetitive statements in their own right:

- Sun in Aquarius square to its modern dispositor Uranus (sudden changes, break-ups or breakdowns in her life path and with men).

- Pluto in the 7th square the MC in Scorpio (powerfully transformative partners).

- MC ruler Mars in its own sign of Aries conjunct Ascendant ruler Saturn (backbone, hard work, and industrious Mars-type men).

These sets of aspects are central to the chart's dynamics and are seen in her life story (which was outlined in Penny Thornton's book *Romancing the Stars*, aka *Suns and Lovers*). Kathy met her first husband at age fourteen and by seventeen had given birth to two children. Two years later (12 December 1959), her husband was killed in a car crash, which later resulted in Kathy suffering a breakdown (Uranus). She moved into modelling and was introduced to a world of glamour, the rich and the famous (Neptune).

At 30, she met powerful industrialist Henry Ford II and spent five years 'underground' (Pluto) as his mistress, until the press (Neptune) broke the story in February 1975 of their affair. With her natal Mars in Aries conjunct Saturn (plus Kathy's need for genius and

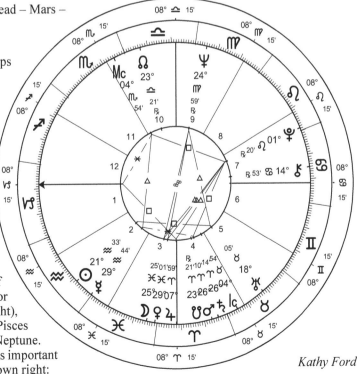

Kathy Ford

glamour in relationships – Sun–Uranus and Moon–Venus–Neptune), he was no simple motor mechanic, he was an empire-builder who introduced her to the high life! They were married in October 1980. When Ford died in September 1987, Kathy almost had a nervous breakdown and, along with the grief over her loss, had to contend with a vicious court battle with Ford's children from his first marriage. She later became a professional photographer.

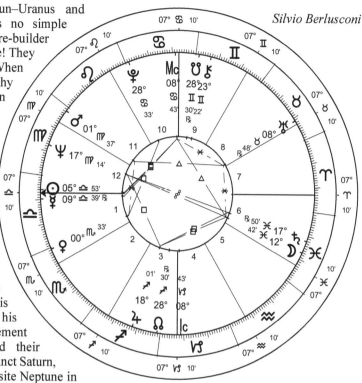

Silvio Berlusconi

Absolute Power Corrupts...
Although there is some dispute over the birth time of former Italian Prime Minister **Silvio Berlusconi**, the tight T-square of his horoscope (right) remains the same in any chart calculated for his birth date. Like Sinatra's chart, his configuration is a repetitive statement involving Jupiter, Neptune and their signs: the Moon is in Pisces (conjunct Saturn, and possibly ruling the MC) opposite Neptune in the 12th and both planets square Jupiter in the 3rd. Berlusconi is the media's champ of corruption. Scandal is Neptunian, and the Jupiter emphasis (as the focal planet of the T-square) suggests *huge* scandal and publicity, as well as the accusations of his *taking advantage* of his high position (Jupiter) through corruption and bribery (Saturn–Neptune).

There is also a strong Libra overtone (especially if Libra is also his Ascendant) and the dispositor Venus is powerfully placed at the first degree of Scorpio and square to Pluto. Unlike most leaders of countries, Berlusconi is a powerful entrepreneur (Pluto), a property baron and media magnate (worth $8 billion), owning TV stations and publishing companies (Jupiter) – he is *everywhere* (Neptune). A born salesman and former crooner, Berlusconi is known for his vanity and large ego (the Sun rises in Libra), and for the fierce personal loyalty he commands from his entourage and staff.

A True Uranian Spirit
Another example of a dominant planetary theme can be found in the horoscope of writer **Germaine Greer** (opposite page, top). For many, Greer embodied the second wave of feminism upon the publication of *The Female Eunuch* (Moon–Uranus) in December 1970 (when Pluto was at 29°

Virgo, and ten months before it began its stint in Libra).

A brash, intelligent personality, Greer has a chart with a fascinating example of a repetitive Uranus–Aquarius theme: the Sun and Ascendant are in Aquarius and are squared by Uranus, which conjuncts the Moon. Simply put, Uranus contacts the three major points in the horoscope – an important factor for a double Aquarian. Greer is certainly a Uranian Aquarian rather than a Saturnian one.

In *Eunuch*, Greer challenges women to reject negative body images and to free themselves from the confines of their domestic role (Moon–Uranus). Aquarius is a sign that attacks patriarchy (Leo). Greer wrote of women, 'She must recapture her own will and her own goals, and the energy to use them, and in order to effect this some quite unreasonable suggestions, or demands, may be necessary.' Given Greer's prominent Uranus, *Eunuch* was a subversive, revolutionary volume for its time. Not surprisingly, Pluto and Scorpio also figure as an overtone: Mars is at 29° Scorpio; Pluto is trine Mars and square the MC in Scorpio and widely opposite (and at the midpoint of) the

Sun and Mercury. A generation of women had been waiting for someone to put voice to their discontent, yet in retrospect there seems to have been a disenchantment with Greer's work as a feminist voice (Venus in the 11th squares Neptune) that has made her a somewhat isolated reformist (Uranus) now most often seen on chat shows, where she nevertheless combines wit with common sense and a fierce intelligence.

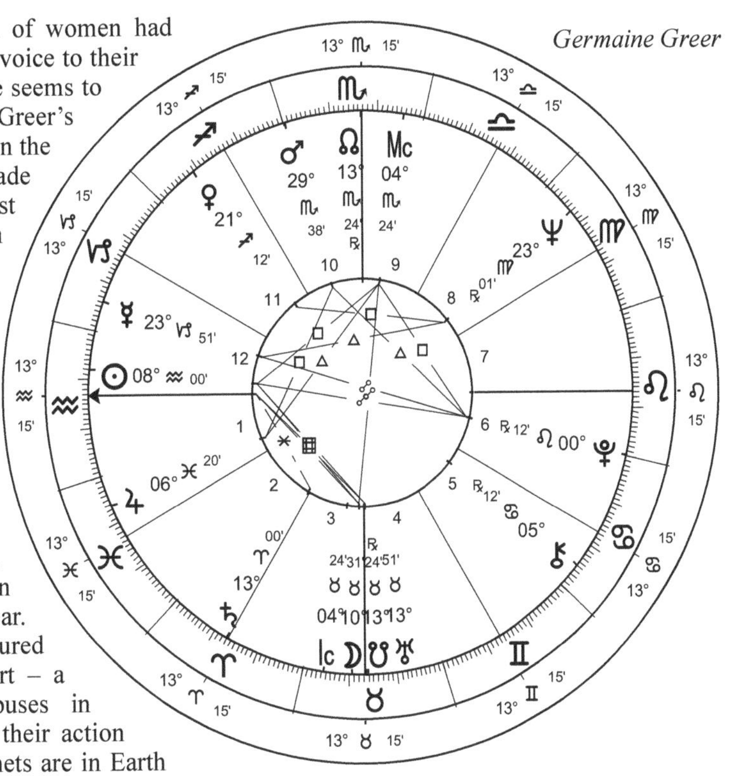

Germaine Greer

The final example is a chart for the first **Earth Day** (pictured below), an annual event to inspire awareness (Full Moon) and appreciation for the planet's natural environment (Taurus, Earth). Over twenty million people participated that first year. Founder Gaylord Nelson favoured a decentralized, grassroots effort – a 'teach-in' organized by campuses in which each community shaped their action around local concerns. Five planets are in Earth signs. 'Sustainable' Taurus dominates and three planet oppositions (awareness) emphasize the Taurus–Scorpio polarity (physical and emotional potency, regeneration and healing): the Sun in Taurus (on the MC) opposes Jupiter in Scorpio (on the IC), and the Moon in Scorpio opposes both Saturn and Mercury in Taurus. Two other oppositions stand out: Mars in Gemini opposes Neptune at 0° Sagittarius (actively forming links to band together for a common cause) and Uranus in Libra opposes Chiron in Aries (waking up group awareness of the individual's role in healing the collective wound). Marking the 25th anniversary in 1995, Nelson spoke this chart's main themes:

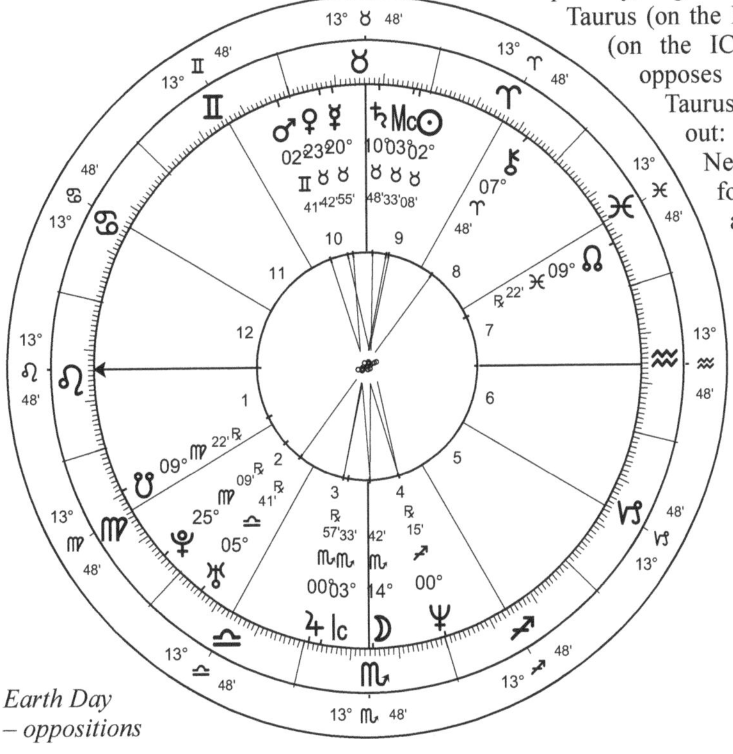

The opportunity for a gradual but complete break with our destructive environmental history and a new beginning is at hand… I am optimistic that this generation will have the foresight and the will to begin the task of forging a sustainable society.[9]

Earth Day – oppositions

In the last section, we considered the key areas to examine when making initial notes on any horoscope:

- The distribution of planets

- Links between the four angles

- The Big Three – the Sun–Moon–Ascendant – and their connections and trails

- The elemental and modal balances

- Major aspects

- Aspect configurations

- Major chart themes and overtones

One of my favourite writing jobs is for the UK Astrological Association's *The Astrological Journal*, first edited by my fellow Aries pal John Green and now Gemini Victor Olliver. When John took over in 2008, he invited me to write a regular column. I didn't want to wax lyrical on just one chart or feature, so I suggested a collection of thoughts and observations on a specific area for each issue. I called the column Horoscope Snapshots.

This next chapter takes our study further with short profiles – snapshots – of famous people. It is not my intention to provide in-depth profiles at this stage, but rather to show at least one good example of the following five possible chart themes (or 'signatures') and how one (or more) of these themes can be seen in biography. I hope you find these snapshots interesting.

Horoscope Snapshots

Any chart you study will contain at least one of five themes:

1. A dominant or missing element or mode (e.g. no planets in Earth, lots of planets in mutable signs).

   Patty Hearst

2. A sign or house emphasis.

   Liza Minnelli and Lorna Luft
   Mina and Anita Bryant

3a. A planetary overtone (a repetition, e.g. Capricorn Ascendant with Saturn opposite Moon in the 10th; or a planetary theme, e.g. Virgo Ascendant, Sun–Mercury conjunct in the 6th House and Moon in Gemini)…

3b. Or a set of planetary overtones (complementary or contrasting themes revealing opposing dynamics).

   Elizabeth Taylor
   Ted Kennedy
   Linda Goodman
   Sarah Ferguson
   Paul Newman
   Johnny Carson
   Anne Perry (Juliet Hulme)
   Justin Bieber
   John DeLorean
   Evel Knievel

4. A major configuration tying up signs, planets and houses ('pockets') of the chart.

   Jim Jones
   Brigitte Bardot
   Margaret Thatcher
   Queen Elizabeth II

5. A pivotal aspect or feature central to the chart's action.

   Whitney Houston
   Shirley Temple Black

Dominant or Missing Elements and Modes: Patty Hearst

Patty Hearst's chart is dominated by mutability, with a Jupiter–Pisces and (lesser) Mercury overtone. Seven of the nine points fall in mutable signs. The rulers of the four angles (Mercury and Jupiter) are in mutable signs and in exact square to, and mutual reception with, each other. Air and Water are strong, which suggest being moved to an emotional response by ideas and ideology.

Heiress to a newspaper fortune (Jupiter in Gemini in the 10th), nineteen-year-old Hearst was abducted on 4 February 1974 by the Symbionese Liberation Army, a group of radicals intent on helping 'political prisoners' escape from prison. High on media attention garnered by the kidnapping and stoned on public infamy, the SLA saw themselves not as countercultural renegades but as patriotic, Robin Hood revolutionaries. These urban militants embarked on a two-year crime spree that saw their political ideology run amok. In choosing Hearst, they picked someone whose chart suggests a search for a guru (Pisces/7th) and a need to be rescued. Instead, she was seduced, controlled, then mentally and physically used and abused (Pisces).

Patty denounced her parents on audiotape and within two months was seen involved in a bank robbery orchestrated by the SLA. Whether she was obeying orders, a victim of brainwashing or a rich girl-turned-gun-toting fugitive, her mutability (especially Pisces/7th) suggests how susceptible her chameleon-like personality was to demolition and reconstruction. When apprehended, Hearst claimed she was the victim of trauma and sexual assault and had lost her free will (Sun in Pisces square Mars). Her trial raised an important ethical question: are victims (Pisces) responsible (the mutable challenge) for their actions while victimized? And her refusal to testify against SLA members brought Stockholm Syndrome (empathy/loyalty towards one's abductors – Pisces/7th) to the public's attention.

Stationary Mercury in Pisces square Jupiter in Gemini is the chart's tightest, most important aspect, and it played out in a number of ways. Society saw Hearst as a vacuous, pretty rich girl (early Gemini and Pisces are linked to 'It' girls and tabloid sensations) and, later, as a celebrity victim. Her kidnapping became an overplayed sensation, a media frenzy of the worst excesses of journalism (Mercury in Pisces square Jupiter in Gemini). Even her names underscore this aspect: Patricia (meaning 'noble' – Jupiter) and her militant SLA name Tania (derived from Tatiana, a martyred saint – Pisces – who was also the patron saint of students – Mercury/Gemini). Symbionese is derived from *symbiosis* – a relationship of mutual benefit (Jupiter in Gemini) or merging/becoming dependent (Mercury/Pisces/7th). To top it all, the legal advocate (Mercury–Jupiter) hired to defend her also acted out this square. During the trial, nervous and appearing drunk (Pisces), he knocked a glass of water onto his trousers, looking like he'd wet himself – just as he began to give his closing argument!

Hearst later married her bodyguard (the Pisces and Descendant emphasis) and on 20 January 2001 was pardoned by President Bill Clinton (TR Jupiter reached 1° Gemini, just past her MC and square to her Sun in Pisces).

Patty Hearst

Sign or House Emphasis: Liza Minnelli and Lorna Luft

Liza Minnelli and **Lorna Luft**, daughters of the legendary entertainer Judy Garland (see page 72), both have charts with Moon–Mars conjunctions that emphasize the 3rd House (and the IC) the 9th House (and the MC). Both conjunctions have a strongly Saturnian flavour.

By the time Liza was eleven, she was responsible for running virtually every detail of the home and taking care of her mother. In Minnelli's chart (right), Mars–Saturn–Moon in Cancer is conjunct the IC at 19° Cancer (which is the degree of her mother's Venus and next to her half-sister's Uranus.) Fittingly for her Sun and Moon placements, Liza says, 'My mother gave me my drive. My father gave me my dreams.'

In Luft's chart (below), the Moon is in Capricorn conjunct Mars in Aquarius on a Capricorn MC, and the dispositor of all three points is Saturn (conjunct Neptune).

Liza Minnelli

Lorna Luft

Both daughters went on tour with their famously competitive, nonstop workaholic mother (Moon–Mars), both inherited her work ethic and never-say-die philosophy, both grew up accustomed to a life of high drama and violence, and both followed their mother into show business and (for a period) into addiction.

The Moon–Mars–Saturn links to their MC–IC reveal similar parental influences, but in Luft's case she has had to fight to be recognized (Mars–MC), escape the spectre of her mother's legend (Saturn–Neptune square MC), and live with comparisons to her older, more successful sister (Mercury in Sagittarius). Charts like these remind us that successful people don't always have planets in the 10th House or conjunct the MC, as some books would have us believe. Motivation, drive and success can originate from the IC and other areas, too.

Sign or House Emphasis: Mina and Anita Bryant

Those born on the same day or at the same hour have always fascinated me, particularly non-twins. It always reminds me that the horoscope shows a number of *energy patterns* that can come to fruition (often at similar times) in various ways depending on opportunity, education, society and many other external factors. The 'astro twins' here were born just over 7 hours apart but, due to time zones, they have very similar angles. Note the emphasis on steadfast, sensual Taurus, the pivotal Venus–Uranus conjunction on the MC, as well as Mercury in Pisces opposite Neptune. The Moon changes sign but still forms a powerful T-square configuration with Saturn and Pluto.

To the right is the chart of enigmatic Italian singer **Mina**, who is famous for her eclectic career (spanning sixty years), her fashions, her sensuality, the adoration of her gay fans and for reinventing her image.

Mina

Anita Bryant

In April 1963, her baby was born out of wedlock, shocking Italy (Venus–Uranus); the scandal saw Mina banned from TV for a year (TR Neptune conjunct IC). In August 1978 she fled the spotlight and has since produced albums from her Swiss hideaway.

To the left is the horoscope of **Anita Bryant**, the singer and former beauty queen who became a born-again Christian and, from January 1977, an outspoken activist against gay rights (Venus–Uranus). Fearing that children would be recruited by homosexuals, she formed Save Our Children. Though vilified by the gay community, Bryant stood firm (Taurus) against boycotts, blacklisting, hate mail and threats (Mars–Uranus), but finally declared bankruptcy in 1997. Bryant was told that she couldn't have children, so she adopted a child in September 1963, only later to give birth to three.

A Set of Themes: Elizabeth Taylor

It's no surprise to find a Neptune–Jupiter overtone in the chart of luminous, larger-than-life legend **Elizabeth Taylor**. Taylor's three planets in Pisces oppose their dispositor Neptune. Her life story epitomizes the glamour of Hollywood stardom – and its pain (as seen in the much-publicized tragedies, addictions and illnesses that befell her personally). Charts awash with Neptune or Pisces can see their owners swim upstream in a search for ultimate meaning and interconnectedness, or slide down the plughole into the realm of unreality or addiction. But Pisces is the survivor of the zodiac. Jupiter is also key here (her motto was 'the more the better'). As Chart Ruler, it disposits the Pisces planets and squares the Moon from the 9th House.

Neptune–Jupiter is the seller of big dreams and fantasies, but it also conjures up images of excess, addiction, glamour, gluttony, opulence and extravagance – words that describe the public view of Elizabeth Taylor, her eight marriages, her weight battles and substance abuse, her enormous diamonds and million-dollar salary for *Cleopatra*. Her chart lacks Earth but there's an anchor of sorts:

the Moon is in enigmatic, *fixed* Scorpio. But this intense, emotionally turbulent Moon is square Jupiter, is posited in the 12th House and in the Pisces decan (i.e. middle ten degrees) of Scorpio.

As a child, Taylor – with 'knowing' Scorpio Moon eyes and a stunning beauty beyond her years – was raised on movie myths. Leaving for Los Angeles in late April 1939 (following TR Uranus opposite Moon), her big break came in early 1943 when she was cast in *Lassie Come Home*. The movie *National Velvet* made her a star on its release in December 1944. Elizabeth grew up at MGM where, she later said, 'everything was in the realm of fantasy'. Every 'spontaneous' childhood moment was captured by studio publicists, and on screen she acted a life she wasn't allowed to live in reality.

Elizabeth became highly strung and depressed, and was frequently ill. Wilful and restless, her only escape was horse riding (Sagittarius), which offered a sense of abandon and freedom away from the control of the studio and her fiercely ambitious mother. Later, her escape would be Neptunian: dating and marrying a range of alcoholics, gamblers, singers and playboys. After the dramatic death of husband Mike Todd on 22 March 1958 (TR Pluto opposite Mars), she turned to married entertainer Eddie Fisher. The resulting scandal began the tabloids' and public's life-long fascination with her tumultuous personal life. In September 1961 (TR Pluto opposite Sun–Mercury), she met Richard Burton and the public were spellbound by their chemistry and the on-off drama of the toxic 'Battling Burtons' (Venus–Uranus in Aries seemed to relish the confrontations and fights). They married in March 1964, when TR Uranus was at 7° Virgo.

Neptune–Jupiter is also seen in Taylor's philanthropic 'rescue' work to publicize causes, her attraction to enigmatic 'misfits', and even her perfumes. It is seen in her great sensitivity to suffering – as well as the public's perception of her turning her own suffering and survival into an art form.

Elizabeth Taylor

A Set of Themes: Ted Kennedy

Born just five days before Elizabeth Taylor, **Edward Kennedy** has a chart that is, however, less mutable with some notable differences: the Moon is in Virgo and the Asc–MC duo is Capricorn–Scorpio, a 'heavier', more arduous and political combo. Mercury and Mars are in socially aware Aquarius, connecting them both to Uranus and to Saturn, which is in Capricorn in the 1st House and is also his Chart Ruler. Although the chart has a major Neptune–Pisces overtone (a Full Moon chart with the Sun in Pisces opposite the Moon and Neptune), the Saturn influence suggests a chart more grounded and linked with structure, reality and anything 'establishment' (Kennedy was also a staunch Catholic).

Kennedy entered the Senate in November 1962, a year before his brother, President John F. Kennedy, was assassinated. Following the murder of a second brother, Robert, Ted was favoured to follow in their footsteps and aim for the White House. But on 19 July 1969, three days before JFK's dream to put a man on the Moon was realized, Ted was involved in a controversial incident – the death of a passenger in a car he was driving. It was said to have quashed any future presidential ambitions.

Looking at this incident in Chappaquiddick, we encounter the strong Neptune–Pisces theme. That night, Kennedy accidentally drove his car off a bridge. He managed to extricate himself but passenger Mary Jo Kopechne suffocated. Kennedy escaped, fled the scene (Pisces) and failed to report the incident immediately. A week later, he pleaded guilty to leaving the scene of an accident after causing injury and received a two-month suspended sentence. Despite rumours, he denied being intoxicated or in a personal relationship with the deceased. TR Saturn was close to his IC, TR Neptune was widely square to Mars and TR Mercury was conjunct his Pluto in the 7th. By Solar Arc, Pluto was opposite natal Mars, Venus was conjunct Chiron in the 5th, and Saturn had passed an opposition to Moon–Neptune.

Kennedy and his first wife both suffered from chronic alcoholism (Moon–Neptune). Ted was the last *surviving* (Pisces) son of Joseph Kennedy's political dynasty – the only one to have avoided paying the ultimate price for his ambitious father's unyielding pursuit of money and power – and in his 'quest for redemption' (Neptune) Ted was able to fulfil much of his personal destiny in a public way.

Moving more towards Saturn in his later years, Kennedy settled into a career as an effective and respected senator, able to work with both sides ('a prodigious cross-aisle dealer', according to *Time* magazine). As a senator he carried out a lifelong crusade to enable universal health care (Moon–Neptune in Virgo), which he called 'the cause of my life'. The theme of his autobiography, *True Compass*, published posthumously, was encapsulated in a review in *The New York Times* (3 September 2009), which describes his Neptune and Saturn themes: 'Persistence, perseverance and patience in pursuit of a cause or atonement for one's failures can lead to achievement and the possibility of redemption.'

Ted Kennedy

Conflicting Themes: Linda Goodman

With Sun–Venus in Aries opposite the (Full) Moon in Libra across the Ascendant–Descendant, the chart of **Linda Goodman** is dominated by the Aries–Libra polarity. Opposite signs are different sides of the same coin; they have much in common and much to learn from each other. Aries–Libra is the axis of conflict vs. cooperation, putting oneself first vs. considering others, declaring war vs. making love, and rudeness vs. tact. The polarity is concerned with removing the expectation that another can provide a missing 'half' to complete us, and yet realizing that our *whole self* can only be discovered while we are in relationship.

In *Love Signs*, Goodman wrote that everyone 'has a spiritual obligation to retain the positive integrity of his or her own Sun sign in this incarnation and also to respect that right in others.' This encapsulates a major theme in the Aries–Libra balancing act.

'The Goddess of Astrology', Goodman made millions fully aware (Full Moon) of the potency of Sun sign ('self'-centred) and relationship astrology. Her first book, *Linda Goodman's Sun Signs*, is the best-selling and most influential book on the zodiac *of all time*. She reinvented Sun sign astrology for the masses. (Her remarkable impact and success demonstrate that a retrograde and unaspected Mercury need not hamper its owner.) Her talent was an ability to write in such a personal, magical style that readers felt she understood, accepted and encouraged their innermost selves, dreams and desires. This is the wonder of a double Aries with the Sun and Ascendant trine Neptune, which also befits her belief in miracles, the illusory nature of time, and immortality.

Aries–Libra is seen in the nature of her first radio show, *Love Letters from Linda*, in which she read correspondence between soldiers and loved ones. Fans relished her thousand-page poem, *Gooberz*, which was in part a plea for the return of her lover, marine biologist (Neptune) Robert Brewer, who had deserted her and to whom she remained devoted (note Venus square Pluto).

Neptune's aspects and placement on the 5th House cusp feature strongly in the mythology of her life – from her ambiguous statements surrounding her birth date to the nebulous reports of her daughter Sally's alleged overdose in December 1973. Linda invested years and her fortune searching for proof of a cover-up and spent the rest of her life longing for Sally's return. Haunted by the disappearance of both daughter and lover *in the same year*, her philosophy nevertheless was to turn 'sadness to gladness'.

The Aries–Libra oppositions are square to an elevated Jupiter in Capricorn (Jupiter–MC is common in the charts of Sun sign astrologers who reach large audiences). This, along with the very close Sun–Neptune trine, is encapsulated in her words: 'The two most important things a human can learn on this planet are: to distinguish between weak hope and rock bound faith, which can, depending on its intensity, move mountains and... how to love... I expect a miracle for that is the one true and sure way that a miracle will manifest.'

Linda Goodman

Conflicting Themes: Sarah Ferguson

Pluto–Scorpio and Mars–Aries overtones dominate the chart of one-time royal **Sarah Ferguson**: Scorpio rises, Pluto culminates, while Mars is conjunct the Sun, and the Moon (the handle of the chart) is in impulsive Aries. There is also a Venusian theme but it is dominated by Pluto and Mars: two planets in Libra, but one is Mars, and Venus is elevated on the MC but also conjunct Pluto (her motto is 'out of adversity comes happiness'). And to add to the drama and scandal, there is a Neptune–12th House focus with four planets in the Equal 12th House, including Mercury (ruler of the MC) conjunct Neptune.

Upon her engagement to Prince Andrew, the Duke of York, her life became a carnival, and the public warmed to her fun and zany spirit. But soon, her over-exuberant, headstrong behaviour was starting to be considered vulgar and unbefitting a royal demeanour. The press, who unkindly dubbed her 'the Duchess of Pork', were soon on the alert and ready to pick up on her verbal gaffes (the Venus–Pluto conjunction is square to Jupiter in Sagittarius in the 1st) as well as forays into fashion faux pas.

On 1 August 1992, the tabloids finally got the royal scoop of the decade. The *Daily Mirror* posted pictures of her on holiday – still married – appearing to have her toes sucked by her American boyfriend. By Solar Arc, Neptune (sleazy tabloid fodder) was square her all-important Venus on the MC. It rocked her status, and overnight she became *persona non grata* in the Royal Family (the comment attributed to senior Palace staff – 'the knives are out for Fergie in the Palace' – reflected the mood). The Moon (from its natal position in impulsive Aries in the frolicking 5th) had directed to oppose Mercury in Scorpio (natally conjunct Neptune).

If sister-in-law Diana's tabloid escapades appeared to be a cry for attention and a manipulative way of crucifying her husband, Sarah's seemed to suggest a lack of discretion and flagrant errors in judgement (Jupiter). Perhaps having every whim catered for ended up feeding her greed (Jupiter in Sagittarius in the 1st House)? Whether she was taking advice under pyramids from psychics and from astrologers who later sold their stories, appearing in the embarrassing *It's a Royal Knockout*, or offering an undercover journalist 'cash for access' to her former husband in April 2010 (SA Mercury had reached the very end of Sagittarius), Sarah's decisions were, for many years, harmful to her reputation.

Venus–Pluto elevated shows the very public demolition of her marriage and status. Her fall from grace and lapses in judgement (she became known as 'rent-a-royal') have been painful to observe, particularly since Sarah has poured much energy into reinventing her image and bringing order into her life, and has shown much courage to pay off her enormous debts (Jupiter square Venus–Pluto).

In Britain, we seem to love our royalty and leaders to personify Saturn. With Mars, Pluto and Venus dominant in Sarah's chart, Saturn in the 2nd plays a secondary role but shows that she's had to pay dearly for every single mistake she's made.

Sarah Ferguson

A Pair of Themes: Paul Newman

What stands out in this horoscope? I am drawn to the three planets in Capricorn straddling the Ascendant. Underscoring the Capricorn influence is the sign's ruler, Saturn, on the MC in Scorpio. So, the dispositor of the Capricorn planets is in Scorpio, and all the planets in Capricorn oppose a powerful Pluto on the Descendant. Together, this gives a Saturn–Pluto overtone. Keywords for Saturn, Pluto and their signs are respect, privacy and control, and those with this overtone are often drawn to politics or activism, or find a way to express an innate civic responsibility in their lives.

With Aquarians, it's useful to ascertain whether the person is a Saturnian or Uranian type. In **Paul Newman's** horoscope, Uranus does little, but Saturn is conjunct an angle and, along with its sign Capricorn, dominates the chart and his biography. Newman was known to be an unpretentious man: serious, hard-working, gracious and wry; he also loved practical jokes (a Capricorn pastime). Often described as a class act, he was an independent, professional actor who exuded dignity and decency. Like many with Capricorn strong, he came into his own after thirty and went on to age well. He studied Method Acting (Saturn) and his style was minimalist and understated; throughout his career, he wanted to achieve through merit, not looks.

Capricorn battles against authority at an early age only to later assume a role of influence on its own terms, while Aquarius has little experience of early authority (often the father is absent in some way) but must make the transition from people-pleasing to feeling comfortable with its differentness. Both signs have their conservative, non-rebellious sides but, to succeed, Capricorn must operate within a hierarchy and work its way up. When it chooses to rebel, it does so on matters of morality. With Aquarian James Dean, the rebel was without a cause; with Newman – a Saturnian Aquarian – he was a new kind of anti-hero: cool and cynical. Yet Newman has said that he's not anti-establishment: 'I'm absolutely square. I'm just anti-idiocy and anti-dishonesty.' His on-screen characters often reflected his own sensibility: men whose moral convictions forced them to work outside the law or against the system.

Newman was born into middle-class privilege; his father co-owned a sporting goods store named Newman-*Stern* (Saturn–MC). When his father's health declined, son Paul suspended his acting ambitions to look after the family business. Later, he slowly built his acting reputation and developed his craft. Success followed his Saturn Return and meant he could enjoy a charmed life (he became a star from a boxing film aptly titled *Somebody Up There Likes Me* – Jupiter–Ascendant).

Content with his wealth, he pursued philanthropic interests including a food business (since its launch in September 1982 – when TR Jupiter crossed his MC – it has donated $300 million to charities), and his name and image are synonymous with quality and integrity (the challenge of Jupiter but Saturn's natural forte).[10]

Paul Newman

A Pair of Themes: Johnny Carson

Like Paul Newman, US TV legend **Johnny Carson** has a strong overtone of Saturn–Pluto (and their signs) in his chart. Saturn is conjunct Mercury in the 1st and widely conjunct the Ascendant, while the Moon is in Capricorn in a powerful T-square. Pluto is involved in the same T-square, and the Ascendant, Mercury and Saturn are placed in Scorpio. Like Newman, Carson has Saturn and Pluto inextricably linked (and, as a matter of fact, both suffered the devastating, tragic loss of a son). With Carson, Saturn is in Scorpio, while Scorpio's rulers Pluto (disposited by the Moon) and Mars are in a T-square with the Moon in Capricorn.

In Carson, we meet the reserve, control, authority, discretion and dignity of Saturn. With Pluto, attitudes to these aspects of his personality can become obsessive. Pluto also adds the potential and desire to sway the masses and influence one's generation (many celebrities, particularly comedians, credited Carson for their success).

Saturn types are reliable 'anchors' and stalwarts. Carson's popularity as a TV talk show host was the backbone to a whole network's success. Saturn and Pluto (along with Scorpio) speak of being in control, having 'staying power' and *endurance* – regardless of fleeting fashions or trends on television. Carson's *Tonight Show* was a cultural centrepiece for almost thirty years (a Saturn Return) from 1 October 1962 to 22 May 1992.

Carson understood that people watched to be entertained, not educated. An 'ordinary' man who put guests at ease, he was one of the great straight men of comedy. He was laconic, deadpan and wry (with Mercury–Saturn in Scorpio, he said, 'Never use a big word when a little filthy one will do').

'I love the applause… the manipulation [of TV]… the sense of power, the centre of attention,' Carson once said. With the Sun on the Ascendant and a Leo MC, the 'King of Late Night', Carson and his monologues (Leo) sparkled on TV through the years, but he was distant, surly, shy and unable to engage in small talk once the cameras were off (suggestive of the Saturn and Pluto influence). He considered his private life as sacrosanct, and he was almost fanatical in his desire to keep the divide between public and personal.

It's been said that there was 'always a barrier which prevented him from establishing a closeness with others,' although the Sun and Mars in Libra needed 'another' (either a guest or co-host) to interact with and create the magic his audience adored. Carson understood the image he projected: 'The word that's always applied to me is "aloof", or "private"… that's me.'

As expected with Saturn, Pluto and their signs, loyalty was a major theme. Ed McMahon worked with Carson for 34 years (McMahon has the Moon at 6° Scorpio). Carson had favourites (Bette Midler, with her Moon at 9° Scorpio and Sun at 9° Sagittarius, was one), but when guest host Joan Rivers, who had been given her big break on Carson's show, set up her own late-night talk show, Carson considered it an act of betrayal and never spoke to her again.

Johnny Carson

A Pair of Themes: Anne Perry

In the horoscope of writer **Anne Perry**, Pluto and Saturn dominate: Pluto conjuncts the Ascendant and squares the Sun in Scorpio; Saturn, placed on the MC, is square to the Moon in Capricorn. So, arguably this chart has both Saturn and Pluto overtones. Both planets have their sinister sides and dark, heavy reputations. Perhaps this is why I introduced the Saturn–Pluto signatures in the charts of Paul Newman and Johnny Carson before I began to tell the story of this notorious woman!

Anne Perry began life as Juliet Hulme, the daughter of a physicist (Saturn–MC). Juliet suffered from tuberculosis and from age eight was sent to various warm climates to improve her condition. At thirteen, she rejoined her family, who had moved to New Zealand. There, in May 1942 (TR Jupiter opposite Sun), the Duchess, as she was known by classmates (Leo Rising), formed an obsessive and intensely close relationship with classmate Pauline Parker (born 26 May 1938). Together the inseparable teens collaborated on fantasy novels they hoped would be sold to Hollywood. When Juliet's parents planned to divorce and send her

to South Africa on 3 July 1954 (partly out of concern over the close relationship between the girls), Pauline's mother forbade her daughter from relocating, too. Together the girls planned to do away with Pauline's mother. The brutal attack – 45 blows to the head – occurred on 22 June (note Juliet's Moon–Chiron–Mars T-square).

They stood trial and were convicted on 29 August 1954 (as TR Saturn conjoined Juliet's Sun). The girls served five years, and one condition of their release was that they never make contact again. Hulme changed her name in 1959, managed to bury her past, rebuild her life and remain undetected for decades. Gradually she built a following as the crime novelist Anne Perry. Her first novel, *The Cater Street Hangman* (1979), was described by *The Chattanooga Times* as an 'ingenious mystery… of manners and caste systems of the Victorian era' (Saturn–MC). Perry's focus on detective stories stems from an interest in seeing 'masks being ripped off, and to see what people will do under pressure, when they are afraid' (Pluto).

Perry received shocking news on 29 July 1994 that her secret was out and a film, *Heavenly Creatures*, was to be made about the relationship and murder (TR Sun and Jupiter were in square that day: TR Sun was on her natal Ascendant square to TR Jupiter on her natal Sun and 4th House cusp).

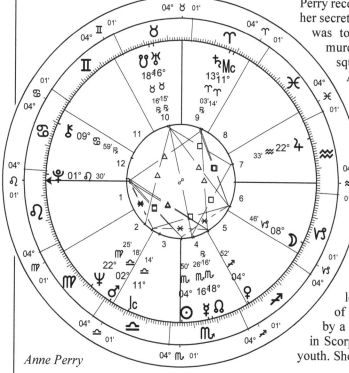

Anne Perry

Perry's chart is not presented to 'prove' that Saturn and Pluto have the potential to be a gruesome twosome. The example demonstrates that this combination can show how someone, who carried an enormous stigma and weighty reputation (Saturn–MC), underwent a metamorphosis and re-emerged with a new identity (Pluto–Ascendant). Perry's story is one of survival, reinvention and a determination to leave her past behind so that her body of work could avoid being overshadowed by a rash, violent and macabre act (Mercury in Scorpio opposite Uranus) perpetrated in her youth. She almost succeeded.

A Pair of Themes: Justin Bieber

Outer Planet People (OPPs) – those with hard major aspects (or close trines) from the outer planets to the inners – are often in sync with the zeitgeist. Or they are impacted by it or find some way of channelling it through their work or lifestyle. They create their own personal stamp this way; it's an external expression of a inner compulsion to influence the masses.

To my generation and above, he's the boy who had one of those bad haircuts, but to millions of teens **Justin Bieber** has been the biggest thing in pop music for ten years. In 2016, he became the first artist to surpass *ten billion views* of his videos on Vevo. Not surprisingly, his horoscope is a mix of Pluto and Neptune overtones: Bieber has Pluto rising in Scorpio and Pluto square Mercury–Venus, and three planets in Pisces with Neptune square to his Moon. Bieber's is also a predominantly Water–Air driven horoscope.

So often, successful people in control of their business and/or influencing their generation have Pluto prominent (in particular, conjunctions or hard aspects to the Moon or Mercury). In addition, publicly successful people often have Ascendant and Midheaven complexes in dialogue (e.g. the MC ruler conjunct the Ascendant or its ruler) or making repetitive statements (e.g. MC ruler in major aspect to the MC). Bieber has a Scorpio Ascendant with co-ruler Pluto closely conjunct, and both are squared by Mercury (the MC ruler) conjunct Mars (co-Ascendant ruler) in Aquarius in the 3rd.

With Pluto strong and Mercury–Mars in the 3rd, you don't want to mess with this guy. When a hacker 'meddled in his life a bit' and invaded his privacy, Bieber posted the boy's mobile number (claiming it was his own) to his 4.5 million fans on Twitter, resulting in the boy receiving over 26,000 text messages.

Bieber is truly a child of the Internet. He was discovered in late 2007 (TR Uranus opposite his MC) when music manager Scooter Braun (working with R&B singer Usher) came across homemade videos of the fourteen-year-old on YouTube, which Bieber's mother had started posting on January 2007 (following TR Uranus conjunct Sun). Bieber signed to Island Records in October 2008 (TR Saturn conjunct MC – *who says Saturn takes time?!* – and TR Uranus conjunct Venus), and Braun (born 18 June 1981) has managed him ever since.

A strong Neptunian overtone helps a performer sell their message, transcend genres and age groups (often through word of mouth) and saturate the market. Neptunian celebrities are gossiped about endlessly, too. Left-handed Bieber has three planets in Pisces at the base of his chart and the Moon square Neptune. 'Bieber fever' began to spread after his first single release in July 2009 and an album in autumn 2009 (when TR Neptune made its last conjunction to MC ruler Mercury). The intensity of his fame continues.

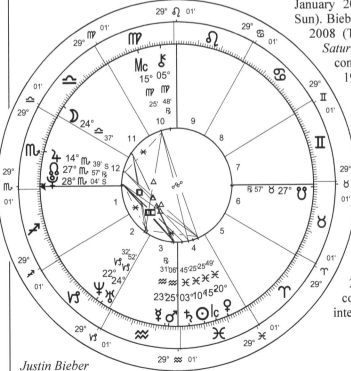

Justin Bieber

Numerous Themes: John DeLorean

John DeLorean's chart has three themes: Mars–Aries, Jupiter–Sagittarius–9th and Capricorn. Mars rising in Aries is the apex of a powerful cardinal T-square involving Sun–Jupiter opposite Pluto, suggesting a highly competitive, controlling and predatory personality, an indomitable will and, in particular, a *belief* in his invincibility.

A maverick and pioneer? Or a con artist, rogue and (according to one judge) corporate bandit of 'barefaced, outrageous and massive fraud'? To many, DeLorean epitomized all of these. This is the chart of a highly ambitious, overconfident empire-builder with big dreams and bigger promises. The Aries–Capricorn square indicates his urgent need to succeed, to do things *his* way, to attain individual acclaim, as well as his workaholic nature. Yet, in DeLorean's chart, Aries–Mars must yield to the experience and wisdom of Capricorn (the two symbols – the Sun and MC – that suggest vocational fulfilment and destiny/destination are placed in this sign). The message is to 'play the game', to make an impact in an existing corporate structure, to change things from the inside.

DeLorean moved swiftly up the ranks from engineer at Packard to executive (and youngest ever vice-president) at General Motors. Skilled at identifying new markets, he launched 'muscle' cars with youth appeal (Aries) for those with a need for speed (Mars), class and style (Capricorn). He was forced to resign from GM in spring 1973 – unable to conform and dogged by questions about his ethics. But showing enviable Jupiterian confidence, he went solo, embarked upon a jet-set celebrity lifestyle and proceeded to fire up investors with his independent, grandiose schemes, idealistic dreams and bold enterprises. He seduced £97 million out of the British Government and built a manufacturing plant in Northern Ireland.

Fittingly for his T-square, DeLorean found himself playing out his huge ambitions as a charismatic figurehead and leader of industry (Sun–Jupiter in Capricorn) in a terror-ravaged region of Northern Ireland – a country divided by religion (Jupiter), war (Mars), politics and terrorism (Pluto). In his autobiography, DeLorean wrote, 'For them, we represented hope… for a renewed chance at self-respect through meaningful work with a future.'

Had he listened to his Capricorn side (or had a strong Saturn – giving an awareness of the laws of cause and effect), instead of following the rashness and selfishness of Mars–Jupiter, he may have created an enduring legacy, rather than becoming a parody of the GM executives he so despised. By February 1982, his dream was in tatters, his Belfast-based factory in receivership. Eight months on, he was arrested on charges of smuggling cocaine. The ensuing celebrity prosecution was a huge public spectacle (Jupiter–MC) – but all in vain. He eluded conviction, successfully arguing entrapment.

With Jupiter–MC, DeLorean escaped being held accountable for his schemes. He remained largely unscathed, the only price being his honour (Jupiter). After years of evading creditors, the flamboyant businessman and ceaselessly inventive con artist declared bankruptcy in September 1999.

John DeLorean

No Dominant Theme: Evel Knievel

When no single theme dominates, there can be an *ongoing search* for a lifestyle that offers enough scope for the person to engage in an array of possibilities and to experience the many facets of their personality. One such example belongs to daredevil performer **Evel Knievel**. Here are some observations (using the method on pages 86-88):

- Venus/Libra/7th: the Sun conjunct Mercury in Libra, Venus conjunct the MC, the Moon in the 7th House.

- Jupiter/Sagittarius/9th: MC ruler Jupiter in the 1st closely trine the Sun (and Mercury) in the 9th, Venus conjunct a Sagittarius MC.

- Uranus/Aquarius: Aquarius Rising and ruler Uranus in a square aspect to the Moon, and square Jupiter in Aquarius in the 1st.

These major aspects are also important: Sun–Mercury square Pluto; Mars conjunct Neptune; Pluto conjunct Descendant and trine Venus–MC. So, let's play detective to see what biography reveals of the man and his accomplishments.

Growing up as a loner and individualist (Aquarius Ascendant), Knievel drifted for many years before he found his niche. Even though he was a gifted salesman, no career had held his attention until he decided to combine risk and daring (Uranus, Jupiter) with entertainment and flair (Venus).

Known as 'hell on wheels', Evel Knievel became the ultimate sporting showman of the 1970s, renowned for his incredible, death-defying motorcycle stunts. When we consider sport as *entertainment*, Venus ranks above Mars in the horoscope. In Sagittarius and conjunct the MC, Venus is a key player and disposits the Sun. Its close trine to Pluto on the Descendant suggests the thrill of danger – the excitement and euphoria Knievel felt when he jumped and engaged his audience. Each stunt meant either an entertaining victory (Venus–MC in Sagittarius) or death in front of the crowd (Pluto in Leo on the Descendant). His Moon in Leo in the 7th loved to play to the gallery, and its square to Uranus suggests an instinct for excitement (Moon–Uranus) as well as a need to shock others (Uranus) to receive attention and acclaim (Moon in Leo). The Moon in Leo and the Sun trine Jupiter are indicative of a man skilled at self-promotion – his white leather outfits with patriotic stars and stripes were part-Elvis, part-Liberace.

With Jupiter in the 1st trine the Sun, Knievel was lucky physically, surviving many astonishing jumps and numerous injuries. Mars–Neptune suggests he was able to ignore and anaesthetize the pain he endured. This conjunction also suggests his craftsman-like preparation (Virgo), the few restraints he put on himself and his stunts (creating the illusion that he was immortal), and the clean-cut, anti-drugs and glamorous image of masculinity he personified for many young boys across middle America (he was born at the exact Neptune Return of the USA's 4 July chart). This charismatic icon also generated millions of dollars through the merchandising of his image (note that the rulers of the 2nd House are in the 1st and 8th).

Evel Knievel

A Major Configuration: Jim Jones

In cases of extreme behaviour, we astrologers are forced to consider the more sinister sides to the planets – facets not usually explored in most charts. Biography paints a portrait of **Jim Jones** as a religious maniac: a paranoid messiah who promised his flock heaven on earth but turned their lives into a living hell – culminating in the mass suicide and murder of 913 followers in 'Jonestown', Guyana. His horoscope has a powerful cardinal T-square of Saturn retrograde in Capricorn in the 1st opposite Jupiter–Pluto in the 7th, both square to Venus–Uranus in Aries in the 4th (the Moon is also conjunct this apex). Here are some ways the T-square manifested in his disturbing life:

- Born to an old, weak and sick father, Jones was a lonely child (Saturn); a surrogate mother (Moon–Uranus) introduced him to church and he found solace in the Bible, giving sermons to classmates (Jupiter).

- He was drawn to Socialism (Uranus) and began to deny the existence of God, feeling that social justice was more important than belief in a higher power (Uranus square Jupiter–Pluto). Later, he adopted a 'rainbow family' of Asian children.

- Jones became a preacher and was able to sway his congregation (Jupiter–Pluto) through compelling rhetoric, magnetism and charisma. Committed to civil rights, he risked personal danger by integrating his flock in Indianapolis (the home of the Ku Klux Klan); he attracted a devoted following of African–Americans (Jupiter–Pluto in Cancer in the 7th).

- Jones built up political clout and influence, and in December 1976 was named Chairman of the San Francisco Housing Authority (Saturn opposite Jupiter–Pluto in Cancer).

- Paranoid and fearful of a nuclear holocaust (Uranus–Pluto), he relocated to safe locations in Brazil and then California. In 1974, he moved his flock to Guyana (the country's Independence Chart has Venus at 23° Aries and Jupiter at 4° Cancer). There, Jones pioneered an agricultural commune, a 'promised land' for his People's Temple (Moon–Uranus in Aries in the 4th); his Utopia demanded rigorous work, seen by many as slave labour (Saturn–Pluto).

- 'Father' Jones accumulated financial and military potency (his fixed Sun in Taurus squares Mars – both angular through Jonestown). He exerted tyrannical control over his people (who were beaten and intimidated) and engaged in 'free love', forcing sexual relations with male and female followers (Venus–Uranus–Pluto).

- By 1978, extreme tests of loyalty had become frequent; he was also paranoid that the US Government was conspiring to kill him. On 18 November 1978 (TR Pluto at 18° Libra, aspecting natal Uranus square Jupiter–Pluto), Jones led his people to commit a 'revolutionary act' of mass suicide (Uranus–Pluto) – a cataclysmic event in a country with Uranus–Pluto exactly conjunct in the 7th. All three outer planets had reached 17–18° of their signs and were contacting four of Jones's natal planets.

Jim Jones

A Major Configuration: Brigitte Bardot

With four planets in Libra and Sagittarius Rising, actress **Brigitte Bardot** was 'a woman who represented liberty but for whom freedom was always out of reach'. With the Sun widely conjunct the MC in Libra, she was the image of Aphrodite, moulded into a legendary screen beauty, a creation of her Svengali husband-director Roger Vadim (whose Saturn at 16° Sagittarius held dominion over Bardot's Ascendant). On film, she was either the ingenue (Virgo) or siren (Libra) and forged a reputation as a sex kitten (Mars in Leo!). Bardot was hunted and hounded by the paparazzi, eventually becoming a recluse and, to many, a wrinkled, embittered symbol of faded beauty.

She retired and became an animal rights activist, saying: 'I gave away my beauty and my youth to men. I am now giving my wisdom and my experience, the best of me, to animals.' Her Mercury–Jupiter in Libra in the 11th suggests ideas – philosophical, humanitarian or religious – for an *equal society* and an ability to speak up when unfairness or injustice is perceived. But *God Created* Bardot with an incendiary T-square of Mercury–Jupiter with uncompromising Uranus and Pluto, which can blow apart any attempts at diplomacy. Speaking out, speaking up or just opening one's big mouth (Mercury–Jupiter) can provoke enormous opposition and controversy (Uranus) or accusations of extremism (Pluto), and Bardot's words have left her former image in tatters and seen her widely misunderstood and condemned. Her views on immigration, opposition to horse meat (Jupiter/Sagittarius!) and attacks on Islam have landed her in French courts, convicted of 'inciting racial hatred'. Uranus 'disturbs the peace' of Saturn and is often censored, banned or outcast for its 'truth'. Jupiter's presence guarantees publicity and the exaggeration of facts (Mercury). With Saturn in Aquarius in the 3rd opposite Mars, Bardot was punished by society for politically incorrect opinions. Pluto in Cancer in the 8th as the apex (target) underscores her views on inter-racial relationships and her apparent hatred of Islam (Pluto) in her home country (Cancer). In *A Scream in the Silence* (2003), she wrote:

> Over the last twenty years, we have given in to a subterranean, dangerous and uncontrolled infiltration, which not only desists adjusting to our laws and customs but which will, as the years pass, attempt to impose its own.

And as is often the case with 'outrageous' or shocking Uranian ideas, society comes around to incorporating or recognizing them. On 11 April 2011, weeks after Uranus made its final current ingress into Aries, Bardot's France was the *first* European country to prohibit the niqab and burqa – the *banning* (Uranus) of *face* (Aries) veils.

With Uranus in the 5th (and Moon square ambivalent Neptune), Bardot once revealed (to the horror of many) that she wasn't attached to her child (Nicolas-Jacques Charrier), whom she later abandoned (Bardot's Mercury–Jupiter opposition to Uranus falls across her son's Ascendant–Descendant axis). The aspect also speaks of her ideas on the mass sterilization (Uranus in the 5th) of stray dogs (the square to Pluto).

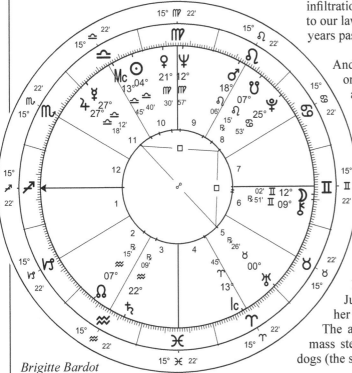

Brigitte Bardot

A Major Configuration: Margaret Thatcher

Much has been written of **Margaret Thatcher's** Saturn rising in Scorpio (the Iron Lady who was 'not for turning'), the elevated Moon in Leo within a degree of Churchill's Moon and conjunct her Neptune (the domineering Attila the Hen who handbagged ministers into submission and had a vision to restore Britain to its 'Victorian greatness'). And there have even been some comments as to the personal allure of her Venus in the 1st House ('femininity is what she wears, masculinity is what she admires'). A summation of the latter placement – along with Scorpio Rising – is perhaps best left to François Mitterand, who said she had 'the mouth of Marilyn Monroe and the eyes of Caligula'.

But in Thatcher's chart, there is a powerful T-square: an exact Jupiter–Pluto opposition that squares both Mars and the Sun in Libra. The apex's exact mid(dle)point is 14° Aries and Libra, which itself is the midpoint of Thatcher's Sun and Mars. I wouldn't consider the Sun and Mars to be conjunct (10° is too wide), but each planet had a pivotal part to play in expressing the potent Jupiter–Pluto

contact throughout her professional life, particularly when transits hit Mars (9°), the apex/midpoint (14°) or the Sun (19°) in Libra. With this T-square, she has been elevated and praised for greatness (Sun, Jupiter) and vilified and hated with a venom usually reserved for tyrants (Mars, Pluto). It reveals a woman of enormous energy, indefatigable spirit and seeming invincibility (with 'an intense, some have said arrogant, certainty that she was right'). Not a revolutionary chart, Thatcher's is a powerfully transformative one.

Jupiter opposition Pluto can be seen in a number of her resolute opinions and hardline policies. From free market globalization, privatization and the creation of a Yuppie consumer society, to her alliance with Reagan against the Soviet 'evil empire' and her determination to free enterprising individuals from a controlling state, she was seen by many as an inflexible 'conviction politician' on a mission. In the charts of leaders, Jupiter speaks of where there can be expansion (and overexpansion) during their tenure. In Capricorn in the 2nd opposite Pluto, there was a focus on revitalizing the economy, encouraging entrepreneurs by owning shares and buying their council houses (stone-cladding – Capricorn – was one popular method at the time!), a credit and (over-)borrowing boom, the demolition of the welfare state (originally based on the Libran principles of equal opportunity and the equitable distribution of wealth), and the 'denationalization' of British industries.

This opposition speaks of the trials she faced from the miners (Jupiter–Pluto represents 'deep exploration'), the trade unions, the Falklands War and the IRA assassination attempt (Jupiter opposite Pluto in Cancer suggests religious, patriotic extremism). Her shadow government jobs were also apt: pensions and National Insurance, the Treasury, fuel and power, transport, and education. Her white paper, *Education: A Framework for Expansion,* was published on 6 December 1972, two weeks before her *Jupiter* Return in *Capricorn.* One exact Jupiter cycle later her

*Margaret
Thatcher*

government privatized British Telecom, the first major act of selling off the nation's companies.

Transits to these important degrees of Libra (9°, 14° and 19°) would prove to be instrumental in the key times of Thatcher's political life:

- 9° – Saturn conjunct natal Mars after her second consecutive election defeat (25 October 1951) at Dartford.

- 14° – Saturn stationed at 14° Libra when she resigned as a candidate for Dartford in early 1952. One Saturn cycle later, it was the Argentines who surrendered, ending the Falklands War.

- 9° – Uranus reached 9° Libra in mid June 1971, when her plans to end free milk for schools received opposition (she was dubbed 'Thatcher milk-snatcher').

- 14° – When Uranus reached 14° Libra and headed towards her Sun, several events occurred that would later hold significance for her politically: in October 1971, Parliament voted in favour of entry into the EEC. A miners' strike followed, as did Bloody Sunday – which escalated antagonism towards the IRA – and unemployment figures surpassed one million (during her 'acid reign', they would later surpass three million – for the first time since the 1930s).

- 9° – When Pluto hit 9° Libra, she battled Edward Heath (born with Venus at 7°, the Sun at 17° and Saturn at 19° Cancer) for the Tory leadership and won. Reagan's election win and the Jupiter–Saturn conjunction of Dec 1980 at 9° Libra (Ronnie's rectified MC is 12° Libra) heralded a decade of expansion for the rich, 'Reaganomics' and 'Thatcherism'.

- 14° – When Neptune reached 14° Capricorn in 1990, Thatcher faced various challenges to her leadership, including much criticism over her stance on the Euro and the Tory 'poll tax'. These led to her resignation in November 1991 (her successor, John Major, has Jupiter at 15° Cancer, possibly on the Descendant). Tony Blair, who kept Thatcherism alive with New Labour, has Venus at 15° Aries square Uranus at 15° Cancer. (The father of the modern Conservative Party, Benjamin Disraeli, was born with Saturn at 15° Libra. David Cameron's Sun is at 15° Libra.)

In each of her major battles – and some were titanic power struggles (Jupiter–Pluto square to the Sun and Mars in Libra) – the mission, as far as she was concerned, was to restore balance and democracy (Libra), to defend 'values and freedoms fundamental to our way of life', and to reinstate the 'great' in Britain. The break-up of trade union power (apex Mars in Libra in the 11th), the marginalization of Socialism and the reversal of Britain's economic decline were her key battles. She saw herself as a figurehead (Sun) for this crusade (Mars), yet so many of her policies and decisions contributed to a vastly different and unequal legacy.

At her birth, the Sun and Mars were rising in the Falkland Islands – the place that was to cement her reputation for leadership, iron will, strength and dominion (Sun, Mars) when the Brits won the Falklands War on 14 June 1982 (as Saturn stationed at 15° Libra). (War had been declared on 2 April, with Mars at 9° and Saturn at 19° Libra.)

Jupiter opposite Pluto is also indicative of the vast money her husband made – firstly through his preservatives firm, then its sale to an oil company (oil is often linked to Pluto) – as well as his international business ties and support of South Africa under apartheid. It was his financial support that enabled her to train as a barrister, and Denis (born with Venus at 15° Aries) was her cornerstone while she worked her way up in Parliament. The couple had met in February 1949, as TR Saturn was on her MC and TR Neptune at 14° Libra – some weeks after she had been selected as a Tory candidate for Dartford. They married on 13 December 1951, when TR Saturn was at 13° Libra.

With Mars in Libra, Thatcher never had much interest in *debate* but she did thrive on *argument*. At its best, Mars in Libra cherishes its own ideal of democracy, equal opportunity and a free society and economy. Rather than the rashness that so often characterizes Mars in its own signs, in Libra there's a firmness of resolve towards a logical argument, a clever combative stance, a skilful persuasiveness and a strong rationale (Air) behind decisions made and kept.

> The codes of right and wrong lie at the bottom of every decision... They account for her inflexibility... and for the lack of imagination or real interest in debate.[11]

A Major Configuration: Queen Elizabeth II

Queen Elizabeth II's Saturn–MC in Scorpio says so much about her dutiful 'job for life' as monarch, and it is part of a fixed T-square that dominates her chart. Let's look at the anatomy of this configuration and how biographical statements and events that shaped Elizabeth's life are reflected therein:

Mars–Jupiter in Aquarius
   fighting for social change and modern causes; coming together during wartime; a great desire for personal freedom

opposite **Neptune in Leo**
   glamour; a weakening of the monarchy; longing for the imperial greatness of yesteryear; royal scandal

both square **Saturn–MC in Scorpio** (the apex)
   holding firm by holding the 'firm' together; a steely resolve; an unbending moral code; impenetrable defences and a stoic, dour public face that conceals emotions; burdened by expectation; a feeling of no escape from her destiny – a dutiful job for life/until death

Queen Elizabeth II

• At the time of Elizabeth's birth, a class war in Britain threatened the establishment; Britain was on the verge of revolution, troops kept peace on the streets and a General Strike was announced a few days after her birth (Mars–Jupiter in Aquarius square Saturn).

• Elizabeth was the most famous child in the world, a special princess (Moon in Leo); much hope was invested in her for the future (Jupiter–Neptune–MC). She soon understood that her job was to be sensible, grown-up, sober and utterly reliable (Saturn–MC).

• Elizabeth found herself in line to the throne because of 'male instability' (Mars opposite Neptune). Her uncle's desertion of the throne and of his responsibilities (Jupiter opposite Neptune, both square Saturn) when Elizabeth was ten meant that her father acceded to the throne. Closeted in the confines of Buckingham Palace, she was isolated and cloistered (the SA Moon conjunct Neptune at age ten), primed for her sacred, religious role.

• Raised in an old-fashioned, Victorian England by her father, she was told that change was dangerous (fixity, Saturn). Her life changed suddenly on 6 February 1952: her father died while she was holidaying near Nyeri in Kenya (close to her Uranus–Ascendant line).

• The Government wanted the people to be a part of her coronation celebrations – to create the biggest national party ever (Mars–Jupiter in Aquarius), but tradition, pomp and ceremony dictated the event (Saturn–MC). The televising of the coronation in June 1953 was the Palace's only major concession (television is known as the democratic medium – Jupiter in Aquarius). A later agreement to film the Royal Family behind the scenes – to show their ordinariness – backfired and led to an unprecedented level of press intrusion that fed the media's hunger for royal titbits and scandal. This TV documentary (which aired on 21 June 1969) washed away the last remnants of royal mystique (TR Neptune was conjunct Elizabeth's MC).

- The new Elizabethan age was marketed as an era of social change (Mars–Jupiter in Aquarius) but this was an illusion (Neptune); Elizabeth's reign has since involved maintaining a delicate balance between preserving the monarchy and adapting to changing times and the cries of popular opinion (Mars–Jupiter in Aquarius). But, under Elizabeth, it has been a passive institution focused on preservation (Sun at 0° Taurus), and she has been a traditional, distant monarch unwilling to modernize (Saturn).

- As Head of the Commonwealth (*common wealth* – Jupiter in Aquarius), she attained status as the most powerful woman in the world. By the 1950s, though, what she controlled were the remnants of an empire; it was a dwindling, imperial inheritance (Neptune in Leo), but one that she has held together for 60 years (Saturn–MC as apex). There has been no escape from her destiny nor any wavering from her pledge at age 21 to devote her whole life to the service of her country. To-the-letter duty involves sacrifice (Saturn square Neptune) but at what cost to her own freedom (Mars–Jupiter in Aquarius)?

- The T-square is at play for husband Prince Philip of Greece, who gave up his cherished naval career and position for marriage. He, Elizabeth's father and grandfather were all naval officers – Mars opposite Neptune – and even her beloved Royal Yacht *Britannia* (a giant pleasure boat designed, but never used, as a hospital ship for use in wartime), is depicted by Mars–Jupiter–Neptune.

- During her reign there has been a reduction in the prestige and influence of the monarchy. Respect has faded and royal ways have been challenged, undermined or made redundant (Saturn square Neptune). Changing times have seen the slow death of tradition and an institution (Saturn–MC in Scorpio). The Royal Family of the 1950s expected complete deference (Saturn) from the press (Neptune), but this was to be eroded (Saturn square Neptune). In the 1950s, to criticize the monarch was to condemn England. In August 1957, Lord Altrincham's personal criticism of Elizabeth and his advocacy of a more 'classless' society provoked outrage, and he was physically attacked in the street for daring to speak against her. At the time,

TR Neptune was at 0° Scorpio opposite the Queen's Sun – where it had been the year before, during the Suez Crisis, which revealed Britain's weakening of political power and respect. The next time Neptune reached that degree – by Solar Arc – was in 1997 when Diana died, and the Queen was criticized for being out of touch with a grieving nation.

- A ruler in the age of divorce (Saturn square Neptune), critics believe this issue to have been the biggest threat to her monarchy – before and during most of her reign. Early on, the Queen spoke out against divorce – it was anathema to her – but her family would challenge this, particularly in the 1990s, as TR Pluto moved over her MC. Her own position has been undermined to some extent by the extramarital exploits and tabloid scandals of her family (Mars–Jupiter opposite Neptune) – perhaps hindered by marriages to 'commoners' (Aquarius). Her heir has seemed both ambivalent to, and burdened by, his future role – and Charles's first marriage to a glamorous 'superstar' almost wrecked his status (as seen in his mother's T-square).

The Windsors were set up as a paragon of ideal family life (Saturn) – but scandals, affairs and a lack of discernment (Mars–Jupiter opposite Neptune) would turn them into the world's most famous dysfunctional family. It began with wilful sister Margaret (see her chart on page 65), who brought the first sign of trouble to Elizabeth's reign when she fell in love with a divorced man around the time of Elizabeth's coronation (both Margaret and the coronation chart have tricky Mercury–Mars aspects). The Queen preferred to duck the issue and bury her head in the sand (Mars–Neptune can be an emotional ostrich), leaving Margaret's difficult choice to the Constitution. In doing so, the press felt that the people's voice should be heard and began to pry into royal affairs.

Yet, the royals continue to fulfil many Britons' need for sovereignty: as an expensive ornament, a costume drama for tourists and a final link to a once-respected empire. In the final analysis, Elizabeth's duty first Saturn–MC apex appears to have won out, but the precarious balancing act of the T-square has made this a difficult ride. With the Sun at 0° Taurus and the Leo Moon, she has always been a model of orthodoxy and a powerful, national symbol of a stubborn resistance to change.

Two Pivotal Features: Whitney Houston

Didn't she almost have it all? Textbook definitions of success in the horoscope are seen all over the chart of the late, talented singer **Whitney Houston**. Venus (conjunct Sun) and Jupiter (conjunct Moon) are in Grand Trine with the Midheaven. (Jupiter rules the Ascendant and MC.) This Grand Trine is a pivotal feature of her chart – it ties the lights and benefics in with the MC (reputation, status). Trines to the MC help promote one's talents and agenda to the outside world; they are indicative of early success and recognition – the MC 'tunes in' and receives the message of the planet clearly. In Houston's case, talent and opportunity (the trines, Venus and Jupiter) combined to further her sense of accomplishment in the outside world (MC).

Growing up around noted R&B and gospel singers (Moon–Jupiter, Sagittarius MC), Houston had a musical pedigree that set her apart, and exceptional opportunities were offered to her. Record mogul Clive Davis launched and guided her career. His own chart ties in with Houston's Grand Trine: his Sun–Uranus (on her Moon–Jupiter) trines Jupiter in Leo (on her Sun–Venus). Houston's confidence, poise and sophisticated model looks set her apart (Sun–Venus in Leo trine Jupiter and MC). Whitney was promoted into the commercial stratosphere, surpassing her female predecessors. (The launch was expertly timed, coinciding with TR Uranus moving over Houston's MC in 1985–6.)

So, how does someone so supremely confident and talented throw most of it away? Tied into the Grand Trine, her Sun makes an opposition (the aspect of 'relationship') to Saturn. Simply put, her long-term marriage affected her health (6th) and played a part in her undoing (12th). This is the second pivotal part of her chart and perhaps the sternest test in her horoscope. (If we include the wide Saturn–Neptune square, it becomes a T-square.) We can speculate as to how much this opposition has to do with a life-long need to prove herself (Saturn) to her father (Sun), who died in February 2003 (as TR Pluto crossed her MC). Houston found a husband with the Sun at 16° Aquarius to 'help' her to unravel her life, climaxing in a personal and professional meltdown (she moved from elegant diva to finger-jabbing fishwife more at home on *The Jerry Springer Show*). Aside from their shared substance abuse and strong sexual attraction, the symbiotic, tempestuous couple became a drug to each other (note her Sun square Neptune, and Uranus–Mercury–Pluto on her Descendant).

'Bad boy' Bobby Brown (Mars conjunct the MC at 12° Scorpio, the degree of Houston's Neptune) met the diva on 12 April 1989 and later claimed that it was *she* who introduced him to hard drugs. Whatever the truth, by the time their daughter was born in March 1993 (a month after Houston's Saturn Return), they had begun to hit rocky ground because his career was in hiatus while Houston was enjoying the greatest success of her life with the film *The Bodyguard*. Houston finally quit Brown, and an announcement of her intention to divorce was made in mid September 2006 (TR Saturn opposed natal Saturn and had just passed her Sun). Sadly, she died at age 48, as TR Pluto squared Mars in the 8th.

Whitney Houston

Two Pivotal Features: Shirley Temple Black

Two features stand out: Saturn as the handle of a Bucket horoscope, and the focus of planets in the 5th House (mostly in Aries). The key to the latter is the Mercury–Jupiter conjunction. Why? Because, like Richard Nixon's chart (see page 58), **Shirley Temple's** horoscope has her four angles in mutable signs, so their traditional rulers (Mercury and Jupiter) become pivotal.

Throughout her life, Shirley Temple has been an embodiment of Saturn retrograde in Sagittarius in the 1st House. Born just 18 months before the Wall Street Crash of 1929, her arrival onto the movie scene at three years old coincided with a time of national despair and yearning for escapist entertainment. Little dimpled Shirley Temple was a diamond in the Great Depression of breadlines, soup kitchens and Apple Annies. She personified hope and optimism, making Americans feel good about themselves (Sagittarius). She brought a bubbly, irrepressible energy and sparkle to her screen roles. (Mercury–Jupiter in Aries in the 5th House says much about her precocious talent.)

A child mature beyond her years, with a knowingness and the work ethic of an adult (Saturn squares her Virgo MC), Temple was a Goldilocks goldmine: she became the world's most bankable and marketable movie star for four years in a row (as TR Neptune roamed over her MC). She single-handedly reversed the fortunes of the Fox studio and earned herself a fortune (Saturn rules her 2nd House).

This prominent Saturn is evident in her life story. Her first roles were in the Baby Burlesks films: a series of satires of well known films with children playing adult roles (Saturn). Later, Shirley was often cast as a poor little orphan (Saturn) in order to melt the hearts of audiences and encourage them to embrace and parent her. In addition, her birth certificate was altered to shave a year off her age. Yet, the studios couldn't avoid her inevitable move into adolescence: by May 1940, as TR Jupiter and Saturn crossed her Sun, movie mogul Darryl Zanuck announced her retirement from Twentieth Century Fox. She continued to act for a few years, entered a four-year marriage (filing for divorce on 5 December 1949, as Saturn crossed her MC and squared natal Saturn), and officially retired a year later upon her marriage to Charles Black.

Shirley Temple Black showed little sign of wanting to cling to her childhood fame. She moved from national treasure to a valuable corporate asset. But with her prominent Saturn natally retrograde (see pages 36–8), she had a pause, then a second peak, evolving into a conservative Republican political figure – an activist for the cause of civic responsibility – who took moral stands against pornography, was appointed the first woman Chief of Protocol of the United States, and held diplomatic posts in Ghana and Czechoslovakia (note Saturn in Sagittarius). She was also the first high-profile celebrity to state publicly that she had breast cancer (in the autumn of 1972, as the Solar Arc MC moved into Scorpio); she spoke out about her setback and physical loss (a mastectomy) with a dignity and candour worthy of her pivotal Saturn placement.

Shirley Temple Black

Astrology comes alive when we engage in a dialogue with clients. When we hear clients *speak their charts* (i.e. describe their lives and characteristics in ways that reveal the themes of their horoscopes), we have the chance to work with them to make meaningful connections between the cosmos and their own lives. It is one of the most rewarding, educational experiences we have as astrologers and one of the most productive as consultants. It consolidates our understanding of the major astrological principles at work and broadens, refines and personalizes our knowledge of astrology.

Often such revelations during a consultation are the client's way of letting us know which area of their life and chart has assumed particular importance at the time of their appointment. In other words, *they* lead us directly to the most important areas of their horoscope. And, of course, the client's own perception of themselves may change over time, but what they share in the session is valuable and pertinent to our inquiry.

Before I introduce some extended biographical profiles and more in-depth horoscope interpretation in Part Six, in this section I'll be focusing on how to:

• Build a planetary profile from biographies.

• Explore how a specific aspect can manifest in numerous ways.

• Have fun with astrological correspondences.

• Connect one area of life (e.g. crime) to various astrological significators.

• Spot that various compositions (from musical to literary to oratorical) are ways for their creators to speak their own charts.

The Essence of a Placement

Astrology is both a language and a study of patterns. By engaging in empirical research, we are looking for meaningful observations and correspondences: we notice themes under similar transits or natal placements, and we begin to document lives at key planetary periods and cycles. When clients or public figures 'speak their charts', we collect gems that inform our practice. The more charts we study – ideally with the client or with a biography about someone whose life fascinates us – the less we are inclined to rely on a narrow model of presumed astrological signatures.

I've always loved aphorisms – they often get to the heart of an astrological concept in a way that pages of interpretation simply cannot. Back in 1999, I published *Shorthand of the Soul: the Quotable Horoscope* by David Hayward. It taught me that concise, clever and pithy statements are often the best way to communicate an idea to a student or client. I use my Twitter account (go figure!) to share ideas and list quotes that speak to me and sum up astrological principles. Here are a few:

Advice for Aries:
   To finish first, you must first finish.

What Scorpios know:
   Silence may not be the best defence, but it is certainly the most annoying.

The 'truth' about Aquarius:
   I love mankind; it's people I can't stand.

Hard aspects in the horoscope:
   God gives every bird its food, but he does not throw it into the nest.

A lesson for the Virgo–Pisces polarity:
   'He has a right to criticize, who has a heart to help.' (Abraham Lincoln)

Mercury in Capricorn:
   Ask them the time and they'll tell you how a watch is made.

From Mars to Mercury to Neptune:
   There are those who make things happen, those who watch things happen and those who don't know anything has happened!

Negotiating aspects between Jupiter and Saturn:
   'We don't receive wisdom; we must discover it for ourselves after a journey that no one can take for us or spare us.' (Marcel Proust, born with Jupiter opposite Saturn–MC in Capricorn)

Saturn and squares in the horoscope:
   One reason why so few recognize opportunity is because it is disguised as hard work.

Earth signs learning from the Fire signs:
   Better to remain silent and be thought a fool than to speak and remove all doubt.

Fire signs responding to the Earth signs:
   We know what happens to people who stay in the middle of the road. They get run over.

On Gemini:
   Gemini is the zodiac's magpie. He knows a lot about plagiarism when he puts pen to paper. His two writing styles? Cut and paste.

And my own advice on keeping Leos happy:
   Stay on the subject of Leo, and Leo will be kind to its subjects.

Exploring Biographies

When studying charts, the main tools for developing our knowledge are reference books and biographies. We can also explore life histories by collecting personal accounts of loved ones, clients and colleagues. If we don't have these, we never really know how people 'inhabit' their charts, how relevant our observations are, or how the major themes of their horoscopes play out in their lives and in the people and events around them.

Let the person or biography *speak their chart*. Don't force the chart to fit rigidly onto the person. With a good planet and sign vocabulary, when we listen to life stories we don't have to look far to see these in the person's horoscope. For example, I've found that the Moon sign and its major aspects are 'heard' most clearly when clients describe their emotional needs and responses, their early shaping experiences, their gut instincts and general temperament. When clients reveal their personality characteristics – those employed to meet and greet the world one-to-one – they're speaking their Ascendant and any planets conjunct that angle. The Sun is often expressed by clients as an inner awareness of an identity or calling, while the Midheaven is often how they are described by others in a 'social shorthand' or their own image of one facet of their social persona (the Ascendant being the other). Each planet has a role, but T-squares, major aspects (conjunctions, squares, oppositions) and planets on angles form the main 'headlines' in the life story.

The Gauquelins (see page 49) worked with keywords to build planetary profiles, and they helped to redefine (and refine) the natures of the planets. Their research found, for example, that keywords given by astrologers for a Sun-like temperament were more often linked to biographies of those with a prominent Jupiter. But often, on their own, keywords are not enough. They are also open to misinterpretation. Biographical statements about a person will sometimes lead us down the wrong path, and we need to be clearer about what is being signified. Words such as 'musical' could imply the person is melodic, harmonious, tuneful (suggestive of a Venusian temperament) or could in some contexts suggest a talent for music or rhythm. Neptune is a planet so often linked to musicians. But is it strongly placed in the charts of musicians? I've only found it prominent in those who have, for example, battled addiction, created personas (Neptune is the chameleon) or attempted to transcend daily life or convey a spiritual message with their compositions. Under the 'music' umbrella is also timing, practice and scales – areas that fall under Saturn. My research suggests a strong Saturn in the charts of opera singers who must have *discipline* to *train* their bodies like athletes to be able to perform (interestingly 'opera' is a Latin word meaning 'work' or 'labour'). And the signs have something to say, too. The drama, passion and tragedy of opera can be likened to signs of Leo and Scorpio.

Shock! Horror!
The word 'shocking' immediately suggests something outrageous (Uranus) or scandalous (Neptune); an incident that jolts, stuns or surprises us (Uranus). Yet when we consider the charts of people who 'speak out' or do truly shocking things, we may not always find Uranus prominent by aspect or in relationship to the angles. Why not? Firstly, we must ask what the *motivation* is behind the shocking behaviour and, while the *impact* it has is important, *how* the person *translates* people's response to them is more significant.

The 'shocking' drag queen and actor **Divine** (his horoscope is on the next page) has a weakly placed Uranus – a few wide trines in the chart from Uranus and a sextile to the MC can't explain a man who was elevated by the gay community to diva status for having 'no shame, no compromise'. Looking further, the most significant parts of the chart are the collection of planets in Libra and an all-important angular aspect: Mercury rising in Scorpio square to Pluto on the MC. The truly shocking nature of Divine (who notoriously ate real dog faeces in the cult film *Pink Flamingos*) is the foul-mouthed vulgarity that made him 'the filthiest person in the world' (Pluto is associated with dogs, faeces, black comedy and cults; Mars and its signs are associated with vulgarity). The impact (shock, disgust, revolt) may have been Uranian in nature at the time (and remains so), but this is not the chart of a Uranian man nor was it a Uranian time for Divine. At the film's release in March 1972, Solar Arc Jupiter was on his Ascendant and TR Pluto was conjunct his Venus – the dispositor of the Sun – in Libra. He became a cult, underground star (Pluto) who generated much publicity for his larger-than-life persona (SA Jupiter to Ascendant).

Divine

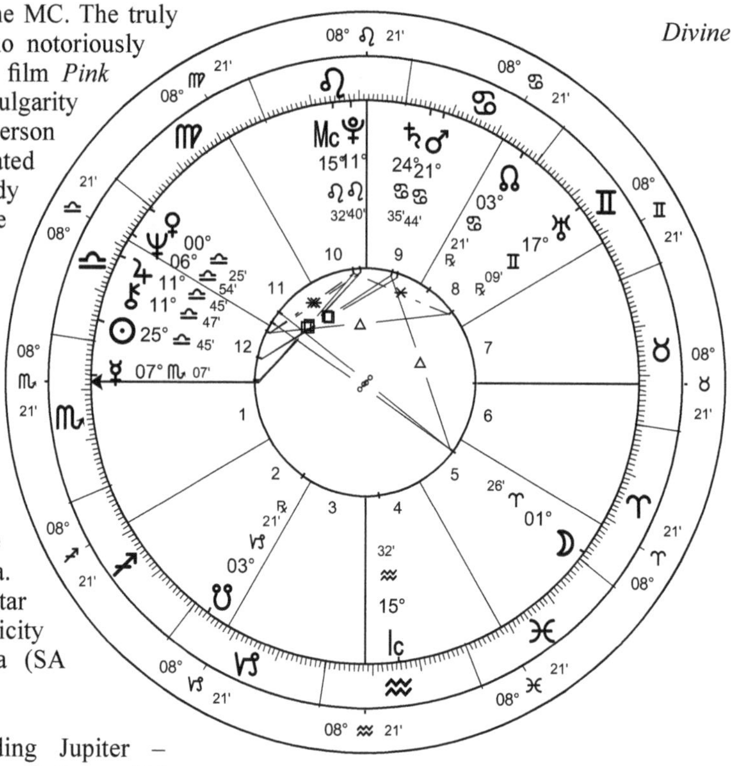

His planets in Libra (including Jupiter – *divine*) would account for the descriptions of his persona being over the top, decadent, indulgent, extravagant – and the epitome of bad taste (Libra can run the gamut from tasteful to tawdry). Divine idolized Elizabeth Taylor (who also ran that gamut) and his Venus–Neptune straddles her MC in Libra. He was once described as looking like Taylor 'if she'd been locked up in a candy store for three months'. The real Divine (Harris Milstead) craved acceptance. He was Venusian: soft-spoken, courteous to a fault, lazy, insecure and 'in need of constant reassurance of commitment'.

Horror films and movies that shock may, in theory, be Uranian in nature, but what of the charts of those who create them? Research suggests that Pluto and Scorpio are primarily concerned with the build-up and manipulation of suspense and the horror of the demonic – letting the audience (and sometimes the characters) know that something is out (or under) there. Alfred Hitchcock had a Moon–Jupiter conjunction in Scorpio (note also his use of icy blonde temptresses in his films); director Wes Craven (*A Nightmare on Elm Street, Scream*) has a Sun–Venus–Pluto conjunction in the 8th; *Dracula* actor Christopher Lee has a Venus–Pluto conjunction on his MC; and Roman Polanski (see pages 81–2), director of *Rosemary's Baby*, has an

appropriate Moon–Pluto conjunction on his MC in Cancer (square to Uranus). Writer Stephen King and director Steven Spielberg (*Jaws*), both masters of shock, have major Sun–Uranus hard aspects. Three lead actors who terrified audiences in horror films have Uranus strongly accented: Kathy Bates (the psychotic fan of a novelist in *Misery*) and Sissy Spacek (the telekinetic teen in *Carrie*) both have Uranus on a Gemini MC (for more on their charts, see page 127), while Robert Englund (the razor-gloved serial killer Freddy Krueger in *A Nightmare on Elm Street*) has Sun–Uranus in Gemini (hands).

Building a Profile

If we take Saturn, for example, and study quotes and biographies from those who have a strong Saturn overtone in their horoscope (including the sign Capricorn), how can it expand our understanding and get to the essence of the planet and its sign?

Researching the life of actor **Anthony Hopkins** (chart opposite), we encounter the solitary, inhibited and melancholic side of Saturn and a liking for the Spartan, bleak or austere. Hopkins grew up hating authority figures and left school with a drive to achieve fame and money, to be a 'somebody'. It appears that Saturnian personalities must often struggle on through an early 'lack' or handicap – a feeling within that they are *without* something automatically afforded to others. (Capricorn knows little of the nepotism employed by its polar sign of Cancer.)

Hopkins articulated the Capricorn emphasis and its ruler Saturn in Pisces in his (Equal) 3rd House for a TV profile, *A Taste of Hannibal*:

I love the bleakness [of travelling by car across America] because it is part of myself. I love the coldness of life. I love the inevitability of it all. When I went to school I discovered I was on the wrong planet because I was so academically retarded. I guess I misused my education… I was the one who didn't fit in… It's a romantic fantasy I have of the loner, the lone wolf who doesn't need any affection. That's part of my life, actually, I think I can do very well without any affection and love… I am capable of withdrawing from people and closing myself off. Maybe it's a form of martyrdom.

Saturn types aim to redress early hardship by becoming an established authority in their field. Recognition for one's achievements in society is often a key motivation. For Capricorn, this is a personal journey into a public realm: recognizing a need to 'play the game' and work within systems in order to climb up the ladder. Capricorn knows it must endure a long apprenticeship, abstain, deny or hold in check the personal needs (its opposite sign is Cancer) in order to attain the rank and respect it craves. Yet, the early rebelliousness of Saturn and Capricorn against the establishment (a motivation often overlooked by astrologers) becomes tinged with irony when such people eventually 'succeed' and become an image of the authority figure against whom they once fought.

Hopkins shared some insights into his psychology with *Vanity Fair* in 1996:

I think success has been very important to me. I wanted it to heal some inner wound of some kind. I wanted revenge; I wanted to dance on the graves of a few people who made me unhappy – and I've done it… I can be a tyrant; I'm ruthless, single-minded. I want what I want… I'm just very, very selfish. If somebody doesn't like what I am, I don't hang around trying to win anybody's approval… I'm a roamer. I think I'm a bit of a nihilist, really.

Hopkins would later achieve great recognition in Merchant–Ivory films by playing emotionally repressed characters determined to ward off intimacy (Saturn), and he has also excelled in creating portraits of simmering, smouldering restraint and terrifying menace (note the Scorpio MC, too, which is descriptive of his most famous portrayal – the psychiatrist and killer Hannibal Lecter in *The Silence of the Lambs*).

The Saturnian character does not share the frivolity of its contemporaries. There is patience, prudence, sobriety, control, shrewdness, ambition, a methodical approach, conformity and the priority of duty over pleasure. Biography also reveals an innate reserve, a need for privacy, an aloof

Anthony Hopkins

self-containment and a desire to be an authentic person of 'substance' and character. In Saturn, a profound sense of isolation or detachment combines with a heavy responsibility to do the right thing and, later, to maintain hard-won integrity and respect.

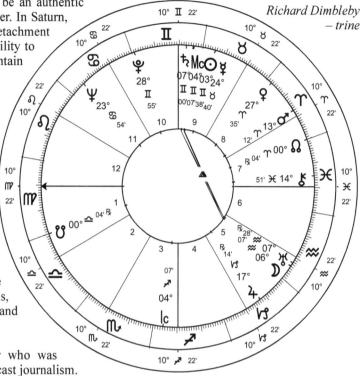

Richard Dimbleby – trine

Richard Dimbleby (chart, right) was the personification of TV current-affairs broadcasting in the 1950s and 60s at the BBC (itself Saturnian, with the Sun in Capricorn and the Moon exactly conjunct Saturn). He joined the BBC as a radio news observer in 1936 and became their first war correspondent, bringing the reality of warfare into the homes of millions of Britons. When he moved to TV, he covered important state occasions, such as the funerals of Kennedy and Churchill.

Dimbleby was a standard-setter who was instrumental in developing broadcast journalism. He was a much-trusted interviewer and defender of public interest who was lauded as a 'bastion of fairness and perspicuity in political debate'.

Demonstrating how an aspect like a trine can work between two sets of planets, here's a vivid quote (found by astrologer Pamela Crane) from his son, journalist Jonathan Dimbleby, demonstrating his father's Moon–Uranus in Aquarius in the 5th House trine Sun–Saturn in Gemini on the MC:

> It fell to Richard Dimbleby to take the television audience by the hand and guide it gently into more tolerant, liberal ways. Intuitively sensitive to public attitudes, frequently sharing them himself, he had an acute sense of what was felt to be proper. Sharing many of the doubts and anxieties of his audience, having discarded yesterday the prejudices they held today, he was the perfect television mentor... His instinct was to inform and entertain, while gently pushing back the barriers of ignorance and intolerance... So accurately did he touch the public pulse that he soon attained the status of a televisual father of the people.

Writer and fellow broadcaster **Joan Bakewell** (chart opposite, top) described her relationship with her mother and the damage caused by a beating she received as a child for stealing:

> I was one of the results of my mother's efforts... I was required to have perfect manners, good school reports... and to maintain a reputation for moral behaviour that brought credit on the family... [After the beating] I grew adept at concealing these petty errors while my mother, suspicious but without proof, couldn't break my resolve... That early tension survived. And with it went the knowledge that she would, if she could, impose her own will on mine.[12]

In this deadly, unspoken battle for control between mother and daughter, we can hear Bakewell's Moon in Capricorn opposite Pluto (and squares to the Aries planets). The pressure to maintain morals and manners can be seen in this Capricorn Moon plus Jupiter culminating at her Virgo MC. The latter aspect describes the context of her TV show, which debated contemporary moral dilemmas; it was called *The Heart of the Matter* – a phrase that encapsulates the essence of Aries–Virgo.

Joan Bakewell – opposition

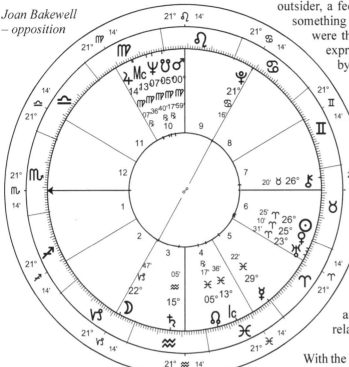

outsider, a feeling of continually groping toward something just beyond one's reach – these were the themes he knew and had already expressed, always superimposed upon by irony and disillusion.'[13]

Sondheim grew to be the master of the acerbic lyric in witty and ironic musicals, a genre for so long dominated by sentimentality or satire. Expressing the Capricorn–Cancer polarity, he is fond of saying that he believes in sentiment (a sincere, refined sensibility) rather than sentimentality (an affected, excessive or mawkish sentiment). Some of his most famous songs, such as 'Being Alive' and 'Send in the Clowns', speak of mismatched lives and the ambivalence that lies at the heart of relationships.

With the benefit of experience and a first-hand understanding of the laws of cause and effect, Saturn and Capricorn are at their most fruitful in the later chapters of life. After almost sixty years

Another early portrait of Saturn–Capricorn and its impact on later years comes from research into the life of composer **Stephen Sondheim** (right), whose chart has themes similar to Bakewell's, with a Capricorn Moon (conjunct Saturn) opposite Pluto. By most accounts (including Stephen's), his mother was a narcissistic, controlling, self-centred woman prone to embarrassing Stephen in public. When she attempted to seduce the ten-year-old following her husband's desertion of her, it created in the boy a deep distrust of his mother; he was at her mercy – abused by, and dependent on, her obsessive love and loathing of him.

Sondheim grew up as the 'boy in the bubble', an 'institutionalized child' in a wealthy environment that supplied everything but human contact. He was neglected emotionally, withdrawn and solitary. One biographer spoke of: 'Loneliness, the sense of being an

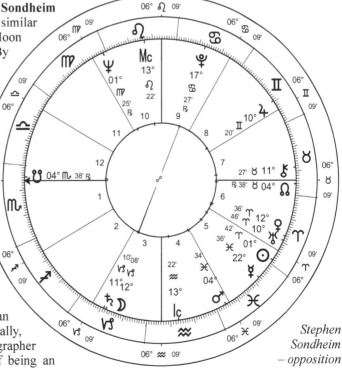

Stephen Sondheim – opposition

of unalleviated obscurity, ridicule and abuse, writer **Quentin Crisp** (chart on right) became an infamous, eccentric gay institution (a self-appointed 'Stately Homo of England') upon the publication of his autobiography, *The Naked Civil Servant*.

Quentin Crisp

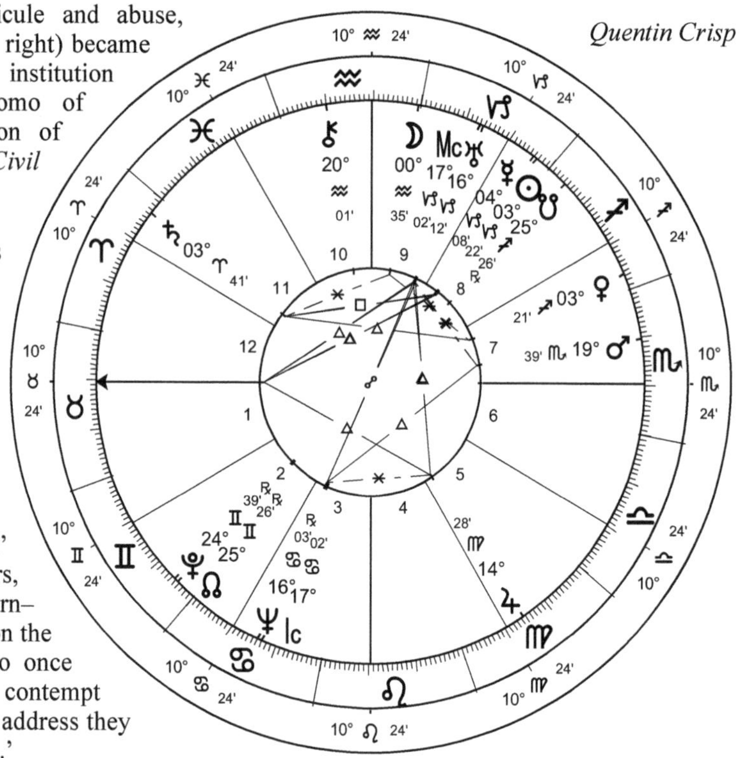

When a Saturnian overtone is melded with a Uranian one in a horoscope, there can be both a *rejection* of what society demands and a *courting* of its approval – a need to speak one's provocative truth but a sober awareness of the limits of and delays in societal acceptance. Labelled by Allen Ginsberg as 'a gay Uncle Tom' who sided with his oppressors, Crisp realized – in true Saturn–Uranus fashion – that 'Time is on the side of the outcast. Those who once inhabited the suburbs of human contempt find that without changing their address they eventually live in the metropolis.'

This planetary contradiction is best summed up in his advice to those trying to keep up appearances (Saturn). It is Uranus at its most humorous and contrary: 'Never keep up with the Joneses. Drag them down to your level.'

Playing Detective with One Aspect

By looking at one specific aspect – in the events *and* in those born at the time of the aspect – we can garner greater insights into its manifestation. The Sun and Jupiter are conjunct every year and there will be some 'themes' in the news each year that reflect this. But the *sign* in which the conjunction falls will have much influence over how the aspect manifests.

Using an 8° orb, the Sun and Jupiter were conjunct in Aries on nine separate occasions in the 20th century, for a cumulative total of 149 days. That's only five months in a period of 100 years! This conjunction recurred in late March to mid April 2011.

Considering keywords for all three principles, we might expect the news to feature stories about an

abundance of courage, heroic acts, conquests and causes worth fighting for, spirited adventures, issues of sex and morality, and people fighting with missionary zeal or evangelical fervour for their identity and principles.

The cardinal Fire sign Aries breathes new life into an existing form. It is an innovator (from *innovare*, 'to renew') rather than an inventor or an original, creative mind. Representing the initial fiery spark of interest, of contagious enthusiasm, Aries the Pioneer forges ahead with courage – daring to rush in where angels fear to tread. A pacesetter, it chalks up 'firsts'. With the Sun–Jupiter combination, we can expect news about successful enterprise, exploration, adventure and innovation – on a grand scale and always first class.

Here are some examples of events during periods in the last century when the Sun and Jupiter were both in Aries and within 8° of each other:

• Henry Royce produces his first car (1904), one month before meeting Charles Rolls. These were to become no ordinary motorcars but large, lavish, luxurious Sun–Jupiter models – symbols of authority, wealth, ostentation; the byword for all that is of the highest quality.

• Women win the right to vote in Norway (1916) and, after a revolution, in Bolivia (1952).

• The first successful transatlantic flight (1928).

• Pioneering African-American leader–educator Booker T. Washington is the first man of colour to be depicted on a US postage stamp (1940).

• Malcolm X delivers his 'The Ballot or the Bullet' speech, a 'call to arms' to end the disenfranchisement of African-Americans (during a two-day conjunction in 1964).

• One day after the transit period in 1964 (when Jupiter, still conjunct the Sun, moves to 0° Taurus), Sidney Poitier becomes the first African-American man to win an Oscar.

• Bill Gates founds Microsoft on the day after the 1975 conjunction. (Two cycles later, his fortune is reported to be over $100 billion.)

• An agreement is reached to construct the huge Euro Disney theme park, now Disneyland Paris (1987).

• The Dow Jones closes above the 10,000 mark for the first time in history (1999).

Aries is a sign associated with violence and confrontation. During these Sun–Jupiter phases, there is often news of major invasions, big fires, assassination attempts on political leaders, and legal cases fighting for justice and individual freedom. The Sun–Jupiter conjunction is linked to larger-than-life father figures and influential starmakers or Svengalis.

• Aleister Crowley channels *The Book of the Law* from his 'holy guardian angel' in Cairo (1904).

• The autocratic last Emperor of China and 'Father of the Warlords', Yuan Shikai, abdicates and the Republic of China is restored (1916). (It appears that there are strong links between this Sun–Jupiter cycle in Aries and significant events in Chinese history. Astrologer Sy Scholfield has observed that during the 20th century, the Year of the Dragon roughly coincided with times when Jupiter was in Aries.)

• *The Matrix* is released (1999) – the first of a highly successful and influential trilogy. This science fiction action film tells the story of a ruling system of machines that sap human energy to use for fuel. As 'The One' (Aries), a young man has been chosen to awaken humanity from its dream state (symbolically, Aries emerges on the first day of spring after the winter hibernation of Pisces).

Large jewellery is a potent symbol of wealth, influence, excess and greed. (Jupiter says, 'It's too much. But is it enough?') Sun–Jupiter can be extravagant, ostentatious, grandiose, superior and elitist ('the ruling classes'), while the gemstone linked to Aries is the diamond. During the conjunction in Aries in 1987, the Duchess of Windsor's jewellery was sold for a record £31 million. Items included a 31-carat diamond ring, which was bought by Jupiterian actress Elizabeth Taylor (Sun in Pisces, Sagittarius Rising, Moon square Jupiter), who was born with Venus in Aries (see page 96 for her horoscope and profile).

Sun–Jupiter in Aries Personified
What of those born under this conjunction? In Aries, the Sun–Jupiter person may have a naïve, somewhat innocent take on the world – a blind faith and perhaps a passionate belief that their personal truth will be embraced by others. With this combination, there's a generosity of spirit, an innate faith in life, an all-consuming hope that's inhaled at the start of each new day, a fresh quality of exuberance and a thirst for adventurous enterprise. One may have a strong sense of destiny, of being on a mission – taking up a quest – but sometimes an exaggerated sense of one's importance (haughty arrogance), a need to play God or to overextend oneself and live life in the moment but beyond one's means.

There may be high expectations and a desire to be seen as the front-runner, an urgent need to claim one's birthright, and an eager pursuit of affluence and influence. Novelist, former MP and disgraced peer Jeffrey Archer (see pages 44–5) bristled with ambition to be Number One and bounced back after bankruptcy, a sex scandal, political resignations and jail. While in Joseph Campbell and Maya Angelou (see over), we see healthy, spiritual embodiments of the Sun–Jupiter principle.

Horoscope Snapshot: Joseph Campbell

Joseph Campbell was the inspirational storyteller, philosopher and mythologist who encouraged people to take delight and joy in saying 'yes' to life, and to embark upon a journey of questioning. As with many Aries, he breathed new life into an old idea: he made his passion relevant to modern existence, and the simple yet profound statement that *what you want must come from you* is summed up by his phrase 'follow your bliss'.

Campbell's most influential book is *The Hero with a Thousand Faces*. His 'Hero's Journey' (monomyth) is Sun–Jupiter in Aries at its most creative. At the start, the Hero (a warrior–explorer–adventurer of the mind) feels something is missing in life, responds to the call to adventure, and makes a break from the past to embark upon a journey alone. With the help of a mentor (Sun–Jupiter) he moves forward with strength and courage – meeting many tests and trials – and on his way to his initiation, he crosses the point of no return and seizes the ultimate treasure.

Here are some Sun–Jupiter in Aries quotes by him:

When you follow your bliss you begin to meet people who are in the field of your bliss and they open the doors for you.

The conquest of fear yields the courage of life. That is the cardinal initiation of every heroic adventure – fearlessness and achievement.

I don't believe people are looking for the meaning of life as much as they are looking for the experience of being alive.

Life is without meaning. You bring the meaning to it. The meaning of life is whatever you ascribe it to be. Being alive is the meaning.

The way to find out about happiness is to keep your mind on those moments when you feel most happy, when you are really happy – not excited, not just thrilled, but deeply happy. This requires a little bit of self-analysis. What is it that makes you happy? Stay with it, no matter what people tell you. This is what is called following your bliss.

Joseph Campbell lived a full, authentic life of integrity and in accord with nature. His message was for us to seek the courage to participate in life and to renounce petty desires for the divine harmony of the greater, true self. His Sun–Jupiter conjunction (along with Mercury) is the apex of a T-square involving Uranus opposite Neptune. He is quoted as saying, 'God is a metaphor for a mystery that absolutely transcends all human categories of thought.'

Exactly one year after Campbell's birth, Viktor Frankl was born in Vienna. Jupiter had moved on to Taurus, and the Moon was in Sagittarius, but the Sun in Aries remained the apex of a T-square with Uranus opposite Neptune. Frankl wrote of his experiences in a concentration camp in *Man's Search for Meaning*, and many of his words – including his focus on a 'will to meaning' – speak of 'reaching out beyond ourselves for something other than ourselves'.

Joseph Campbell

Horoscope Snapshot: Maya Angelou

Another example of Sun–Jupiter in Aries is acclaimed poet and activist **Maya Angelou**, who had a Grand Passion for life and remains an inspirational example of embracing one's potential, putting one's heart into life. 'Life loves the liver of it,' she often said.

In seven volumes of autobiography, Dr Angelou writes of the triumph, frustrations, hopes and joys of the human experience. The theme of her work encapsulates the positive message of Sun–Jupiter in Aries: the refusal of the human spirit to be hardened. *Current Biography 1994* notes her 'inexhaustible capacity for renewed hope, determination and love'.

Essentially, her philosophy is to engage in and experience life with *courage*. Angelou says, 'You may encounter many defeats but must not be defeated.' In true Aries style, she notes, 'One must learn to care for oneself first, so that one can then dare to care for someone else.'

This quote about Angelou speaks her Sun–Jupiter:

She has the innate and compelling grace of a woman who has constructed a full life, one lived without concession or false excuse.[14]

Her first volume of autobiography, *I Know Why the Caged Bird Sings*, recalls with candour her early years surviving poverty and segregation in a place where the racist townsfolk were so powerful they had no need to disguise themselves with white sheets and hoods. Angelou was raped as a child and the subsequent murder of her attacker led to a self-imposed six-year silence, broken only when Maya fell in love with the spoken word. During that time, her senses 'rearranged themselves', making her acutely aware of the world around her (note Mercury–Venus in Pisces and Neptune Rising).

Angelou grew into a charismatic, 6-foot empress of African-American pride (whose father was 'much too grand for his colour' – Sun–Jupiter). She stood tall as an imposing, positive embodiment of a Sun–Jupiter conjunction (ruling her Leo Ascendant and 5th House): a woman of honesty, integrity and dignity, living a full life without false modesty. In her colourful life, she journeyed from being the first female and first 'negro' trolley conductor in San Francisco to a dancer, actress and nationally treasured symbol of hope, whose literature, poetry and speeches touch that which is human and universal in all of us. With Neptune Rising, she often said, 'As human beings, we are more alike than we are unalike'.

Dr Angelou's poem for President Clinton's first inauguration, *On the Pulse of Morning*, was a soaring call for peace, justice and harmony. She read this poem at the ceremony on 20 January 1993 (as TR Jupiter in Libra opposed her Sun–Jupiter, and her progressed A*C*G [astrocartography] Jupiter–Ascendant line closed in on Washington, DC). She spoke of the Sun–Jupiter conjunction's philosophy of being present and vigilant in living life to the utmost: 'Give birth again to the dream… lift up your hearts. Each new hour holds new chances for new beginnings.'

Maya Angelou

Having Fun Playing with Astrological Correspondences

John McEnroe – Grand Cross

We can get so focused in our attempts to infiltrate the horoscope, describe the psychology of a person and figure out their motives, that we can miss having fun with correspondences. Take, for example, bad boy **John McEnroe's** (chart on right) infamous outbursts and petulance on the tennis court. These can be seen in his Moon–Mars conjunction in Gemini opposite Jupiter in Sagittarius (anger expressed bluntly in big emotional verbal scenes) and in a Grand Cross to Pluto opposite Sun–Mercury (an obsessive and compulsive need to be 'right'). Note, too, the Ascendant in Libra – his disputes were always around issues of fairness. And quite simply and aptly, with Saturn in Capricorn in the 3rd, his most famous expression of disbelief towards the umpire (Saturn–Capricorn) was 'You *cannot* be serious!'

Actors appear to be drawn to playing the characters personified in their charts, and these roles are usually written in their horoscope's major themes, such as T-squares and planets on angles, or in their Sun, Moon, Ascendant or MC signs. And when an actor becomes intrinsically linked to a role – where the line between personal/public personas becomes blurred – we are also likely to see major plotlines show up by transit, progression or direction in the actor's own horoscope.

Some years ago, I visited the set of *Coronation Street*, a well-known TV soap in the UK, to read the hands and the horoscopes of some of its actors. I remember being alarmed to see transits and directions that suggested sadness and loss associated with one actress's partner early the following year. Although I made no mention of this, I was surprised to discover later that it was her *on-screen husband* who was written out of the soap the following January because of the ill health of the actor, who died some six weeks later.

Actors have the best jobs in the world – and arguably the most therapeutic in terms of exploring their inner landscapes. They find themselves chosen to play out roles that are 'written' in their horoscopes; roles that appear to have been scripted for them. The clients of mine who are actors never cease to be amazed by astrology's ability to describe the parts they've been chosen to play – and astrologers could certainly debate how much 'choice' there is in this matter.

Actress Pauline Collins has Saturn (in Taurus) also in the 3rd (by Equal house) trine Sun–Mercury in Virgo in the 7th. In *Shirley Valentine* she played a character stuck in a dull, monotonous marriage and reduced to talking to the wall (Saturn) in her kitchen. With Pisces Rising, her character has dreams of escaping her mundane life and travelling to Greece for a holiday.

Linda Gray (opposite, top) became famous as Sue Ellen Ewing, the long-suffering wife of J.R. Ewing (played by Larry Hagman) in the cult soap *Dallas*. Gray's role was that of a neurotic alcoholic whose husband used and abused her for years in what became the most watched, most talked-about show of the 1980s. With an array of facial tics and her quivering lips and huge, expressive eyes, Gray played the drop-down-dead drunk for over 300 episodes (April 1978 to May 1989). The character was a former Miss Texas who survived vehicular manslaughter, (near) dry spells in sanatoriums, and all sorts of show-ups from drunk-related stupors. In the chauvinistic world of *Dallas*, where few women kept their dignity, viewers were invited to enjoy Sue Ellen's numerous humiliations, and only occasionally was she allowed to outwit her husband by sleeping with his arch rival or using their son in their sadistic, salacious game of matrimony. Speaking her Sun–Mercury–Neptune, Gray has said,

Linda Gray

> Most people in a television series play themselves because it's easier… [but] when the cameras start rolling I not only get an accent, I walk differently, talk differently, I look different.

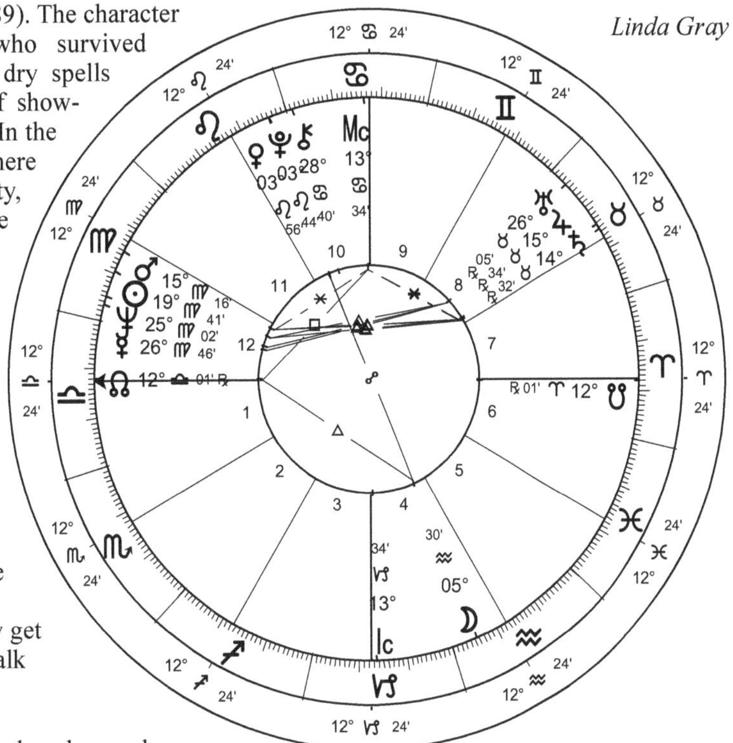

But Gray's horoscope not only shows her character's addictions but also the enormous impact she had in the role and how she eventually became an inspiration to women who realized they, too, could survive destructive marriages and addictive routines: Venus–Pluto in partile conjunction in Leo in the 10th House (marriage to the ruthless oil baron!) opposite the Moon, plus the planetary cluster in Virgo in the 12th with the Sun flanked by Mars, Neptune and Mercury. The character eventually left the series in 1989 as a successful businesswoman and film-maker.

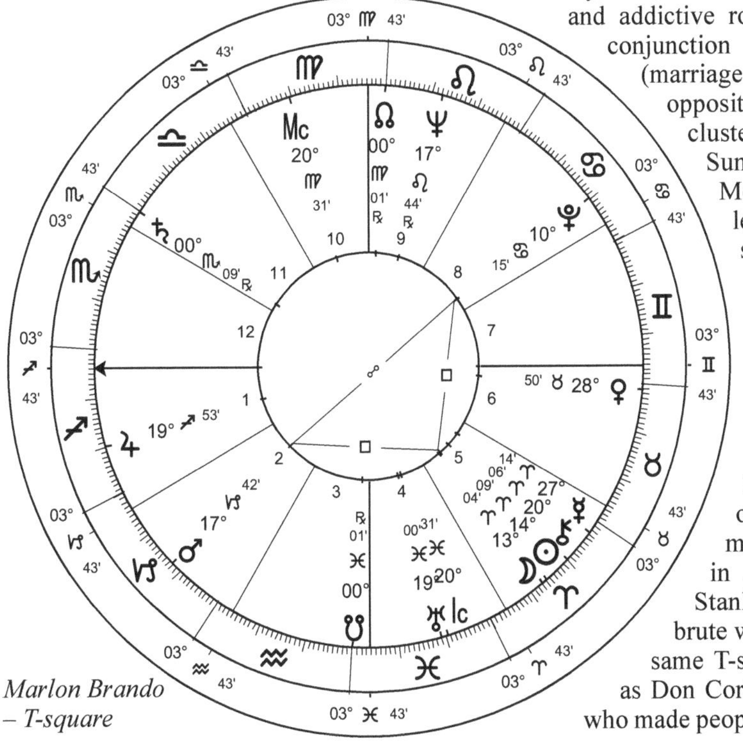

What of other actors and their most famous creations? With Sun–Moon in Aries in the 5th House as the apex of a T-square involving Mars and Pluto, **Marlon Brando** (chart on left) brought a new type of masculinity to the silver screen in *A Streetcar Named Desire* as Stanley Kowalski, a brooding bully, a brute with raw sexual magnetism. That same T-square is descriptive of his role as Don Corleone in *The Godfather* trilogy, who made people 'an offer they couldn't refuse'

Marlon Brando – T-square

(Pluto – and if you're wondering about Neptune… it makes people an offer they can't remember!).

Jack Nicholson (Sun–Uranus, and Pluto Rising) played the unhinged, self-destructive Jack Torrance struggling with demons in his head in *The Shining*. Nicholson's character in *One Flew Over the Cuckoo's Nest* inspired a rebellion (Uranus) in a mental institution. Nicholson's Moon in Virgo is best seen in his role as the obsessive-compulsive novelist in *As Good As It Gets*.

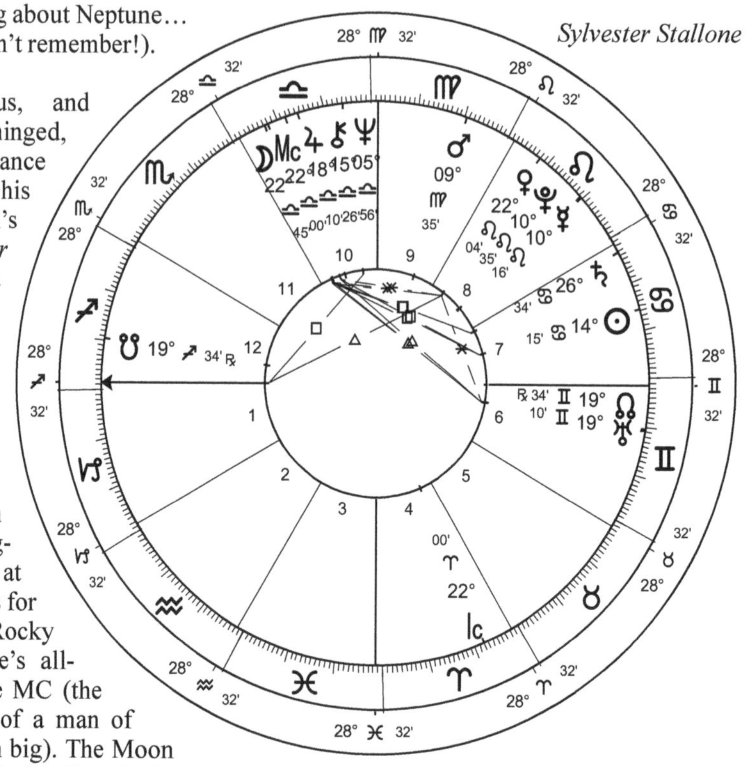

Sylvester Stallone's (chart, right) working class hero in *Rocky* was an American flag-waving pugilist who tugged at audiences' sentimental fondness for the underdog. In some ways, Rocky Balboa is depicted in Stallone's all-important Moon–Jupiter on the MC (the inspirational, patriotic victory of a man of the people who was able to win big). The Moon disposits his Sun, while Jupiter is the Chart Ruler.

Sylvester Stallone

Stallone's other famous character is John Rambo, the violent Vietnam veteran consumed with rage and revenge. His philosophy is 'live for nothing or die for something'. (Stallone was born on the same day as George W. Bush.)

Clint Eastwood's taciturn, enigmatic loner – 'the man with no name' – embodied the strong silent type of anti-hero, demonstrated by his Scorpio Ascendant and Neptune–MC. (Later, Eastwood played a vigilante who pursued a serial killer called Scorpio in the film *Dirty Harry*.)

Elfin and waif-like, **Audrey Hepburn** (chart, left) gave a naïve and innocent portrayal of liberated hedonist Holly Golightly in *Breakfast at Tiffany's*. It represented an escape for women cinemagoers who wished to break away from the stringent 1950s' ideals of womanhood and domesticity. Hepburn was born with the Moon in Pisces in the 1st House widely opposite Neptune–Descendant.

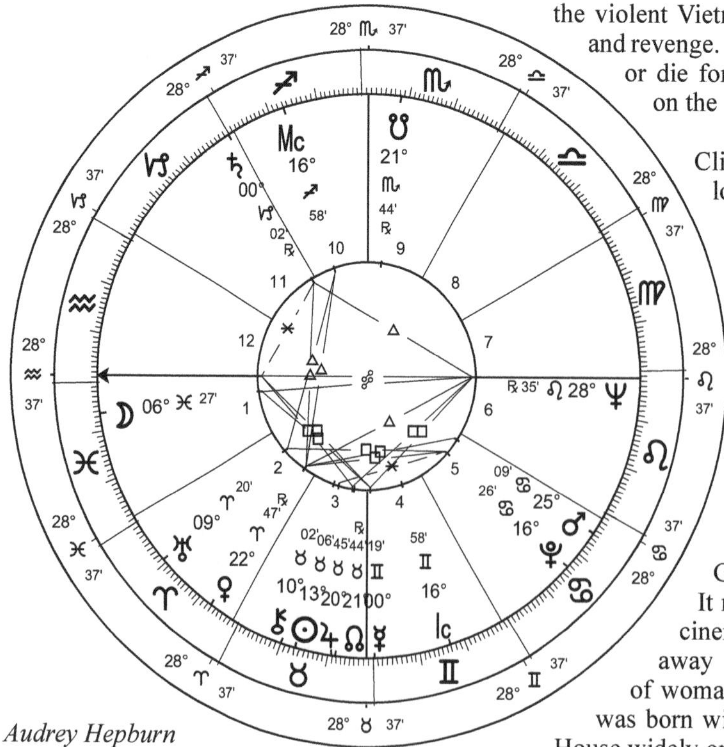

Audrey Hepburn

Best known for roles in Stephen King films, **Sissy Spacek** (chart, right) and **Kathy Bates** (chart below) were *both* born with Uranus conjunct a Gemini MC (Spacek's Uranus is in Cancer), as well as Mars rising in Virgo and the Moon in Pisces.

Spacek played the alienated, socially outcast teen who, through telekinetic powers, wreaks revenge on her tormentors in *Carrie*. Her mentally unstable, fundamentalist and puritanical mother gets her just desserts, too. Kathy Bates played the unpredictably violent and psychotic fan, Annie Wilkes, who rescues, cares for, holds captive then tortures her favourite author in *Misery*.

Author Stephen King has Mars Rising, and a Sun in Virgo–Uranus in Gemini square at very similar degrees to both actresses' Mars–Ascendant and Uranus positions.

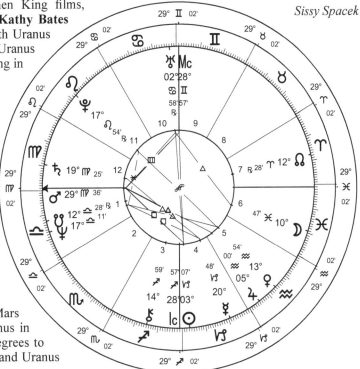

Sissy Spacek

Kathy Bates

Whatever work we pursue, whichever types of relationships we encounter, our chart is a vivid description of the people, life stories, events, names and situations we meet. The major themes of our horoscope can be seen in almost every aspect of our lives. The whole chart is working *all* the time – through the energy of our endeavours and pursuits to the projection onto loved ones, favourite pop stars and book storylines that enact key themes of our horoscopes for us.

We all find ourselves drawn to roles that are written in our horoscopes, but actors are chosen to play these parts and act out these themes on behalf of us all. Characters created by actors, writers and directors clearly personify the stereotypes and archetypes written in their charts, offering them a chance to tackle their horoscope's key themes and dynamics.

Big Dreams and Bigger Hair:
the Career and Birth Chart of a TV Mogul

By most accounts, producer **Aaron Spelling** (chart below) was a gracious, amiable and discreet boss, who knew how best to win over prima donnas and difficult thesps, as well as play patriarch to wayward adolescent actors who had bought their own hype and 'gone Hollywood'. With an unaspected Sun crowning the MC in Taurus, he was an enduring symbol of substantial material wealth: a man who consolidated power over forty years and whose influence on pop culture came through the medium of TV and into people's homes (note the Moon–Pluto conjunction in Cancer). Interestingly, Sun–MC people are often well known and highly visible in their professional sphere, but they prefer to hide in the shadows of their elevated solar position. They also consider their private lives sacrosanct.

With Sun on the MC and Leo Rising, Spelling was a televisual Wizard of Oz – an uncanny little man in an enormous office who re-created the MGM (Leo) magic and glamour for the small screen. But the major themes of his professional life can be seen in his T-square: Mercury in Taurus in the 10th opposes Jupiter in Scorpio in the 4th, both square Neptune rising in Leo. (The fixed Mercury–Jupiter

opposition is the backbone of a kite formation, too.) A former scriptwriter and actor, Spelling became a prolific independent producer, a TV mogul who sold Jupiter–Neptune drama, fantasy, escapism, extravagance and guilty pleasures to the masses in the 70s and fed the clamour for glamour in the 80s. Such was the mass appeal of his shows that the identity and mythical lifestyle of America that he exported to homes (Moon) worldwide was the defining image the world had of the USA in the 1980s (Spelling's Moon is closely conjunct the position of the USA's 4 July Sun).

Fascinatingly, the principal premises of his TV shows – the on-screen dramas he created and oversaw – are shown in remarkable detail in this T-square, too. And even the characters (usually three protagonists) can each be described by one leg of the T-square! Let's find out how.

The Mod Squad was Spelling's first smash (September 1968, as Solar Arc Venus moved into his Equal 10th House, and the MC squared Uranus). It helped advertisers to recognize the importance of the youth demographic on TV (Mercury–Jupiter–Neptune). The show featured three young, hip crime fighters ('one white, one black, one blonde', the ads proclaimed) who worked with the system to avoid being incarcerated. Dropouts on probation, they were given a second chance and an opportunity to redeem themselves (Neptune) by working undercover to infiltrate the counterculture (Mercury opposite Jupiter in Scorpio). They comprised a rich kid (Mercury in Taurus), an intense, brooding African-American (Jupiter in Scorpio), and, in Spelling's words, a vulnerable 'canary with a broken wing' (Neptune rising in Leo).

Spelling's most successful show was *Charlie's Angels*, a story of three female crimefighters. The pilot aired on 21 March 1976, with the Sun in Aries square Mars in Cancer. Spelling's Solar Arc Venus had reached Mercury – appropriately, the show would create a media and promotional frenzy and be labelled 'jiggle TV'. The plot and characters epitomize Mercury in Taurus, Jupiter in Scorpio

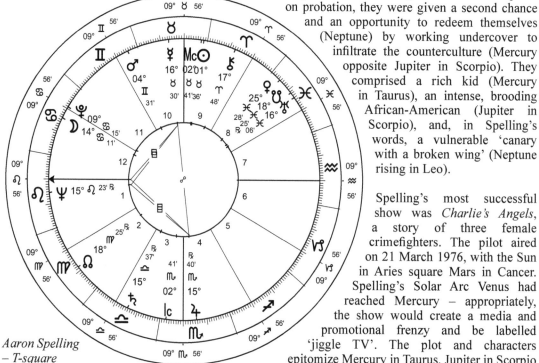

Aaron Spelling
– T-square

and Neptune in Leo: three women leave tedious desk jobs with the police to become glamorous private investigators assigned to undercover work (in bikinis and high-fashion, expensive clothes). They work for an elusive, womanizing millionaire recluse whom they've never met (they only ever hear his voice). There's the no-nonsense, savvy and practical one in turtleneck sweaters with the raspy voice (Taurus); the dark, sexy, streetwise but vulnerable abused orphan (Scorpio); and the glamourpuss racecar driver (Leo) with a super-big golden mane (the 'Farrah Flick' and its iconic cover girl became a national phenomenon).

In the most decadent decade of the century came **Dynasty** (chart below), which began on 12 January 1981, two weeks after the Jupiter–Saturn conjunction. Note Spelling's T-square once again: a small-town stenographer marries her oil tycoon boss and feels lost on entering a hostile world ruled by extravagance, wealth and snobbery. She later does battle with a vengeful, scorned ex-wife (also note Spelling's Moon–Pluto in Cancer square Saturn in Libra). Viewers were treated to over-the-top storylines about the power struggles of a capitalist family living in a huge, 48-room mansion. (With Jupiter in Scorpio in the 4th, Spelling's own 123-room, 56,000 sq. ft home,

built in 1991, remains the largest single-family home in California.) With super-rich people behaving badly in glamorous gowns, *Dynasty* was camp. 'Camp' is Jupiterian and, according to essayist Susan Sontag, it 'converts the serious into the frivolous. The hallmark of camp is the spirit of extravagance.' *Dynasty* went through the ratings roof in 1983–4, when Solar Arc Mercury reached Spelling's Moon.

In *Fantasy Island*, an enigmatic overseer of a mysterious island and his pint-sized sidekick help people to act out their long-held fantasies for a substantial amount of money. In *Hart to Hart*, a self-made millionaire marries a freelance journalist and together, in between making whoopee, they embark upon a glamorous, jet-set lifestyle as amateur detectives. In *Beverly Hills 90210*, suburban teenage twins relocate to Hollywood, encounter culture shock and subsequently bond with a group of poor-little-rich-kids from a star-studded, excess-laden community. In *Charmed*, three sisters discover they are descended from powerful witches and defend the innocent while coping with the practical issues of life, love and work. One can move objects with her mind (Mercury in Taurus), another can control others by freezing them in time (Scorpio is fixed Water – the ultimate deep freeze!), and the third can see future events, has premonitions and empathic powers (Neptune).

Premises for other Spelling shows *The Love Boat* (giving viewers comedy, romance and sentiment aboard a luxury cruise liner named *Pacific Princess*), *7th Heaven*, *Vega$* and *Sunset Beach* are also depicted in his T-square. Even the characters in *Starsky and Hutch* are illustrated: the soft-spoken, clean-cut cool one, the streetwise, sardonic one, and the flamboyant snitch.

It's sometimes too tempting to zoom in on the psychological dimensions of a chart and miss jokey 'cosmic correspondences' between life and the horoscope, where the symbolism of the birth chart is manifested literally in the events and situations and people in our lives, whether in 'real life' or on television.

'Dynasty'

Cosmic Compositions

When a singer writes and/or records a song with a particular message or noteworthy theme, we astrologers can see this in their horoscope, especially if the tune is strongly associated with that performer.

The Icon Is Barry White

With his MC in Scorpio (and its co-ruler Mars straddled by Venus and Neptune in Libra), Barry White filled CDs with his deep, passion-soaked R&B baritone, and the silky sound of his lush orchestral arrangements set the mood for men with seduction on their mind.

Originally a producer and arranger for his band Love Unlimited (Venus–Neptune), White was drawn into the limelight with such songs as 'You're the First, the Last, My Everything', 'Can't Get Enough of Your Love', 'I'm Qualified to Satisfy You', 'Love Serenade', and albums *The Icon Is Love* and *Staying Power*. White, dubbed 'the Walrus of Love', described his music and velvet voice as 'tough but gentle, macho yet sensual, huge yet intimate, manly, but in a humble way'.

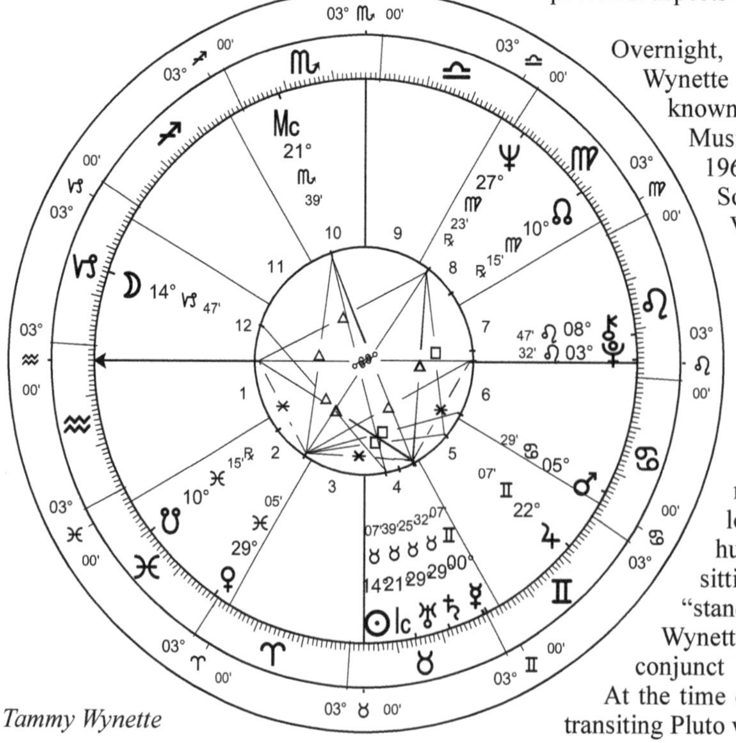

Many career-defining songs are written or released at times when the singer is having appropriate transits or directions.

Tammy's T-square of Trouble

Singing with a teardrop in her voice, country music legend **Tammy Wynette's** (chart below) career-defining tune of loyalty and solidarity, 'Stand By Your Man', was not a step back for gender equality, she and co-writer Billy Sherrill argued. After an antagonistic response from feminists, they spent much of their careers defending their composition. Sherrill said, '[It's] just another way of saying "I love you" – without reservations.' It was a call to overlook the many shortcomings of men ('After all, he's just a man').

The song painted a picture of forgiveness and tolerance, not of a woman as a domestic doormat – although both are possible manifestations of Wynette's natal Venus at the final degree of Pisces and opposite Neptune, both widely square Mars in Cancer. And the song never hinted at the volatile conjugal and medical soap opera its singer was living off-stage. With Pluto–Descendant, a Scorpio MC and the Venus–Neptune opposition, Wynette handed over control of her life and career to her various husbands instead of using these powerful aspects to take charge.

Overnight, 'Stand By Your Man' elevated Wynette to superstar status (she became known as the Queen of Country Music). It was released (September 1968) when both Uranus and the Solar Eclipse opposed her natal Venus. With Uranus linked to break-ups and splits, the song might have been just what she needed at the time.

The song and the singer gained further notoriety when a usually tight-lipped future First Lady Hillary Clinton made reference to it while showing loyalty to her philandering husband. Clinton said, 'I'm not sitting here – some little woman "standing by my man" like Tammy Wynette.' Clinton's Mercury is exactly conjunct Wynette's MC at 21° Scorpio. At the time of the gaffe (26 January 1992), transiting Pluto was at 22° Scorpio.

Tammy Wynette

Belief, Faith and Going 'Loco': Pisces MC

Pop survivor **Cher's** (chart on right) comeback single, 'Believe', was Piscean in name and in the novel use of a sound distortion/ pitch correction. It was released at a time when Midheaven co-ruler Jupiter was transiting near her Pisces MC. Cher's signature song with then-spouse Sonny Bono, 'I Got You Babe', spoke of teenage love defying societal expectation ('They say we're young and we don't know. We won't find out until we grow… They say our love won't pay the rent…'). In her chart, the Ascendant and Descendant rulers are in mutual reception and opposite each other: Moon in Capricorn in the 7th and Saturn in Cancer in the 1st House.

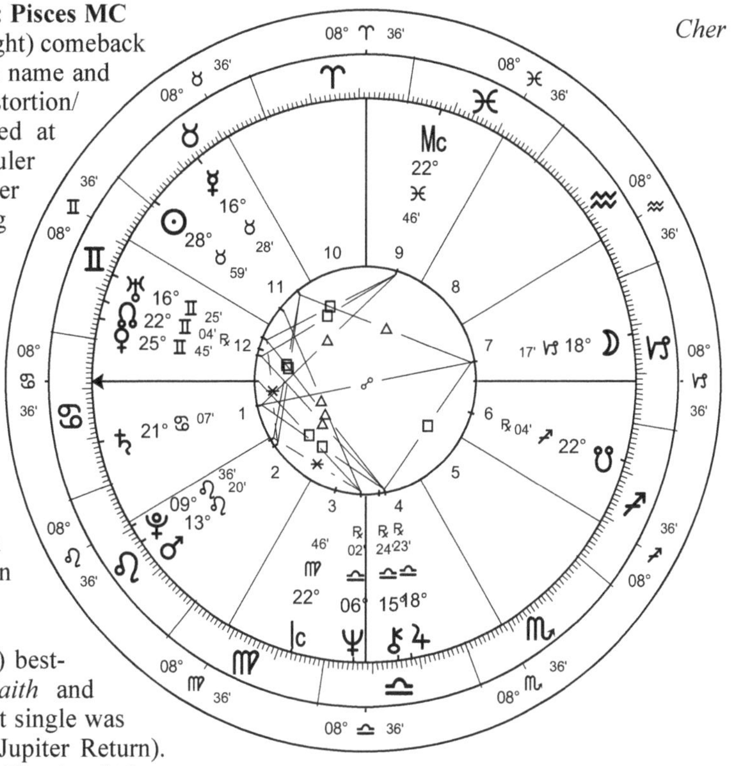

George Michael's (chart below) best-selling album was entitled *Faith* and launched his solo career (the first single was released a few weeks after his Jupiter Return). Other songs such as 'Praying For Time' and 'Jesus to a Child' also conjure up facets of his MC in

Cher

Pisces. In 2011, he released 'True Faith' during another Jupiter Return in Aries. (The Pisces MC has provided much tabloid fodder over the years: when TR Jupiter reached his MC in April 1998, he was arrested for lewd conduct in a toilet and, when TR Uranus was close, he was involved in a series of drug-related car crashes.) Looking elsewhere in his chart, Michael's 'Careless Whisper' is suggested by Mercury–Venus in Gemini in the 11th square Mars–Pluto ('Time can never mend the careless whispers of a good friend'), and 'Fast Love' (natal Venus in Gemini square Mars) was released on 22 April 1996, the day of his Venus Return.

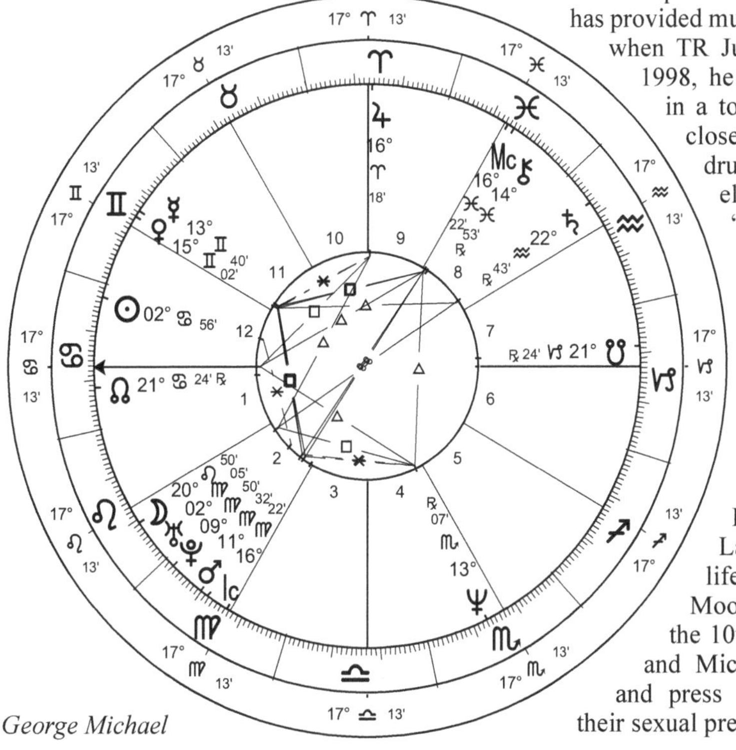

Ricky Martin's pop hit 'Livin' La Vida Loca' ('living the crazy life') reflects his Pisces MC and a Moon–Mars conjunction in Pisces in the 10th. For many years, both Martin and Michael experienced much gossip and press speculation (Pisces MC) over their sexual preference.

George Michael

A Titanic Hit

I associate Jupiter–Neptune with illusions (and delusions) of grandeur. Consider the legendary *RMS Titanic*. So much of its symbolism is Jupiter–Neptune: the Olympic-class passenger liner, designed for the rich, hailed as the grandest, most luxurious, opulent passenger steamship ever built.

On its maiden voyage, it hits a massive iceberg in the Atlantic Ocean. When 1,500 people drown, it becomes one of the biggest maritime accidents in recorded history and will result in changes to maritime law.

With Mercury and Jupiter retrograde, a void Moon conjunct Uranus, the Sun square Neptune and Venus in Pisces square Mars–Pluto, even its maiden voyage must count as one of the biggest, most spectacular and disastrous starts to anything!

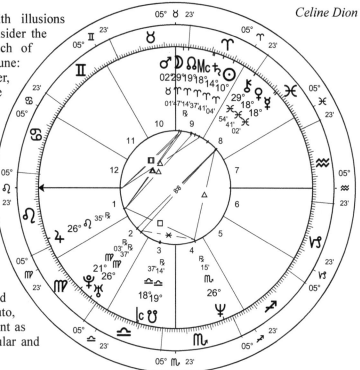

Celine Dion

In 1997, its story was made into the most expensive (at the time) and Oscar-honoured film of all time – an epic steered by director–producer James Cameron, born on 16 August 1954 during a Jupiter–Neptune square). Its movie theme, with a Neptunian title of its own, was the biggest selling single *in the world* in 1998 (Neptune is nothing if not ubiquitous). 'My Heart Will Go On' (a song about the eternality of love) was sung with drama by **Celine Dion** (chart above), born with Jupiter in Leo *exactly square* Neptune in Scorpio.

The film turned Leonardo DiCaprio into a movie superstar (and Neptunian 'Leo-mania' followed). He too was born with an exact Jupiter–Neptune square.

The 'H' Factor

Jupiter–Neptune is also heard in Leonard Cohen's mournful, biblical classic 'Hallelujah', revived in 2008 by contestants on

Jeff Buckley

TV's *American Idol* and *The X Factor*. A double Virgo, Cohen nevertheless has a Pisces Moon, MC ruler Mercury conjunct Jupiter, and Venus exactly conjunct Neptune.

Jeff Buckley (chart opposite page, bottom), whose version is perhaps the definitive recording, was born when Jupiter in Leo had risen in the 12th. With a natal Sun–Mercury–Venus–Neptune stellium in Scorpio, Buckley described his sensual rendition as a homage to 'the hallelujah of the orgasm'. The *American Idol* contestant, Jason Castro, whose performance on the talent show prompted the resurgence of Buckley's version, was born with the Sun conjunct Jupiter in Aries square – you guessed it – Neptune.

Some Further Cosmic Connections
Nina Simone's mellow tones and political voice in the civil rights movement can be seen by her MC in Scorpio and Moon opposite Pluto (see her horoscope on page 77). Perhaps her most famous songs are 'I Put a Spell on You', a torturous threat of revenge ('I don't care if you don't want me, I'm yours right now'), and the infectious 'My Baby Just Cares for Me'. Other Scorpio-tinged tunes include 'To Be Young, Gifted and Black', 'Strange Fruit' (made famous by another Scorpio MC, Billie Holiday), 'Ne Me Quitte Pas', 'I Wish I Knew How It Would Feel to Be Free' and the legendary 'Mississippi Goddam'.

And without wishing to tread on sacred ground, enjoy the astrological symbolism in these titles: Jimi Hendrix's 'Electric Ladyland' (Venus opposite Uranus); Patti Smith's punk-rock/underground debut album *Horses* (MC ruler Venus conjunct Jupiter in Scorpio, Sagittarius Rising); Joan Baez's 'Love Song to a Stranger', 'Prison Trilogy', 'Sweeter for Me' and 'Diamonds and Rust' (Neptune conjunct the Descendant and Aries Rising); the powerfully simple, social message of John Lennon's 'Imagine' (Moon in Aquarius opposite Pluto, T-square Mercury); Tina Turner's 'A Fool in Love' (Jupiter opposite Neptune, both T-square Venus in the 5th, plus Mars in Pisces in the 7th); and Paul McCartney's 'Hey Jude' and the longing of 'Yesterday' (Sun square Neptune–Ascendant). And only a Gemini with Sagittarius Rising like Bob Dylan with Uranus conjunct the Sun, Moon, Jupiter and Saturn ('the old road is rapidly ageing') could have written the hypnotic hymn 'The Times They Are a-Changin''.

Judy Garland's 'Somewhere Over the Rainbow' describes her Pisces MC and its dreams and longings for 'a land that I heard of once in a lullaby'. (Her Uranus–MC conjunction in Pisces describes not only the emotional rollercoaster of her public life and private sorrow, but also how her death triggered the Stonewall riots – a rebellion [Uranus] of a repressed minority [Pisces] who could no longer tolerate abuse from the police.)

A little more complex is the symbolism found in **Doris Day's** chart (left). The song 'Que Sera Sera (Whatever Will Be Will Be)' – letting go of future plans and allowing events to happen naturally – will always be associated with her. Day's MC ruler is Mercury in fatalistic Pisces opposite controlling Virgo on the Ascendant. Mercury is square to the Moon in Gemini (on the MC), and Mars is in philosophical Sagittarius on the IC: in the song, her mother (Moon) tells her 'the future's not ours to see, que sera sera'.

Doris Day – Grand Cross

Horoscope Facts in Works of Fiction

When we consider the horoscopes of writers of fiction, we find that in developing characters, depicting life as they see it, and constructing plots, authors undoubtedly speak their charts, too. Literary themes and areas that intrigue or inspire a writer are seen in their natal chart, as well as in progressions/directions at the date s/he engages in constructing the work and at the time of its publication.

In Her Prime: Finding Jean Brodie

Muriel Spark (chart below) is considered one of the great literary creators of 20th century fiction. After a disastrous marriage and a nervous breakdown, Spark became a Roman Catholic in 1954 – a conversion credited as being a catalyst in 'creating a stable, intellectual force in her life'.

Originally a poet, Spark wrote books that are, in many instances, commentaries on domestic disquiet and the unsatisfactory state of being female in the world (note natal Moon–Mars in Libra and Venus–Uranus in Aquarius). Many of her works display a curt, waspish tone. They reveal an incisive, malicious wit that pierces cliché and reveals unpleasant truths (MC ruler Mercury in Capricorn,

and Moon–Mars in Libra square Pluto) – truths that are often packaged in a deceptively simple way.

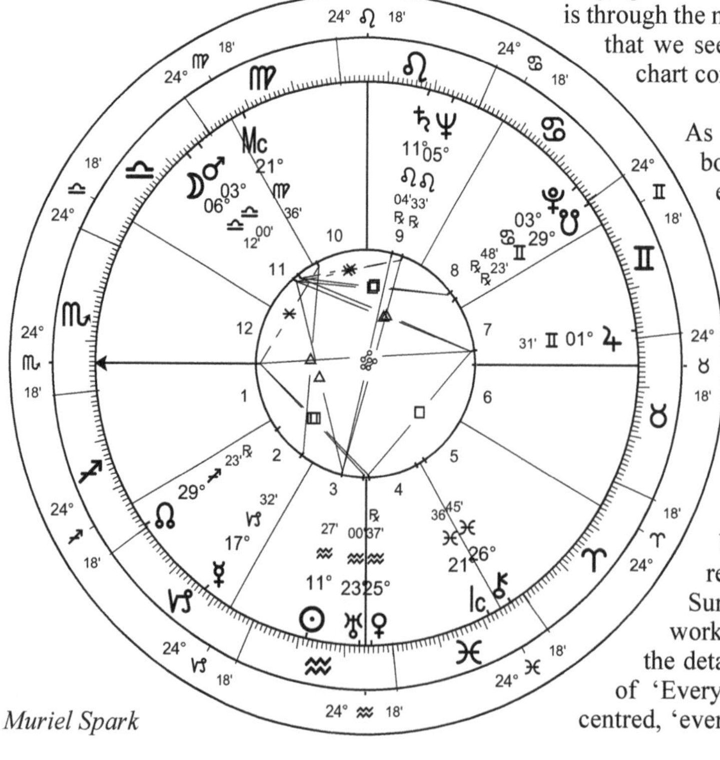

The main themes and major aspects of Spark's chart appear to be:

• An Aquarian overtone (Sun in Aquarius and Venus conjunct Uranus in its own sign) underscored by an emphasis on the Air signs and Air houses, as well as the fixed signs.

• Sun in the 3rd opposite Saturn–Neptune in the 9th; Venus–Uranus square Jupiter on the Descendant; Moon–Mars square Pluto.

Spark's most iconic character remains Jean Brodie, the charismatic, progressive schoolteacher in *The Prime of Miss Jean Brodie*. A story of morality and manipulation, the book was first published in its entirety in serial form by *The New Yorker* (from its 14 October 1961 issue). Spark, who had struggled in vain to be published regularly in this magazine, submitted the book in August 1961 when Uranus was at 25° Leo, opposite her Venus–Uranus conjunction and into her 10th House. It was the breakthrough she had worked so hard to attain. The novel turned Spark's life around, bringing her success, acclaim and renown. And it is through the memorable creation of Jean Brodie that we see the principal themes of Spark's chart come to life.

As I've written elsewhere in this book, there is much to be said for engaging in and living out the essence of our Sun sign. If we don't follow the message of our Sun, we can wallow in the very worst of its opposite sign. The shadow of each sign is usually the unpalatable side of its polar opposite. Writers often use both ends of this polarity to form a multifaceted identity on the written page. Readers of Paul Wright's book *The Literary Zodiac* will recognize the importance of the Sun in the key themes of writers' works. In Spark's creation of Brodie, the detached idealism and egalitarianism of 'Everyman' Aquarius masks the self-centred, 'every man for himself', divine right-

Muriel Spark

to-rule of Leo. As the leaders of the revolution in *Animal Farm* declared, 'All animals are equal,' later adding, '...but some are more equal than others.'

When the Sun (the ruler of individualistic Leo) is found in the group-spirited sign of Aquarius, we have an intriguing and difficult paradox: how can an individual be 'self-centred' (in the truest sense) when the group's ideals demand priority? The intellectual detachment and humanitarianism of Aquarius can be compromised when the individual no longer represents the group – or elevates themselves to role of mentor, guru or Svengali. Many Aquarians fight for *liberté, égalité, fraternité* but secretly feel superior to the common folk whose rights they defend. We soon learn that Jean Brodie has high ideals *and* an elitist sensibility. She is dedicated in her prime to her handpicked group of girls but imposes on them her way of thinking.

> Give me a girl at an impressionable age and she is mine for life. – Jean Brodie

Manifestations of the Aquarian shadow include favouritism (the need for a clique), omniscience, a desire to be a 'personality' and the elevation of a heroic figure that is admired or emulated. Brodie cultivates an exclusive following, a special 'Brodie Set', whom she proclaims, no less, as 'the crème de la crème'. She dominates the herd by sheer force of personality ('She thinks she is Providence,' states the insightful Sandy, who later betrays her mentor). Brodie attempts to exert control over their lives, fantasies and aesthetic tastes. She introduces them to the ideals of Fascism and attempts to create the girls in her own image, even playing God (Jupiter–Descendant) by pigeonholing them ('Sandy is dependable' and 'Jenny will be painted many times') and attempting to enforce a rigid predestination by mapping out plans for their futures. The reader understands that Brodie is living her life vicariously through them and that she even manoeuvres one of her girls to replace her in her ex-partner's bed.

The book's message reveals the key aspect in Spark's horoscope: the Sun in Aquarius in the 3rd House opposite Saturn–Neptune in Leo in the 9th. In the classroom (3rd House), the charismatic Brodie encourages her students to think beyond the confines of their school and society (note Uranus posited in the 3rd, too). She is strong-willed, forceful and unorthodox in shaping their lives. We later discover that inspiration (Neptune) has a dangerous side and fatal allure, as she pushes one student into joining her brother to fight for Mussolini, which leads to the girl's death.

Brodie's progressive teaching is in contrast to the rigid, traditional Marcia Blaine School for Girls in 1930s conservative Edinburgh (in addition to the opposition, Saturn rules the 3rd House in Spark's chart). Her lessons are not on the curriculum. Her classes focus on aesthetics, art, poetry and her romanticized love life and personal dramas (Hugh, her suitor who fell on Flanders field, is lionized in her stories). Yet Brodie's own relationships with men are complex: she is torn between the conservative music teacher, who wishes to commit to her (Saturn), and the romantic but married artist (Neptune), who is infatuated with her and longing to reignite their clandestine affair. At the book and film's conclusion, she remains independent and unattached to either (Sun in Aquarius).

Brodie's interest in Fascism – particularly in romanticising its leader, Mussolini – is reflected in Spark's key opposition. But what of the ideology and its leader? **Benito Mussolini** (chart overleaf, top) began climbing the political ranks in 1917 and early 1918 – the time of Spark's birth – under a Saturn–Neptune conjunction in Leo (over his Sun–Mercury conjunction in the 9th House). Principally an authoritarian ideology (Saturn–Neptune), Fascism was both traditional and revolutionary in that an elite (Leo) 'protected' shared societal goals and opposed discrimination based on social class (Aquarius). In *The Doctrine of Fascism* (1932), Mussolini wrote of its collectivism (as opposed to individualism) – the interdependence of humans and the priority of group goals over individual needs. Here, in his words, we can sense the Leo–Aquarius polarity and the Saturn–Neptune conjunction: 'The Fascist conception of the state is all-embracing... Fascism is a religious conception in which man is seen in his immanent relationship with a superior law and with an objective Will that transcends the particular individual and raises him to conscious membership of a spiritual society.' Yet Mussolini – like the fictional Brodie – became a law unto himself, dismantling most of the constitutional restraints on his power.

Mussolini's own chart has some fascinating links to that of Brodie's creator, including 20° Scorpio

Rising (near Spark's own Ascendant), Pluto at 1° Gemini (conjunct her Jupiter), Uranus at 20° Virgo (on her MC) and, perhaps most clearly, a Sun–Mercury conjunction in Leo in the 9th House (within an acceptable 5° orb of Spark's Saturn–Neptune conjunction in the 9th).

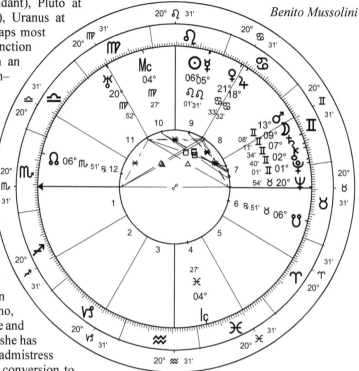

Benito Mussolini

The links to Mussolini may end there, but Spark's most famous novel can be seen as an allegory of Fascism. With little awareness of irony, Jean Brodie's totalitarian personality demands her students think independently by conforming to her ideals. In the book, Sandy likens the Brodie Set to Mussolini's soldiers. Yet Brodie is blind to the perils of Fascism and to dissent in her own ranks. She is betrayed by Sandy who, in refusing to become a Brodie clone and in converting to Catholicism, feels she has a moral obligation to inform the headmistress of Brodie's agenda. (Spark's own conversion to Catholicism in 1954 occurred soon after another

conjunction of Saturn and Neptune.) Perhaps motivated by jealousy, it is Sandy who 'puts a stop' to her manipulative teacher. Accused of teaching Fascism, Brodie is dismissed from Marcia Blaine and (in the book) spends the rest of her life trying to determine the identity of her 'assassin'.

Christina Kay (chart on left) was a teacher at Spark's own school and the inspiration for Brodie. Kay had revolutionary Uranus at 26° Leo (opposite Spark's Venus–Uranus and had her Uranus Return during the book's publication in October 1961) and other very telling synastry with her student: MC at 27° Aquarius (on Spark's Venus–Uranus), Saturn at 1° Aries (opposite Spark's Moon–Mars), Pluto–Mercury at 25° and 28° Taurus (on Spark's Descendant), and Jupiter at 6° Aquarius (near Spark's Sun).

Christina Kay

In May 1966, Vanessa Redgrave played Brodie in a West End play based on the novel. Redgrave's Ascendant is 24° Leo and, remarkably, actress and author have Suns conjunct and Mercury placements conjunct, too. Redgrave was born at a Saturn–Neptune opposition. On 2 March 1969, the Oscar-winning film starring Maggie Smith was released, bringing Spark further international fame. This occurred at a Jupiter–Uranus conjunction (2–3° Libra), which was conjunct Spark's Mars and opposite her progressed/directed Sun at 2° Aries (Solar Arc Mars was on her Ascendant, too). Even without a birth time for Smith, there is fascinating synastry: Smith's Sun–Mercury opposes Spark's Pluto, her Mars is at 7° Libra (conjunct Spark's Moon–Mars), Venus at 15° Capricorn (conjunct Spark's Mercury at 17°) and Saturn at 24° Aquarius (conjunct Spark's Venus–Uranus at 23° and 25°).

Although Muriel Spark's book is highly autobiographical of her years at school, it is Brodie the protagonist – the repressed, arrogant maverick – who is identified most clearly in the dynamics of Spark's horoscope, and whose chilling portrait has left an indelible mark on literature.

Much of Spark's work is about judgements, and it alerts the reader to the fallibility of people and the perils of misplaced faith in them (Saturn–Neptune in the 9th opposite the Sun in Aquarius). There's often the suggestion that it would be wiser to put one's faith in God.

In an apt description of Spark's Aquarian Sun opposite Saturn–Neptune in Leo in the 9th, Carl MacDougall wrote that a later book by Spark, *The Driver's Seat* (1970), was a story where 'fairytale romance is subverted in the same way as the drive towards individualism has produced isolation and cults have replaced spiritual fulfilment. Chaos has replaced moral certainty and pseudo-spiritual experiences and beliefs are exposed as little more than fads which deprive and subvert social and spiritual values.' In her *Guardian* obituary (14 April 2006), Alex Clark wrote, 'You could argue that Muriel Spark's body of work was most effectively characterized as the study of charisma and the deceptions that can be carried out, almost unstoppably, under its auspices.'

A Multitude of Planetary Culprits

There's no part of the chart that immediately identifies someone as a 'builder' or 'ice hockey champion', particularly now that there are so many professional choices. People feel less condemned to accept their lot and are more *aware* of a need to pursue work that expresses who they are (whether they do so or not). Astrology reveals the motivations, the qualities, the passions that lie beneath a person's work and form the major aspects of the character. In the UK, barristers in the Law, for instance, do a different job from solicitors. They have the 'right of audience' and, instructed by a solicitor, they are in the business of advocacy before a judge. But although Mercury may govern advocacy, the birth charts (and Mercurys) will be as varied as the individual motivations, professional styles and communication skills of the barristers. These styles, rather than the actual job, are the areas, I believe, that can be grouped under particular planetary signatures. It is more fruitful, in my opinion, to find a common link in the charts of workers who share a *set of traits* and, more importantly, a *set of motivations* associated with such work. Here are some observations on the astrology of crime.

In the introduction to *Profiles in Crime* (Data News Press, 1991), Lois Rodden wrote:

> The criminal act – that which offends the laws of man or injures the rights or well-being of another – runs a gamut in both nature and degree. If a criminal is one who has broken a law, most of us law-abiding citizens fall within that definition by dint of a traffic citation, of shading our income-tax to our benefit, of exaggerating an expense-account, of taking home items of our employer's product. There are sins of commission or omission that we forgive in others in order to forgive them in ourselves; basically the average person has a moral standard of conduct that is developed through the socialization process.

As astrologers, once we've seen a few horoscopes of 'evil' people, it can be easy to demonize a set of planetary placements – forgetting that we're looking at a *moment in time* that contains no apparent morality or judgement. In a recent project I commissioned for an astrological magazine on a mass murderer, one of the contributors wrote of 'the maximum effect' – an unusual amount of concurring testimony present in a chart that 'would produce' a serial killer. This was written in earnest, forgetting that the serial killer had a twin born five minutes earlier who lived a very different life – a life that was ended by his twin brother.

In my opinion, it is easy to forget that our study can only show how people use their 'contract' – to paint a life story with their particular palette of tools – within the constraints of society, opportunity, their time in history and other external factors. In studying the charts of criminals, perhaps more than any other group, we are reminded that so many other non-astrological factors come into play in the development of a personality and lifestyle. We also are aware that if an act can be committed by one human being, it becomes a human act capable of being performed by all of us. Put in astrological terms, we would say that everyone's chart contains the same set of planets, signs and houses.

Despite the fact that the natal chart cannot show guilt or a clear pattern that says 'criminal', I have found it useful to study those criminals who share similar traits and experiences, and then to look for common planetary or sign denominators. The astrology of crime is a huge subject and cannot

be covered here, but I shall attempt to share a few observations and examine some themes from the psychology and horoscopes of perhaps the most fascinating of all lawbreakers: serial killers.

Mutability

Dana Holliday collected the birth data of dozens of serial killers (many obtained by writing to them incognito while they were in prison) and, some years ago, she left me her files, charts and correspondences in her will. Dana found that serial killers have charts that are usually heavily mutable, particularly with the Sun, Moon and/or Ascendant (plus additional planets) in the signs of Gemini or Sagittarius. (In *Jupiter and Mercury: An A to Z* [Flare, 2006], Paul Wright notes the strength of Sagittarius and Jupiter in the charts of mass murderers who are known for the sheer enormity of killings.) With this in mind, I began to look at the psychology of the mutable signs and soon saw a link between mutability and the issue of avoidance and repetition.

The word 'series' means 'a number of similar or related things coming one after another'. It derives from the word *serere*: to join, link, bind together. It could be said that the function of the mutable signs is to join events, link information and bind people together; and to create or make sense of a chain of similar events that can be understood through their sameness. And a serial killer by definition is one who has escaped detection (mutable) and been able to repeat a similar crime against a victim, usually picked at random, who has something *in common* with the previous victim (mutable signs are known as 'common' signs). Some killers are more organized than others, and with these the challenge is to outwit, cover their tracks and escape detection – to play a psychological game of cat and mouse, in which the mutable signs are adept.

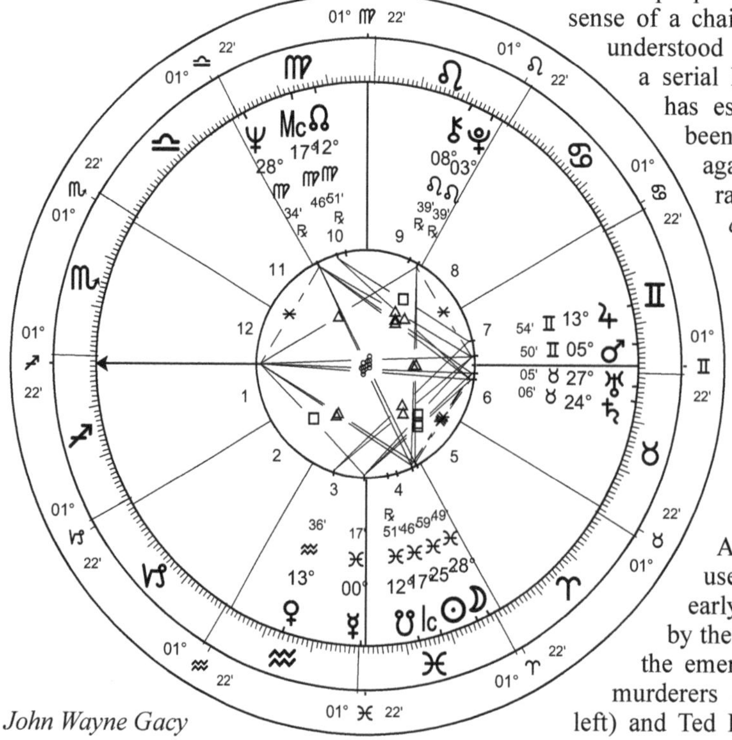

Apparently, the phrase 'serial' was used in connection with murders as early as 1930 but became a term used by the media by the late 70s following the emergence of the high-profile mass murderers **John Wayne Gacy** (chart on left) and Ted Bundy. Gacy, menacingly often

John Wayne Gacy

pictured in a clown's outfit, was born with Sun–Moon (plus Mercury) in Pisces, Sagittarius Rising, Virgo MC and Mars–Jupiter in Gemini. Bundy was born with the Sun and Moon–Mars in Sagittarius. He was attractive, charming, well mannered and seductive (Venus is conjunct Jupiter in Scorpio on the IC); when arrested, Bundy refused a plea of insanity, preferring to be hailed as 'brilliant' (Sagittarius).

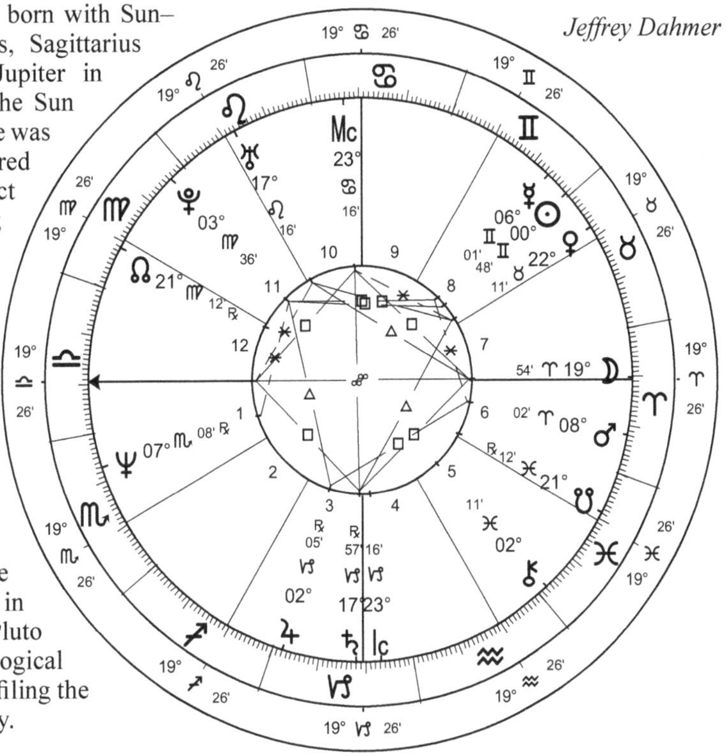

The man who coined the term 'serial killer' in the USA was said to have been criminal profiler Robert Ressler. He was born on 15 February 1937 with only a Saturn–Neptune opposition in mutable signs, the Sun in Aquarius square Mars in Scorpio, and Mercury opposite Pluto – aspects suggesting a psychological interest in understanding and profiling the violent and the criminal in society.

Jeffrey Dahmer

Profiling

Of course, an emphasis on mutable signs does not a serial killer make! Profilers have created a list of characteristics said to identify a serial killer. Consider the most appropriate planet(s) for each of the following characteristics:

- Antisocial behaviour; a short attention span.

- A lack of accountability for their actions; a failure to learn from experience.

- A sporadic sense of conscience; a feeling of victimization.

- A need to lie or steal habitually.

- A lack of empathy or guilt.

- An avoidance of intimacy; a strong, early sexual (often voyeuristic or sadomasochistic) fantasy life.

- An inability to control their impulses; a need to satisfy their desires.

- Fears and phobias from childhood; fearful of appearing weak; low self-worth combined with a sense of superiority over others; a desire for power and domination (often seen early in cruelty to animals).

- An ability to charm, manipulate and exploit, often hiding behind a 'mask of sanity'.

- A rejection of the family (often from a family with a weak father, dominant mother); a seeking out of others who are compliant with their domination or relationships of mutual exploitation.

Interestingly, studies suggest that the childhood environment is not the cause of criminal behaviour in serial killers. Nor does it appear to be physiological. For instance, after notorious killer **Jeffrey Dahmer** (chart above) was murdered in prison, his mother asked that his brain be studied, but it was found to be 'normal'. Most serial killers are single, white males with high intelligence.

Although many are on a mission or 'hear voices' (see Neptune, below), others are termed 'hedonistic' serial killers – those who seek thrills and derive pleasure from killing. Sometimes the thrill- and pleasure-seeking murders are motivated by lust (thus combining the elements of Venus and Mars). Another type of motive is material gain – the 'comfort' serial killer – and poison is often the murderous means by which they carry out plans to commit theft, fraud or embezzlement (taking advantage of others for this purpose appears to be Jupiterian in nature).

The issue of power, domination and control is a major one for some serial killers. This is most often seen in horoscopes with a dominant Pluto or Scorpio emphasis. With some killers there's a provocative motive (other than sexual) to induce pain or incite terror, which provides excitement (Uranus) for the killer during the hunt and capture. Often this kind of killer will be attempting to commit the perfect crime (Uranus is linked to the perfect ideology).

David Berkowitz

Neptune and a Cause

Neptune is often prominent in the charts of terrorists and those with a 'cause', a dedication to an '-ism'. There may be a break with reality and 'voices' may compel them to commit murder. 'Son of Sam' killer **David Berkowitz** (chart above, right) had Neptune

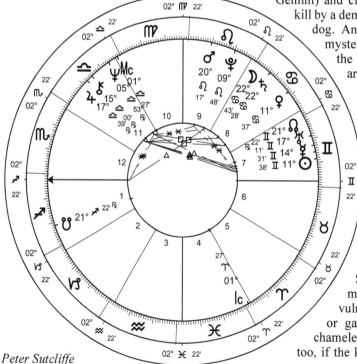

Peter Sutcliffe

Rising (plus Sun–Jupiter and Mercury–Mars in Gemini) and claimed to have been instructed to kill by a demon who possessed his neighbour's dog. And with Neptune, there's often a mystery or tabloid frenzy surrounding the killer's identity long before they are discovered.

Peter Sutcliffe (chart on left) was born with Neptune on the MC, and terrified the public for years as the elusive Yorkshire Ripper before eventually being caught. According to Sutcliffe, voices in his head called out to him to kill prostitutes. The Neptunian serial killer is often on a mission to rid the world of a particular 'type'.

Strongly Neptunian killers may choose people who appear vulnerable or lost, may use poisons or gases, and may have an array of chameleon-like disguises. Expect Gemini, too, if the killer has an alias or is known by a pseudonym, such as 'The Hillside Strangler' (Angelo Buono, Gemini MC, Neptune Rising). Neptune is prominent in the charts of those who appear to be martyrs or wrongly accused like Derek Bentley (Pisces Rising, Neptune conjunct the Descendant) or 'patsies' like Lee Harvey Oswald (Neptune opposite the MC in Pisces).

Uranus: the Perfect Crime
Uranus is linked to sporadic, explosive, sudden crimes – often defended as 'temporary insanity' (a strong reaction to a build-up of frustration or years of abuse, however, is more Mars–Pluto in nature). Uranus is linked to manic-depressive behaviour, plus the destructive idea of purification – attempting to create a 'perfect' society, a master race – or extreme solutions such as sterilization of the lower working classes. Both Hitler and cult leader **Charles Manson** (chart on right), who tried to incite a race war, were born with Uranus Rising, while Harold Shipman, a doctor who murdered over two

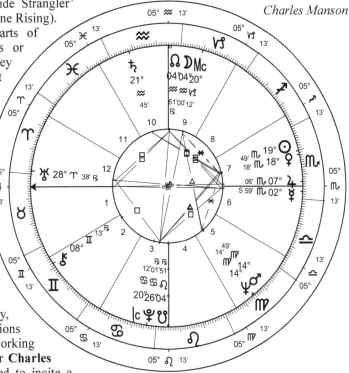

Charles Manson

hundred of his patients, was born on 14 January 1946 (no birth time known) when the Moon was conjunct Uranus all day.

Social reject and (rumoured) paedophile **Thomas Hamilton** (chart below) was born with Uranus rising in Cancer. Hamilton walked into a school in Dunblane, Scotland, one morning in 1996 and massacred sixteen young children, an event that shattered the Scottish town and for which no real motive was established (Hamilton had the Sun in Taurus opposite the Moon in Scorpio in the 5th, T-square Pluto). The event occurred during his Venus Return (natally opposite Mars) and days after transiting Mars squared the Solar Arc directed Venus–Mars opposition at 19° Gemini–Sagittarius.

Jupiter and Criminal Crusades
Jupiterian criminals are often charismatic and have greed or fame on their mind. There's

Thomas Hamilton

sometimes a sense of moral righteousness, a misguided belief (especially if Neptune is in the mix) or some crusade (if combined with Mars). Confidence schemes, grand theft and other big corner-cutting plans fall under Jupiter's remit. Definitions of the psychopathic personality align with observations of the nature of astrological Jupiter, too. Often there is a pathological egocentricity, a love of risk, excessive sensation-seeking, a lack of shame, remorse or moral sense, plus poor judgement, a failure to learn from experience and a reluctance to honour financial obligations.

Perhaps one of the most atrocious acts of betrayal and avarice is that of a fraudulent doctor, **Marcel Petiot** (chart on right), who offered to move Jews to safety during the Second World War for 25,000 francs. Instead, he injected his victims with cyanide and disposed of their bodies. Petiot was born with Jupiter on the MC in

Marcel Petiot

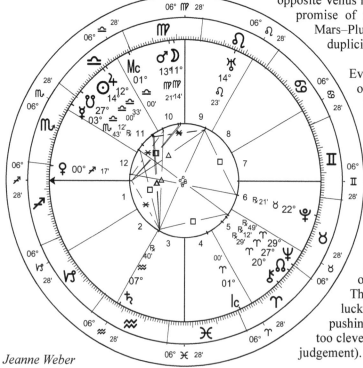

Jeanne Weber

Virgo (the reputation/honour of a man of service) opposite Venus in Pisces on the IC (the fraudulent promise of rescue). Note, too, the apex of Mars–Pluto–Neptune (in that order) in duplicitous Gemini in the 7th House.

Evangelists on both sides of the law often have very strong Sagittarius/Jupiter and Pisces/Neptune charts (see the profile starting page 182).

Jupiter is traditionally the lucky planet and many murderers (with prominent Jupiter placements or close trines from Jupiter) have evaded the authorities through lucky escapes or avoided getting caught due to oversights or careless errors by the police. That is, until Jupiter runs out of luck (usually for Jupiterian reasons: pushing their luck, feeling superior or too clever, tripping up or making errors in judgement).

A number of children (including three of her own) died while in the care of **Jeanne Weber** (chart on opposite page, bottom), born with Sagittarius Rising and the Sun conjunct Jupiter in Libra (plus a Moon–Mars conjunction, ruling the 8th and 5th, in Virgo). Insufficient evidence and conflicting testimony resulted in an acquittal. She disappeared but was found the following year when she registered the death of another child. Weber was tried but released when the doctor misdiagnosed the death. She was later declared criminally insane after choking a child (while being allowed to work in a children's hospital). Weber died with her hands around her own throat.

In my early twenties, I was the foreman in the jury trial of a taxi driver accused of assisting drug smugglers. He pleaded ignorance of what he was transporting. The inept police in the Caribbean, plus a flimsy case from the Crown Prosecution Service, established reasonable doubt and, although we felt he probably turned a blind eye to what he was carrying, we found him not guilty. As I left the court, there was a document that had his birth date on it. He was born a lucky man with the Sun conjunct Jupiter in Sagittarius.

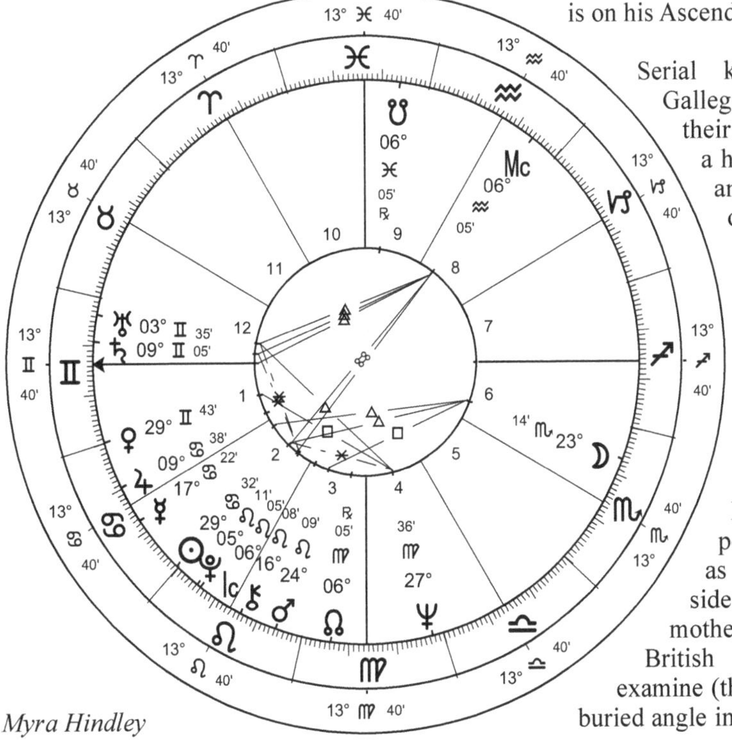

The research carried out by the Gauquelins revealed the presence of Jupiter around the four angles (in the cadent houses) in the horoscopes of prominent Nazis (many of whom were born during the 'propaganda' aspect of Neptune conjunct Pluto in Gemini). It's also easy to forget that these men, branded war criminals because they were on the losing side, are those who attained great rank, status and power in their time and place.

Sun Conjunctions

Sun–Jupiter individuals are often associated with an influential or powerful ally: for example, Rudolf Diels, who was appointed the first Chief of the Gestapo by Hermann Goering. Diels was born with Sun–Jupiter conjunct in Sagittarius opposite Neptune and widely opposite Pluto.

Sun–Pluto would suggest powerful, influential male role models or father figures, particularly when found in Leo. Certain behavioural patterns might have stayed dormant if not triggered by another person. Serial killer Caril Ann Fugate, just fourteen, murdered her family with boyfriend Charles Starkweather before embarking on a killing spree. Fugate was born with the Sun in a partile conjunction to Pluto in Leo, and Libra Rising. Her Ascendant is on Starkweather's Mars, her Mars is exactly on his Uranus, and her Moon is on his Ascendant.

Serial killers Gerald and Charlene Gallego kidnapped love slaves for their sexual gratification. Charlene, a habitual liar, would lure the girls and then Gerald would dispose of them. Born with the Sun conjunct Neptune, Charlene has Mars on Gerald's Descendant (and opposite his Mars rising in Virgo, which is conjunct her Venus). Their MC-IC axes are reversed to within 1 degree.

Myra Hindley (chart on left) had the Sun in Cancer conjunct Pluto in Leo. She was – and perhaps always will be – depicted as the epitome of female evil – a side of the Cancerian caregiver/mother shadow that members of British society would prefer not to examine (the conjunction is on the IC – the buried angle in her chart). Her Sun was exactly

Myra Hindley

conjunct her lover and killing partner Ian Brady's Pluto at 29° Cancer. Interestingly, her Jupiter was opposite his Sun in Capricorn (the elevation and projection of a powerful authority figure), his Jupiter was on her MC and opposite her Sun, and Hindley's Venus was conjunct his Chiron. The Jupiter interaspects are apt as both killers considered themselves invincible and boasted of their exploits.

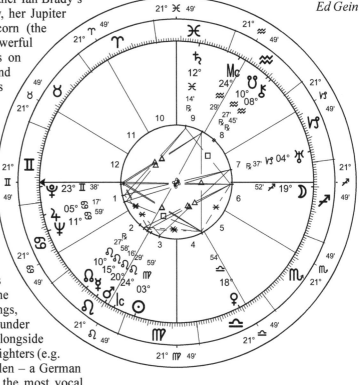

Ed Gein

Mars and Violent Crime

The link to Mars and murder is as simple and direct as the planet itself: 65 per cent of murders are crimes of passion or violence that explode from pent-up stress in domestic or other everyday situations (although these are not usually the triggers for serial killers). Stabbings, guns and physical violence fall under Mars. Mars is often strong alongside Uranus in those who are freedom fighters (e.g. the Resistance). Clemens von Galen – a German Cardinal Archbishop and one of the most vocal opponents of Hitler – was later removed from his position and placed in a concentration camp. He was born with a Moon–Uranus conjunction in the 10th square Mars–Pluto in the 7th (with his MC conjunct Hitler's Saturn, and Neptune–Descendant on Hitler's Sun). Anti-Nazi politician, Wolf von Harnack, was born with Moon–Uranus on the MC in Libra and the Sun square Mars in Libra (on Hitler's Ascendant).

Pluto, Scorpio and the Unspeakable

Reading about Pluto killers is not for the faint-hearted. Pluto and, more commonly, Scorpio are prominent in killers who have extreme tastes and brutal behavioural patterns. Dominant, masterful and manipulative, these are serial killers who exert control and power over others (cult leaders can be included in this description). Vengeful crimes (the Kray twins had the Sun at 0° Scorpio opposite Uranus, T-square Pluto), Mafia-style killings, sadomasochism, necrophilia, bestiality, butchering and dismemberment, sodomy, debasement, mutilation and cannibalism are all Pluto- or Scorpio-linked.

Necrophiliac and cannibal **Ed Gein** (chart above) was the 'inspiration' for Buffalo Bill in The

Silence of the Lambs, Norman Bates in *Psycho* and the evil depicted in *The Texas Chainsaw Massacre*. A Virgo, he was born with Pluto rising in Gemini opposite the Moon setting in Sagittarius. Upon the death of his domineering, God-fearing and fanatical mother (Moon in Sagittarius opposite Pluto) on 29 December 1945 (when Saturn was at 22° Cancer), he found himself completely alone. Ed kept his mother's bedroom in pristine condition as a shrine to her, and began his descent into madness (Solar Arc Neptune was now conjunct Mars). Gein dug up graves, skinned the corpses and dressed them in the skin and hair of the unearthed women. When this night-time activity no longer thrilled, he began killing.

He was apprehended on 16 November 1957 – SA Uranus was conjunct his MC (TR Uranus arrived on his MC when the film *Ed Gein* was released in the US in May 2001). Police found souvenirs in his Wisconsin home: a drum of human skin, bedposts made from skulls, and a fridge filled with a heart and other human parts.

Writer Robert Bloch was in Wisconsin at the time of the gruesome discoveries and wrote the novel *Psycho* (1959) – and made his reputation – from the stories being published in the newspapers at the time (Bloch's MC at 4° Virgo is conjunct Gein's Sun). The book and the Hitchcock film (June 1960) were released when TR Pluto reached 4° Virgo, giving Gein an international, macabre fame.

Peter Kürten, the Monster of Düsseldorf, was a sadist who killed and dismembered more than 68 women. Labelled the 'king of sexual perverts', Kürten had the Sun in Gemini conjunct Saturn, as well as Pluto, which was rising.

Cult leader Charles Manson (see page 141), who mesmerized his followers into committing a series of brutal killings, was born with four planets in Scorpio (either conjunct the Descendant or in the 7th House). Night Stalker Ricardo Ramirez was a devil-worshipping serial killer who kidnapped, sodomized and butchered indiscriminately and bragged that Satan watched over him. Ramirez was born with the Sun and Moon–Mercury in Pisces and Jupiter rising in Sagittarius; the Sun was opposed by Pluto.

The horrific actions of **Marc Dutroux** (chart above), who was born with Pluto on the MC and Sun–Mercury rising in Scorpio, will never be forgotten in Belgium. He kidnapped, raped and then starved children in his basement. With 'fortunate' trines from the Moon and Mars in mutable signs (avoidance) to the MC and Ascendant, respectively, he remained undetected for years. This was in spite of Dutroux having been imprisoned for rape some time earlier (only serving three years of his thirteen-year sentence). The gross negligence and amateurism of the police and officials involved in the investigation kept his secrets safe for years.

Pluto crime can also cast a black cloud over a person's life, leaving them feeling victimized or at the mercy of others (see, for example, the chart of Louise Woodward, who has Pluto conjunct her MC, on page 88).

Some Final Observations
In many of the charts of brutal and sadistic killers of women, there are conjunctions, squares or

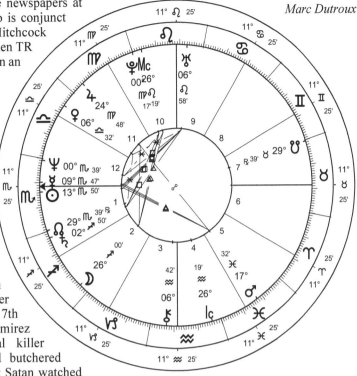

Marc Dutroux

oppositions from the outer planets to the Moon and Venus. And in many killers, Saturn (the conscience and anchor or morality in the horoscope) is often unsupported by aspect or weakly positioned – unless the killer has the Saturnian temperament or has felt the burden of expectation or parental subjugation.

Famed astrologer Dennis Elwell pointed out the degrees of sadism (20–23° Cancer–Capricorn axis) in some killers and sadists (Brady, Kürten, Sutcliffe, Dennis Nilsen, Shipman, and even de Sade himself). From my own research, the area around 19° Libra is common in those who are noted for killing or those who are fascinated by serial killers. For example, two of the most notorious serial killers in recent years, Dennis Nilsen and cannibal Jeffrey Dahmer (for his chart, see page 139), have Ascendants at 19° Libra. Nilsen has the Sun at 0° Sagittarius and Dahmer has the Moon at 19° Aries, and the Sun at 0° Gemini square Pluto. Astrologer Dana Holliday was a treasured colleague, a wonderfully funny lady, and a dedicated data collector – fascinated by criminals and horoscope signatures of crime. When she died, I found her horoscope in the notes she left to me. Her Sun was at 19° Libra.

Political Speeches – Their Timing and Impact

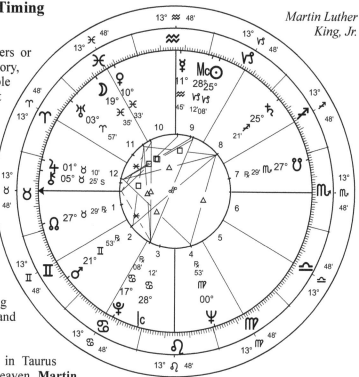

Martin Luther King, Jr.

If we consider speeches by leaders or influential personalities in history, we note that they carry a double astrological message. An important speech will be reflected in the horoscope of the orator (natally as 'potential' and by transit, progression and direction), as well as in the transits in the sky at the moment of the speech, which will show its key themes, impact and place in history. Essentially, a speech is of its time and made by those seen to shape the times (even if the rhetoric is written or fine-tuned by others). So, what can we learn of astrology in action during historically important speeches and interviews?

With the Ascendant and Jupiter in Taurus and the Sun on a Capricorn Midheaven, **Martin Luther King, Jr.** (natal chart above) gave an address on the steps of the Lincoln Memorial on 28 August 1963 that had a monetary tone:

> We have come to our nation's capital to cash a cheque. When the architects of our republic wrote the magnificent words of the Constitution… they were signing a promissory note… But we refuse to believe that the bank of justice is bankrupt… We have come to cash this cheque, a cheque that will give us upon demand the riches of freedom and the security of justice.

It's no surprise that Neptune appears by transit, progression or direction when people reveal the romantic longings, ideals and dreams composed in their natal charts. King's soaring, virtuous and rhythmic 'I Have a Dream' speech – addressing his hope of ending racial segregation and letting go of discrimination, anger and bitterness – was delivered when TR Neptune crossed his Descendant at 13° Scorpio, and his Sun had just progressed/directed into the sign of Pisces.

The True Essence of Libra
A meeting of minds (Gemini Sun) and the coming together of both sides for peace (Libra

Rising) were the main themes of charismatic John F. Kennedy's inaugural address on 20 January 1961, a time of TR Pluto in Virgo squaring his Sun in Gemini. He asked that:

> Both sides begin anew the quest for peace… [but] we dare not tempt them with weakness… [Remembering that] civility is not a sign of weakness… Let us never negotiate out of fear. But let us never fear to negotiate… Let both sides join in creating a new endeavour – not a new balance of power, but a new world of law – where the strong are just, and the weak secure, and the peace preserved.

That speech, given when transiting Mars was *retrograde* in nationalistic, patriotic Cancer, included his famous reversal: 'Ask not what your country can do for you; ask what you can do for your country,' also revealing his natal Saturn conjunct his Cancer MC.

As a mediator to warring sides, Libra understands the art of diplomatic negotiation and arbitration. But Libra knows that the concept of compromise is overrated: no one gets what they really want. (Jimmy Carter – Sun in Libra and Libra Rising –

once said, 'Unless both sides win, no agreement can be permanent.') Upon closer inspection, cardinal Libra has an agenda. It seeks agreement through the full acceptance of its needs by the other. At first, it attempts to have those needs met through the line of least resistance – gentle, logical persuasion and charm (Libra sends you to hell in such a way that you actually look forward to the trip). But when faced with stubborn obstruction or an impasse, Libra reveals itself to be an iron fist in a velvet glove by sending in the troops.

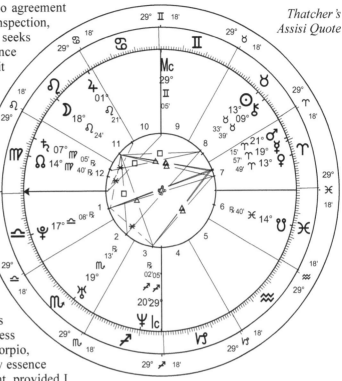

Thatcher's Assisi Quote

Former British Prime Minister Margaret Thatcher was born with a Sun–Mercury conjunction in Libra and Mars in that sign as well. Although her remark that 'the lady's not for turning' speaks of the firmness and inflexibility of Saturn rising in Scorpio, many of her remarks convey the very essence of Libra: 'I am extraordinarily patient, provided I get my own way in the end' and 'I don't mind how much my ministers talk, so long as they do what I say.' Politician Roy Jenkins said, 'She does have the advantage of being almost totally impervious to how much she offends other people.' Upon her **arrival at Downing Street as Prime Minister** on 4 May 1979 (chart above, set for the time of the following words), this Libran paraphrased another Libran, St Francis of Assisi:

> Where there is discord, may we bring harmony.
> Where there is error, may we bring truth.
> Where there is doubt, may we bring faith.
> And where there is despair, may we bring hope.

It was not to be. After the speech, she walked into Number 10 and 0° Libra was rising and, although Jupiter had returned to its position in the UK's 1801 Chart, Mercury was conjunct Mars in Aries and both were opposed by Pluto in Libra. Over the next eleven years, Thatcher would go to war against Argentina and do battle with the miners, the labour unions, the IRA and members of her own cabinet. Libra attempts resolution and reconciliation and aims for a course of action that's free from strife, but this sign is usually found at the heart of ongoing conflict – where it's needed and where it is most effective.

Rivers of Blood

Pluto addresses the unspeakable; it unearths buried information (be it treasure or toxic waste), broaches the taboos of sex and politics, and satirizes its target with an uncompromising, irrevocable candour.

When British politician Enoch Powell took to the stage at 2:30 p.m. on 20 April 1968 in Birmingham (Mars on the MC and Mercury in Aries quincunx Uranus), he delivered his infamous **'Rivers of Blood' speech** (chart overleaf, top) and spoke with the full power of someone with a politically aware Scorpio MC and inflammatory Mercury conjunct Pluto in Gemini (and at a time when TR Neptune was retrograding back towards his natal MC).

Powell acted as a mouthpiece of Pluto by prophesying a total transformation of England, and he stirred up people's fears by speaking openly on an area that the establishment wanted to remain hidden and unspoken (Pluto).

Following anti-discrimination laws and legislation introduced earlier that year which extended immigration rights to Commonwealth nations (including citizens from the Caribbean and India),

Powell gave a provocative speech that addressed his concerns over mass immigration. It was to be the defining moment of his career.

> We must be mad, literally mad, as a nation to be permitting the annual influx of some 50,000 dependants… It is like watching a nation busily engaged in heaping up its own funeral pyre… As I look ahead, I am filled with foreboding; like the Roman, I seem to see 'the River Tiber foaming with much blood'.

On the day of the speech, stationary Jupiter in Leo (exactly square to Neptune in Scorpio) assured much publicity, and the fear of public condemnation resulted in Powell's immediate removal from office. This, in turn, incited workers – who felt that their livelihoods were under threat from immigrants – to strike in protest.

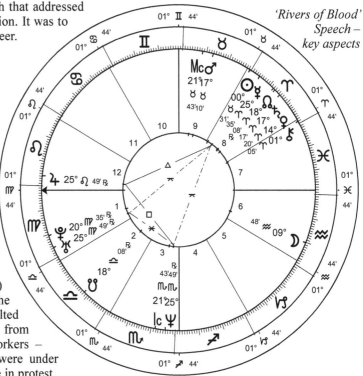

'Rivers of Blood' Speech – key aspects

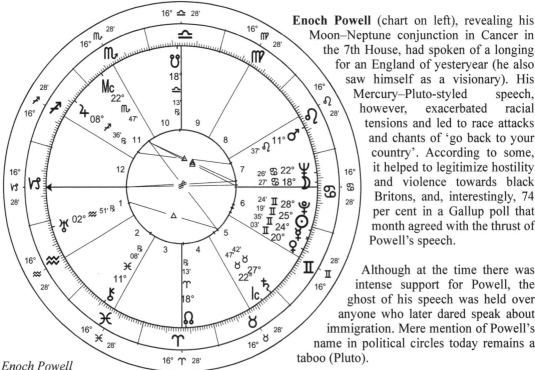

Enoch Powell

Enoch Powell (chart on left), revealing his Moon–Neptune conjunction in Cancer in the 7th House, had spoken of a longing for an England of yesteryear (he also saw himself as a visionary). His Mercury–Pluto-styled speech, however, exacerbated racial tensions and led to race attacks and chants of 'go back to your country'. According to some, it helped to legitimize hostility and violence towards black Britons, and, interestingly, 74 per cent in a Gallup poll that month agreed with the thrust of Powell's speech.

Although at the time there was intense support for Powell, the ghost of his speech was held over anyone who later dared speak about immigration. Mere mention of Powell's name in political circles today remains a taboo (Pluto).

Noble Mansions

Jawaharlal Nehru's **'Tryst with Destiny' speech** (chart on right, set for midnight), on the eve of his becoming Prime Minister to a newly **independent India** (around midnight of 14–15 August 1947), captured the spirit of determination and triumph worthy of the statesman's fixed Leo–Scorpio horoscope and his people's hundred-year struggle for freedom: 'Long years ago we made a tryst with destiny and now the time comes when we shall redeem our pledge.'

At an exact Saturn–Pluto conjunction in Leo, it was time for India to separate and form a new alliance with its autocratic, colonial father, whose empire was now fading. India, once the jewel in Queen Victoria's crown, was being reborn as a self-ruling republic at this 'solemn moment', when: 'The soul of a nation, long suppressed, finds utterance… The responsibility rests upon this assembly, a sovereign body representing the sovereign people of India.'

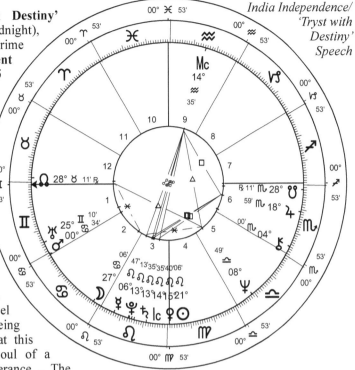

India Independence/ 'Tryst with Destiny' Speech

Jawaharlal Nehru

Mahatma Gandhi (Moon in Leo and possibly Scorpio Rising) may have been the spiritual father of India, but **Nehru** (chart on left) was the patriarch of the nation and, along with his dynasty, wrote the script and shaped the drama of a politically unstable and violent India for decades to come. Both Nehru and his wilful daughter, Indira, were born with Leo Rising and a Scorpio Sun near the IC. Leo and Scorpio hold on to rank and power, and may *only* trust their family (Scorpio–IC). In his speech, Nehru said, 'We have to build the noble mansion of free India where all her children may dwell.'

Independent but partitioned India (with more than a 1000 languages and dialects at that time) arrived with 0° Gemini Rising and the IC flanked by five planets in Leo, most of which were in square to Jupiter in Scorpio. Much of Nehru's legacy rests in his development of educational institutions and universal primary education (Gemini–Leo, 3rd House).

When **Diana, Princess of Wales** (chart on right) said, 'There were three of us in this marriage, so it was a bit crowded,' she was confirming the state of her ill-fated soap-opera union. She was also depicting her horoscope's dramatic T-square: Moon opposite Uranus (plus Mars) and both square Venus. Each of these planets could, in its own way, describe all three players in the love triangle. For instance, Diana's Moon in Aquarius indicates the troubled kindergarten teacher in need of affection, the aloof husband unable to provide emotional comfort, and the other woman/ best friend of Charles.

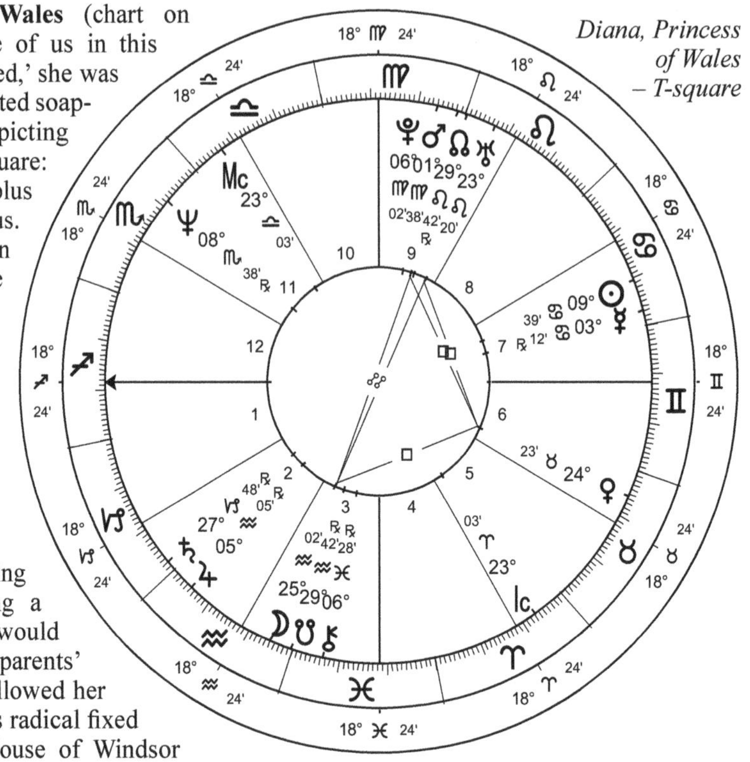

While all three were committing adultery, Diana was following a self-destructive course that would see her replicate her own parents' acrimonious divorce (which followed her mother's affair). And using this radical fixed T-square to blow open the House of Windsor and its Pandora's box of secrets, the interview on

Diana, Princess of Wales – T-square

the BBC's *Panorama* TV show would prove how ill-suited she was to the royal role expected of her by the establishment.

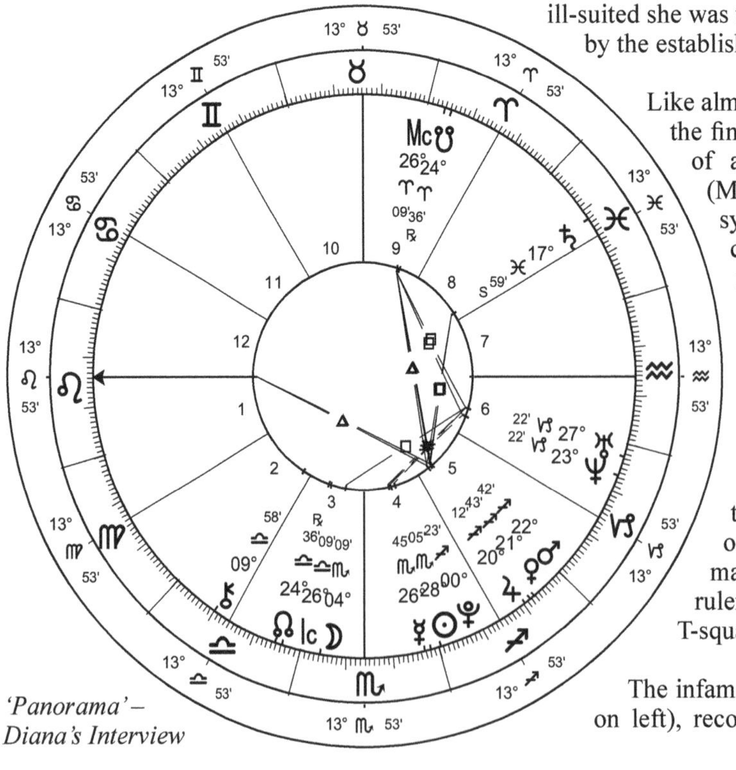

Like almost everything else Diana did in the final years of her life, this course of action divided public opinion (Moon–Uranus). Many had sympathy for a vulnerable victim caged and abused by a heartless monarchy, while others felt scepticism towards a loose cannon and arch-manipulator seemingly hell-bent on using the media to exact revenge. Moon–Uranus can also be seen as one cosmic 'sign' of Diana's bulimia: an ongoing cry for help that she described as a 'release of tension' as she negotiated her marriage and public role (Venus, ruler of the MC, is the apex of the T-square).

'Panorama' – Diana's Interview

The infamous ***Panorama* interview** (chart on left), recorded in secret, was announced on Prince Charles's birthday (apparently elected by Diana's astrologer, with TR Jupiter on Diana's Ascendant), six days before it aired on 20 November 1995 (her in-laws' wedding anniversary!). As always, public sympathy was mostly on her side (natal Moon in Aquarius) and, as her former private secretary once said, 'Diana had a genius for knowing, on an emotional level, what mattered to people.' But larger transits were at play that month. It was *her* royal status that was rocked (TR Uranus conjunct natal Saturn, TR Saturn square natal Ascendant), and her revelations and lack of discretion led to the removal of the title Her Royal Highness (TR Neptune square her Libra MC). Interestingly, with MC-ruler Venus in the fixed sign of Taurus as the apex of the T-square, her status could have been assured, but perhaps on some level the emotional volatility of Moon–Uranus wanted to shatter a rigid system (the monarchy) and, in so doing, sabotaged her very wish to remain royal.

The chart for the interview reveals the public airing of royal/celebrity dirty laundry (Sagittarius, Leo, Scorpio). The target of Diana's revenge is clear: the links to Charles's natal chart are numerous, particularly Scorpio/Pluto ones. Both charts have the Sun in Scorpio and Leo Rising, the programme's Ascendant is close to Charles's Pluto, the Moon in Scorpio in the 3rd is conjunct his Mercury, the Sun is on his Chiron (which is conjunct his natal Sun, highlighting his supposed 'unfitness' to be king). Pluto is 0° Sagittarius and the Descendant is a degree from the position of TR Jupiter when Diana was killed less than two years later. The trio of planets in Sagittarius is crowded into the 5th House ('three of us in this marriage') and is close to Diana's Ascendant (and Charles's Mars), suggesting the publicity and indiscretion in speaking about the infidelities, and the private regret she would later feel over giving the interview.

Pivotal Moments

The following three cases show astrology in action, with reference to a specific time in history.

The Kennedys of Asia:
The Fall of the Marcos Regime

On 7 February 1986, after twenty years of bleeding the country dry, after abolishing its constitution and declaring martial law, Ferdinand Marcos of the Philippines held the first open election in years. Despite the resounding victory of Corazon Aquino, the widow of his former political rival, Marcos declared himself the winner. For two weeks he refused to concede defeat.

The culmination of a three-year people's revolution saw hundreds of thousands of citizens march through Manila between 22 and 25 February to call for Marcos's removal from office. Suddenly he and his queenly wife Imelda faced the end of their 'conjugal dictatorship' of the Philippines and fled their palace in Manila. Offered asylum in the USA by President Reagan, they were helicoptered to Guam and then on to Hawaii with an entourage of eighty. With a gift for expressing the dramatic in song, Imelda was said to have warbled 'New York, New York' all the way into exile.

The **Marcos Flight** chart (below) – one day after a Full Moon – has two mutable T-squares:

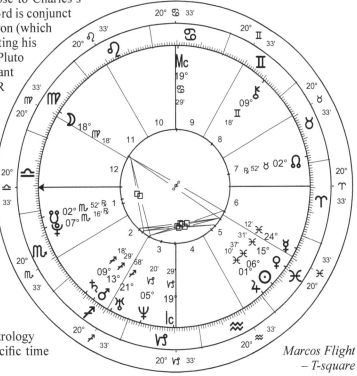

Marcos Flight
– T-square

1. The Moon in Virgo opposite Mercury–Venus in Pisces, both square Uranus in Sagittarius. (Mars is also implicated.)

2. Saturn in Sagittarius opposite Chiron in Gemini, both square Sun–Jupiter in Pisces.

All nine planetary bodies involved are mutable and seven are in succedent houses (the 2nd, 5th, 8th and 11th). This implies great change, unsteadiness and 'flight' (mutable) in areas where energy has been fixed, consolidated or stuck (succedent). This is underscored by the presence of seven planets in Jupiter's signs of Sagittarius and Pisces, linked to each other in two sets of squares. As a combination, Sagittarius–Pisces suggests big hopes and dreams, religious charisma, fervour and elevation, as well as running/travelling/fleeing/escaping to another country. Together they are the signs of the evangelist and the con artist able to sell a dream or vision. As this event occurred at the time of a Full Moon in practical Virgo, the wasteful extravagance of this combination was being exposed. The dream is over, the people have woken up to the fraud and seen the reality of their poverty (Full Moon in Virgo square Uranus, and Moon square Mars in the 2nd).

At its worst, Sagittarius–Pisces indicates abuse from an elevated position – taking advantage of goodwill extended and opportunities handed on a silver platter. The combination has the 'feeling' of provoking moral outrage due to the exploitation of faith and trust. The people of the Philippines were sold an ideal by their magical First Couple – in reality, the 'royal couple' royally looted their country of its resources and felt they had a divine right to rule. This sign combination shows the escape of the charismatic but fraudulent despot/dictator as well as the birth of new hope (Sun–Jupiter) – and, interestingly, it also suggests the huge national longing of many Filipinos for the return of their idols.

When journalists and political commentators looked at the extraordinary, non-violent events of February 1986, the matter became a simple polarization befitting a Full Moon: the Marcoses were an evil needing to be purged by the forces of good (as seen by Corazon Aquino). Even their first names reflect the good vs. bad stereotype: the Aquinos are Sun–Venus–Jupiter (Corazon means 'heart' and Benigno means 'kind' and 'benign'), while the Marcoses are Martian (the name Imelda

derives from 'battle' and 'warrior' and Ferdinand has links to the word 'courage').

The new president's chart has links to the Flight chart, too. Corazon Aquino's Mars is at 20° Virgo (near the chart's MC ruler, the Moon – the people) and her Pluto is at 22° Cancer (near the chart's MC and 10th House). With no prior political experience, she was known for making humble speeches and putting forward the image of a decent, honest, simple citizen, after the glamour and deceit of the Marcoses (note the Virgo–Pisces polarity in the Flight chart).

The seeds of the EDSA ('People Power') Revolution had been planted three years earlier on 21 August 1983, the date of the assassination of Benigno Aquino. (His chart has planets in mutable signs close to the Flight chart's degrees, including the Sun at 4° Sagittarius square Mars at 5° Virgo.) Aquino had returned from exile to challenge the Marcos regime but was shot dead as he stepped off his plane. Immediately he became a martyr to a new cause and his wife soon became the person to run against Marcos. TR Jupiter was at 1° Sagittarius and Uranus ahead at 5° Sagittarius – both square the Marcos Flight chart's Jupiter and Sun, respectively. In late August 1983, Saturn, having just moved away from a near conjunction with Pluto, was at the final degree of Libra – surely the degree that can suggest the point at which diplomacy and cooperation break down. What were once rumblings of dissatisfaction – appeased by the hope promised in Aquino's return – became a series of non-cooperative acts that would lead to full-scale civil disobedience against the Marcos era of intimidation, electoral fraud and the fleecing of national funds.

Political couples are always intriguing, but none more so than the Marcoses of the Philippines. Yet, it is Ferdinand's wife, **Imelda Marcos** (chart on opposite page, top), who is the more fascinating of the pair. Cast and recorded in history as the scheming, extravagant and vindictive First Lady, this former model's antics and high-glamour greed make for fascinating copy.

Imelda Romualdez revealed her personal ambition early in the game: on losing a beauty contest in 1953, she went to the Mayor of Manila with claims of corruption and persuaded him to overturn the result (though the original winner was reinstated soon after). On 6 April 1954, she caught the eye of an obsessively ambitious congressman, Ferdinand Marcos, and they married eleven days later. Ferdinand, considered a brilliant and spellbinding orator, would become her teacher and Svengali, forcing her to study and memorize history and current political names. She would go on to suffer a nervous breakdown and be diagnosed manic-depressive in the late 1950s, finding her role as political wife and the public intrusion too stressful. But she emerged with an attitude change and went on to become a major political asset – what her husband would describe as his 'secret weapon'.

When, on 30 December 1965, he became the tenth President of the Philippines, Imelda was poised to become one of the most powerful and richest women in the world. (His victory coincided with the Uranus–Pluto conjunction at 19° and 18° Virgo – very close to the Moon of their Flight chart.)

Imelda Marcos

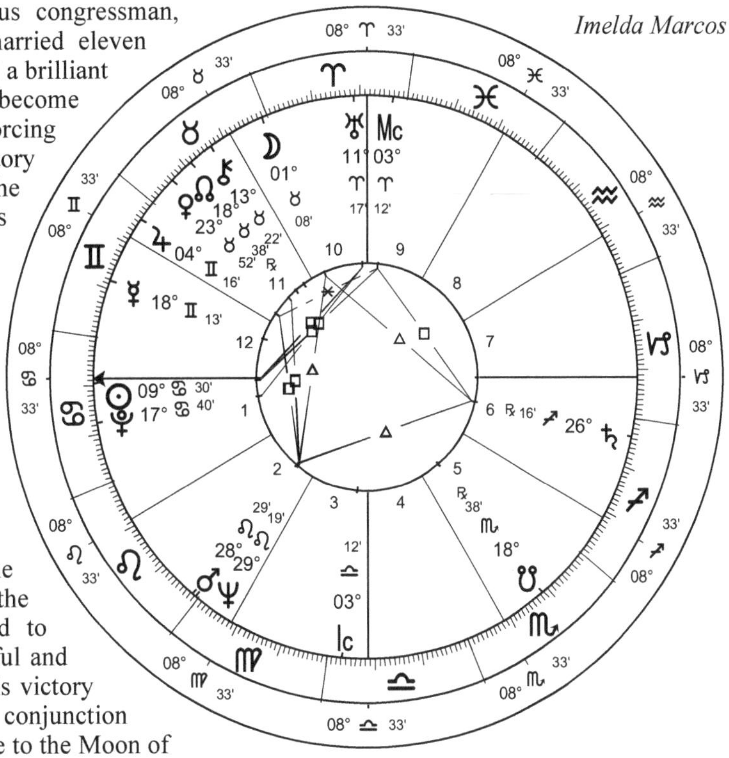

Ferdinand Marcos

Imelda considered herself a caring mother to her people (Sun in Cancer). But with Venus in Taurus square Mars–Neptune in Leo, Imelda's greatest personal attribute was star power. She brought the Filipino people much-needed Hollywood glamour. They seemed to forgive or condone her queenly capriciousness, even when her jet-setting shopping sprees across the world for designer labels were exposed. She and her husband **Ferdinand Marcos** (chart on left) were the Kennedys of Asia and put the Philippines on the world map. Her singing, statuesque beauty and humble origins won the hearts of crowds, who warmed to this Camelot Cinderella.

More than a conspicuous consumer who spent astronomical sums on jewels, clothes and property, Imelda became a formidable political force taking on a diplomatic role to charm Castro, Mao and Gaddafi!

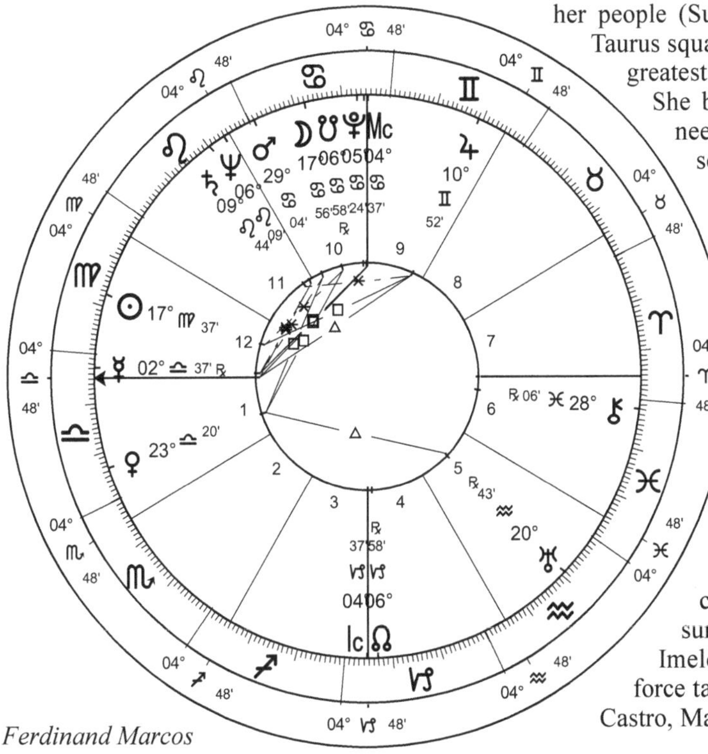

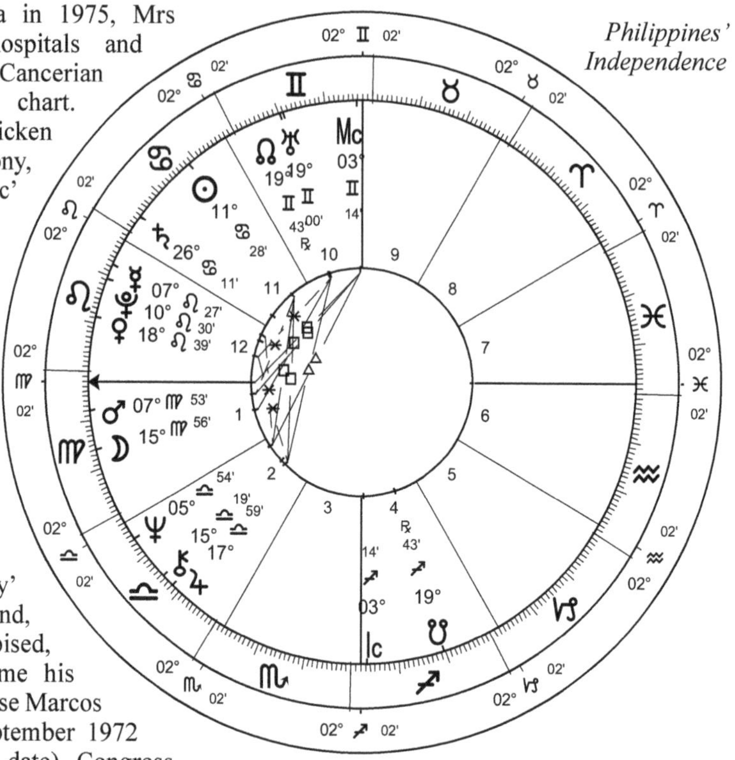

As Governor of Metro Manila in 1975, Mrs Marcos inaugurated many hospitals and cultural buildings, fulfilling the Cancerian and Venusian aspects of her chart. While 'serving' her poverty-stricken people, she revealed, without irony, her unapologetic 'philanthropic' philosophy:

Philippines' Independence

> Never dress down for the poor. They won't respect you for it. They want their First Lady to look like a million dollars.

> I have to look beautiful so that the poor Filipinos will have a star to look at from their slums.

The glamorous 'Steel Butterfly' was faring better than her husband, who was becoming a much-despised, ruthless dictator. Unable to tame his opponents, as an act of last recourse Marcos declared martial law on 21 September 1972 (using numerology to select the date). Congress was abolished and his enemies thrown in prison. On the date of martial law, Mars was at 23° Virgo (opposing the Marcos Flight chart's Mercury) square Saturn at 20° Gemini (opposite the Flight's Uranus at 21° Sagittarius). Perhaps more importantly, the **Philippines' Independence** chart (above) was activated by TR Uranus conjunct Jupiter in Libra (breakthroughs in – or breakdowns of – individual freedoms and liberties), TR Chiron in Aries opposite Chiron, and TR Neptune on the IC and square the Ascendant.

Consider how close the aspects of the Flight chart – reflecting the end of a twenty-year glamorous, pilfering, cruel and repressive regime – are to the Independence chart (including a Uranus opposition and Neptune square). There are also strong links, of course, to the horoscopes of the Marcoses.

Another national chart for the Philippines could be set up for the date General Aguinaldo proclaimed Philippine independence from Spain (12 June 1898, Kawit, Philippines). This chart shows a Sun–Neptune conjunction at 21° Gemini (opposite the Flight chart's Uranus) and Saturn at 8° Sagittarius (conjunct the Flight's Saturn at 9° Sagittarius). This chart has strong links to the Marcoses' charts, too.

In October 1988, a Grand Jury in the USA indicted the pair, who stood accused of stealing hundreds of millions of dollars and illegally investing money in holdings in the USA. With Ferdinand's health in sharp decline, Imelda faced the charges alone and was acquitted on her birthday in 1990 (Ferdinand had died on 28 September 1989, when TR Neptune opposed Imelda's Sun). Upon her return to the Philippines in 1991, she ran (unsuccessfully) for president, later became a congresswoman, and continues to fight numerous corruption charges brought by eager government opponents.

Back to 1986. After the toppling of the Marcos dictatorship, Malacanang Palace was opened to the public and thousands queued patiently to get a foot in the door. What they saw was the vulgar opulence that the Marcoses had once enjoyed – but they were also surprised by the palace's air of gloom and decay. A major feature of the Marcos Flight chart for that February evening is the collection of four planets in Pisces, most notably the Sun–Jupiter conjunction in the 5th House. What is remembered most by foreigners and always mentioned by the media about the events around their exile? Surely it must be the 2,700 pairs of shoes (Pisces) that Imelda left behind.

The infamous discovery (itself an exaggeration, no doubt) was a sign of her extravagance, opulence, waste and arrogance (Sagittarius–Pisces). In her defence, Mrs Marcos later said that she had accepted these gifts to support and promote the nation's shoe industry and keep the economy afloat. Aside from the shoe collection, there were 2,000 ball gowns, 500 bras, and boxes of handbags still unopened. One order of clothes from Rome for $80,000 had been placed days before their departure.

But time wounds all heels – or does it? Defiant and adamant that she played no part in any wrongdoing, Imelda often said, 'When they went to my closet, they did not find skeletons – only shoes.'

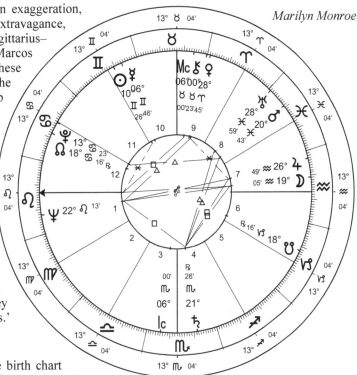

Marilyn Monroe

The Lost Goddess

Much has been written about the birth chart of **Marilyn Monroe** (at right).[15] Marilyn's all-important T-square of Moon–Jupiter in Aquarius in the 7th House opposite Neptune in the 1st, with both square Saturn in Scorpio in the 4th, speaks of her luminous glamour queen 'projection', the elusiveness, the chronic lateness and addictions, and her unhappy, abusive home life, as well as the dream of having a loving family and escaping her 'solitary, suspended state of suffering'. With Venus in Aries on a Taurus MC, she was picked to play the seemingly-innocent gold-digger who believed that 'diamonds are a girl's best friend', but Marilyn's natural comedic skills and childlike charm were blurred by the haze of the frenzied attention that surrounded her from the start of her immense celebrity (Neptune conjunct the Ascendant in Leo). She said, 'I think that when you are famous, every weakness is exaggerated,' speaking her pivotal T-square.

But there's one potent aspect in her horoscope that has not been explored in depth – one that does not, on the face of it, seem to tie in with the Marilyn with whom the public most identifies: her Sun–Mercury conjunction at 10° and 6° Gemini respectively in the 10th House. It is a particularly important duet (a conjunction unaspected by any other planet), because the Sun is her Chart Ruler, and Mercury disposits the Sun.

How did this aspect manifest in her life? Firstly, the identity of Marilyn's father was a mystery, which 'held a hollow, bleeding place in her soul... *a cry that would never be answered*' (Sun–Mercury in Gemini). Two grandparents were rumoured to have 'lost their mind', and her mother was emotionally erratic. It could be argued that Marilyn was born to *make sense* (Sun–Mercury in Gemini) of the legacy of instability and madness that ran in her family (suggested by the T-square).

Perhaps, in an attempt to define herself, Marilyn sought out men to personify this conjunction, each one a stronger manifestation than the last. It began with marriage at sixteen to James Dougherty in June 1942, a few weeks after transiting Saturn and Uranus both entered the sign of Gemini. She wed him so that she could avoid returning to the orphanage in which she'd been placed. (Later that year, Marilyn was told her father's identity, but he rejected her attempts to make contact.) Marilyn and Jimmie were both too immature and argued a great deal, and he often teased (Gemini) his insecure wife. In July 1944, when TR Uranus conjoined her Sun, she began to receive attention from photographers. It woke up (Uranus) her ambition (Sun in the 10th), and stardom beckoned

– but it also sounded the death knell for her marriage. It is – at this first juncture – that we can see an opportunity for Marilyn to live out this important conjunction herself by fulfilling her own life purpose.

But what ensued – while she was becoming a celebrity for her looks (Venus–MC) rather than her talent or intelligence (Gemini) – was a succession of high-profile relationships with older *important men*, all of whom embodied the Sun–Mercury in Gemini in the 10th House.

The list started with Joe DiMaggio, 'Joltin' Joe', known as the *greatest all-round* baseball player of his day. He was indifferent and sullen and wouldn't speak to her, so their marriage soured (above all, Gemini needs to communicate and be heard). Then followed marriage to Arthur Miller, one of the *most respected* American *playwrights*. Marilyn, who wanted to be seen as an intellectual, was dazzled by his intelligence but felt insecure and intellectually inferior. And then there were strong rumours of a dalliance with President John F. Kennedy — again, another prominent, successful man. Kennedy had the Sun in Gemini, too, and was a *powerful orator*. But wait, there's more! He also had a charismatic sibling (Mercury), Robert Kennedy, and Marilyn was said to have dated *both* men (Gemini).

It is interesting that Marilyn stated, to much ridicule, that she considered her hero to be the 'father of psychology' himself, Sigmund Freud. She had so many unanswered questions (Gemini) and sought to understand, illuminate and articulate her true self (Sun in Gemini). Freud's Moon was a handful of degrees from her Sun in Gemini. Marilyn had sessions with his daughter Anna, who had the Sun at 11° Sagittarius exactly opposite Pluto at 11° Gemini, again linking into Marilyn's chart. She also had high-profile acting roles with male co-stars Laurence Olivier (Ascendant at 15° Gemini) and Tony Curtis (Sun at 12° Gemini).

There was a fascinating moment when she lived out a facet of her Sun that was *truly for herself*. It was a transit from Jupiter that reached her Gemini Sun in late June 1953. On 26 June, Marilyn cemented her fame and fulfilled a childhood dream by leaving her handprints (Gemini) in the sidewalk outside Grauman's Chinese Theatre in Hollywood. Being asked to do so is recognized as a sign of great celebrity (Jupiter).

In his book *Outliers: The Story of Success* (Little, Brown, 2008), author Malcolm Gladwell states that success is not simply defined by talent, personality or drive. It is a result of parentage and patronage. Successful people, he argues, are 'beneficiaries of hidden advantages and extraordinary opportunities and cultural legacies that allow them to learn… and make sense of the world in ways others cannot.'

Using the emergence of the personal computer age in January 1975 as an example, Gladwell states that people who were already working in the computer field (born before 1952) were too old and probably already entrenched in other jobs; those who were born from 1958 onwards were too young to take advantage of this revolution. Those ready to jump into the new field were the undergraduates and postgraduates born between 1953 and 1956. He found that many of the key players in the development of the personal computer (such as Steve Jobs of Apple) were born during that time.

Simply put, success is about being ready to blossom at a time when society encourages and rewards that activity. As astrologers, we see this in the outer-planetary transits through a sign or over a planet, which draw out the potential of the natal chart for that window of time. Looking back on a life, we may discover, as James Hillman wrote in *The Soul's Code* (Warner, 1997), that events have conspired to bring our particular calling (as carried by the daimon – the soul or guardian angel) to the fore, to fulfil its function. Getting in touch with our calling is a matter of defining it and being in a time/place/environment that allows it to be nurtured into manifestation. Oprah Winfrey sums it up well: 'Luck is a matter of preparation meeting opportunity.'

The Chart of a Young Girl
Pour forth words and cast them into letters…
For words have wings; they mount up to the
heavenly heights and they endure for eternity.
                                    – Rabbi Nachun Yanchiker

People with the Sun in Gemini are 'born' to understand the power of the written or spoken word, to be reporters and chroniclers of facts and events, go-betweens receiving and simplifying messages. Gemini seeks to make sense of conflicting information and to unite seemingly contradictory aspects of Gemini's nature. Gemini often finds itself in 'foreign' situations where it is misunderstood in order for it to become a communicator and clarify its message.

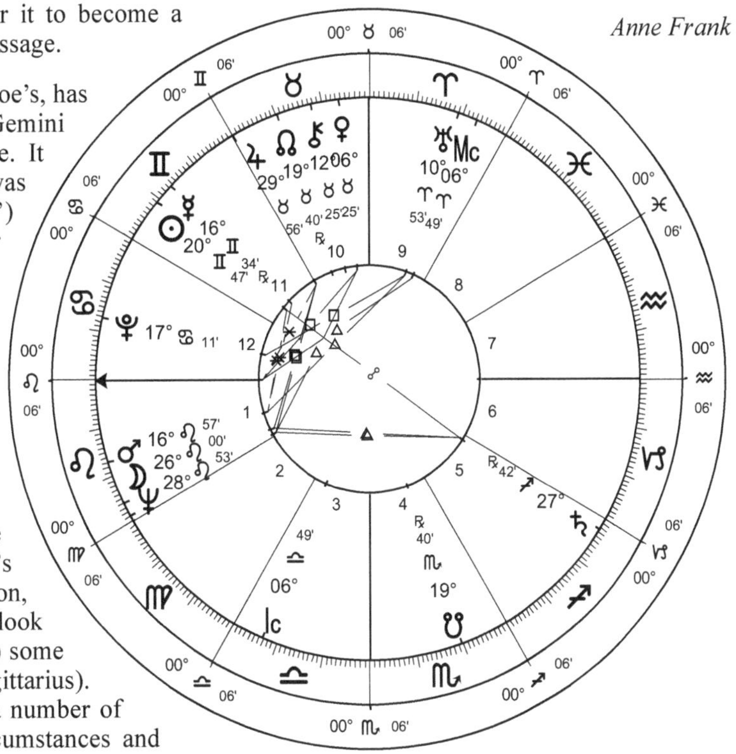

The chart to the right, like Monroe's, has the Sun conjunct Mercury in Gemini but they are in the 11th House. It would suggest someone who was born (and perhaps felt 'called') to speak for/with her group or community. The opposition from Saturn in Sagittarius reveals a potential religious or moral obstacle to this calling, yet this tension (opposition) could manifest as something tangible and lasting (Saturn). 'Life' is challenging her to do something with the information she has amassed; to do more than merely pass it on (Gemini's remit). With Saturn's opposition, she would need to go deeper, to look philosophically, to ask (Gemini) some of the bigger questions (Sagittarius). This could have developed in a number of ways, depending upon her circumstances and opportunities and the times in which she lived.

Anne Frank

But *when* would this calling have been ignited or woken up? Just weeks after Saturn and Uranus moved into the sign of Gemini (interestingly, the same month – June 1942 – that Marilyn married her first husband), this young girl received an autograph book for her thirteenth birthday and turned it into a diary.

It also 'happened' to be just a few months before the girl – **Anne Frank** (chart above) – and her family were forced into hiding to escape the Gestapo. The diary would prove to be a lifeline during this period, particularly since she was forced to be silent during daylight hours. It could be argued that Anne was given the diary *just in time* to begin manifesting her vocation (Sun). Under extreme hardship and severe restrictions, she began fulfilling some of the potential written in her chart.

When TR Saturn reached Anne's Sun on 4 April 1944, she wrote in her diary of her journalistic aspirations and a need 'not to be forgotten', to 'go on living even after my death!' She wrote, 'I think I shall succeed, because I want to write!' Anne had already adapted some of the diary with the intention to publish it after the war. (This period was also a time of Anne's sexual awakening.) Certainly the circumstances and her time in history were demanding that someone 'pour forth words' and create a document of the times.

Anne's personal story, up to her death in a concentration camp, is well known. For two years in a secret annexe, hidden behind a movable (mutable) bookcase (Gemini), Anne chronicled her experiences in order to escape the banality and confines of her extraordinary conditions. The diary was quintessentially Gemini: flippant, joyful, feisty and self-analytical with a searching self-criticism. Skilled at mimicry, Anne revealed herself to be sharp-tongued and easily irritated, mocking anyone who annoyed her. In her father, we see the opposition from Saturn. He was described as a serious, dry man with a strong work ethic, who read Dickens. Showing great restraint and acting as a calming influence, her father possessed a 'self-control almost amounting to self-sacrifice'.[16]

With the Sun opposite Saturn in Sagittarius in the 5th, Anne was unable to play freely outdoors, yet in spite of the oppressive Nazi regime and dogma that surrounded her (where 'God is dethroned and replaced by evil principles'), she had a positive philosophy of life and still believed 'in spite of everything, that people are truly good at heart'. On 27 November 1943, as TR Jupiter conjoined her Moon, she began writing of how oneness with God and nature was now soothing her fears. The idea of God soon became a refuge and provided her with 'a figure embodying the moral authority she would not allow in any human being', in order for her to 'find her way back to herself' and 'obey [her] own conscience'.

The rest of Anne Frank's chart reveals remarkable correspondences with her life story:[17]

- Uranus conjunct the Aries MC: Anne was considered feisty and ruthlessly honest. After her death, she symbolized the power inherent in being a singular voice of courage and candour amid the background of war (Aries) – one voice that represented many individuals and would serve as a provocative, undeniable argument against Holocaust deniers. The MC and Uranus are 4° apart, as are the Sun and Mercury: at age four, in February 1934, following the election of the Nazis and the boycott of Jewish businesses, Anne joined her family in Amsterdam, where the story unfolded. Uranus–MC in Aries can also be heard in her poignant observation, 'How wonderful it is that nobody need wait a single moment before starting to improve the world.'

- The Moon conjunct Neptune in Leo: the diary (Moon) was, in fact, an autograph book (Leo), and letters were addressed to 'Kitty' (Leo). Anne dreamt of being an actress; on her bedroom walls were photographs of movie stars and the family trees of European royalty. She had an ambivalent relationship with her mother, whom she felt suffered like a martyr, and she yearned to respect her as a parent.

- Diurnally, Pluto in Cancer has risen into the 12th: the Gestapo (a law unto themselves in charge of investigating espionage and treason) were on the rise and *on the horizon*, hunting down, infiltrating and exterminating families (Pluto in Cancer), while the Moon–Neptune below the horizon in the 1st suggests a family longing to emerge into the sunlight, but instead cloistered and caged in silence.

- The Sun in Gemini opposite Saturn in Sagittarius: after Anne's father received the diaries in the summer of 1945 (TR Uranus on her Mercury), he overcame many obstacles to get the book published and, indeed, fought battles in the years ahead to prove their authenticity.

Neptune is strongly placed in the charts of writers who connect to the parts of us all that are profound, unfathomable, immeasurable and eternal. Irrespective of the reader's age, creed or experience, the writings of Neptunian authors seep into mass consciousness. The work shares an understanding of the *fragility of the human condition*, as well as its enduring strength in the face of suffering. The sadness that hits the reader of Anne Frank's diary is that we know what Anne couldn't possibly know: she wouldn't survive. The book is, in effect, an unfinished symphony.

SYC: DIY

In the final part of this section, let's look at a couple of charts and some lengthy quotes from or about the owner of the horoscope. In each case, which areas of the horoscope do you think are being described? First up are quotes from the late stand-up comedian **Marti Caine** (chart on opposite page, top):

[My mother] drank to forget the pain and then it was too late, she was hooked on booze... [Being molested by my grandfather] damaged me and gave me a streak of recklessness. He was responsible for so many of my rash actions, getting pregnant at 16 for instance... My real name is Lynne Stringer and Lynne is different to Marti Caine. Marti is arrogant and pushy, the one that gets me into trouble. She's the one that opens her mouth and says the wrong thing. I'm aware when she takes over. It's conscious schizophrenia because the face alters and the chin comes forwards. Marti Caine is infinitely more aggressive than I am and she's saved my bacon a lot of times.
        – Marti Caine in the *Daily Mail*,
                19 August 1995

My confidence is totally on the surface. I sometimes feel the softness I inherited from my mother and I have to hide it deliberately because I don't want to be crushed. You can bleed for people and my mother did. She took on the worries of the world... I'm always

grateful for my tough childhood… So many people in show business come from a deprived background you've got to laugh or you'd go mad. Adversity breeds either comedy or bitterness.
– Marti Caine in the *Daily Mail*, 6 November 1995

The next set belongs to actress **Stephanie Cole** (chart below):

I admire [Stephanie's] enthusiasm and curiosity about things… [During *Tenko*] she was very funny, witty, dry; and passionate about her work. But she had a very short temper if people weren't as professional as she was… She was meticulous on detail – I remember how she relished her character's greased-back hair, yellowing teeth and sores around the nose! It didn't matter how unattractive she looked as long as it was authentic.
– Friend Veronica Roberts, *c.*1995

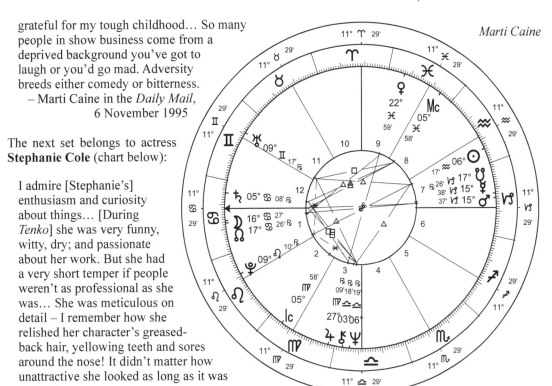

Marti Caine

I was lucky, because I had some fire inside me that made me fight the injustices… I think if anything could drive me really mad it would be to find myself again in a place or a situation of deep injustice about which I could do nothing… I'm an optimist, a fantasist and an idealist, which is not a frightfully realistic combination. That is to say, I'm very practical, and have my feet on the ground, except where matters of the heart are concerned. Ever since I was a child, I would weave dreams and fantasies around people… I absolutely believed, despite many contradictions to the contrary, that marriage was wonderful and that everybody always lived happily ever after.
– Stephanie Cole in her autobiography, *A Passionate Life*, Hodder and Stoughton, 1998

Stephanie Cole

In this section, I'll start with some basic 'worksheet' information derived from the approach introduced in this book, and then go further by presenting five short astrological biographies. These profiles blend biographical information with astrological significators in an attempt to focus on one or two areas of the person's life.

Following my lengthy profile on Barack Obama, I have written about the lives of four fascinating women in accordance with my dedication at the front of the book. These are all profiles of women whose life stories, temperaments and horoscopes have intrigued me. I've greatly enjoyed researching them.

The following worksheet is a checklist – a way in to understanding the key areas of each horoscope and the major drives inherent in its owner. It pulls together everything we've learned in the book so far.

Let's keep a look out for:

- The general distribution of the planets.
- Imbalances in modes or elements.
- Clusters of planets in signs or houses.
- Planets that are strongly placed in the horoscope.
- Major aspects and configurations.

And we'll play detective by looking for planetary overtones and confirmation in biography.

I have included only the major aspects in the horoscope wheels, although there are times when I refer to minor aspects such as the quincunx. And opposite, I've outlined the key parts of the worksheet that precedes each biography.

Five Extended Profiles

The profiles begin with a piece I wrote on **Barack Obama** in late 2008, after he was elected President of the USA. I have included it here as an example of how to take a handful of major chart factors while exploring biography in some detail, and then watch the chart come alive. The four profiles that follow are shorter – often focusing on a couple of key overtones or aspects.

- **Tammy Faye Bakker** – the tale of how the one-time televangelist moved from being a figure of fun to falling from grace, only to re-emerge a tv personality before fighting a brave battle against cancer.

- **Irene Cara** – the fascinating story of a triple threat talent who shone brightly as a singer, songwriter and actress but who, at the height of her career, experienced the ugly side of fame.

- **Mary Tyler Moore** – a personal look at America's comedy sweetheart who became a symbol of the 70s independent woman and faced numerous family tragedies and personal truths.

- **Martina Navratilova** – a profile exploring the complexities and contradictions of this celebrated tennis champion and gay rights campaigner.

But before I introduce the profiles listed above (along with their chart and analysis worksheets), opposite is the layout of the chart worksheet. This is followed by six additional worksheets of well known women. Full profiles on these women will follow – but at some other time in some other book!

The Worksheet

	Cardinal	Fixed	Mutable
Fire			
Earth	*Listed here are the main nine points (Sun to Saturn plus the ASC and MC) with the outer planets in brackets*		
Air			
Water			

Chart Ruler

Sun Dispositor

SUN   MOON   ASC
*Glyphs for these
are listed here and above*

Four Angles and Links

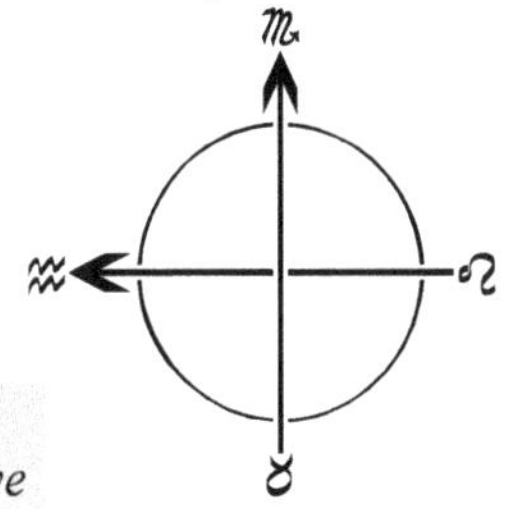

Major Aspects

Listed here are conjunctions, squares and oppositions (to planets, ASC and MC). Orbs are as outlined on page 39, but only tight trines (under 3°) are listed here. No aspects between the outer planets are listed (see below under 'Generational Aspects')

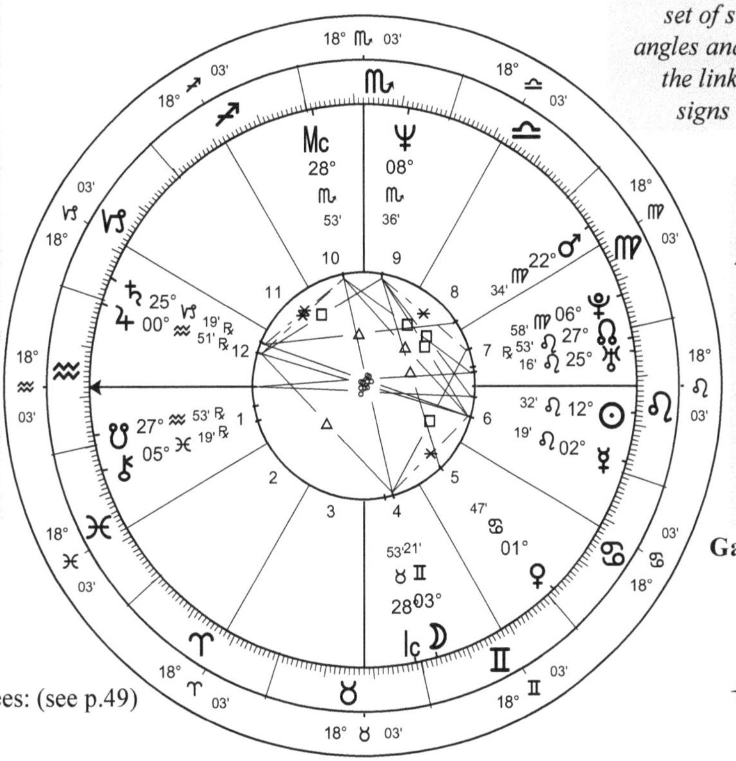

Above shows the particular set of signs on the four angles and listed here are the links between these signs and their rulers

Planets in the Gauquelin Zones are listed below. Those bracketed are those found not to be statistically significant in the Gauquelin research

Gauquelin Zones

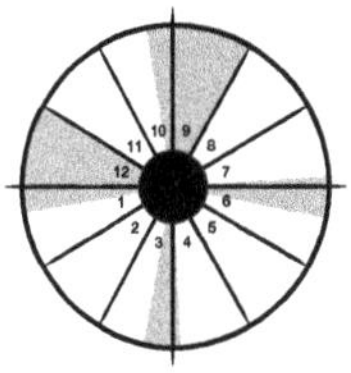

Other Notes
Stationary:
Retrograde:
0°:   29°:
Discovery Degrees: (see p.49)
Unaspected:
Generational Aspects:
Sequential Conjunctions:

*Above is an Equal house chart
(aspect lines between planets – showing major
aspects to all but the Nodes or Chiron – are
shown inside the inner wheel)*

*Any major
aspect configurations are
drawn here*

Major Aspect Configurations

Jane Fonda: The Worksheet

	Cardinal	Fixed +	Mutable
Fire +		☽	☉♀
Earth	☿ASC	(♅)	(♆)
Air		♂♃	
Water	(♇)	MC	♄

Chart Ruler
♄♓2nd/3rd

Sun Dispositor
♃♒1st

SUN	MOON	ASC
♐	♌	♑

Four Angles and Links

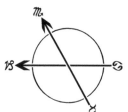

Major Aspects

☉□♄
☽☍♂
☽□MC
♀□♆
♃☍♇
♃☌ASC
♄☍♆
♄△♇
♇☌DSC

Cardinal and Fixed. Earth and Water.
ASC ruler ♄△♇ (MC co-ruler). DSC ruler ☽□MC
DSC ruler ☽☍♂ (MC co-ruler)
MC co-ruler ♇☌DSC

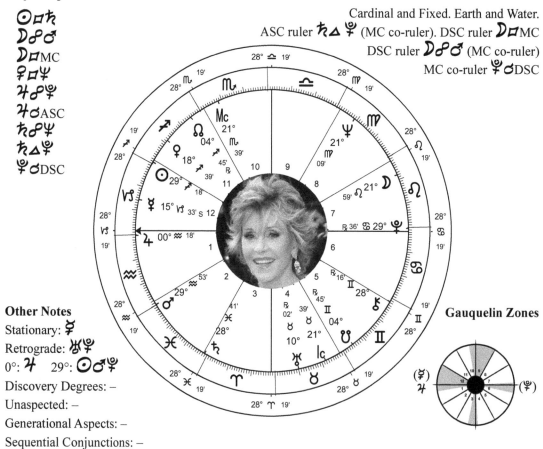

Other Notes
Stationary: ♀
Retrograde: ♅♇
0°: ♃   29°: ☉♂♇
Discovery Degrees: –
Unaspected: –
Generational Aspects: –
Sequential Conjunctions: –

Gauquelin Zones

(☿)
♃ ⸺ (♇)

Major Aspect Configurations

Leona Helmsley: The Worksheet

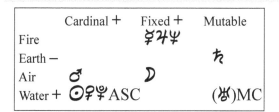

	Cardinal +	Fixed +	Mutable
Fire		☿♃♇	
Earth −			♄
Air	♂	☽	
Water +	☉♀♆ASC		(♅)MC

Chart Ruler
☽♒7th

Sun Dispositor
☽♒7th

SUN	MOON	ASC
♋	♒	♋

Four Angles and Links

Cardinal and Mutable. Earth and Water.
ASC ruler ☽☍♃♆ (MC rulers)
MC co-ruler ♃♂♆ (MC co-ruler)
MC co-ruler ♆♂☿ (IC ruler)

Major Aspects

☉♂♀
☉♂♇
☉♂ASC
☽☍♃
☽☍♆
☿♂♇
♀♂♇
♀♂ASC
♃♂♆
♄☍♅

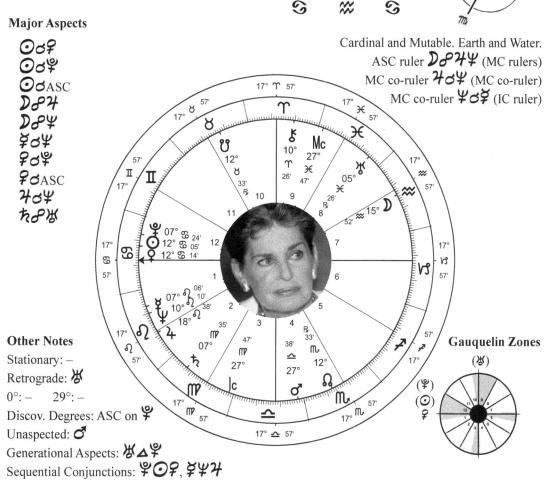

Other Notes

Stationary: −
Retrograde: ♅
0°: −   29°: −
Discov. Degrees: ASC on ♇
Unaspected: ♂
Generational Aspects: ♅△♇
Sequential Conjunctions: ♇☉♀, ☿♆♃

Gauquelin Zones

Major Aspect Configurations

Nancy Reagan: The Worksheet

	Cardinal +	Fixed	Mutable
Fire −		☽(♆)	
Earth		♀	♃♄
Air −	ASC		
Water +	☉☿♂(♇)MC		(♅)

Chart Ruler
♀☿8th

Sun Dispositor
☽♌10th

SUN	MOON	ASC
♋	♌	♎

Four Angles and Links

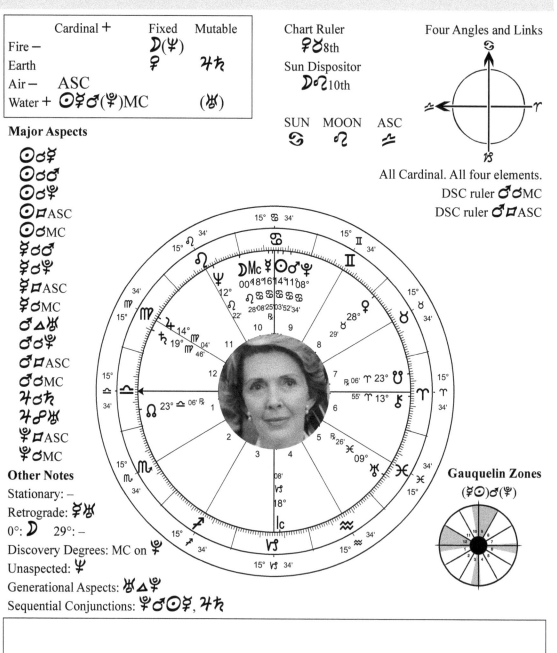

All Cardinal. All four elements.
DSC ruler ♂☌MC
DSC ruler ♂□ASC

Major Aspects

☉☌☿
☉☌♂
☉☌♇
☉□ASC
☉☌MC
☿☌♂
☿☌♇
☿□ASC
☿☌MC
♂△♅
♂☌♇
♂□ASC
♂☌MC
♃☌♄
♃☍♅
♇□ASC
♇☌MC

Other Notes
Stationary: −
Retrograde: ♀♅
0°: ☽   29°: −
Discovery Degrees: MC on ♀
Unaspected: ♆
Generational Aspects: ♅△♇
Sequential Conjunctions: ♀♂☉☿, ♃♄

Gauquelin Zones
(♀☉)♂(♆)

Major Aspect Configurations

The Supremes, Diana Ross: The Worksheet

	Cardinal	Fixed +	Mutable +
Fire +	☉☿	♃(♀)	
Earth		☽	MC
Air	(♀)		♂♄(♅)
Water		ASC	♀

Chart Ruler
♂♊8th, ♇♌9th

Sun Dispositor
♂♊8th

SUN	MOON	ASC
♈	♉	♏

Four Angles and Links

Fixed and Mutable. Earth and Water.
ASC co-ruler ♂□♇ (IC co-ruler)
DSC ruler ♀♂IC
MC ruler ☿△♃ (IC co-ruler)

Major Aspects

☉□♂
☉☍♇
☉△♇
☽□♃
☽□♇
☽♂DSC
☿△♃
♀□♅
♀♂IC
♂♂♄
♂□♇
♃□ASC
♅□MC

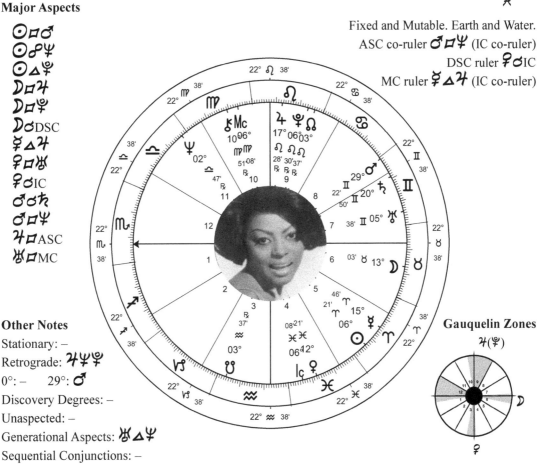

Other Notes

Stationary: –
Retrograde: ♃♇♀
0°: –   29°: ♂
Discovery Degrees: –
Unaspected: –
Generational Aspects: ♅△♇
Sequential Conjunctions: –

Gauquelin Zones
♃(♀)
♀

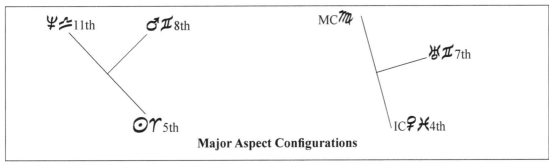

Major Aspect Configurations

The Supremes, Florence Ballard: The Worksheet

	Cardinal +	Fixed −	Mutable +
Fire	♂	♀(♇)	
Earth −			(♆)
Air +			☽☿♄(♅)
Water +	☉♃ASC		MC

Chart Ruler
☽♊ 12th

Sun Dispositor
☽♊ 12th

	SUN	MOON	ASC
	♋	♊	♋

Four Angles and Links

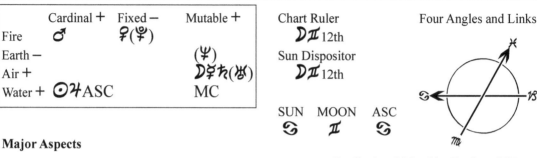

Major Aspects

☉☌ASC
☉△MC
☽☌☿
☽☌♄
☽☌♅
☽□MC
☿☌♄
♀△♂
♂□♃
♃☌♆
♅□MC
♆□ASC

Cardinal and Mutable. Earth and Water.
ASC ruler ☽□MC
ASC ruler ☽☌☿ (IC ruler)
ASC ruler ☽☌♄ (DSC ruler)
DSC ruler ♄☌☿ (IC ruler)
MC co-ruler ♆□ASC

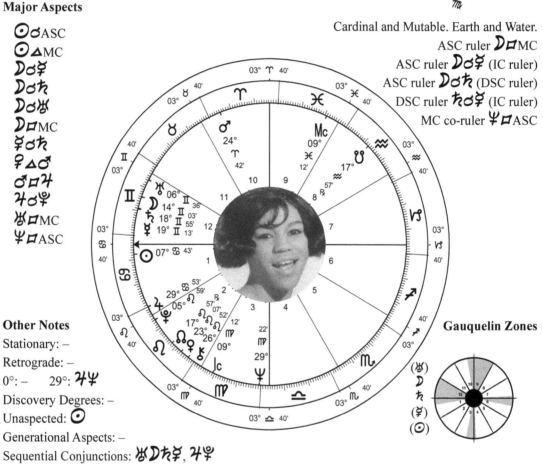

Other Notes

Stationary: −
Retrograde: −
0°: −   29°: ♃♆
Discovery Degrees: −
Unaspected: ☉
Generational Aspects: −
Sequential Conjunctions: ♅☽♄☿, ♃♆

Gauquelin Zones

(♅)
☽
♄
(☿)
(☉)

Major Aspect Configurations

The Supremes, Mary Wilson: The Worksheet

	Cardinal −	Fixed +	Mutable +
Fire		☽♃(♀)	
Earth	MC	ASC	
Air	(♆)	♀	♂♄(♅)
Water			☉☿

Chart Ruler
♀♒10th

Sun Dispositor
♃♌4th, ♆♎5th

SUN	MOON	ASC
♓	♌	♉

Four Angles and Links

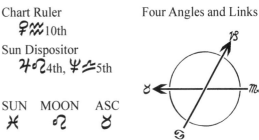

Major Aspects

☉□♂
☉□♄
☽♂♀
☽♂♥
☽□ASC
♀□♅
♀△♂
♀♂♃
♀△♄
♀□ASC
♂♂♄
♃□ASC
♆□ASC

Cardinal and Fixed. Earth and Water.
ASC ruler ♀□ASC. ASC ruler ♀△♂ (DSC co-ruler)
ASC ruler ♀△♄ (MC ruler)
ASC ruler ♀♂☽ (IC ruler)
DSC co-ruler ♥□ASC
DSC co-ruler ♂♂♄
(MC ruler)
DSC co-ruler ♥
♂☽ (IC ruler)
IC ruler ☽
□ASC

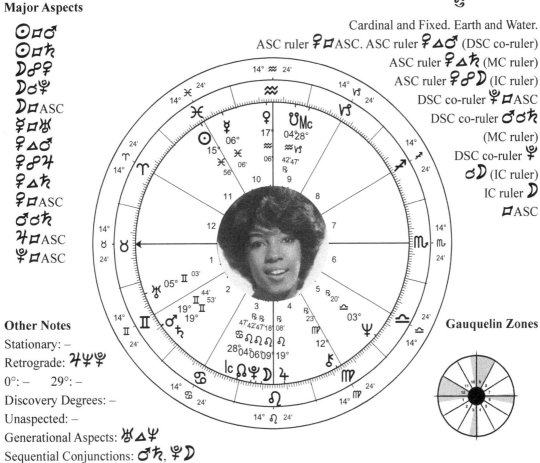

Other Notes

Stationary: –
Retrograde: ♃♆♥
0°: –   29°: –
Discovery Degrees: –
Unaspected: –
Generational Aspects: ♅△♆
Sequential Conjunctions: ♂♄, ♥☽

Gauquelin Zones

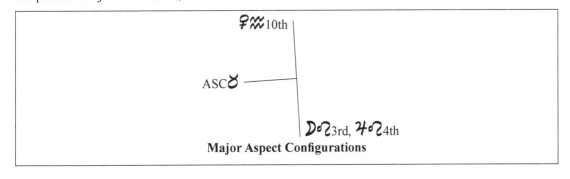

♀♒10th

ASC♉ —————

☽♌3rd, ♃♌4th

Major Aspect Configurations

Barack Obama: The Worksheet

	Cardinal	Fixed +	Mutable
Fire		☉☿(♅)	
Earth	♄		♂(♇)
Air +		♃ASC	☽
Water	♀	(♇)MC	

Chart Ruler
♄♑12th, ♅♌7th

Sun Dispositor
☉♌6th

SUN	MOON	ASC
♌	♊	♒

Four Angles and Links

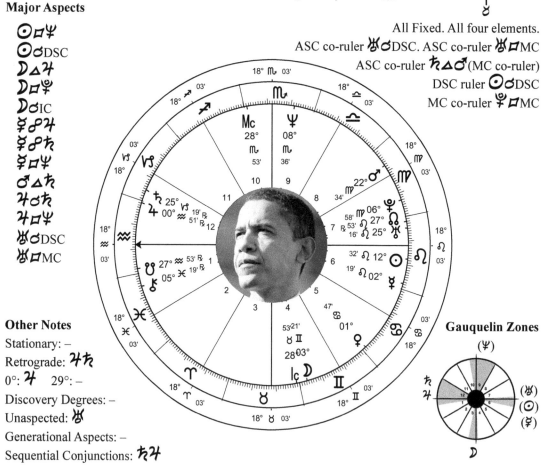

All Fixed. All four elements.
ASC co-ruler ♅☌DSC. ASC co-ruler ♅□MC
ASC co-ruler ♄△♂(MC co-ruler)
DSC ruler ☉☌DSC
MC co-ruler ♀□MC

Major Aspects

☉□♇
☉☌DSC
☽△♃
☽□♇
☽☌IC
☿☍♃
☿☍♄
☿□♇
♂△♄
♃☌♄
♃□♇
♅☌DSC
♅□MC

Other Notes
Stationary: –
Retrograde: ♃♄
0°: ♃   29°: –
Discovery Degrees: –
Unaspected: ♅
Generational Aspects: –
Sequential Conjunctions: ♄♃

Gauquelin Zones

Major Aspect Configurations

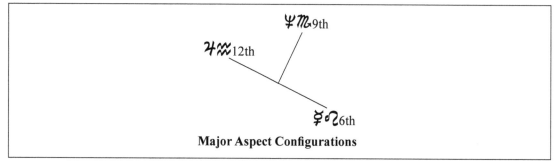

Putting it All Together: Barack Obama

Using Barack Obama's chart as an example, the following is a method – a checklist, a way in – for understanding the key areas of a chart and the major drives inherent in its owner. This pulls together everything we've learned in the book so far.

1. The Distribution of Planets
Four planets are either in the house of health and service (6th) or the house of relationships (7th); three of the planets are in Leo. Although it could be argued that this is technically a Locomotive chart (Jupiter and the Moon are +120° apart), the dissociate (out of sign) Jupiter–Saturn conjunction operates like the handle to a Bucket shape because both planets are the only residents in the eastern hemisphere. They are both in an all-important Gauquelin Zone. These features make this conjunction a highly important aspect in the horoscope even though neither planet is a personal one.

2. The Set of Signs on the Four Angles
The orientation is fixed and the links between the planetary rulers of the angles lead us mainly to the Sun and Uranus, which straddle the Descendant in Leo. Although the Sun and Uranus are too far apart to be considered conjunct, their presence around the Descendant makes this angle the most important of all four. Both rulers of the MC (Mars and Pluto) are in the fastidious, detail-driven sign of Virgo.

3. The Sun–Moon–Ascendant Trio
Two of the Big Three are in Air, all are in positive (Fire/Air) signs. Interestingly, if we take Uranus to co-rule Aquarius, all three dispositors are in the sign of Leo, once again highlighting the important collection of planets in this sign. Using the forecasting method of Solar Arc directions, the degrees between these three planets in Leo should indicate key years in Obama's early life (Mercury to Sun at 10, Mercury to Uranus at 23, and Sun to Uranus at approximately 13 years of age).

4. Elemental and Modal Balances/Imbalances
The elements are reasonably balanced, although Fire and Air are stronger (the ability to articulate a vision). Fixity comes out the strongest, suggesting staying power and stubborn determination.

5. Major Aspects
Looking at conjunctions, squares, oppositions and very close trines (within a 3° orb), the aspects I would single out are: the Sun and Mercury both square Neptune; the Moon square Pluto; Mercury opposite both 'handles' of the horoscope (Jupiter and Saturn); the Jupiter–Saturn conjunction (because it stands alone and is the pseudo Bucket shape's handle); and the three planets on an angle: Sun and Uranus either side of the Descendant, and the Moon on the IC.

6. Major Aspect Configurations
The T-square is rather wide (the Jupiter square Neptune aspect is almost 8°), and I wouldn't usually take this into consideration. This is a fixed configuration with Neptune as the apex. There is a Jupiter–Neptune (rulers of Pisces) theme to the T-square, as Jupiter is in Neptune's (and its own) house, while Neptune is in Jupiter's natural house. The T-square underscores the 'selling of dreams', the big promise of hope and salvation, the desire to serve, and the celebrity star power that we see elsewhere in the horoscope. If we include Chiron, there is another T-square of Chiron–Moon–Pluto.

7. Spotting Overtones
The focus on the fixed signs and three planets in Leo are two important factors to consider. And with the Sun conjunct the Descendant, there's a Sun–Leo theme. Two of the three Leo planets (the Sun and Mercury) are tinged by squares from Neptune, the apex of the wide T-square, suggesting a Sun–Leo–Neptune overtone. A secondary 'subtone' belongs to Mercury: the Moon is in Gemini, Mars in Virgo and the Sun and Mercury in the 6th House.

What follows is a profile written in December 2008 and first published (in a slightly edited form) in the April/May 2009 issue of *The Mountain Astrologer*.

America's last hope.

An embodiment of the American dream.

An earnest, eloquent man whose visions lack specificity.

A politician with grandiose plans compensating for a father's unfulfilled dreams.

A prideful, iconic symbol of male African-American achievement.

An heir to Martin Luther King as the moral voice of black America.

Just Google him. President Barack Obama has been labelled, misrepresented, accused, lauded, elevated and deified on his way to the highest post in American politics.[18] But what does biography say about the man behind the beaming smile and unflappable exterior? What do his own words reveal of his drives, needs and temperament? And where does he fit, astrologically, into the scheme of American politics and the ongoing fight for racial equality?

In the murky, cynical climate of Uranus in Pisces, in which we are all dizzy from political 'spin', is it possible for a politician to embody integrity? Can he remain in power without his ideals being corrupted? And, on an individual level, will our desire for someone to truly succeed and fulfil their promise outweigh our cynical need to watch them prove our suspicions right by falling from grace?

It is said that most things Uranian eventually become Saturnian in nature, i.e. any thing or person on the cutting edge or acting as an instrument for change will, in time (Saturn), either be accepted into the mainstream or cut out, barred, censored or censured. If Uranus remains on the outside then, by its very nature, it continues to have a revolutionary influence and a pertinent function. If it is accepted and becomes part of the fabric of the inner walls of society, it loses its ability to wake or shake up, or to kick-start us into moving forward. Barack Hussein Obama (named after his father) is a conduit for change who has been elected at a time in history that is growing ever more conservative: he's an outsider working in the mainstream. His

own father's vision of Kenya was at odds with the politics of tribe and patronage, and this cost Obama Senior his political ambitions. Elected under the first of the current sequence of Saturn–Uranus oppositions, will Obama Junior, born with chart rulers Saturn and Uranus in a tense 150° aspect (indeed, the chart's closest aspect), manage to achieve the ultimate cosmic juggling act?

As an aside, it is not my intention to debate the possibility of assassination. It is a sobering fact that America does not have a history of treating well its political visionaries of colour: Dr Martin Luther King (murdered 4 April 1968), Medgar Evers (murdered 12 June 1963) and Malcolm X (murdered 21 February 1965) are three such examples. What follows is a profile of Obama the man, his role as he emerges onto the world stage and his place in the history of African-American culture.

Although we can bring dozens of techniques (old and new) to a horoscope, its fundamental components – sign positions of the angles and inner planets, hard aspects, angular planets, T-square configurations – come to life when we hear someone speak their chart. The individual's words and experiences (or accounts from a well researched biography) reflect the chart's major themes and overtones.

With this in mind, research into the life experiences and character of Barack Obama reinforces the following key components of his horoscope:

1. A strong Neptunian overtone.

2. Fixed angles and a Leo–Aquarius polarity.

3. A Jupiter–Saturn handle to the chart.

4. A secondary, Mercurial overtone (Moon in Gemini, Mars in Virgo, Sun and Mercury in the 6th).

Some individual major aspects should also be taken into account: Moon square Pluto, Mercury opposite Jupiter–Saturn, and the setting Sun and Uranus (rulers of the ASC–DSC axis) straddling the Descendant. Finally, a Mars–Neptune theme runs through synastry and forecasting.

Barack Obama, 44th President of the United States
Photo: mistydawnphoto/Shutterstock.com

The Neptune Trail in Biography

Every man is trying to live up to his father's expectations or make up for his mistakes. In my case, both things might be true.[19]

Barack Obama

Barack Obama was born to an immigrant black father, who was an unfulfilled economist from Kenya, and a white mother, a 'naïve, wandering spirit' from Kansas. Obama's early life and immediate family history read like a textbook description of the Sun in the 6th House square Neptune in the 9th:

- A glamorous idealization of the father followed by a shattering of illusions.

- A nebulous, absent father; seen as a lost soul or victim yearning for a better life.

- A father who, to his detriment, puts his personal quest (be it work, education or religion) before family.

- A distorted or unreal image of male figures and one's own identity.

- A 'perfect vision' of one's destiny and a continuous struggle to remain grounded.

One of the first to benefit from a US education initiative in the early 1960s, Barack's father was airlifted from Kenya to study economics in Hawaii, where he took a second wife in February 1961. Barack was born six months later. As the boy's Midheaven progressed and Solar Arc directed from fixed Scorpio into mutable Sagittarius (in the autumn of 1962), his ambitious father left the family to study at Harvard University. What appeared to be a move to better the family's future turned out to be a father's desertion. Soon after, Barack's mother returned to Hawaii and filed for divorce in January 1964, as transiting Neptune edged closer to the EQHS 10th cusp.[20]

Nevertheless, Barack's mother created a personal mythology around his father, building him up to be a powerful, successful and moral character. She encouraged the young boy to read esteemed black authors who wrote of the powerlessness and anger of the black male experience. Barack was introduced to the lives of prodigious black men in history who embodied integrity and stood firm against racism. With an MC in late Scorpio, Obama reflected, 'To be black was to be the beneficiary of a great inheritance, a special destiny, glorious burdens that only we were strong enough to bear.'

The young Barack was to see his father just once more, at Christmas 1971 (a few months after SA Neptune had crossed over the cusp of the EQHS 10th). Obama Senior visited the family and the boy learned of his father's remarriage and his half-siblings. Although he found his father to be a debonair man with a commanding presence, his mother's carefully crafted image of a god-like hero was starting to be eroded. Barack researched the Luo tribe and found that his father's life was less than ideal. The boy was confused by the visit and became more starkly aware of his father's abandonment of familial duties.[21]

Years later, as TR Jupiter crossed his IC in Taurus, Barack took off to Kenya for a five-week trip to meet many of his relatives for the first time.[22] His first autobiography, appropriately titled *Dreams from My Father*, chronicled his father's ancestry in Kenya, Barack's own experiences with race relations and racism in America, and his search to find his racial and spiritual identity. The book was first published on 18 July 1995, as TR Pluto crossed over his MC in Scorpio,[23] and became the most influential account of a search for African ancestry since Alex Haley's trilogy of Roots books.[24]

In the years to come, Barack would describe himself as an orphan, revealing his early feelings of abandonment and isolation. (His mother had sent him back to Hawaii when her second marriage was disintegrating.) He became acutely aware of his estranged father's grandiose plans and unfulfilled life – an all-consuming ambition (a trait he shares) pursued at the expense of the family. Obama Senior had followed a career as an economist in Kenya, but conflict with the then President Kenyatta put paid to his own political ambitions. He ended up destitute and drinking heavily. His daughter later described him as a 'victim of the clash between the Kenyan and Luo cultures and the Western culture and the expectations that were on him' (Barack's Sun in Leo squares Neptune in the 9th). Barack believed his father to be a victim of 'his inability to truly reconcile his past with modern life.'[25]

The Leonine myth of Parzival is one that has been played out, in part, by both father and son: the young, ambitious man (who is fatherless and ignorant of his origins) embarks on a quest for personal identity. He squanders an early opportunity to discover his unique destiny and promise, and must spend much of his life trying to rediscover and reclaim his birthright.[26] It is a myth that Obama Junior appears to have worked hard not to repeat. Unlike his presidential predecessor (Bush has Leo Rising), he has taken pains not to inherit the sins of his father. It could be argued that, if George W. Bush was re-elected at his Saturn Return in Cancer to complete his father's unfinished plans (chiefly, the oil war against Iraq), Obama has been elected to realize much of what was unfulfilled in his own father.

With an awareness of what his father might have been, young Barack grew up with a strong sense of destiny and personal ambition – a desire to will himself to be anything but ordinary. If we look to the present day, his political mission is to encourage Americans to aspire to greatness, to claim their own birthright.[27]

Barack's Mercury squares Neptune in the 9th, so he and his half-sister Maya yearned to experience life beyond their island.[28] In June 1985 (as TR Jupiter stationed near his Ascendant in Aquarius), Barack moved to Chicago and was soon drawn to community organizing in some of the city's poorest districts. Barack became writer, editor and finally president of the *Harvard Law Review* (5 February 1990: TR Pluto conjunct the Equal 10th House cusp). After graduation, an idealistic, somewhat naïve Barack joined a law firm specializing in civil rights and discrimination cases – a move that was to ignite his political ambitions.

Navigating with a Fixed Compass
In Obama's chart, there are fixed signs on all four angles. If we consider the angles of the horoscope to be our personal compass, then Obama's orientation is fixed: unswerving in his certainty and rightness, unapologetic of his principles.

Fixed signs on the angles suggest a framework – a life structure – that is implacable, constant, dedicated and unafraid to be 'in it for the long haul'. There's a stubborn, uncompromising view of, and interaction with, the world. With Aquarius on the Ascendant, the worldview is idealistic, detached and concerned with issues of tolerance and intolerance.[29] Yet Aquarius is a sign resistant to any change imposed upon it, recognizing instead the potential in the group to change its own dynamics from within.

If Sagittarius were on the MC with an Aquarius Ascendant, faith and education would be two avenues for exploration, and the life direction would be less rigid. But with a combination of an Aquarius Ascendant and a Scorpio MC, the individual must seek out *depth* rather than breadth of experience – life is marked more by crisis, such as the death or absence of a mentor. The individual is called on to assume a powerful, transformative role in society and there is an awareness of the gravity of one's calling and professional status. Rather than assuming the role of wanderer or eternal student (MC in Sagittarius), this ASC–MC combination suggests intensity, focus and bravery in tackling some of the tougher, darker issues encountered in society.

Biography suggests Scorpionic themes: an overwhelming need to control his own destiny, to live a life that is, most importantly, *authentic*. With Taurus on the IC, he has come from a firm foundation of dogged principles, a strong awareness of right and wrong. His early experiences and exposure to a multiplicity of cultures offered fertile soil for education and enquiry (Moon in Gemini on the IC in Taurus). This has provided a rock-like foundation to help pursue a purposeful role with conviction and confidence. The calling of a Scorpio MC is self-mastery; to probe, dig deep in order to emerge into the world with an awareness of one's potency (something that can elude those with Scorpio Rising). What can result is a charismatic, formidable public image – an in-it-till-the-end, succeed-or-die-trying image of unflinching courage. It is also suggestive of a 'sexy' public image (in terms of personal magnetism), but there is often an impenetrable guard of one who is suspicious of inviting intimacy. Always a tough negotiator and shrewd political player of the game, Barack might expect life to be punctuated by extreme tests of fortitude that trigger personal and professional metamorphoses.

When all four angles are fixed, a difficulty can arise: one's purpose and direction in life becomes so set that there's an inability to see the benefits of altering course, of obtaining a different perspective. For someone in a position of influence, this can be characterized by a need to be right and a reluctance to relinquish control. It is also a warning to avoid sticking with a select group of advisors who have amassed power and who serve their own interests at the expense of initial ideals.

Leo and Aquarius: An Uneasy Union

Every man is a moon and has a side which he turns toward nobody: you have to slip around behind if you want to see it.
Mark Twain, 'The Refuge of the Derelicts', published in *Fables of Man*

I took a lot of inspiration from the civil rights movement and the way the movement brought ordinary people into extraordinary positions of leadership.
Barack Obama

Reflecting on his time at college, Obama said: 'I noticed that people had begun to listen to my opinions [Mercury in Leo]. It was a discovery that made me hungry for words [Moon in Gemini]. Not words to hide behind but words that could carry a message, support an idea.' This emerging sense of importance and growing influence carry the dilemma of the Leo–Aquarius polarity, which Obama's chart exemplifies, with Sun in Leo, and Aquarius Rising.[30]

How can a man educated in elitist institutions (Leo) be a man of the people (Aquarius)? When an individual, who speaks for the group, becomes elevated as their leader, he is no longer in a position of equality with the other members. Aquarius declares he is a 'man of the people': an Everyman. But this can easily become 'every man for himself' when elected to lead (Leo) the people for whom you're fighting (Aquarius).

Both signs are concerned with authority (Leo: personal; Aquarius: collective). Both can have an uneasy relationship with the father (the first symbol of authority). The difficulty arises with the concept of specialness and ordinariness. Leo is signified by the monarch; Aquarius by the common, average folk. Leo senses its own uniqueness within but can't accept the Aquarian principle that no one person is any more special than the next. Yet the shadow side of Aquarius is Leonine superiority. Secretly, Aquarius will fight for the group but doesn't feel comfortable sitting among the common folk. It may fight for the right to equality, but doesn't consider itself to be one of the crowd. How can Barack Obama negotiate a craving for recognition with a need to serve the community? And how will he cope with the constraints that 'celebrity' has imposed on his freedom to be an ordinary member of society? To balance the Leo–Aquarius polarity, this self-absorbed, introspective journey of self-discovery needs a wider focus – a cause greater than himself. In this, Obama has found his calling, but an awareness of both sides is required. The idealistic socialist (Aquarius) loses track when the leader (Leo) becomes the dictator seeking only personal glory.

Longing for a Saviour

[Obama] is an exceptionally gifted politician who, throughout his life, has been able to make people of wildly divergent vantage points see in him exactly what they want to see… It is his easygoing public temperament and ingenious lack of specificity that perhaps have most abetted his career in politics.

David Mendell

How has an African-American male attained the most influential position in the land? In the course of his rise, Obama has been labelled 'too white' for the black voters yet just 'white enough' for the white electorate. His background has not been that of an average African-American (Aquarius Rising and Uranus square the MC/IC are never run of the mill), yet he has been accepted by the majority of black voters (95 per cent voted for Obama in November 2008).

With Pluto now in Capricorn, the times are undoubtedly moving towards the deeply cautious and conservative, and this has worked to his advantage. His vision of hope (Jupiter in Aquarius) is combined with a strategy to maintain and work within the system (Saturn in Capricorn). It is an establishment chart,[31] yet not without its rebellious aspects (Uranus–Descendant squares his MC). This is a horoscope that seeks to build, consolidate and preserve (fixity), but Obama's message is, in essence, Neptunian: to *recapture* the greatness squandered by a nation with so much promise.

Obama was elected under a wave of Neptunian longing for something better, more ideal; a time of deep dissatisfaction with the status quo. Neptune is connected to those areas of life which are indefinable or unquantifiable, yet speak to our very essence and our need to connect with something greater than ourselves. (It is interesting to note that

Obama's father had rejected Islam and become an atheist.)

If the message of Uranus shatters barriers, Neptune dissolves boundaries by seeping through, infiltrating, permeating all it touches – its reach knows no limits. Like those entertainers who have 'crossed over' into other genres, the Neptunian politician offers something for everyone. In his own words, Obama is 'a blank screen on which people of vastly different political stripes project their own views.' Where we find Neptune, we sense the gist of a nebulous message, a wide spectrum of possible meaning, and we interpret it according to our own emotional frame of reference.

The US has now tuned into his wavelength, been seduced, been sold a dream and is waiting to be swept away. Obama's message – his call for hope – has transcended fears of his Islamic background and the colour of his skin. Herein lies the difficulty: Neptune has enabled him to be accessible to all, even if this has meant 'a tendency to disappoint people in his own crowd – blacks and progressives – by not being more strident in his demeanour or behaviour.' (Obama's response has been that blacks should infiltrate the mainstream power structure and work from inside to effect social change.)

In practice, as he cannot be all things to all people, he is bound to disappoint sections of his supporters, who may feel duped or disillusioned during his presidency. His principle theme of encouraging the US to attach itself to a larger ideal – and essentially to redeem itself – will backfire if the people of America (Aquarius) expect this to be done *for* them rather than take a personal role (Leo) in this journey. (Enacting the Drama Triangle: The Victim, unable/unwilling to be saved by the Rescuer, then turns Predator, making the Rescuer a Victim.) With Uranus in Leo on the Descendant, Obama's message is to reawaken others to the need to change their own lives.

Neptune's transit through Aquarius calls for recognition of a common humanity. Once the transit had made its last pass over his Ascendant in early 2007, Obama announced his candidacy for the Democratic nomination. His *raison d'être* and personal message (Sun and Mercury) were distilled and ready to be sold to the American people – the collective mind – through the filter of Neptune.

A Promise for the Future

People don't come to Obama for what he's done. They come because of what they hope he can be.

Bruce Reed, president of the
Democratic Leadership Council

If we are products of our parents, then their messages, involvements and desires are seen all over the horoscope (not just in the 4th or 10th Houses). But the Sun and Moon, as well as the MC–IC axis, are good places to start the trail. On the face of it, Barack's mother is represented by the Moon in Gemini conjunct the Taurus IC. She is portrayed as being intellectually curious and a voracious reader, traits she passed on to her son. Yet, if we explore biography further and listen to Barack's own reflections, we can hear her as Mercury opposite Jupiter in Aquarius. She was a woman who embraced a different, idealistic worldview, and later became an anthropologist. The Moon's dispositor is Mercury, found in Leo and opposed by Jupiter in Aquarius: **Ann Dunham** (later Soetoro) preached the importance of honesty, independent judgement and a life of service to the community. She opened her son's eyes to the powerful potential of multiculturalism (seen in both his Moon position and Jupiter) and social amelioration, and helped him to recognize the commonality in people. She fired Barack's imagination with stories of inspirational African-American heroes of integrity, yet significantly (with Mercury in Leo square Neptune), she also weaved a fantasy around his father's history and importance.

(Dunham's chart – pictured right – reveals some pertinent synastry with her son: her Mercury–Sun–Ascendant opposition to Uranus lines up with Barack's Moon; her MC conjoins his Mars and her Mars conjoins his EQHS 10th; and her Moon in Leo sits on his Descendant.)

'To encourage a country with only rhetoric is not a promise of hope. It is a platitude,'

countered John McCain, speaking against Obama. In the lead-up to the election, Obama personified a cool, poised politician of conviction (his campaign was unofficially known as 'No Drama Obama'). With Mercury in Leo opposite Jupiter in Aquarius, Obama made speeches that fired up Americans to take on an individual role to change the community. During election year, America witnessed the supreme confidence of a man boosted by an overwhelming sense of personal destiny, a man poised to take up the mantle of power, to assume his birthright. It is this Mercury–Jupiter message of hope that was so pivotal to his campaign, along with a refreshing 'off the record' candidness rare in politicians. It is interesting to note that the 'Yes We Can' speech during the New Hampshire primary (8 January 2008) occurred as TR Mercury conjunct natal Jupiter at 0° Aquarius. Mercury returned to that exact position on the day of Obama's inauguration (along with the Sun and Jupiter).

Erudition and confidence aside, though, with the Moon and Ascendant in Air signs, there's a temptation to *talk* about feelings rather than to actually feel them. (The same can be said for Mars in Virgo, where the challenge is to *experience* rather than simply enquire, report, distil or

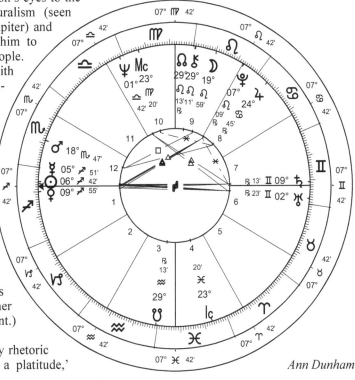

Ann Dunham

analyse.) With the Moon in Gemini square Pluto, the instinct may be to intellectualize one's deepest stirrings or touch upon a cauldron of emotions on a superficial level. (Given such a Mercurial temperament, there may also be a need to calm the nerves: Obama is known to be a private smoker.)

Yet, it is not surprising that the public has been swept up by rhetoric and the promise of a better tomorrow. If we look into the etymology (the history and development of words – fitting for a man with the Moon in Gemini) of his name and the word 'promise', we can see Sun–Neptune, Mercury–Jupiter and the preponderance of Air in his chart: 'Barack' means 'a blessing from God that the individual may pass on to others as a benefit to them.' The word 'promise' originates from *promissum* (a 'pledge' or 'vow') and *promittere* ('to send forth', 'foretell') – an affirmation or a declaration about the future.

Jupiter in Aquarius signifies hope and optimism towards a better, brighter, bigger future – Jupiter in the horoscope is also where we show great *promise*. But the Air signs all have this 'promise' in common, too: before making a commitment or a promise, Gemini must select, connect or unite two separate aspects that show promise; Libra's chief aims are to respond (*respondere*: to promise in return) and *compromise* (to make a mutual promise); and finally, Aquarius seeks to set forth a pledge, a promise for the future.

Obama's pledge has attracted powerful allies, too. His presidential election campaign was given a global platform by Chicago-based, one-woman media empire Oprah Winfrey (born 29 January 1954). His vision was shared and promoted by Winfrey, whose own Mercury sits on Obama's Ascendant. Another person instrumental in Obama's political rise is his advisor David Axelrod (born 22 February 1955), who also has Mercury a few degrees from Obama's Aquarian Ascendant. Axelrod's advice when Obama delivered his speeches was to visualize the people he had met, to 'invoke more humanity in his speeches' by bringing their stories to life (essentially a Mercury–Aquarius Ascendant message). Only Obama's association with the controversial Reverend Jeremiah Wright (born 22 September 1941) has come close to tarnishing Obama's otherwise excellent judgement in choosing associates.[32]

The Audacity of Hope: Mars and Neptune
Many young men… engage in self-destructive behaviour because they don't have a clear sense of direction.

Barack Obama

The themes of service and dedication to a cause are seen in some striking synastry and forecasting that link Mars and Neptune. Obama's natal Mars conjuncts the US (4 July 1776) Neptune at 22° Virgo (which makes a tight square to its own Mars). Natally, his Mars is semi-square Neptune. And by Solar Arc direction, his Mars reached a once-in-a-lifetime conjunction to Neptune in Scorpio in the 9th shortly following the inauguration (exact early March 2009).

The symbolism of Mars in Virgo–Neptune in Scorpio is rich. Spurred on by a sense of destiny, his father's failures and by inspirational stories of men of colour, Mars–Neptune is a call to set forth a collective promise and fulfil his own; to serve and heal; to put ideals into practise; to embody a new type of (African-American) man; to answer the yearnings and illusions of the collective; to rescue the underdog and victims of war and violence. It also warns of sacrificing one's life and desires, or being seduced or manipulated by others.

America and a Setting Sun
Once a president is elected, we can consider that person's chart (or the chart of any country's principal leader) to embody the country as a whole. Obama's birth chart *becomes* a symbolic representation of the US as it stands: the America into which he was elected, as well as the future of America during Obama's term as President. The President's vision, role and impact can be found, once again, in the major chart themes and planetary placements. Consider the Presidencies of Kennedy and Clinton:

John F. Kennedy (chart opposite, top)
Sun in Gemini; Ascendant in Libra;
Saturn–Neptune on a Cancer MC

With Neptune on the MC (in both John and his wife Jackie's charts), it is not surprising that JFK's brief period as President and the promise of a better America were idealized and later encapsulated into one word: Camelot. (In addition, Neptune was

John F. Kennedy

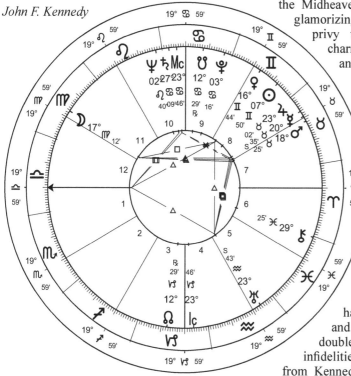

the Midheaven), there's a risk of idealizing or glamorizing his legacy, but we are now also privy to Kennedy as the charismatic, charming serial womanizer (Libra Rising and Chart Ruler Venus in Gemini).

Bill Clinton (chart below)
Sun in Leo; Ascendant in Libra conjunct Mars, Neptune and Venus; Cancer MC

For much of his presidency, Clinton was a public relations expert with a huge capacity for empathy, a genuine interest in people and an ability to make people feel at ease. In many ways, Bill Clinton's Venusian and Neptunian chart matches Kennedy's: both were popular leaders with personal charisma who had mastered the art of the soundbite, and both came as a power-packed double act with their wives. But Clinton's infidelities happened during an era different from Kennedy's: an America fed on salacious insights into the sex lives of the rich and famous (Clinton's Mars, Neptune and Venus rise in Libra).

setting at his inauguration.) Neptune accounts for the couple's projection into the media (through TV) and their influence on the fashions of America. They were a stellar *couple* (he had Libra Rising). Saturn–MC called for patriotic responsibility ('Ask not what your country can do for you; ask what you can do for your country') and put a Catholic into the White House for the first time. Kennedy is remembered as a powerful orator (Sun in Gemini). His America was a time when civil rights were in the process of being renegotiated (Libra), and America called for a cool head during some major conflicts (Gemini–Libra). Upon reflection, the elevated Saturn–Neptune conjunction could describe America's disillusionment (Neptune) with the system (Saturn) following his assassination. The conjunction is also descriptive of *conspiracy theories* surrounding his death and connections to the Mob. Because Neptune culminates (is near

Bill Clinton

Personal boundaries such as privacy had now been eroded. Neptune permeated all aspects of his chart and presidency (and it was culminating at his inauguration),[33] while Saturn and Jupiter (two reference points on our moral compass) are less dominant. On reflection, it appears that personal discipline was lacking (plus an ability to filter personal desires) and this overshadowed the promise of his presidency.

Both Kennedy's and Clinton's natal charts are very different from the Mercury–Pluto themes running through the charts (and Americas) of Richard Nixon and George W. Bush. And if we consider Bush's seismic inauguration chart (around noon, 20 January 2001, Washington, DC), with Mars setting in Scorpio and Moon conjunct Pluto in Sagittarius in the 8th, it is not surprising that America ended up with a president with Mercury–Pluto rising in Leo.

Looking at Obama's natal chart as a reflection of the America he sees and of the America he was chosen to lead from January 2009, we can recognize a dis*heartened* country that has lost faith in its leadership (Sun in Leo square Neptune). In choosing Obama, it has rejected the fractured leadership of recent years and is yearning for a more idealistic father/leader/saviour (Sun–Neptune). To borrow the title of astrologer Jessica Murray's book, we can see a *Soul Sick Nation*[34] in need of healing – one yearning for a spiritual practice on an everyday, grass-roots level (Sun in the 6th square Neptune in the 9th) and a people desperate for community (Aquarius). Its resources – emotional and financial – have been sapped by a political war overseas (Neptune in Scorpio in the 9th rules Obama's 2nd House).

In short, Obama's chart shows the US as a country ultimately responsible for itself – one that needs to be aware of its power to create and destroy. (Leo can be a benevolent source of light or a tyrannical bully.) If Mercury square Neptune in the 9th suggests a country that feels deceived or misinformed about foreign affairs in an attempt to distract from day-to-day matters (Mercury in the 6th), the Moon in Gemini square Pluto is hungry to unearth the truth. And given Neptune in Scorpio in the 9th, we have a country, to quote Obama, that needs to 'finally end [its] dependence on oil from the Middle East... Now is the time to end this addiction.'

The Sun has set in the chart. The monarch – the great power (Sun) – has descended into darkness, and the people (Moon) are approaching their nadir. It is an America needing to be guided through some of its darkest days ahead. The future for America is likely to be a sobering period of reconstruction and re-*establishment*. Yet, there's the hope of an Aquarian horizon; a dawn of collective understanding and social responsibility. (Jupiter and Saturn have risen into the 12th – the cavalry arriving over the horizon just in time.) Obama has offered an example: 'Right now we have a society that talks about the irresponsibility of teens getting pregnant, not the irresponsibility of a society that fails to educate them to aspire for more.'

At best, Jupiter in Aquarius conjunct Saturn in Capricorn can construct a framework and workable vision for the future. The conjunction is a pivotal part of Obama's chart. It is, in effect, the handle of a bucket chart, a conjunction in a powerful Gauquelin Zone and the only two planets found in the eastern hemisphere. It locks him into the 20-year Jupiter–Saturn cycle, making him especially sensitive to this cycle. Not surprisingly, at the time of his election, the Jupiter/Saturn midpoint was at 18° Scorpio – his EQHS 10th cusp.[35]

When looking at conjunctions, consider the planet that rises first (i.e. the one that is in the earliest degree/sign of the zodiac). Significantly, Saturn in Capricorn rises before Jupiter in Aquarius. The conservative building and the restructuring must take place before a new brotherhood of man – a brotherly compassion, a spiritualized humanity – can be born.

If, at the starting point of 20 January 2009, we direct (or progress) Obama's MC from its natal position at 28°53' Scorpio, we see that it moves symbolically into Sagittarius in the spring of 2010, when TR Mars moves direct at 0° Leo and just a short time before TR Jupiter and Uranus ingress into Aries. These developments should herald new initiatives, a renewed sense of vitality and enthusiasm, and provide a target and a cause to fight for. (There is also the potential for violence against leaders, civil disobedience and social militancy.) In addition, by regular secondary progression from his birth, the Sun moves into Libra in the autumn of 2010 (perhaps suggesting an armistice followed by further negotiation or conflict), and progressed Jupiter moves direct for the first time in Obama's life on 4 January 2011.

US Presidential Inauguration (First)

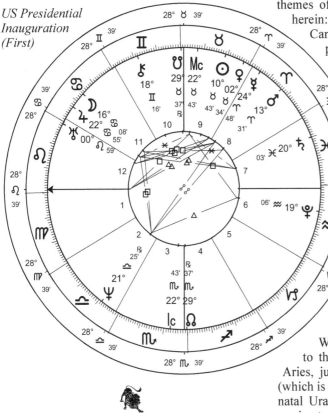

One Chart for All Presidents

Although we can use a number of charts to illustrate synastry between Obama and the US,[36] it is useful to look at the original chart for **the swearing in of the first president of the United States** on 30 April 1789 (see above). This chart would define the spirit of the position, the principles behind the role and the burden of leadership.

Back in 1789, the primary characteristics outlined for the role were wisdom, moderation, dignity and reserve. The presidency called for George Washington to be the 'father of his country' and his image was promoted everywhere (Leo rises, Chart Ruler Sun in the 9th in Taurus) – and, soon after, a national bank was established. In recent times, the presidency has been described as 'less of an office than a performance'.[37]

In many ways, this chart offers more than the 1776 chart when researching key political events during a president's tenure ('It would be the precedents [George] Washington set that would give practical substance to the theories set down in Philadelphia.').[38] Yet a number of the aspects and themes of the Declaration chart(s) are mirrored herein: the apple pie and patriotic Sun–Jupiter in Cancer of 1776 is replicated as a homespun philosophy of Moon–Jupiter in Cancer. The dreams of democracy, equality and independence are also written here: Mercury in Aries opposite Neptune in the 2nd. But with Mars in Aries square the Moon in Cancer, the people expect vigorous leadership from their president – someone who can fight to defend his country.

The links to Obama's natal chart are revealing: Uranus at 1° Leo (conjunct his Mercury) and Pluto at 19° Aquarius (on his Ascendant) suggest that Obama can bring forth some of the original principles of both outer planets, as discussed elsewhere. It is more telling that the Solar Arc (SA) Ascendant for Washington's inauguration chart, directed to the time of Obama's inauguration, is 2° Aries, just 1° off Obama's own SA Ascendant (which is minutes from a conjunction to Dr King's natal Uranus in Aries in the 11th). Both charts are in step to welcome in this dawning of a new political and presidential era.

The Pluto Generations Then and Now: The Emergence of Earth

On his way to the White House, Obama (from the Pluto in Virgo generation, 1956–72) successfully took on Hillary Clinton (Pluto in Leo) and John McCain (Pluto in Cancer). On many levels, his victory is a call for the Pluto in Virgo generation to finally grasp the reins of power. Clinton's 'in it till the bitter end' campaign is characteristic of her generation's refusal to relinquish its position at the helm. In mundane terms, and from Bush to Obama, Pluto has moved from Fire to Earth. The US is ready for (and in need of) a new generation of leadership. To be glib, after the party (Leo), someone has to clean up (Virgo). After the imposed 'thy will be done', the Virgo healing and decontamination processes must begin. And in global terms, after the over-extension and outreach of Sagittarius, some Capricorn sobriety, discipline, accountability and responsibility (the *ability* to *respond*) are called for. Fittingly, Obama's election comes at a time when America draws slowly closer to its Pluto Return (although this won't be exact until 2022).

Each of the Earth signs must build on, temper or make concrete the dreams envisioned by the Fire signs that precede them. Keeping the flame alive with realism, and a need for expediency, usefulness and practicality, is the mission of the Earth signs. Leo delivers fanfare, charisma and establishes a system (fixed) to believe in (fire) – i.e. the monarchy – but Virgo understands that for a system to keep functioning, it needs order and attention to detail. It can do this in a quiet, understated manner. After all the Leo pomp and ceremony, the band marches on – still in tune but more in step. Obama's natal Mars in Virgo speaks of the workaholic, the perfectionist unable to delegate authority; at a time of crisis, Mars in Virgo can be fiddling (with detail) as Rome burns. But with the Sun in Leo and MC co-ruler Mars in Virgo, who better than Obama to outline a step-by-step, workable vision of the future in these conservative, hard-line times?

The Roots of Black Culture

Several astrologers have linked Pluto with black culture and the struggle for racial equality for the African-American community. Pluto signifies both the powerful and the oppressed: for example, 'plutocrats' so powerful that their wealth, influence and names are hidden, as well as the disenfranchised, subjugated members who form the underbelly of society. The path from the time when African-Americans were sold into slavery up to the election of the first black president of the US is a trail of Pluto through the generations. The ingress of Pluto into Capricorn has thrust a black man into a position of power and administration.

It is interesting that the emergence of Obama onto the world stage took place during Pluto's initial foray into Capricorn, but the election victory came when Pluto was at 29° Sagittarius. I was intrigued and began to look for this degree in landmark dates of the black experience in America. Two seemed particularly significant: 29° Sagittarius is almost exactly opposite the natal Pluto of Rosa Parks (born 4 February 1913), and Dr King's landmark 'I Have a Dream' speech, the climax of his March

on Washington (28 August 1963), began at 4 p.m. when 28° Sagittarius was rising and Mars had culminated in Libra.

In addition, Obama's own direct midpoints (which I use sparingly) show the following:

- Saturn/MC is 27°07' Sagittarius
- Neptune/Ascendant is 28°20' Sagittarius
- Jupiter/MC is 29°53' Sagittarius

When Pluto moved into Scorpio in 1983–84, there were positive black role models reaching out into mass consciousness: from Jesse Jackson (his bid for a Democratic presidential nomination was launched days before the ingress) to Bill Cosby (whose #1 rated *The Cosby Show* was first screened when Pluto was at 0° Scorpio) to Oprah Winfrey (who emerged as a talk show star in early 1984).

Outer planetary activity (such as Saturn or Uranus aspects) to Pluto appears to show defining moments in the timeline of blacks and African-Americans in the US. Three other factors feature prominently in the charts of key figures who have either broken down race barriers in America or are symbols of black pride, rebellion and excellence:

1. The sign of Scorpio.

2. Mars–Pluto aspects (a combination suggestive of formidable, regenerative power to overcome suppression).

3. The last ten degrees (final decan) of the fixed signs. The fixed signs have staying power; they represent a powerful force of resistance, and immovable objects; strong willpower; a refusal to yield or go against one's principles. The third decan leads to the mutable signs: indicators of changing goalposts.

There are more examples than space can allow, but consider the following:

On 1 December 1955, weeks before Neptune went into Scorpio, Rosa Parks was arrested for refusing to move to the back of a bus. Saturn at 25° Scorpio was square Pluto at 28° Leo, Mars at 1° Scorpio was square to Uranus at 2° Leo. Parks was born with Saturn at 27° Taurus. (Neptune's transit through Scorpio saw the gradual dissolution of race discrimination by law; in November 1956, when Neptune had entered Scorpio, the Supreme Court ruled in Parks' favour.) But the unsung, forgotten teenager whose arrest preceded Parks' was Claudette Colvin (5 September 1939, with Mercury at 27° Leo square Uranus in Taurus). Colvin first refused to budge on 2 March 1955, when Mars was in late Taurus opposing Saturn in Scorpio, T-square Pluto in Leo. This led to the Montgomery (Alabama) bus boycott.

Uranus and Pluto made a series of stunning conjunctions in the mid-60s (at times opposed by Saturn and Chiron), which saw the formation of the Black Panthers (15 October 1966) and the explosion of the civil rights movement across America, along with the assassination of Malcolm X, born with Mars conjunct Pluto (19 May 1925). A few years later, Dr King was gunned down as Jupiter in Leo squared Neptune at 26° Scorpio.

With Obama's Uranus at 25° Leo square the MC at 28° Scorpio, it suggests that he was born to change the image (MC) of black men in America, to assume a leadership role in politics. After all, America was not electing Jesse Jackson or Al Sharpton. America was voting for a visionary activist, not a militant or radical. As reinforced by the Mars–Neptune connections (Obama's synastry with the US chart and his own SA Mars conjunct natal Neptune), they elected a man of colour – of many colours – integrity, vision and belief who is able to work with (and within) the system.

In the lead-up to the 2008 election, a catchphrase was doing the rounds:

> Rosa sat so Martin could walk;
> Martin walked so Obama could run;
> Obama is running so our children can fly.

Tammy Faye Bakker: The Worksheet

	Cardinal −	Fixed +	Mutable +
Fire −		(♀)	ASC
Earth −		♄ (♅)	(♆)
Air +	MC	☿ ♀	♂ ♃
Water +		☽	☉

Chart Ruler
♃ ♊ 6th

Sun Dispositor
♃ ♊ 6th, ♆ ♍ 10th

SUN	MOON	ASC
♓	♏	♐

Four Angles and Links

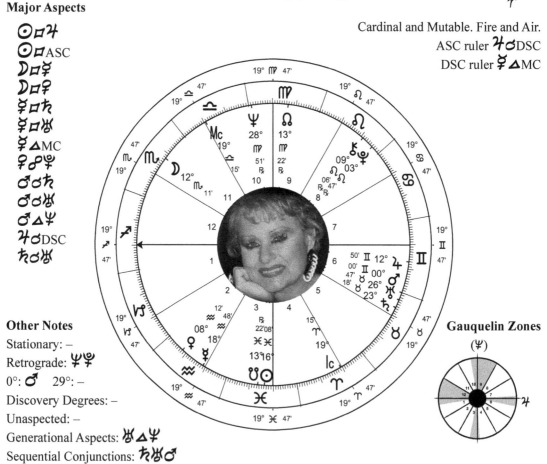

Cardinal and Mutable. Fire and Air.
ASC ruler ♃ ☌ DSC
DSC ruler ☿ △ MC

Major Aspects

☉ □ ♃
☉ □ ASC
☽ □ ☿
☽ □ ♀
☿ □ ♄
☿ □ ♅
☿ △ MC
♀ ☌ ♅
♂ ☌ ♄
♂ ☌ ♅
♂ △ ♆
♃ ☌ DSC
♄ ☌ ♅

Other Notes
Stationary: −
Retrograde: ♆ ♀
0°: ♂   29°: −
Discovery Degrees: −
Unaspected: −
Generational Aspects: ♅ △ ♆
Sequential Conjunctions: ♄ ♅ ♂

Gauquelin Zones
(♆)

Major Aspect Configurations

ASC ♐ ——————
          ♃ ♊ 6th
☉ ♓ 3rd

MC ♎
          ♃ ♊ 6th ☌ DSC
☿ ♒ 2nd/3rd

Putting it All Together: Tammy Faye Bakker

1. The Distribution of Planets
The planets are scattered around the zodiac with one concentration in the 6th House in the signs of Taurus and Gemini (three of these planets are in trine to Neptune in Virgo, the natural sign of the 6th). The most important of these four planets is Jupiter, the Sun co-ruler and Chart Ruler, which is conjunct the Descendant and (just) in a Gauquelin Zone.

2. The Set of Signs on the Four Angles
The orientation is both cardinal and mutable. The four angles are either Fire or Air – very different from the luminaries, which are found in Water (the Sun in Pisces, Moon in Scorpio). All four angle rulers are in Air signs (Mars and Jupiter in Gemini, Mercury and Venus in Aquarius), again a contrast to the Sun–Moon watery combination. Both Jupiter and Mercury (rulers of the Ascendant and Descendant) aspect the angles. The rulers of the four angles are either in the house of money (2nd) or the house of routine and health (6th). The angles have more subtle links that underscore the importance of Jupiter, the Sun co-ruler and the Chart Ruler: Jupiter is widely trine the MC and Venus, which rules the MC. It is also in a (wide) Grand Trine with Mercury (its dispositor) and the MC. In addition, Mars is conjunct Saturn and Uranus, which are the dispositors of Mercury and Venus (rulers of two angles) in Aquarius.

3. The Sun–Moon–Ascendant Trio
Both the Sun and Moon are in Water (and in a 4° trine to each other). The Sun and Ascendant share a ruler, Jupiter, and both the Sun and Jupiter are located in mutable signs and positioned in houses associated with Mercury (the 3rd and 6th), with Jupiter in Mercury's sign of Gemini. Again, stressing the importance of Jupiter, it is the Ascendant ruler, the only planet on an angle, in square aspect to the Sun (both the Sun and Jupiter aspect the Ascendant), and in a tight quincunx aspect to the Moon.

4. Elemental and Modal Balances/Imbalances
The luminaries are in Water signs and there are four planets (plus the MC) in Air (the art of conveying empathy and an ability to express one's feelings through language). Of the seven planets and two angles considered for weighting the elements and modes, only Saturn is in Earth (suggestive of a lack of grounding, a fear of poverty, and an overcompensatory desire for financial stability and status symbols) and only the Ascendant is in Fire (a consuming need to keep enthusing others in her work). Cardinality is weak and her first husband (Jim Bakker) was born with the Sun in Capricorn and Moon in Libra.

5. Major Aspects
Looking at conjunctions, squares, oppositions and very close trines (within a 3° orb), the aspects I would single out are: the Sun square to Jupiter and the Ascendant (ruled by Jupiter); the fixed inner planet squares from the Moon to Mercury and Venus; Mercury in tight dialogue with the angles and square to Saturn; MC ruler Venus opposite Pluto; Uranus–Mars trine Neptune.

6. Major Aspect Configurations
There's a wide Grand Trine in Air that links the rulers of both the Ascendant and Descendant to the MC. The Grand Trine has a Mercurial 'feel' to it, with the closest aspect being Mercury–MC and the third leg (Jupiter) in Mercury's sign (Gemini) and house (6th). (Mercury is technically on the cusp of the 2nd and 3rd House, another house linked to Mercury.)

7. Spotting Overtones
As already seen, this chart has a strong Jupiter signature (overtone) with a Mercury subtone (Mercury is strongly linked into the chart and angles, the 6th House emphasis, two planets in Gemini, and the Sun in the 3rd). Both planets rule the four mutable signs, of which there is a predominance in this chart. With all of the Big Three linked to Jupiter by rulership or aspect (including the tight quincunx), this chart belongs to a Pisces who is more Jupiterian than Neptunian (see the chart of Louise Woodward on page 88 for a similar Piscean signature, but where Neptune is more influential than Jupiter).

God-fearing folk in organized religion – who follow a vengeful creator (whose respect they must earn) and believe in the notions of guilt, atonement, confession, penance, being born into sin, and a 'you reap what you sow' type of karma – would fit the Saturn-type personality, and have horoscopes that correspond to this. But Jupiter's connection to religion relates to the concepts of faith, belief and an almighty, benign deity. Jupiterians with religious convictions *know* that life's mission is to embark upon an expansive quest – until we make the transition to the hereafter and begin another explorative journey.

Evangelists are those who 'spread the Gospel'. Originally travelling preachers, they are, essentially, missionaries who *sell and promote their vision of God* (Jupiter). As 'messengers of good news' (the etymology of 'evangelist'), those who become evangelists must have persuasive personalities, for their work as proselytizers often involves stirring up 'emotional excitements' and convincing non-believers of a need to be saved in time for Judgement Day.

Proselytizing and selling, and rescuing and redeeming, relate to Jupiter and Neptune respectively; both planets and signs are strong in the charts of evangelists. An influential Mercury is often present (the tools to articulate/persuade) and the mutable signs, which are all messengers and connectors of some kind (and ruled by Jupiter, Neptune or Mercury), are usually pronounced.

One of the more colourful characters in religious broadcasting was televangelist Tammy Faye Bakker (later Messner). With husband Jim, she formed a powerful religious TV satellite network, PTL (Praise the Lord), and together they were trailblazers in Christian television (the 'electric church'). At its peak their daily show (the inspirational mouthpiece of their charismatic ministry) reached 50 countries and 20 million viewers. For many years, the Bakkers were the darlings of the evangelical circuit, dining with presidents and living the high life in the 1980s era of prosperity and conspicuous consumption. Then, in 1987, their Jupiter bubble burst and their empire crumbled amid accusations of corruption and sordid sex trysts. On 24 October 1989, Jim was sentenced to 45 years in prison (later reduced

to 18), but Tammy, proving to be the Cher to his Sonny, survived four years of depression, divorced Jim and reinvented herself as a gay icon, chat show personality and host.

As already noted, Tammy's chart has a Jupiter signature: Sagittarius Rising and the Sun in Pisces square Jupiter. And, along with Chart Ruler Jupiter in the sign of Gemini, her chart also has a Mercury subtone. Jim's chart (see page 187) has more of a Jupiter–Neptune flavour than his former wife's, befitting his role as dream-maker and scapegoat, too, as the decade of greed neared an end.

The Bakkers first met in 1960 and were married on April Fool's Day the following year. They shared a passion for preaching the Gospel and saving lost souls. As with many couples who live and work together, their synastry is strongly angle-based: Jim's Moon is on Tammy's MC, and Jim's MC on Tammy's Ascendant (plus Venus conjunct Venus, both opposite their Pluto placements). Together they were a seemingly unstoppable partnership that generated up to $130 million annually for their ministry, and viewers adored them:

> Jim and Tammy had a childlike quality, an innocence and spontaneity that drew the eye and warmed the heart. They were without irony or self-consciousness. They just loved Jesus… There was a vulnerability behind Jim's charm and practised TV manner… But he was the man with the vision… Tammy was the tough, vital spark for the show. Whether she was streaking her mascara with copious tears or laughing uncontrollably at some on-screen disaster, she lived on the edge, with an unpredictable quality that kept people tuned in.[39]

A winning double act, they would pioneer all that became powerful in religious TV. Yet, when each of their TV enterprises became a successful money-maker, they were let go, forced out in a boardroom coup, sacrificed or betrayed (Pisces).

The Bakkers started out at a local TV station for Pat Robertson and created a new format: an unscripted and joyful Christian programme, *The Jim and Tammy Show*. They also began the first religious evening talk show (*The 700 Club*). Jim would preach, Tammy would sing and interview, hug audience members, and entertain the children with hand puppets. To viewers, both seemed like puppets themselves: Jim the straight man

Tammy Faye Bakker, later Messner
Photo © Erica Berger/Corbis

(Capricorn) with a Howdy Doody grin, and Tammy a baby-voiced bubble of energy with Kewpie Doll make-up. Like her heroine, Dolly Parton, Tammy Faye was the girl next door... if you happened to live next door to an amusement park.

If Neptunians fare better on stage and film, Jupiterians are born for TV *broad*casting, especially infomercials (of which the Bakkers were masters) and live television that calls for spontaneity, salesmanship and non-stop chatter (Tammy has Mars at 0° Gemini). On TV, Jupiterians exude natural enthusiasm, promote direct to camera and sparkle with 'personality'.[40]

On 3 April 1978 (TR Neptune on Tammy Faye's Ascendant), PTL began broadcasting 24 hours a day, and that year their theme park, Heritage USA, opened. Theirs was an exhausting schedule and workaholic Jim was always preoccupied with the next fundraising effort to build PTL's latest giant construction. At one point, he needed to entice from viewers one million dollars a week in donations. Everything about the couple and their empire was large-scale, excessive and over-the-top.

True to Jupiter, even their fall was spectacular – and a media sensation (Neptune). The seeds of their dizzying descent began on 6 December 1980 (the day before a New Moon on Jim's Midheaven). For three years, Jim and Tammy's marriage had been suffering and they had agreed on a trial separation (TR Neptune was over Tammy's Ascendant and Pluto on her MC). On that December afternoon, Jim was introduced to a young church secretary, Jessica Hahn. In a bizarre attempt to make Tammy Faye jealous (he suspected her of having an affair), Jim embarked on a brief sexual encounter – a twenty-minute tryst that set the script for Hahn's demands for hush money and a threat to expose him, followed by her eventual public revelations. Was Hahn a virginal victim or a gold-digging Bible Belle who cashed in on her notoriety for a cool million dollars (thanks to a September 1988 *Playboy* shoot)? Hahn was born with Jupiter rising in Scorpio and five planets in Leo, including the Moon in Leo square Neptune, and Venus in Leo conjunct Pluto. You decide.

The scandal – both the affair and the now-crisis-ridden finances of PLT – was one of the biggest media events of the year. When news was due to break mid March 1987 (following TR Saturn over Jim's MC, and his Jupiter Return), naïve Jim agreed to resign and sign over control of PTL to evangelical pastor Jerry Falwell (a figurehead for the Moral Majority). His aim was to avoid a hostile takeover and wait until the scandal subsided, but Falwell (keen to acquire PTL's much coveted space satellite) later reneged on his promise to safeguard the empire, declaring PTL bankrupt and washing his hands of it on 8 October 1987 (as TR Saturn returned to Jim's MC and Tammy's Ascendant). As expected, the couple's demise was a soap opera played out on the news shows across America. PTL was soon renamed 'Pay the Lady' or 'Pass the Loot' by comedians anxious for laughs. The biggest losers, though, were the 100,000 'lifetime partners' who had invested in the Bakkers' time share resort, Heritage USA, the third most visited theme park in the world after Disneyland and Disney World.

Back in March, Tammy had been recovering from pill addiction (her crisis began in autumn 1986, with TR Uranus on her Ascendant, and led to a stint with the Betty Ford Center as an outpatient in February 1987, with TR Saturn on her Ascendant). She received the devastating news of Jim's fling and of the Falwell deal *on the same day*.

Growing up poor and among small-minded folk, Tamara Faye La Valley prayed that her life would be anything but dull. At three, her father had an affair and fathered another woman's child. Tammy's mother threw him out but her decision to divorce drew criticism from critical locals in their deeply religious township. (Significantly, at the time *her father deserted* the family, by Solar Arc Tammy's Sun in Pisces had moved into the Equal 4th House, mutable Jupiter was exactly square the Sun, and Chiron was square the Moon in Scorpio.)

Divorce was anathema to Tammy but, while Jim was in prison, she found solace in the arms of Roe Messner, a former building contractor for Jim who had been involved in the construction of Heritage USA. Tammy Faye split from Jim in January 1991 (when TR Uranus conjunct his Sun). She married Messner on 3 October 1993 (TR Jupiter had just passed her MC in Libra). In a remarkable example of history repeating itself, Tammy's Pisces-named husband *Roe Mess*ner(!) followed Bakker to prison in 1996, tainted by his links to his former

boss and convicted of bankruptcy fraud. Note the literal manifestation of Tammy's Venus in the 2nd opposite Pluto in the 8th.

Jupiter personalities (and those with a Libra MC) are often taken less seriously, forgiven more quickly, and able to get away with *far* more than others. The mud rarely sticks, and Jupiterians often escape closer scrutiny because they come across as lovable rogues, chancers or liberty-takers who 'mean well underneath'.

Public opinion, the tabloids and the criminal courts were much tougher on Capricorn Jim. Jupiterian Tammy, however, was seen as a gullible figure of fun (Sagittarius), and a deeply emotional, tolerant woman who had lost everything, been betrayed, humiliated and vilified (Sun in Pisces, Moon in Scorpio). Her over-the-top fashions and wigs, false eyelashes and a trowel of cosmetics ('Put on with a butter knife,' shrieked spiky comedian Joan Rivers) were all mocked, and even her lavish lifestyle and overspending were forgiven by most ('Shopping is cheaper than a psychiatrist,' Tammy once quipped). Her free-flowing, Piscean tears were ridiculed at every opportunity (although they flowed at every opportunity, too). She was camp, attention-seeking and camera-hungry. But a palpable need to be liked and her fascinating aura of genuine artifice – of superficial sincerity – made her a likeable and popular figure, even more so following her exile and resurgence as an endearing, fun chat show guest and gay icon.

Long before the bedside visits of fellow Sag Rising (one degree apart) Princess Diana, Tammy was hugging victims of AIDS and sharing her lovable dimestore philosophy with viewers. On the seeming paradox of embracing gays as a Christian woman, she often proclaimed, 'I want my life to be a hospital, not a courtroom!' Americans warmed to her upbeat, giggly and infectious 'I will survive' (Pisces) personality, and wept with her in the last years of her life, as she began battles with cancer (March 1996, March 2004, July 2005) with the courage, optimism and honesty fans had come to expect. Tammy Faye passed away in July 2007, just two months after her nemesis Jerry Falwell. Jupiter was retrograde in Sagittarius and Saturn's opposition to Neptune (a death of evangelism?) was occurring in the heavens.

Key Player: Jim Bakker

Jim Bakker's horoscope reveals a battle between a spiritual Good Samaritan (the T-square) and a secular materialist and empire-builder who craves status and an opulent lifestyle (Sun in Capricorn in the 11th, Moon in Libra in the 8th). His chart is dominated by a powerful T-square (pictured) of Mars–Jupiter (the religious zealot and charismatic crusader) opposite Neptune in the 7th (the promise of salvation, the seller of dreams, and the relationship scandal that brought about his resignation), both square the apex Mercury in Sagittarius (the religious messenger of good news) at the Midheaven.

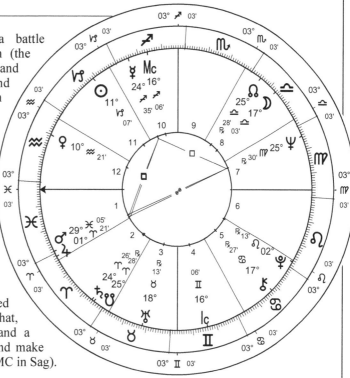

A short, shy boy with deep-seated feelings of insecurity, Jim found that, armed with verses from the Bible and a microphone, he could reach people and make others take notice (elevated Mercury–MC in Sag).

> Jim needed people's acceptance and their respect; he craved it like a drug… Deep down he never felt good enough. He had to go out and prove himself every single day.
>
> He interpreted all criticism as a personal attack, a horrendous failure on his part, the voice of his father belittling him.[41]

With Pisces Rising, Bakker later saw himself as a Christ figure, persecuted by the powers-that-be and a 'patsy' in the era of greed. He put himself under great pressure to accomplish new endeavours for his flock, but these proved financially crippling (Saturn in Aries in the 2nd). Too often he spent time fussing over the minor details when the major structure of his life was unravelling (the shadow of Pisces, Virgo, which can also be seen in his hypochondria and hand-washing obsession). He also had the habit of withdrawing into moods of sullenness, and to cope with the daily stresses he shut out the world (Mars–Neptune).

Jim Bakker wasn't the only Jupiter–Neptune-themed scandal-tainted preacher. Others cashed in on God and worshipped the almighty dollar. (Note the strong Mars when the scandal was sexual.)

- Hypocrite preacher Jimmy Swaggart condemned Bakker, only to engage the services of a prostitute: the Sun in Pisces exactly trine Jupiter, Sagittarius Rising, Jupiter square Mercury. (Mars on the MC in Libra opposite Venus, T-square Pluto.)

- Oral Roberts asked his followers for $4.5 million otherwise the Lord 'will take my life': Sun opposite Neptune and closely trine Jupiter. (Mars is the apex of a T-square involving a Moon–Pluto opposition to Mercury.)

- Aimee Semple McPherson, dubbed the 'Barnum of Religion', had a dubious 'kidnapping' (which she re-enacted for photographers!). This created much negative publicity and innuendo, costing her a huge following: Venus in Sagittarius opposite Neptune (possibly T-square Moon). She was taken up by the media in December 1919, when Jupiter and Neptune were widely conjunct in Leo, and her disappearance occurred on 18 May 1926, a month after the planets were opposed (from Aquarius to Leo).

Irene Cara: The Worksheet

	Cardinal +	Fixed −	Mutable +
Fire +	☿ ♀	(♅)	♃
Earth −	♄		(♀)
Air			♂ASC
Water +	☽	(♆)	☉MC

Chart Ruler
☿♈10th

Sun Dispositor
♃♐6th, ♆♏5th,

Four Angles and Links

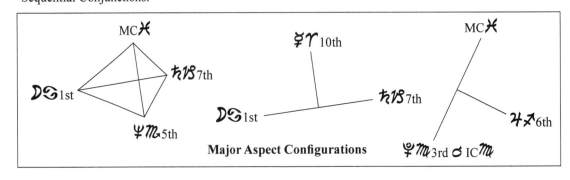

SUN   MOON   ASC
♓   ♋   ♊

Major Aspects

☉□ASC
☽□☿
☽⚹♄
☽△♆
☽☌ASC
☿□♄
☿△♅
♃□♆
♃□MC
♄☌DSC
♆△MC
♀☌IC

All Mutable. All four elements.
Rulers: Mercury and Jupiter.
DSC ruler and MC co-ruler ♃□MC
MC co-ruler ♆△MC

Other Notes

Stationary: ♃
Retrograde: ♅♆♀
0°: −   29°: −
Discovery Degrees: ⚷ on ♀
Unaspected: ♂
Generational Aspects: ♅□♆
Sequential Conjunctions: −

Gauquelin Zones

(♀)

Major Aspect Configurations

Putting it All Together: Irene Cara

1. The Distribution of Planets
With no planetary conjunctions and the ten planets spread over nine houses, the chart pattern is truly a Splash type (adding to the Gemini feeling of versatility and interest in exploring many facets of life). All the personal planets (except the Moon) are above the horizon.

2. The Set of Signs on the Four Angles
The angles are mutable (in tune with the Sun, Mars and Jupiter) and this leads us to the rulers, Mercury and Jupiter, which are in Fire signs and Earth houses (10th and 6th respectively). By SA, these rulers link by trine at eleven years old. Mercury, the ruler of the Ascendant and IC, is strongly positioned as the apex of a cardinal T-square, but it is the MC complex that has more repetitive patterns: its co-ruler Jupiter is stationary in Sagittarius and square the MC, and MC co-ruler Neptune is closely trine to the MC.

3. The Sun–Moon–Ascendant Trio
The Sun and Moon are in Water signs, while the Sun and Ascendant are linked by a square at the end of two mutable signs. Following trails, we discover that all of the Big Three have links to Mars-ruled planets: the Sun's co-dispositor Neptune is in Scorpio (in the Sun's natural 5th House), the Ascendant (Chart) Ruler is Mercury in Aries, and the Moon (in its own sign) is in Mars's natural 1st House and trine Neptune in Scorpio and square Mercury in Aries. Each of the three also has a Saturn/Capricorn/10th House link: the Sun is on the cusp of the 10th; the Moon opposes Saturn in Capricorn; and the Ascendant is opposite Saturn and the Ascendant-ruler Mercury is in the 10th square to Saturn.

4. Elemental and Modal Balances/Imbalances
Water dominates, with the Sun, Moon and MC posited in Water signs, and this is emphasized by the Water Grand Trine. Fire and Air follow, and there's little Earth. Cardinal and mutable signs dominate at the expense of planets in fixed signs, suggesting the importance of moving forward (cardinality) and being in process (mutability). Little Earth and no fixity create issues around money and feeling grounded.

5. Major Aspects
Six planets/points between 1° and 8° of signs can generate many aspects, but I would prioritize the conjunctions, squares and oppositions, and then consider very close trines (within a 3° orb). Here, the aspects I would single out are: the heavily aspected Moon (the square to Mercury and opposition to Saturn, both aspects in cardinal signs); Mercury square Saturn; and the tight Jupiter square Pluto because it is linked to the MC/IC axis and Jupiter rules two angles and disposits the Sun. I'd also consider the wide conjunctions from the Moon to the Ascendant and from Saturn to the Descendant; and Pluto on the IC. I would look at the trines to the MC as part of an aspect configuration (see below), and keep in mind the Chart Ruler's tight trine to Uranus, although I would not give this great weight in interpretation, except to say that it adds to the quickness of the Mercury–Mars theme (see below), which includes Mercury in Aries and Mars in Gemini.

6. Major Aspect Configurations
The Water Grand Trine links two watery planets to the MC, and the Moon opposes Saturn to form a Kite; this opposition is key to utilizing opportunities suggested by the Grand Trine. There's a cardinal T-square (in angular houses) with Chart Ruler Mercury as the all-important apex. The other T-square (if the MC is included) has a Jupiter–Pisces feel to it and is in mutable signs (and cadent houses).

7. Spotting Overtones
Although this chart has many features, there's a Jupiter–Neptune feel to it: the Sun and MC are in Pisces, while co-ruler Jupiter is stationary and in Sagittarius aspecting both the Sun and MC, and co-ruler Neptune trines the MC. There is also a Mercury–Mars subtone, with a mutual reception between Mercury and Mars, two personal planets in Aries and both Mars and the Ascendant in Gemini. Mars in Gemini is also in a Gauquelin Zone, and all of the Big Three have links to the signs of Mars (see above).

The desire for public recognition – the need to be *seen* as someone great and special – is Jupiterian in nature. Neptune describes that intangible *something* that appeals to everyone; it is the lens through which fame is sold, spread and projected. Pop culture guru Andy Warhol – Sun in Leo square Jupiter (possibly on the MC) – identified and shaped the modern cult of celebrity. With a Venus–Neptune conjunction in Leo, he saw fame as the new opiate of the people. Recently there's been *Glee*, *High School Musical* and far too many competitions with showbiz wannabes to recall – or care about. But thirty years ago, there was *Fame*.

It was Irene Cara's contribution to the films *Fame* and *Flashdance* that inspired the teenagers of the 80s to train in the performing arts. But to the children born into the Neptune in Capricorn age that followed (1984–98), the glamour, success and status have always been the goals, rather than a mastery or nurturing of individual talent. To this generation, power is in the image, and image is everything. Yet ironically, Cara, one of the handful of people most closely associated with modern 'fame', has lived a private, almost reclusive, life for many years. Her relationship with fame has always been ambivalent:

> I never really did it because my goal was to be famous. I see how other people react to me being famous and I see what fame means to them. But it doesn't necessarily mean the same thing to me, you know?

With the Sun and Midheaven in Pisces, Irene sees herself as an artist, someone involved in the *process* (mutable) of creating (Pisces), in the joy of performing and *being in the moment*.

> I don't mean to sound immodest, but I never had any doubt that I'd be successful, nor any fear of success. I was raised as a little goddess who was told she would be a star.

A child prodigy raised in the South Bronx, Irene Escalera came from a family of musicians (Pisces MC aspected by its rulers). She began performing for her family around her fifth birthday and was soon a finalist of the Little Miss America contest. By eight she had released her own album in Spanish (*Esta es Irene*). Her father Gaspar (10 Feb 1917 – 13 Jan 1994) was a saxophone player who brought merengue music to America and worked two jobs to fund the family's dreams for their daughter. Her beautiful mother Louise (28 Nov 1923 – 27 Sep 2010), discouraged from a performing career herself, was Irene's greatest champion and the driving force in her life, nurturing her talent, enrolling her in dancing, singing and piano lessons and taking her to auditions (Louise's Jupiter and Sun are at 0° and 4° Sagittarius respectively, tying into Irene's Jupiter–MC aspect). Irene's mother, who had installed in 'Reenie' an admirable work ethic, passed away in September 2010 (TR Jupiter–Uranus conjunct Irene's Sun); her professional 'mother' – former manager Selma Rubin – had died six months earlier.

On 23 October 1968, Irene made her Broadway debut in *Maggie Flynn* and a year later was performing in a tribute to Duke Ellington at Madison Square Garden. Irene was already on her way to developing an illustrious career in showbusiness and becoming a formidable triple-threat performer (Gemini, Pisces). In the process, she was also working to pay for her education.

> That's what is fortunate about my career. I have a ten-year jump on everybody. I didn't have to go to school, graduate and then go, 'What am I going to do?' I knew from the beginning.

In her teens she starred in two African-American movies, including *Sparkle* (released April 1976), and appeared in the original cast of *Ain't Misbehavin'* (February 1978). A year later she was part of *Roots: The Next Generations*, playing Alex Haley's mother (her favourite role).

There's an assumption today that celebrity is the ultimate goal of any aspiring performer. Pop culture historians look back at *Fame*'s exuberant cast list and delight in noting that none of them is still famous; yet the critics fail to see that the film explored the *dreams* and *pursuit* of fame, and its cast members were professionals seeking to learn and perfect their *craft*. In an open letter to the cast, director Alan Parker hoped his film, *Fame* (rel. May 1980), would show both sides of the dream:

Irene Cara singing at the 1984 Grammys
Photo © Bettmann/Corbis

The glamour of the Great White Way of Broadway and the squalor of 42nd Street; the dream of instant success and the constant reminder of failure; the fine line between a Julliard scholarship and dancing topless at the Metropole… A dozen races pitching in each having their own crack at the American dream.

Parker's penchant for spotting and showcasing young and teenage talent in ensemble pieces (*Bugsy Malone*, *The Commitments*) is suggested by his Sun in Aquarius opposite Jupiter in Leo (a 'starmaker' aspect of sorts). The month he cast Cara in *Fame*, his Jupiter had Solar Arc directed to 27° Virgo, exactly opposing Irene's Sun. (TR Saturn reached 27° Virgo at the height of the *Fame* success in the late summer of 1980.)

Irene played the determined Coco Hernandez who, like Irene, was bursting with unbridled ambition, energy and talent. Coco was the tough cookie almost too smart for her own good, who has it all worked out until she's seduced by a sleazy filmmaker into exposing her breasts.

Coco was one of the first bi-racial lead characters in a Hollywood film, and Irene (of African, Cuban, Spanish and French descent) was the movie's breakout star (by Solar Arc, her Moon moved into Leo that summer and the MC edged closer to her Sun). Irene was catapulted into the limelight and it was her image that sold the film. Her electrifying alto dominated the film's soundtrack, which topped the charts and went on to make Academy Award history. (She would later become the youngest woman of colour to win an Academy Award and the first outside the acting categories.)

Shy but intense and passionate about her work, Irene was keen to be understood and to say something meaningful in interviews (Aries, Gemini, Pisces). She presented an open, no B.S. sincerity to the media but her almost childlike honesty was portrayed as cockiness and arrogance; she soon learned to keep quiet to protect herself (Moon in Cancer in the 1st).

The Pisces–Jupiter–Neptune theme in her chart has shone through her media work. Irene's two most successful recordings were exuberant anthems of youthful striving (note the signs of youth, Aries and Gemini, are prominent): 'Fame' and 'Flashdance... What a Feeling'. Both hits were from films that merged drama, music and dance (Pisces) with the inspirational theme of making your dreams happen (Pisces–Aries, *'Bein's believin'... I can have it all now I'm dancing for my life'*). Her 1983 solo album generated hits that were Piscean in nature (from the plaintive victim's cry 'Why Me?', to 'The Dream' and 'Breakdance', written about the dance craze). This was no surprise: as the *Flashdance* theme ruled the airwaves in summer 1983 and Irene won Grammys, an Oscar and a slew of awards in 1984, transiting Neptune passed back and forth across her Descendant and squared her Sun in Pisces. She was *everywhere*: the film was a worldwide phenomenon and Irene's title track became one of the world's most successful singles *of all time*. From being seen as a 'junior Donna Summer' (Saturn), she emerged with her own Piscean voice:

> Whereas Summer was characterized by a rough, almost mechanical sexuality, Cara's singing has a naked, unstudied emotional appeal. It allows her to convey, even in the midst of Moroder's most high-tech synthesized productions, the most basic of human sentiments.[42]

During the Neptune transit, Cara's enormous success made her a victim of industry greed. Al Coury of Network Records had been building his label on the back of the 'Flashdance' song and, after four years together, presented Irene with a cheque for $183. She responded by filing a breach of contract suit for unpaid royalties in February 1985 (when her SA MC moved into Aries). Immediately her career hit a brick wall. Cara's name was blacklisted by industry chiefs, her reputation tarnished by rumours of exaggerated drug use and temperamental behaviour ('fame' originates from *pheme* and *fama*, meaning 'rumour'), and along the way she managed to incur the wrath of ruthless music moguls such as David Geffen.

At the time of the lawsuit, SA Pluto opposed (and Jupiter squared) her Pisces Sun. It would be a dirty fight, one that would last eight years. As a black woman in music, who had too easily given up control and power to others, she was discovering the force of an unclaimed Pluto on the IC:

> I found myself up against something I was totally powerless against... I had enemies I never heard of because of this.

It was a confusing and turbulent time, and no one could help her. Her marriage that began on 13 April 1986 (SA Jupiter to her DSC) to stuntman Conrad Palmisano (born 1 May 1948, with natal Jupiter on Irene's DSC) collapsed under the strain after three years. Irene's inner rage would consume her for a decade. The tight Jupiter–Pluto square contacting her Pisces MC suggests exploitation by the 'men in black', as well as the need to let go of feelings of abuse and victimization. Later, Irene's shamanic teachers would help her to understand that her faith could move mountains (Jupiter–Pluto), and to come to terms with the dark and paradoxical sides of celebrity: the media's simultaneous exaltation and persecution of the famous.

Awarded a relatively paltry $1.5 million on 11 February 1993, Irene's was a moral victory rather than a financial one (most of the assets had been siphoned off) – but she had won the rights to future royalties, putting her on a more solid financial footing (her Sun had directed into Taurus). For a time in the mid 90s, she was unable to sing the songs that had brought her acclaim – there was no joy left, only a disgust that resulted in short-lived psychosomatic illnesses (spring 1996, as TR Saturn conjunct her Sun).

Nowadays, Irene doesn't often dwell on the past. She sees her success in the 80s as the end of an era, the culmination of her work since childhood. The Mercury–Moon–Saturn T-square suggests a need to wrest control and one's identity back from 'parental' figures, and to express a body of work that defines one's true artistic identity (Aries); to *write one's own story*. Her all-girl group, Hot Caramel, reflects a musical rebirth – with Irene in control, financing the CD and making the music her way. *Irene Cara Presents Hot Caramel* is an uncompromising masterwork, a project of a lifetime, bringing together talented women singers and instrumentalists to play jazz, adult contemporary and soul music.

Her early work, 'Fame' and 'Flashdance', will live forever as defining musical moments for a generation. But Pisces, the sign of the true survivor, learns to reject the undue influence of others and draw back into a creative centre, connect to a deeper spiritual process, and then emerge to share its enchanting song with the world.

Key Player: Giorgio Moroder

Famous for his own instrumental (pun intended) sound in the disco and electronic new wave movements of the late 70s, innovative producer Moroder teamed up with Donna Summer in late 1975 and created 'Love to Love You Baby', a 17-minute orgasmic symphony of moans. It made Summer the recognized (but reluctant) international diva of disco and Moroder the principal architect of the short-lived disco revolution that, by 1979, had brought a string of accolades for them both.

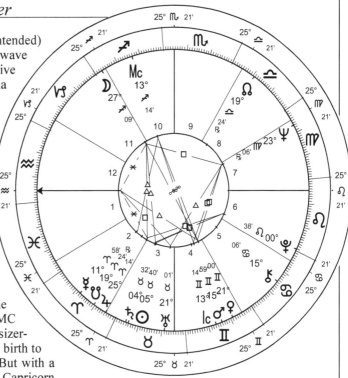

With Sun–Jupiter in the 5th square Neptune, sensual Summer would be dubbed a fantasy 'first lady of love' (her Venus is on Moroder's Sagittarius MC). Together (when TR Neptune in Sagittarius reached their Venus–MC synastry) they composed the synthesizer-driven 'I Feel Love', which would give birth to techno music and change club music. But with a strong Saturn signature (five planets in Capricorn and Saturn in partile conjunction to the Ascendant), 'Ordinary Girl' Summer rejected her erotic image in 1980 for a Born Again lifestyle and opted to use her powerful gospel voice in other musical genres.

Moroder's chart points to a futuristic, mechanical or inspirational message (Aquarius Ascendant, Sagittarius MC) – driving Eurodisco dance tracks and electropop anthems rather than love songs (the Venusian parts of his chart are dominated by the 'malefics': Mars conjuncts his Venus, and Saturn conjuncts the Sun in Taurus). The only planets above the horizon are the Moon and Neptune (in a T-square with Venus), suggestive of an ability to tap into the public mood (Moon–Neptune), package it for a universal market (Venus–Neptune) and carry out daily work in a secluded, womb-like environment (among other things, Moon–Neptune is suggestive of a soundproof recording studio!).

Together with Irene Cara, he created the theme to *Flashdance*, the defining dance movie of the 1980s. Their synastry is fascinating: Mars conjunct Mars in Gemini, Mercury conjunct Mercury in Aries, his Jupiter conjunct her Venus, and his Moon at 27° Sagittarius conjunct Cara's Descendant (and the Sun of *Flashdance* actress Jennifer Beals!). When the movie dominated cinemas and the soundtrack ruled the airwaves *worldwide* in the summer of 1983, transiting Neptune was at 27–8° Sagittarius.

Known for his trademark 'galloping bassline' (appropriate for a Sagittarius MC and Moon), Moroder would later compose for two Olympic ceremonies (I link Sagittarius to the ethos of the Games, the Olympic Flame and igniting passions).

Irene's horoscope is in marked contrast to that of Debbie Allen, the other performer long associated with the *Fame* franchise. Allen has a heavy Saturn signature (Sun, Moon and Mercury in Capricorn, Venus and Jupiter in Aquarius, plus Saturn conjunct the Ascendant and square the MC). With Gemini on the MC, Allen is an actress, singer, dancer, choreographer, producer – and a highly disciplined, renowned task-master (read 'ballbreaker') who introduced a strong work ethic to her *Fame* and *A Different World* troupes with regimented morning exercise workouts. Allen's most famous line (from the TV series) is pure Saturn reality: 'You've got big dreams. You want fame. Well, fame costs and right here's where you start paying – in sweat.'

Mary Tyler Moore: The Worksheet

	Cardinal +	Fixed −	Mutable
			MC
Fire −			
Earth +	☉☿♃	(♅)	(♆)
Air	♂	♀	
Water +	☽(♇)		♄ASC

Chart Ruler
♃♑ 10th, ♆♏ 7th

Sun Dispositor
♄♓ 1st

SUN	MOON	ASC
♑	♋	♓

Four Angles and Links

All Mutable. All four elements.
Rulers: Mercury, Jupiter.
ASC co-ruler ♆□MC
ASC co-ruler ♆☌DSC

Major Aspects

☉☌♃
☉△♅
☽☍☿
☽☌♂
☽☌♀
☿□♂
☿☍♇
♂□♇
♃△♅
♄☍♆
♄☌ASC
♄□MC
♆☌DSC
♆□MC

Other Notes
Stationary: −
Retrograde: ♅♆♇
0°: −   29°: −
Discovery Degrees: −
Unaspected: −
Generational Aspects: ♅□♇
Sequential Conjunctions: ♃☉, ☽♀

Gauquelin Zones

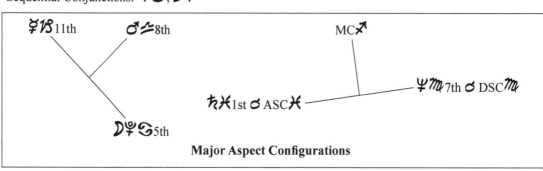

♀♑ 11th   ♂♎ 8th   MC♐

                                                    ♆♏ 7th ☌ DSC♏

                    ♄♓ 1st ☌ ASC♓

♽♀♋ 5th

Major Aspect Configurations

Putting it All Together: Mary Tyler Moore

1. The Distribution of Planets
The planets are scattered around the chart but the eye is drawn to the luminaries and the conjunctions they make: the Sun is conjunct Jupiter (which rules the Ascendant and MC), while the Moon is conjunct Pluto in the 5th House (naturally linked to the Sun).

2. The Set of Signs on the Four Angles
The orientation is mutable and, although the rulers Mercury and Jupiter are not in aspect to each other, they are (like the Sun) both in the cardinal sign of Capricorn, which emphasizes this sign, the strong Saturn (on the Ascendant) and the cardinality that drives this chart. The angle rulers do not contact each other, but the Ascendant co-ruler Neptune is conjunct the Descendant. This is a highly cardinal chart that must work within a mutable framework, which suggests flexibility and, at times, a precarious orientation (Saturn is the anchor that suggests punctuality and a strong work ethic to keep the chaos at bay).

3. The Sun–Moon–Ascendant Trio
The Sun and Moon are in cardinal signs, while the Ascendant and the Moon are in Water. Following trails, we discover strong links between the Sun and Ascendant (suggesting an ability to project an authentic image): the dispositor of the Sun is Saturn, which is on the Ascendant, while the Ascendant (Chart) co-ruler is Jupiter, which is conjunct the Sun.

4. Elemental and Modal Balances/Imbalances
As already stated, cardinality dominates but must work with the mutable angles. The 'love' planets Mars and Venus are in Air signs, but the main focus is on Earth and Water. There is little fixity or Fire.

5. Major Aspects
Looking at conjunctions, squares, oppositions and very close trines (within a 3° orb), the aspects I would single out are: the elevated, earthy Sun–Jupiter conjunction in the 10th House (tightly trine Uranus in Taurus in the 2nd House); the Moon–Pluto conjunction; and the aspects that form the tight cardinal T-square: Moon opposite Mercury, Moon square Mars, Mercury square Mars, Mercury opposite Pluto, Mars square Pluto. Pluto's tight aspects to the Moon, Mercury and Mars make it an enormously influential player in this horoscope. But perhaps the single most important aspect in this chart is the social–outer planet opposition of Saturn to Neptune, as this aligns with the Ascendant–Descendant axis and links to much of the chart's action: there are three planets in Capricorn (disposited by Saturn) and Pisces rises (the Chart co-ruler is Neptune). Trails of this opposition keep *leading us back to the importance of Capricorn*: Saturn is disposited (and mutually received) by Jupiter in Capricorn, Neptune is disposited by Mercury (placed in Capricorn), and the opposition squares the Sagittarius MC, which is ruled by Jupiter, also found in Capricorn.

6. Major Aspect Configurations
Although instrumental in the chart, the Saturn–Neptune opposition is a 'duet' – an aspect that does not dialogue with any other planet. It finds relief through the MC apex (and transits or directions to the MC degree should release this opposition). The second T-square is an 'official', planet-only one: a cardinal T-square in succedent houses (5th, 8th, 11th). Two corners of the configuration have a Scorpio (Mars, Pluto and the 8th House) feel, which can range from family taboos, intimacy issues and creative transformations to crises, taboos, death or life-changing situations relating to children.

7. Spotting Overtones
The Saturn–Neptune opposition across the horizon draws our attention to the Saturn–Capricorn signature (the planets in Capricorn, the 10th House Sun–Jupiter, Saturn Rising and in a Gauquelin Zone). But there is a Jupiter–Neptune subtone to this signature (including Saturn in Pisces, Neptune on the Descendant, both square the Sagittarius MC, and information outlined above in 5). In biography, we should be able to see this interesting battle between Saturnian control and Jupiter–Neptune chaos, excess and addiction.

Cultural or generational influence is usually seen in a horoscope through major aspects from the outer planets to the four angles or inner planets. The Uranian personality works to detonate the status quo, call out for a change in hierarchy and disrupt the establishment. The Neptunian may influence fashion, music and cinema, seduce or scandalize; s/he subtly invades all boundaries and genres, infiltrates consciousness, and puts us back in touch with the longings of a more romantic yesteryear. The Plutonic personality changes irrevocably the ways in which we view life; it pushes our buttons to encourage the process of transformation: a non-negotiable demolition that can, potentially, lead to empowerment.

Born with a powerful Pluto placement, comedy actress Mary Tyler Moore defined and changed the face of women on American television. She was a trendsetter and role model, the girl everyone fell in love with, America's sweetheart who 'turned the whole world on with her smile'.

As the peppy, domesticated 60s wife in *The Dick Van Dyke Show*, she wore Capri pants and was an equal to her husband. In *The Mary Tyler Moore Show*, she was a 70s independent woman who'd 'been around... well... nearby', struggling in earnest to build a career for herself, but happy to be a woman who lived on her own and dated as and when she wanted.

Yet it is the T-square of Saturn–Ascendant in Pisces opposite Neptune–Descendant in Virgo square to the Sagittarius MC apex that is clearly embodied in many of Mary Tyler Moore's experiences and 'scripts' on- and off-camera. In this profile, we shall see how Moore, a Capricorn with Saturn Rising, has lived out this key aspect both personally and in her most memorable acting roles.

Mary's early life was filled with longings for comfort as there was little warmth or affection at home (the Moon in Cancer, Saturn Rising). Later, Mary would crave parental approval for her talents (the Moon in Cancer in the 5th), and the family's move to Hollywood in September 1945 helped to fuel Mary's interest in a performing career. Her father was a reserved, intellectual man – an administrator for a gas company, and a martinet who drove Mary's outgoing but alcoholic mother

to despair (note the pivotal Saturn–Neptune–MC). When times were difficult, young Mary sought refuge with her aunt and grandmother, often staying with both of them. Aunt Bertie offered a calm space, much affection and a solid routine (so longed for by Saturn rising in Pisces, and Moon–Pluto in Cancer). Bertie sent her to a school of dance, which offered Pisces Rising Mary a chance to transform into various characters and hide the quivering mess and fear that she felt lay inside.

At six, she was molested by a friend of the family but, in an act of betrayal that she never recovered from, Mary's mother refused to believe her (MC in Sagittarius) and snapped, 'No! That's not true. It didn't happen.' In her autobiography, Mary writes:

> I never felt the same about her after that. My mother, by her denial, had abused me far more than her friend.

She met Dick Meeker in January 1955, married him later that year (to escape the family) and soon ran an obsessively clean and efficient household, and began to pursue some acting roles. She found out she was expecting a baby a few months after her own mother's surprise pregnancy, and Mary gave birth to Richie on 3 July 1956. The experience of both mother and daughter being pregnant brought them closer together and healed some wounds (Moon–Pluto in Cancer in the 5th).

Mary's marriage failed and she sued for divorce in February 1962, just four months before she married producer Grant Tinker (both events took place during Solar Arc Venus conjunct Saturn). Mary's seventeen-year marriage to Tinker (a father substitute) was an immensely productive pairing (their partnership created MTM Enterprises and a variety of comedy classic shows), but it was an intense one and excluded other friendships.

'The extraordinary thing about Mary is that she is so extraordinarily normal,' Grant Tinker once said. 'I'm not an actress who can play a character. I play me,' was Mary's modest, understated and self-effacing (Saturn) assessment of her talent, which nevertheless won her seven Emmys. As is often the case with strong Pisces/Neptune, millions of viewers thought Mary *was* the character she portrayed. And herein lay Moore's magical gift:

Mary Tyler Moore
Photo © Mitchell Gerber/Corbis

the ability to portray lightness and gentleness at a time in American life when society was torn apart by political strife. The Mary underneath was far more complex. On TV, she represented an escape for the viewer, a Pisces/Neptune refuge of sweetness and good-naturedness. The America of *The Dick Van Dyke Show* (1961–6) was innocent. The America of *The Mary Tyler Moore Show* (1970–7) was looking to recapture its innocence and magic.

Moore's forte was to *react* in a funny way, rather than deliver the hilarious one-liners. Describing her role in her own sitcom, Moore reveals her strong Saturn overtone:

> I was the audience. I was the voice of sanity around whom all these crazies did their dance. And I reacted in the same way that a member of the audience would have reacted.

In *Humour in the Horoscope: The Astrology of Comedy*, I write that the Ascendant complex reveals our personal 'take' on the world and, as such, it has much to say about the types of circumstance and life situations we find funny. With Saturn rising in Pisces, the humour originates

from hard done-by, 'why me?' situations where other people bring chaos into our carefully constructed lives. Saturn is often the 'straight' guy, the stooge or the reactor – the one who is acutely aware of protocol and other people's (often anticipated or imagined) disapproval.

A team player but self-contained and detached (Saturn), Moore has always given credit for the show's success to the talented writers and cast rather than singling out her own contribution, acknowledging that she was lucky to be in a nurturing environment that allowed her talent to blossom. Someone with a Sun–Jupiter conjunction (particularly in the 10th) can be blessed by association or linked to important, powerful people – what Moore called 'the protective canopy of genius' that surrounded her.

One such person was co-star and comedy mentor Dick Van Dyke, the elastic-faced, rubber-limbed clown whose chemistry with Mary made her a star on his show and changed the course of her professional life. Van Dyke is a Sagittarian with his Sun at 21°, exactly on Moore's MC. Mary auditioned for the show in January 1961 (as the Solar Arc 10th House cusp by EQHS conjunct her

Sun) and the show aired on 3 October 1961, as TR Jupiter hit Mary's Mercury. When the series wrapped in 1966, Mary was bereft, feeling as though she had lost the only real family she'd had.

Before her sitcom success, Moore had never tried comedy. A trained dancer (Virgo–Pisces is the axis of dance), Moore was the Happy Hotpoint Pixie in an appliance commercial, and later the voice and legs of a never-seen telephone receptionist on *Richard Diamond, Private Detective* (1957). But she hit her stride in *The Dick Van Dyke Show*, and then as a working girl – an associate producer of a news show – in *The Mary Tyler Moore Show* (19 September 1970 to 19 March 1977).

The most memorable and lauded episode of her own show was 'Chuckles Bites the Dust', which showed the gamut of Moore's comic range – and personified her pivotal Saturn–Neptune opposition. In the episode, the news team receive word that Chuckles the Clown, while dressed as a peanut, has been crushed to death by an elephant. Hilarity ensues and, outraged by their insensitive remarks and lack of reverence, Mary scolds them. During the funeral, as she sits with appropriate solemnity (Saturn) in the hush of the moment, she starts to 'lose it' (Pisces/Neptune). To the horror of everyone around her, Mary's giggling builds until it disrupts the service. Singled out by the minister and asked to stand, a mortified Mary pulls herself together but, when told that Chuckles would have loved her laughter, she collapses into uncontrollable sobbing.

Transiting Neptune's sojourn over her Midheaven in 1979–80 was to coincide with a monumental time in her life, one of both professional triumph and stunning tragedy.

Actor Robert Redford (also born with Saturn rising in Pisces, plus Jupiter on Mary's 10th House cusp) was preparing to direct his first movie and saw Mary walking along the beach, deep in thought. Seeing beyond her broad smile and bubbly public image, he wondered about the darker side of her nature. Soon after, he cast her in a haunting role as the icy mother Beth Jarrett in *Ordinary People*, which premiered on 19 September 1980. Mary gave a powerful, Saturn in Pisces performance as 'a woman victimized by her

own emotional rigidity' who flees the family nest to avoid dealing with the emotional turmoil of one son's death and another's suicide attempt. In her autobiography, she wrote:

> Beth Jarrett's ready smile and cheerful demeanour hid the contempt she felt for weakness, self-doubt, and disorder, all of which lurked inside of her. The woman was constantly struggling for the survival of all she'd been taught to hold dear – winning, self-confidence, and pride... There was very little room for spontaneity in Beth's life. She was a product of her own upbringing, a demanding mother who was so concerned with the externals of a loving home, there simply wasn't the energy left to comprehend the unplanned for, sometimes unattractive, needs of the people she loved.

In Pisces, Saturn fears the chaos of emotional entanglement and exerts a vice-like grip on itself to avoid any emotional leakage. Mary thought she was playing her father, but 'it wasn't until years later that I recognized someone in that role, and it was me,' she confessed.

In December 1979, following the *Ordinary People* shoot, Moore called time on her marriage to Tinker. She then took over the lead role from Tom Conti on Broadway in *Whose Life is it, Anyway?* for three months (from 24 February 1980). Moore played a keenly intelligent sculptor in a useless body, having been paralysed (Saturn) from the neck down. Determined to be allowed to die, the character debates the act of euthanasia (Pisces/Neptune) and to what extent government should be allowed to interfere in the life of a private citizen (Saturn).

Her bravura performances in the film and play (SA 10th House EQHS cusp conjunct Mercury, SA Sun conjunct Venus) stretched her as an actress and opened the door for a truly remarkable range of portrayals in the years to come (*Just Between Friends, Stolen Babies, Stolen Memories*).

Following both career successes, Mary faced the most heartbreaking event of her life. On 14 October 1980 (when the 4th House EQHS cusp reached Pluto by Solar Arc), her son accidentally shot himself dead. Eerily reminiscent of the *Ordinary People* storyline, Moore never recovered from the loss. But for Saturn, life goes on. It has to.

Saturn Rising, the self-contained loner, presents a tough, 'everything's OK' exterior to the world, while the Moon in Cancer wears a protective shell.

> For the longest time I would share only my 'up' moments with my friends. I felt that to let them into my problems, the dreary parts of my life, would be a burden... I didn't understand that it was depriving *them* of a chance to be human.

Moore had always guarded her privacy but in the following years she spoke publicly of her battles with diabetes and alcoholism, and in 1995 she wrote a searingly honest autobiography, *After All*. Her diabetes was discovered in late 1969, when a blood test following a traumatic miscarriage revealed that she had Type 1 diabetes (the SA Moon had entered Virgo, and Mars was at 29° Scorpio).

Of her illness, Moore told Larry King in 2002:

> I live in a kind of controlled awareness. I wouldn't call it fear, but it's an awareness. I know I have a responsibility to behave in a certain way. I'm able to do that.

But with Neptune angular and Saturn rising in Pisces, the veneer of calm, personal control and self-mastery that Mary exhibited in her immediate environment could not be maintained. In September 1984, Mary checked herself in to the Betty Ford Center (sober Saturn was conjunct Uranus in the 2nd House by Solar Arc, and SA Pluto approached an opposition to natal Saturn, unravelling her tightly coiled springs). When she emerged five weeks later (TR Jupiter was conjunct her Jupiter and Sun), she had gained some honest insights into herself and learned much about her relationship dynamics.

Speaking her apex Mars and the survival instinct of Mars–Pluto, she has said:

> Take chances, make mistakes. That's how you grow. Pain nourishes your courage. You have to fail in order to practise being brave.

Later, using the T-square (with the MC in Sagittarius as the apex), she became an outspoken protector of the weak, abused or ill: as an animal rights activist, as an advocate of vegetarianism, and as a spokesperson for the Juvenile Diabetes Foundation in the fight against the illness.

The Saturn temperament demands respect and privacy; on the Ascendant it can display a self-protective hauteur. As Saturn matures, it can get in touch with a playfulness and lost youth – or it can wrap a bitter, cantankerous or ironic cast around itself. For Mary, it seemed to bring inner peace, a contentment with her third husband, Dr Robert Levine, and the horses on their farm, and an acceptance of her remarkable talent – without the inner critic always stepping in.

A classy lady with a rare gift for both comedic and poignant acting, Mary (who died on 25 January 2017) wrote in her autobiography of the 'two distinct inner spirits who live my life for me, playing hide-and-seek at times'. In doing so, she articulated the two key divisions in her horoscope that are encapsulated by the Saturn overtone/Moon–Pluto conjunction, and her strong Neptune theme/Sun–Jupiter conjunction:

> There does seem to be one brooding, paranoid, and pessimistic Mary Tyler Moore. I think she's the one who supplies the comedy. The other Mary is a supremely confident champion. They do battle with each other... I'm like a chameleon in that I take on the colours of success or failure, happy or sad, depending on what's going on, or how it *seems* to be going... emotionally, I am, after all, the chameleon waiting to see what colour I am meant to be.

Martina Navratilova: The Worksheet

	Cardinal +	Fixed −	Mutable +
Fire +	☽ASC	(♅♇)	♄
Earth	MC		♃
Air	☉☿(♆)		
Water −			♂

Chart Ruler
♂♓11th/12th

Sun Dispositor
♀♏5th/6th

SUN	MOON	ASC
♎	♈	♈

Four Angles and Links

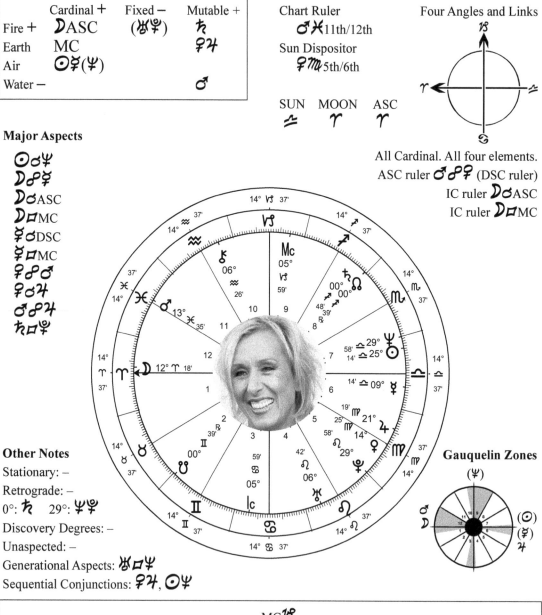

All Cardinal. All four elements.
ASC ruler ♂☍♀ (DSC ruler)
IC ruler ☽☌ASC
IC ruler ☽□MC

Major Aspects

☉☌♆
☽☍☿
☽☌ASC
☽□MC
☿☌DSC
☿□MC
♀☍♂
♀☌♃
♂☍♃
♄□♇

Other Notes

Stationary: –
Retrograde: –
0°: ♄ 29°: ♆♇
Discovery Degrees: –
Unaspected: –
Generational Aspects: ♅□♆
Sequential Conjunctions: ♀♃, ☉♆

Gauquelin Zones

(♆)

♂
☽

(☉)
(☿)
♃

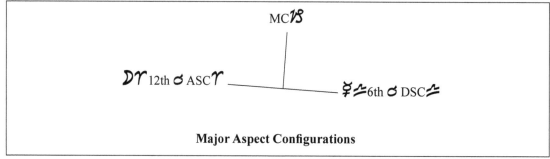

Major Aspect Configurations

MC♑

☽♈ 12th ☌ ASC♈ ——————— ☿♎6th ☌ DSC♎

Putting it All Together: Martina Navratilova

1. The Distribution of Planets
Most of the chart (eight planets) is contained between the 4th and 8th houses, with an Aries- and Mars-themed section of the horoscope (the Moon in Aries and Mars in Pisces) out there on its own and in an all-important Gauquelin Zone. There are emphases on Virgo–6th House (craft, perfection) and Libra–7th House–Descendant (the delicate balancing act in relationships).

2. The Set of Signs on the Four Angles
The cardinal angles tie in well with the luminaries (the Sun in Libra and Moon in Aries) and the general emphasis on cardinality (including the T-square). The Moon (ruler of the IC) is on the Ascendant in a cardinal sign (Aries) and square to the MC. But the driving force in this chart is the horizontal axis: the Ascendant ruler Mars opposes the Descendant ruler Venus, our first indication of a Venus–Mars overtone and the interlinking of the 1st and 7th signs/houses.

3. The Sun–Moon–Ascendant Trio
All three are in cardinal signs that relate to issues of independence vs. partnership, conflict vs. cooperation, me vs. you (Aries and Libra). The Moon is on the cusp of the 1st House (the house associated with Aries) and the Sun is in the 7th (Libra's natural house). The rulers of the trio are Venus and Mars, which are in opposition to each other. Looking further, we can see that each of the Big Three has links to Neptune: the Sun is conjunct Neptune, the Moon is in the 12th House, and the Ascendant's ruler is Mars, which is placed in Pisces on the cusp of the 12th.

4. Elemental and Modal Balances/Imbalances
Fire dominates, with two of the Big Three placed here, while the Water element is left in the hands of the Chart Ruler, Mars. As already noted, the cardinal signs are strong and there is a lack of fixity. We have a signature of cardinal Fire (Aries) and an anti-signature of fixed Water (Scorpio), so it comes as no surprise that Martina's long-time on-court rival Chris Evert has a Scorpio-heavy chart, and mentor Billie Jean King has the Sun in Scorpio.

5. Major Aspects
Looking at conjunctions, squares, oppositions and very close trines (within a 3° orb), the aspects I would single out are: the Sun conjunct Neptune (almost a duet); the Moon–Mercury opposition (underscoring the Aries–Libra axis) which aspects all four angles (making it a key aspect); the Venus–Jupiter conjunction in Virgo and both opposite Mars (the Venus–Mars should be prioritized: it is tighter and more influential by rulership to other parts of the horoscope). Saturn square Pluto is tight and made personal by both planets being sesquisquare the Ascendant.

6. Major Aspect Configurations
The T-square underlines the cardinality in the horoscope, as well as the strong Mars/Aries/Ascendant–Venus/Libra/Descendant theme that runs through the chart.

7. Spotting Overtones
The main themes in this chart are linked to the planets Venus and Mars (their signs and associated angles/houses). In what could otherwise be a simple Venus–Mars polarity throughout, we discover that both overtones have a Neptune coating/wash: Chart Ruler Mars is in Pisces on the cusp of the 12th, the Moon is in the 12th, and the Sun in Libra is conjunct Neptune.

The research of the Gauquelins showed statistically that the position of Mars was linked to the temperament that created eminent sports champions, soldiers and executives. Those with Mars prominent were often described as: active, ardent, combative, daring, dynamic, fearless, reckless and strong-willed. The Moon – which they found to be the psychological opposite of Mars – was linked to noted writers, and was weak in the charts of the Mars professions listed above. Those with the Moon strong were: amiable, generous, good company, impressionable, impulsive and popular. A few years before her death, Françoise Gauquelin approached me to publish a book on planetary combinations in Gauquelin Zones. I warmed to the idea because there were so many people who had planets of contradictory natures in these Zones and who *personified their combination*. The following profile, of the tennis legend Martina Navratilova, is a case in point. So, what sort of temperament emerges from a woman with both the Moon and Mars in key Gauquelin Zones? And what of the other influences in her chart?

The on-court dramas, the supreme athleticism, the publicized love life, and courageous political and ethical stands have made Martina Navratilova one of the most compelling sports figures of all time. With a rising Moon, she has always worn her heart on her sleeve, revealing the triumphs, tantrums and the tears. In the worksheet analysis, the combined influence of Mars and Venus arose as the key theme to the chart of this remarkable athlete – once the outsider and booed for not being feminine, graceful and 'straight' enough; the same outsider who eventually won over the crowds when she was no longer the unbeatable Wonder Woman of tennis, and when the public recognized the 'heart' she had for the game.

When the Moon and Ascendant are in Aries, we might expect the temperament and personality to be focused on winning, being Number One, the champion. More importantly, though, Aries (and its ruler Mars) depicts the need to have a target, to pit oneself against an opponent (or a level of attainment/expectation) – to struggle, to test and *prove* oneself, to *experience* the stark contrast between victory and defeat. In essence and at their best, Aries and Mars are related to perfectionism, to standards of excellence.

With her strong Venus–Libra and Mars–Aries signatures, it could be argued that Martina would meet conditions in the world that reflected this Venus–Mars polarity: the oppression of personal rights, fighting against injustice, taking an individual stand for what is right. She would come to learn the value of independence, the thrill of winning, and grace in defeat. Along the way, she would give total commitment to herself and craft her body into a temple of muscular beauty.

It wasn't long before she encountered situations that brought the Venus–Mars blend to the fore. In an attempt to crush growing political and economic reforms, the Soviets invaded Czechoslovakia in late August 1968. Eleven-year-old Martina was 'ready to fight them with apples' (TR Saturn at 25° Aries stationed directly opposite her Sun in Libra). Seven years later (Saturn), when the Czech tennis authorities restricted her access to tournaments in non-Communist countries, Martina took the ultimate step and sought political asylum (at the time, TR Jupiter had stationed at 24° Aries). Her defection took place on 9 September 1975. As I wrote in an article on sesquisquares in *The Mountain Astrologer* (April/May 2012):

> She was acting out her natal Mars in Pisces on the cusp of the 12th house sesquisquare Neptune in Libra in the 7th. The aspect is descriptive of the 18-year-old's secret and dramatic defection to seek asylum (i.e. refugee status – Neptune, Pisces) in the US, fleeing from a Communist ideology she deemed unfair (Neptune in Libra) and feeling persecuted by gossip and innuendo (Pisces). Once she had defected, Martina 'ceased to exist' publicly in Czechoslovakia. Her combative, independence-seeking Aries Ascendant is sesquisquare both Saturn and Pluto, also descriptive of her personal battle for freedom against a restrictive and harsh regime.

Looking further, MC ruler Saturn in Sagittarius in the 8th could indicate her reputation as a defector and 'naturalized American', as well as her outspokenness about her homosexuality, and the impact this would have on sponsorship endorsements. (The square from Saturn to Pluto in the 5th, and both planets' tight Thor's Hammer aspect to the Ascendant, underscore this.)

In April 1980, her mother, worried that Martina's sexuality might trigger the same manic depression

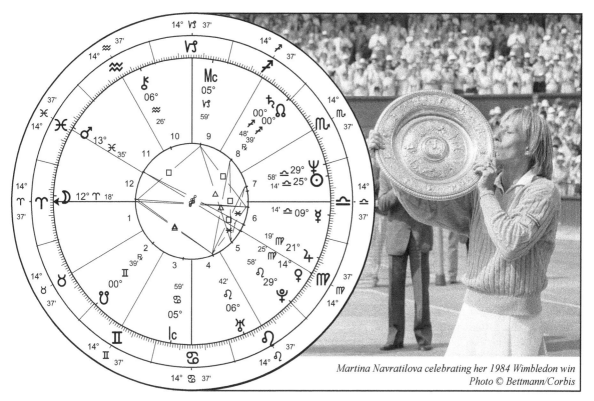

Martina Navratilova celebrating her 1984 Wimbledon win
Photo © Bettmann/Corbis

that had plagued her father, told her daughter the truth: Martina's father had committed suicide when she was eight. Shocked but unwilling to change her lifestyle, Martina eventually came out publicly (firstly as being bisexual) after gaining her US citizenship on 21 July 1981. A staunch advocate for equal human rights, she never apologized for (nor allowed press intrusion into) her sexual preference. And, along the way, she delivered some sharp verbal volleys:

Male reporter: Are you still a lesbian?
Martina: Are you still the alternative?

Labels are for filing. Labels are for clothing. Labels are not for people.

With the Venus–Mars theme and natal opposition, it's interesting that tennis spectators and viewers also tended to *polarize* Martina and her opponent, none more so than when she battled her long-time rival Chris Evert (who has Venus Rising). When they played, it was Mar(s)tina the muscled Amazon against blonde, feminine Chris, the Venusian (but chilly) sweetheart. Yet Martina brought both Mars and Venus to the court: awesome power and aggression, speed, strength and muscles, plus

grace, style, timing, fairness and rhythm. She was a supreme champion in singles (Mars) and doubles (Venus), winning 41 Grand Slams, 167 singles and 177 doubles titles over an astonishing period (1974 to 2006).

Tennis is Venus–Mars – two (or four) players, two sides of the court, serving–receiving, a mix of graceful and winning shots with élan – some with a delicate 'touch', others simply 'muscled', fast and forceful. Tennis is a game of mental combat, and Mercury's position is key in terms of focus and mental strength. But on court, a player's Ascendant complex comes to the fore. There are players with graceful technique and finesse (Roger Federer, Venus rising in Virgo), a single-mindedness and powerhouse strength (Rafael Nadal, Pluto rising in Scorpio), or a commanding presence and speed (Steffi Graf, the Sun rising in Gemini). With Martina, the Aries Ascendant defines much of her on-court play: the serve-and-volley attacking game, the chip-and-charge, the fast reflexes, and matches done-and-dusted in half an hour. It describes her combative and perfectionist streaks, the ruthless elimination of on-court opponents, and the intimidation that players felt because of her sheer physical presence, thigh-slapping, cocky strut and muscular frame. Off-court, there could be a dismissive impatience that suggested dead weight wouldn't be carried and fools would not be entertained.

When matches weren't going Martina's way, an urgent need to put it right *now* would overcome her. 'She goes from arrogance to panic with nothing in between,' said tennis designer and spokesman Ted Tinling. Her perfectionism led to scowling, whining and cursing. With the Moon in Aries on the Ascendant, her feelings were always on the surface, and an edgy, sharp self-protectiveness warned fans and reporters to tread carefully.

The Moon rising in Aries also speaks of how she was the first tennis player in the 1980s to pioneer an exercise regime and diet. After her defection in 1975 (and a Jupiter transit over her Ascendant and through her 1st House), Martina discovered American fast food and ballooned to 167 pounds. Suddenly, she was the Great Wide Hope! Her natural athleticism won through and she captured the first few of her Grand Slam singles titles. But by April 1981 it was clear that she was unfit and not fulfilling her potential. Pluto's transit over her Sun saw Martina reinvent herself by using sports science (a fitness regime and nutritionist) to take her game to a new level, and make her a complete player and winning machine.

But what of Libra? We know from tabloids that Martina's most difficult area has been relationships: issues of avoiding emotional conflict and confrontation, and escaping controlling partners. This (along with her colourful entourage and choice of glamorous women) can be seen in Sun–Neptune in Libra in the 7th (and to some extent in the Mars in Pisces placement). Observers say that when Martina has fallen in love, she gives completely of herself. A frank, open, impulsive and naïve approach to the world (the Moon and Ascendant in Aries) can, of course, leave someone susceptible (Mars in Pisces, Sun–Neptune in the 7th) to control-freaks with other motives.

Writer Rita Mae Brown (Ascendant at 25° Libra, Sun–Mars in early Sagittarius) was her first partner.

When Martina started a relationship with ex-beauty queen Judy Nelson in March 1984, Martina was entering a record-breaking 74-match winning streak – TR Jupiter spent the year around her MC, but Neptune had moved into her MC sign. In love, she signed a non-marital agreement, promising to share her earnings. Nelson videotaped this on 12 February 1986 – TR Neptune was on Martina's MC at 5° Capricorn (Nelson's Mars at 5° Cancer is tightly square Jupiter–Neptune in Libra). The couple split on 3 February 1991, when TR Neptune conjunct Martina's 10th House (Equal) and SA Sun was at 29° Scorpio. Martina had fallen in love with another woman. Nelson sued to enforce their agreement in June (SA Sun square natal Pluto in the 5th) and the court case was in early September 1991 (SA Saturn reached Martina's MC). For Martina, who guarded her privacy so closely, the public scrutiny of her personal life was unbearable.

Mars at 13° Pisces opposite Venus–Jupiter (at 14° and 21° Virgo respectively) points to a devotion to animals, a gentleness and generosity of spirit, as well as the energy Martina puts into fighting for equal rights. Interestingly, the mid mutable degrees of the Virgo–Pisces polarity appear with regularity in the charts of those concerned with the oppressed, including gay rights campaigners and champions and those who personify the various public images of homosexuality.

Nowadays, Martina continues to play tennis at a competitive level and take on new physical and mental challenges (from expeditions to mountain climbs). She has spent much time attending to personal growth, developing a more philosophical, Zen-like approach to life (connecting to the Neptune/Pisces/12th House subtone in her chart). In February 2010 (as TR Pluto conjunct the MC and TR Saturn squared it), she was told she had breast cancer. Having felt in control of her body, diet and fitness for so long, this came as a major blow. She underwent radiation treatment in May and is back to full health.

An inspiration to many, Martina learned one of her great life lessons from her idol Katharine Hepburn – the legendary actress with the Sun in fixed Taurus and Ascendant in fixed Scorpio. Hepburn told her, 'It's not what you start in life, it's what you finish.' Fiery, cardinal Martina summed it up herself, too:

> The moment of victory is much too short to live for that alone.

Key Player: Billie Jean King

With the Moon at 0° Libra and the Sun at 29° Scorpio, Billie Jean King envisioned a new equality for women in sports and fought a long political battle to create a professional tour and generate sponsorship deals. Famously, on 20 September 1973, she struck a blow for women's tennis (and Lib) when she trounced chauvinist pig Bobby Riggs in a 'Battle of the Sexes' match in front of an estimated 50 million viewers. In the sky, Mars was stationary retrograde (square King's Pluto in the 7th), and Saturn in Cancer squared Pluto in Libra. Her SA Sun was 29° Sagittarius. It was a public spectacle, and a gamble that paid off. Always a mentor to Navratilova (note their synastry), King was enlisted by Martina in April 1989 to help her rejuvenate her tennis – TR Uranus was stationary on Martina's MC. It returned to the MC when Martina won her ninth Wimbledon in July 1990 (and SA Jupiter conjunct her Sun in Libra).

Key Player: Chris Evert

Evert vs. Navratilova. One of the great sporting rivalries of the 20th century. From 1973 to 1988, they played 80 times. Their contrast in styles mesmerized tennis fans, and their charts couldn't be more different: watery, fixed Chris; fiery, cardinal Martina. Chris, the more consistent, cast the longer shadow. Martina, the more sensational, radiated the brighter light. Off-court, they were the best of friends. With her Moon–Saturn–Venus rising in Scorpio, Chris had a controlled, industrious and sheltered upbringing. Spectators rarely saw her Sag–Scorp quick wit and dirty sense of humour. Instead, they met the unflappable, tunnel-visioned 'ice princess', the defensive baseliner and counter-puncher (Scorpio) with an unnerving 'nothing personal' steeliness. Adept at long rallies and at her best on slow clay courts (fixity), Evert personified mental toughness and killer instinct (Scorpio).

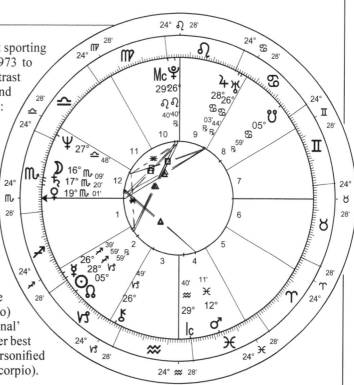

Mystery Chart 1: An Explosive Sportsman

Put your skills to the test to see whether the following statements can be 'found' in each of the following Mystery Charts.

Do transits, progressions or directions confirm the life event dates? Do astrological significators back up these biographical details and personality traits?

- Our mystery man, a self-confessed 'split personality' when under pressure, is known by colleagues for his explosive temperament, risk-taking and fiery emotional outbursts.

- A prodigious youth with great sporting talent, he began to achieve professional recognition in late January 1989 at the age of 17.

- The son of a Catholic engineering professor and his biochemist wife, this man worked to raise money to pay the medical bills for his sister, who had been diagnosed with throat cancer.

- His lowest professional point came in early July 1998, when he spoke of feelings of despair and thoughts of suicide.

- He is known for his charitable work on behalf of children, as well as his love of designer labels and the high life in his adopted home of Monte Carlo.

- Modest, humorous and soft-spoken in private, he is also known to be religious and highly superstitious.

- He has come under attack from political groups and received death threats when his country was at war.

- His work took him all over the world, but he now has strong fears of long-distance travel.

- On 13 September 2001 he was drafted for military service, which took place between November 2001 and May 2002.

- After a two-year stretch of low achievement, injury problems and thoughts of retirement, he surprised pundits by reaching the pinnacle of his career on 9 July 2001.

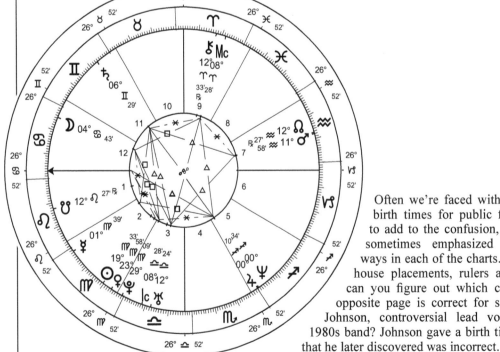

Often we're faced with conflicting birth times for public figures and, to add to the confusion, themes are sometimes emphasized in similar ways in each of the charts. Looking at house placements, rulers and transits, can you figure out which chart on the opposite page is correct for singer Holly Johnson, controversial lead vocalist of a 1980s band? Johnson gave a birth time in 1997 that he later discovered was incorrect.

Mystery Chart 2: Holly Johnson's Two Birth Times

Influenced by Bolan and Bowie, Johnson was the provocative, openly gay front man of the band Frankie Goes to Hollywood, who played their first gig in August 1980. Their first hit, 'Relax', was released on 31 October 1983. The song's sexually explicit lyrics resulted in it being banned from the airwaves on 13 January 1984, ensuring an immediate best-seller and national infamy.

An effeminate man of slight build, Johnson has always been uncompromisingly queer; he became *the* face of Britain in 1984. Unlike Boy George or camp TV stars such as Larry Grayson, Julian Clary and John Inman, Johnson was too threatening and effete to be a favourite with teenage girls and grannies: 'Johnson preened and strutted and sucked up the celebrity with fabulous arrogance. He knew he was made to be admired.' (*The Guardian*)

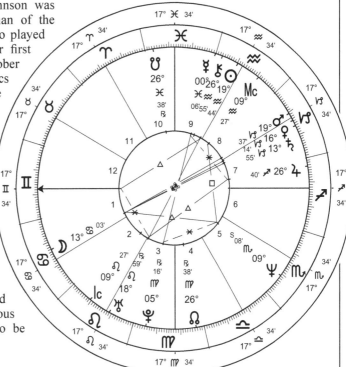

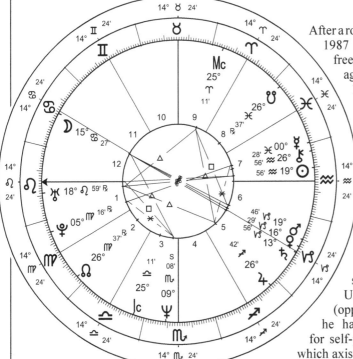

After a rollercoaster ride, the group split in March 1987 and Johnson secured his professional freedom with a landmark legal victory against his record company in February 1988. A few years later he had moved into relative obscurity. He is now seen as an icon of the 80s. In November 1991 Johnson was diagnosed as HIV positive, a condition he revealed in April 1993. He published an honest and witty autobiography in 1994. Johnson is also an artist, inspired by the work of Andy Warhol (Sun at 13° Leo).

Are we looking for a performer whose overt sexuality and provocative songs are described by an Aries MC and Uranus Rising? Or is the Sun on the MC (opp. Uranus) more fitting for the impact he had professionally? Is Jupiter angular for self-promotion and egomania? And across which axis does the Sun–Uranus opposition fall?

Mystery Chart 3: A Soul Survivor

This Mystery Woman has had a life of extreme highs and lows, and she remains a rock and roll music legend.

- This woman is known for her enduring career as a performer, her youthfulness, energy and zest for life, as well as surviving an abusive marriage and having strong religious convictions. Friends have described her as indomitable, dynamic, gutsy, proud and sexy. She describes herself as 'quite domesticated and down to earth; I [have] never left the reality of life.'

- A former friend and ex-personal assistant has described her as cold, tough, uncompromising, haughty, imperious and able to dispense with those closest to her.

- She was abandoned at the age of three by both parents, but was later reunited with them. But at age ten her mother left her, and her father followed suit three years later.

- She met her future husband (born 5 November 1931) in late 1956, and during the marriage they raised four sons.

- She began to work professionally – touring and recording – with her husband in 1959. Their first success came in October 1960, and coincided with a growth in her self-confidence. Her Svengali-like husband, however, grew increasingly controlling, unfaithful, erratic and violent.

- During the marriage she sought out the advice of psychics, tarot readers and astrologers, and became a devout Buddhist following depression and a suicide attempt in mid-1968. Yet it wasn't until Christmas 1973 that she began to gather reserves of inner strength and view her predicament with greater clarity.

- Out of both allegiance and fear she endured years of verbal and physical abuse before leaving her husband on 4 July 1976 in Dallas, Texas. She left penniless and soon accrued debts of $500,000. Rather than considering herself a victim during her marriage, she says that she had the qualities of patience, loyalty and endurance. Her divorce was effectively sealed by November 1977 and decreed final on 29 March 1978.

- She resurrected her career in April 1977, but it took concerts on 25 September 1981 and in December 1982 to lead to a career rebirth and phenomenal solo success from December 1983.

- In September 1984 she reached the top of the US charts and negotiated a film deal. She won recognition from her musical peers in February 1985. In June 1993 her life story was told on film.

- She has toured the world and even made the record books for singing to the single largest audience for a solo performer. On 30 June 2000 she announced she would be retiring that November from her gruelling worldwide schedule. She continues to record and lives an extravagant lifestyle at home in Zurich with her German partner, 17 years her junior.

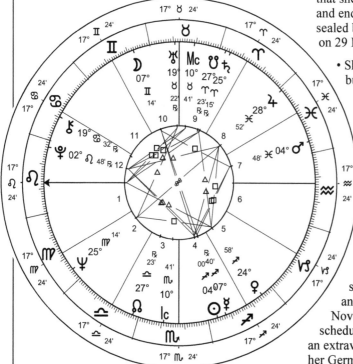

Mystery Chart 4: A Notorious Aristocrat

Whether a cruel, degenerative pervert or a pioneer exposing the darker sides of human sexuality, this Mystery Man challenged and outraged every aspect of civilized society, including the Church and government.

- Our notorious Mystery Man's reputation is that of a sexually insatiable hedonist who mixed sex with violence and torture.

- His mother was abandoned by her bohemian diplomat husband and sought refuge in a convent, leaving our Mystery Man with relatives.

- As a child he was rebellious, haughty and despotic – traits he carried into his adult life. He was also known for his violent temper and explosive tantrums.

- At six he was sent to stay with a debauched uncle who introduced him to a world of cynicism and hedonism. This began a lifelong fascination with sex.

- He became obsessed with pain and whipping after being subjected to physical discipline at school from age ten.

- By his late teens he was indulging his more extreme sexual tastes with prostitutes, feeling free to explore his darkest fantasies without moral constraint.

- His reputation was damaged beyond repair following an arrest for a sexual incident on Easter Sunday, 3 April 1768.

- On several occasions he fled his country to escape punishment. In his absence he was sentenced to death in June 1772 for attempting to sodomize and beat four prostitutes.

- In February 1779 a 'supernatural vision' of an ancestor inspired him to write. His 15 manuscripts would provide insight into the dark recesses of the human soul. He often attacked women, especially mothers, in print.

- After a long marriage he fell in love at the age of 53 with a girl of 22. In his later years he found himself destitute and turned to publishing pornography.

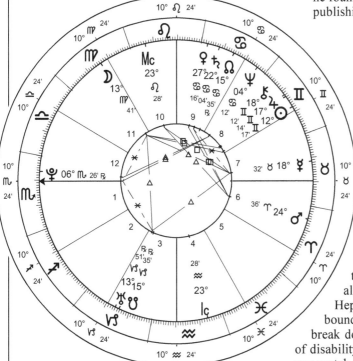

On the next page are the charts of two world-class female athletes with much in common: both are former Olympic champions and record-breakers who turned professional in 1989, both have been described as dedicated, focused, hugely positive and competitive. Both are role models who have been awarded the MBE and OBE. But one is a black all-round athlete who was the Olympic Heptathlon champ, the other a wheelchair-bound sportswoman who has done much to break down barriers and normalize awareness of disability. From the following information can you match the biographies to the correct charts?

Mystery Charts 5 and 6: Two Sportswomen

Which biography belongs to which horoscope?

Sportswoman 1: Born with spina bifida and confined to a wheelchair, this woman won her first race at age 15 in the 100 metres at the Junior National Games. She studied politics and sports at university. She was at the top of her sport for 19 years and has held over 30 world records in events ranging from the 100 metres to the marathon. An ambassador for sports and disability awareness, she won 16 paralympic medals, including 11 Olympic golds (four of which were won at Sydney's Paralympic Games in October 2000). Her autobiography was published on 4 October 2001, and she gave birth to a daughter in February 2002.

Personality-wise, she is modest, enjoys a good laugh at her own expense and does not want to be seen as a pioneer, simply as an athlete. After her retirement in May 2007, she became a TV sports commentator.

Sportswoman 2: From a one-parent family (her father left before her birth), this charismatic athlete was raised by strong, independent black women. As a child, she had singing and dancing aspirations, but started sports training at 14 and turned professional in 1989. Her breakthrough occurred in August 1994 when she won gold at the Commonwealth Games in Victoria, Canada. On 24 September 2000 she won an Olympic gold medal in Sydney in the Heptathlon, a testament to her all-round sporting talent. She became a mother in April 2002. Her autobiography was released in September 2001. In December 2004, she was the runner-up on TV's *Strictly Come Dancing*. She loves being an ambassador for her sport, revels in her glamorous image and enjoys being photographed, having proven to be a natural model and sporting pin-up with her dazzling smile and athletic frame.

Mystery Chart 7: A Graceful Actress

In this Mystery Chart, the features that stand out are: Neptune rising in Leo, the Venusian overtone and the angular Saturn. Our formidable Mystery Woman was born three days after Prime Minister Margaret Thatcher (they share a cardinal T-square), and has been likened to 'a porcelain vase with a hand grenade concealed inside it'.

- In her teens she began acting in Hollywood films, later moving onto the Broadway stage and into long-running TV drama. Her career as a character actress has spanned over 70 years.

- As a child she was taught to be independent and self-reliant. Her mother was an actress who struggled to find work and became jealous of our Mystery Woman's success.

- Her image is one of gracefulness, elegance, poise and dignity. On-screen, she moved from playing the shrew to the villainess and finally to playing the inquisitive, good-natured busybody.

- Broadway has always offered her a lifeline when screen roles are scarce: stage triumphs occurred in April 1964, May 1966, May 1973 and March 1979. In May 2007, she returned to Broadway after a 23-year absence.

- Even with a prominent Neptune she has managed to be untainted by scandal, instead using the placement to develop an enduring body of work. Neptune also attests to her career longevity and stage presence. She has said, 'I love owning the stage and that unbelievable feedback from an audience.'

- In September 1970 her Malibu home was destroyed by fire.

- On 30 September 1984 she began a long stint in her most famous television role.

- She has been married twice, firstly to an actor (who turned out to be homosexual) from 27 September 1945 to 11 September 1946, and later to an agent, from 12 August 1949.

- Her second husband died on 29 January 2003.

- She underwent hip surgery in May 1994 for a second time.

- Of her desire to act she has said, 'I always wanted to act, but not for recognition, nor to think I amounted to something. I did it because I adored becoming someone else, escaping my own personality.'

Mystery Charts Revealed:
1. Goran Ivanisevic
2. The chart on the bottom left is the correct horoscope for singer Holly Johnson
3. Tina Turner
4. The Marquis de Sade
5–6. Sportswoman 1 is Tanni Grey-Thompson, whose chart is pictured bottom left. Sportswoman 2 is Denise Lewis, whose horoscope is top right
7. Angela Lansbury

Three Essays

Before I sign off with some final words in 'Labours of Love', I would like to share three features that were written for *The Astrological Journal* – two from early 2009 and one from late 2011. The first two articles are on Jupiter and Neptune (their conjunction in Aquarius was a major feature of 2009), while the third article is a follow-up of sorts, as it examines some possibilities of what Neptune's move into Pisces might bring. The pieces have been edited slightly for this book.

Vegas, Hollywood and Other Cut-rate Babylons

Making personal links to countries and cities is a fascinating area of study in astrology. Which places resonate with us? Where might we feel at home? Which parts of our charts will be emphasized or drawn out in certain countries?

There are various ways to observe and research the synastry between people and places. There's the direct link of interaspects (e.g. the US's Moon is trine my Ascendant). Or there can be simple sign placements in common – for example, the US's melting pot Moon in Aquarius has attracted and welcomed Brits who have the same Moon sign, from *Phantom* star Michael Crawford, Cary Grant and Vivien Leigh (an Indian-born English star who 'stole' the cherished role of Scarlett O'Hara from hundreds of American actresses) to Princess Diana and the eccentric Quentin Crisp, who emigrated to New York at the age of 70 to become a tourist attraction and self-proclaimed 'resident alien'. And, here in the UK, we tend to like our Royal Family and elected officials to embody Leo and Capricorn, two traditional signs of respect, dignity, rank and class (in both senses of the word). In the midnight 1 January 1801 UK chart, the Sun is in Capricorn and Jupiter and Saturn (royalty/those 'born to the purple' and elected officials) are in Leo (in the 10th and 11th Houses respectively).

There's also locational astrology and Jim Lewis's copyrighted Astro*Carto*Graphy, and although in my opinion neither is a tool precise enough to aid rectification, there are some very vivid examples of their effectiveness. Thatcher's Sun and Mars in Libra rise through her place of 'victory', the Falkland Islands, where she 'restored balance' through war (Libra); Bush Jr.'s Neptune is on the IC through New Orleans (where Hurricane Katrina caused massive flooding and was handled chaotically by his administration); Jane Fonda's publicity-hungry Moon in Leo runs through Hanoi in Vietnam (*Hanoi, I'm home!*); and anti-establishment boxer Muhammad Ali's Saturn passes through the MC in Washington, DC and his Mars–MC line goes through Houston, Texas, where a court found him guilty of draft evasion and stripped him of his boxing title. Sagittarian Walt Disney has his Mercury–IC line near Disneyland, where he sent his employees on holiday with their families, and his big dream project, Walt Disney World (which he never lived to see opened), is on his Neptune–MC line in Florida and was opened on 1 October 1971, two weeks after the Jupiter–Neptune conjunction in Sagittarius.

On a personal note, I have a Virgo Moon rising in Singapore and have always been at home among the lush landscapes and felt comfortable browsing the inexpensive portable electronic delights! And it's so *clean*. But my only problem when I travelled to Singapore as a boy and teenager (six times in seven years) was that my natal Moon–Neptune square was severely tested. I was always being dragged off the street by pushy shop-owners flogging 'copy watches' and other nefarious temptations. My Moon in Virgo square Neptune was under pressure to set firm boundaries (*Learn to say 'no thanks', Frankie*), and to be rude or dismissive if necessary to avoid being harassed and suckered in. Interestingly, a student of mine at the LSA hated Singapore when he visited. He felt very ill at ease with its strict laws, rules and restrictions (there are many). Not surprisingly, he has Saturn on the MC running through the city.

So, with numerous examples in and out of class, I learned that when we travel we have the chance to experience specific areas of our charts (and character) in places where these planets/aspects are angular. (2012: I've just returned from a wonderful trip to Melbourne, where I had the warmest reception while teaching astrology at the FAA Conference. My Sun–Venus conjunction in Aries runs through the city.)

But there's more to locational astrology. We have transits and progressions to these planets/lines, too, pinpointing the 'when' factor in the 'where'. Looking at the transits of 31 August 1997, we know that Princess Diana died at the time TR Uranus was on her natal Jupiter at 5° Aquarius (a transit that could indicate a variety of happenings, from sudden surprises and accidents abroad to changes of fortune, etc.). But her progressed Jupiter had moved back to 0° Aquarius and, in her progressed chart, Jupiter was rising through Paris that year. And even more fascinating, her potent Mars (natally conjunct Pluto, and triggered by the eclipse the day after her death) had moved, in her progressed chart, to a position where it was setting (i.e. on the Descendant) through Cairo and Alexandria, where fellow fatality Dodi Fayed was born. Diana's progressed Moon was on the IC there, too.

There's also the astrology of associations and correspondences. As we know from Nick Campion's encyclopaedic *The Book of World Horoscopes*, countries and cities have birth charts (often several). National charts are fascinating (and interaspects between a country's chart and ours can prove interesting), but these moments of incorporation (often hundreds or thousands of years after the countries were formed) give us only part of the overall picture. We need to see what the country or place *means to us* and to our clients

Certain countries have a particular 'feel' about them – to us but maybe not to others. And which signs or planets are apparent or triggered when we travel to a specific location? For example, Sue Tompkins has linked Australia to the planet Uranus because, from her observations, European clients often emigrate under Uranus transits or Solar Arc directions. We can also make other links to Uranus: the British government sent convicts *down under* to Australia, of course (Uranus turns matters upside down) because of overcrowding (Uranus is associated with space, and Australia has vast amounts of unoccupied space). On 18 August 1786, some five years after the discovery of Uranus and with transiting Saturn conjunct Pluto in Aquarius, the decision was made to uproot a group of 775 unruly outlaws (Uranus) by sending them to Botany Bay. The fleet set sail on 13 May 1787 and arrived on 20 January 1788, the day the Sun moved into Aquarius, opposing Uranus. The penal colonies ran for 80 years, almost a Uranus Return.

But it's easy to stereotype (a function of the planet Saturn), and the following observations are not intended to do that, nor to insult anyone (particularly in this climate of extreme political correctness – the philosophy of Saturn-gone-mad).

Every country has a persona and its people have characteristics that other countries pick up on, insult, mock or exaggerate for effect. Some Brits see the Australians as very comfortable with the planet Uranus, giving a good two-fingered salute to the establishment. For example, *Mad Max* was one of Australia's first international successes at the box office and was set in a dystopian, apocalyptic future where law and order are beginning to break down (Uranus). More recent films (from *Babe* to *Priscilla, Queen of the Desert*) are often stories of the underdog, outcast or other sorts making good and winning over disbelievers. These films often reject the conventional format of a happy ending, too. (Australian film and TV had 'lost its virginity' in the early 1970s with sexploitation, bed-hopping and shocking ribaldry!)

Some of the images that Westerners have of Japan are personifications of Virgo and Saturn, whether or not either of these feature in an 'official' horoscope for the country. They include the valued work ethic and productivity of the country – an industry of hard workers seen as regimented cogs in a wheel; the attention to detail, precision and 'smallness' – from food preparation to origami; the characteristics of humility, 'saving face', courtesy and the importance of manners; the healthy diet; the micro gadgets and electronic accessories; the geisha, and so on.

I lived in Italy for a few summers and the country appeared strongly Gemini–Cancer to me. There's an emphasis on food (so much food), on beautiful coastlines, and the strong unity of church and family. In particular, the influence of *mamma* is foremost (Cancer). And the Gemini aspect is seen in the way Italians speak with their hands, the multitude of languages and dialects (every town, perhaps almost every street, has its own dialect), the sharp division between north and south, and the way Italians speak proudly of avoiding paying taxes! (Mutable signs are about avoidance.)

All these comments may or may not be 'true', and of course each country has every planet and sign at work on some level. But these observations derive from a sort of 'national identity' that is seen by a country's inhabitants and visitors, in the same way that we recognize Ascendant-type personas in horoscope analyses.

While I was in Las Vegas, it felt Jupiter and Neptune (and Leo) personified. I had just seen a client perform on stage: here was an acrobatic showman with the Sun in Leo on the MC who had moved to Vegas a few years before (when TR Neptune opposed his Sun) to accept a job in a fantasy-based aquatic show called *Le Rêve* ('The Dream')! The link between astrological symbolism and life events couldn't have been more apt. So I did some research into the town.

Apparently 'prehistoric' Southern Nevada was a marsh of abundant water (Jupiter–Neptune) and vegetation before its now famous arid landscape. Water trapped underground surfaced and the Las Vegas Valley was born. Discovered by Rafael Rivera in 1830, it would act as an oasis for Spanish traders looking for gold in California. In May 1844, some 14 years later (Neptune's sojourn through one sign), John Frémont's (Frémont means 'noble protector' or 'protector of freedom') expedition arrived and camped at the Springs. Mormons settled a decade later for a few years, but it wasn't until 15 May 1905 that the town of Las Vegas was established (with an exact Mars–Jupiter opposition in Scorpio–Taurus, suggesting enterprise and risk-taking in areas of money).

For a town so identified with gambling, it had unusual beginnings: at midnight on 1 October 1910, a strict anti-gambling law became effective in Nevada (Jupiter was at 21° Libra square Neptune at 21° Cancer and both were aspected by Uranus – *bans* – at 21° Capricorn). Three weeks later, Mars joined Jupiter and a gambling underground was set up, which flourished until a New Moon in Pisces on 19 March 1931 (TR Saturn was at 21° Capricorn, Jupiter was in Cancer) when a legalized gambling bill was written to raise taxes for public schools. This would protect (Jupiter in Cancer) Vegas from the Great Depression (Saturn in Capricorn) of the 1930s. (Vegas had been incorporated as a city on 16 March 1911 – the Sun was in Pisces and its rulers Jupiter and Neptune were in a 5° trine.)

On 3 April 1941, the first casino opened. The El Rancho Vegas Hotel–Casino triggered a boom in the late 40s with several hotel–casinos being built on what is now the Las Vegas Strip. Later, mobster Bugsy Siegel built the Flamingo. And this began the Vegas we now know, which appears so Jupiterian, Neptunian and Leonine: the huge, lavish, no-expense-spared Vegas hotel–casino–resorts with celebrity crooners, magic acts and topless revues. (One of the biggest hotels is the MGM Grand with its *golden lion* at the helm of

the hotel entrance.) Vegas has since been a mix of sleazy, seedy joints and high-rolling members-only clubs, with gambling run 24/7 and no clocks (Saturn) in sight. (Initially, Vegas was famous for being the 'no' town: no minimum, no speed limit, no sales tax, no income tax, no waiting period for marriages. This is both the no-limits of Jupiter and the no-boundaries of Neptune.) And then there are the Mob ties to the town, and the desperation of gambling addicts, the big wins and bigger losses, and the enormous tourist industry (37.5 million people visited in 2008 and spent $42.8 billion). Landing in Las Vegas and staying on The Strip is like being a visitor to another planet – it is an unreal set of monstrous buildings begging us to suspend reality. In many corners, it's the town that taste forgot, but it has its unique, opulent style that attracts so many.

One of the most famous associations with Vegas must be the Rat Pack of the 1960s. Dean Martin had Pisces Rising and his Neptune–Descendant line ran through Vegas. Frank Sinatra had Sun–Mercury in Sagittarius square Jupiter in Pisces, plus Neptune on the MC in Leo. Sammy Davis Jr. had the Sun in Sagittarius, and Peter Lawford was born with Jupiter square Neptune. Other people strongly associated with Vegas are Elvis (Sagittarius Rising, Moon in Pisces, relocated Jupiter rising in Vegas), Celine Dion (Jupiter exactly square Neptune, her high-grossing show started on 25 March 2003, when Jupiter opposed Neptune), and Liberace (Moon in Sagittarius rising through Las Vegas).

Another Jupiter–Neptune–Leo place is Hollywood, Los Angeles (la-la land). It is famous for its movie industry, the celebrity homes, the psychics, the quest for fame, the multi-million dollar movie deals, the bluff, the ego trips and debauchery, the selling out, the casting couch, the greed and excess, not to mention the addiction to therapy and New Age cures to work through other addictions such as substance abuse.

'Tinseltown' is the glittering centre of the movies, huge film studios and powerful moguls, the biggest being Louis B Mayer who created the star system during MGM's golden years. (MGM, the studio associated with the roaring lion, glamorous stars and Technicolor, was founded on 16 April 1924, when Neptune was in Leo trine Jupiter in Sagittarius.) But although the pursuit of fame and fortune goes hand in hand with Hollywood, its Walk of Fame is

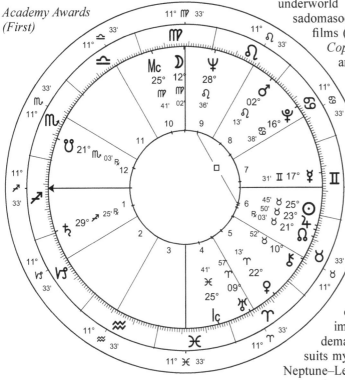

*Academy Awards
(First)*

underworld lifestyle of drugs, prostitutes and sadomasochism as his collection of popular films (*Top Gun, Flashdance, Beverly Hills Cop*). As well as being born with the Sun and Moon in Scorpio square Pluto, Simpson had Sagittarius Rising, ruler Jupiter in Leo and Neptune exactly on the MC. (His Mars in Gemini line sets very close to Los Angeles – the aggressive deal-maker interested in a variety of sexual situations.) Have a read of *You'll Never Eat Lunch in this Town Again* by producer Julia Phillips to really gauge how far and how low Simpson and Jupiter–Neptune have reached in Hollywood.

I've always experienced New York City and New Yorkers, on the other hand, as fast-paced, vibrant, immediate, impatient, pushy and demanding. Very Mercury–Mars, which suits my own chart. If Broadway is Jupiter–Neptune–Leo once more, then the fame and success from New York appear to come from hard work, numerous auditions and juggling three jobs

a sleazy place to walk along. This Hollywood street may be paved with gold, but its gold is the stuff of Jupiter: gold plate that, when rubbed, comes off on your fingers – revealing just below the surface a boulevard of broken dreams.

And of course the **Academy Awards** (chart above) are associated with Hollywood. Oscar night is one out-of-this-world evening of glamour, excess, designer gowns and jewels. It's a far cry from the sedate, private dinner in Hollywood at 8 p.m. on 16 May 1929, when the first awards were handed out. But in the horoscope for that night, the Sun–Jupiter conjunction is square Neptune in Leo: all three significators in aspect and an indication of what was to follow.

Consider the chart of Hollywood producer **Don Simpson** (chart on right), who was as notorious in the 80s for his decadent, excessive

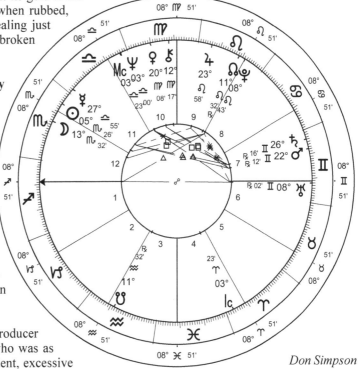

Don Simpson

a day – all Mars and Mercury. People in the frantic pursuit (Mercury–Mars) of the dream (Neptune) of stardom (Jupiter). When you encounter New Yorkers hungry for fame, you get the impression that if they ever did succeed, you might be physically forced to sit down and watch them.

When Oscar Wilde arrived in New York on 3 January 1882, as TR Jupiter conjunct his EQHS 9th, he was on his Jupiter–Descendant line, and later wrote 'America is the only country that went from barbarism to decadence without civilization in between'. It's anyone's guess where US writer Charles Luckman had his Jupiter when he wrote, 'The trouble with America is that there are far too many wide open spaces… surrounded by teeth.'

Reality Bites: One Shot at the Grand Illusion

With the Jupiter–Chiron–Neptune dance in Aquarius present all year [this was written in 2009], I wanted to look at the astrology of celebrity – specifically how the astrology of the times reflects the current over-saturation of minor celebrities and contestants on TV reality/talent shows.

It's a safe bet to say that Neptune's sojourn through Aquarius has reflected the current fashion for the *everyman* celebrity – an umbrella of talented and not-so talented ordinary people (Aquarius) thrust into the spotlight, courtesy of Facebook, YouTube and reality TV shows like *Big Brother*, *The X Factor*, *Pop Idol* and *Britain's Got Talent*. There has also been an endless stream of shows inviting minor celebrities to perform or function out of their comfort zone (*Strictly*, *Dancing on Ice*, *I'm a Celebrity… Get Me Out of Here!*).

It is ironic that during the transit of Neptune in Aquarius so much of the programming has been termed 'reality TV', when in fact it's an editing and structural exercise in moulding, duping and manipulating the audience. By no means a new genre, these reality TV shows have a surveillance, voyeuristic or intrusive slant where personal boundaries are eroded and the illusion of real, ordinary people (Neptune in Aquarius) is sold to the masses and bought by an unquestioning general public (or, if not unquestioning, happy to accept the manipulation). And by putting performers into (albeit heightened) daily routines or training situations, we are invited to see glamorous, 'famous' people being themselves, where no aspect of their lives is left unexposed (Paris Hilton, Anna Nicole Smith and Jordan/Katie Price come to mind). An illusion that they are, when stripped of the make-up, just like you or me. In effect, we are witnessing both the 'elevation' of ordinary people to celebrity status and the reduction of celebrity life to the mundane, routine, dull and (overly) familiar.

The Neptune in Aquarius symbolism is everywhere in the media, as the public at large are duped into believing they have a vote – that their opinion holds some sway. This was seen in the recent phone-fix scandals in the UK (beginning in February–March 2007) when Saturn in Leo opposed Neptune in Aquarius ('Phone-vote scandals rock trust in broadcasters,' the headlines ran).

Each Neptune transit through a sign sells fame and glamour to the previous Neptune generation, and we now have a series of teenagers (with Neptune in Capricorn) who believe that they can achieve fame and fortune by appearing on reality TV, by being a 'somebody' for doing nothing, and gaining recognition by standing out from the crowd (an Aquarian dilemma). The previous generation had *Fame* (the film and series) to inspire them to be wannabes. The fame of the 80s, which required that 'you start paying in sweat', has been replaced by a narcissistic entitlement to being special and rich. (Granted, at best, the Leo–Aquarius polarity knows that specialness is measured by one's creative commitment to oneself and to the group rather than by accolades.) This contemporary craving has resulted in the fifteen minutes of fame promised by Andy Warhol being diminished to about four and a half.

As Chiron approached its first one-degree conjunction to Neptune since 1945-46, Jade Goody, a symbol of this new everyman celebrity, died of cervical cancer. During the last few months of her short life, a woman who was synonymous with confrontational, loud-mouthed ignorance and ranting racism was being seen as a people's princess. Yet, for someone so vilified a few short years ago, her brutal honesty and openness, black-and-white mindset and shoot-from-the-*lip* personality had finally won the respect of many people. And it brought Neptune in Aquarius to the fore with much of the public connecting in a genuine, humanitarian sense of compassion for her suffering.

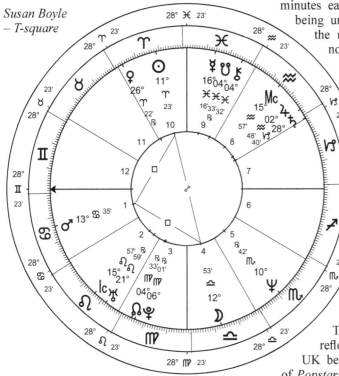

Susan Boyle – T-square

minutes earlier), it warns of over-saturation or being unprotected, taken advantage of or at the mercy of the money-makers of this notoriously shark-infested profession.

With an acerbic, home-truths manner not dissimilar to fellow Librans Judge Judy and Anne Robinson, Simon ('I don't mean to be rude, but…') Cowell was born with a Venus–Pluto conjunction in Virgo square to Jupiter in Sagittarius. He has positioned himself as guru-Svengali and manufacturer of conveyor-belt pop to a whole generation of wannabes. This current set-up of auditions, contests and public voting has almost eliminated alternative routes to national music acclaim.

The first wave of the new wannabes, as reflected by Neptune in Aquarius, in the UK began in January 2001 with the airing of *Popstars*. The winning singers formed a band named Hear'Say – a word that, aside from its legal definition, means 'unverified information heard or received from another; a rumour'. (The word 'fame' originates from *pheme* and *fama*, meaning 'rumour'.) Predictably, the band dissolved soon after their TV victory.

By 2001, the first UK series of *Big Brother* had already hit TV screens (it began on 14 July 2000). As an astrological piece of synchronicity, it's interesting that both the winner and runner-up shared the same birthday (16 October, although in different years) with presenter Davina McCall. Two years later, Jade Goody, a dental nurse born with Venus opposite Neptune, became the series' most successful alumnus, entering the house on 24 May 2002, following TR Saturn conjunct her Sun. She emerged a household name (as transiting Pluto returned to oppose her Sun).

A few weeks later, as Venus retrograded into (and stationed at the final degree of) Pisces, the media found a new working class princess: **Susan Boyle** (chart above). Boyle's singing surprised everyone on *Britain's Got Talent* and she has captured the spirit of the times. Jupiter–Neptune can speak of a global phenomenon. Up to her audition last autumn, Boyle had spent much of her life caring for her elderly mother and subjugating her own ambitions (note the natal Full Moon with Mars in Cancer as the apex of a T-square). But with her MC in Aquarius (and transiting Jupiter having conjunct it some weeks before the show aired), Boyle has become a symbol of the working-class hero and, true to Jupiter–Chiron–Neptune, a reminder not to give up on one's dreams, however wounded or downtrodden one might be. There is an eloquent article on Susan Boyle and her aptly titled rendition of 'I Dreamed a Dream' from *Les Miserables* by the late Robert Blaschke on www.mountainastrologer.com

Yet as the press and public seek to elevate Boyle, there is also the temptation to re-enact the Tall Poppy Syndrome (*build 'em up and cut 'em down*). And with SA Neptune hitting her Descendant in 2010 (or now, in 2009, if the birth time is a few

There's a difference between the 'accidental' celebrity of *Big Brother* contestants and the fame generated by weekly appearances on singing competitions such as *The X Factor* (sold to us by the Cowell fame factory). I do not have access to many of the data of *Big Brother* contestants, but I suspect the popular and best remembered contestants would have charts with a lunar or

Aquarian emphasis (striking a public chord) and the planets of celebrity – Jupiter and Neptune – active during their time in the limelight. The latter would reflect the whirlwind of publicity and the disorientating feeling of having one's anonymity disappear and private life eroded by an intrusive media. A fall from grace or disinterest in their activities usually follows – which is equally disorientating – with further Neptunian symbolism abounding ('where are they now?').

While researching this article, I came across a piece by astrology entrepreneur Robert Currey on his website (www.astrology.co.uk/news/tourettes.htm) about Pete Bennett, the winner of *Big Brother 7*. A wacky, likeable guy with Tourette's Syndrome, **Pete Bennett** (chart above, on right) was a massive hit with audiences. Interestingly, he showed no outward signs of Tourette's in his early childhood. It was diagnosed when he was 14 – at the time he lost contact with his father (SA Mercury squared Neptune, which is natally on his MC). The condition was said to have been later aggravated by an addiction to ketamine, which led him to 'go completely bananas' in 2005, when transiting Pluto journeyed over his MC. Pete was born with the Moon conjunct Venus in Aquarius, and during his stay in the BB house (18 May to 18 August 2006), transiting Jupiter stationed at its own natal degree (Jupiter return).

Pop idols and other custom-made entertainers are more likely, it appears from research, to have Venus prominent. Manufactured pop is Venusian. And when successfully packaged to appeal to the masses – everyone from 8 to 80 – Neptune is very often prominent. For pop idols to have more of a generational impact (or to be a symbol of their generation), Pluto contacts to the inner planets (particularly the Moon and Mercury) appear to be necessary.

Pete Bennett

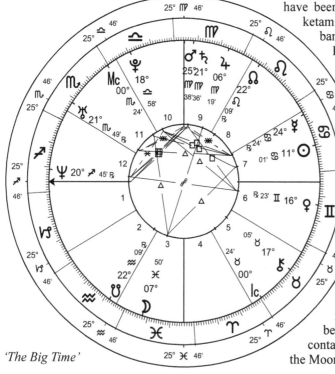

'The Big Time'

Let's take a look at a few talent show winners (mainly from *The X Factor* and *Pop Idol*). Luckily for astrologers, many have been twins or born in Scotland, so their full birth data are available.

Back in 1980, Sheena Easton was packaged for a commercial audience (her Sun is opposite Neptune) with the help of a TV show documenting her bid for fame. ***The Big Time*** (chart on opposite page, bottom) began on 2 July 1980 at 20:10 GDT. Set for London, the chart has Neptune rising in Sagittarius opposite Venus in Gemini – a perfect aspect for its aim: to watch and mould a young, plucky girl as she took her first steps in the music industry. The journey was tough and Sheena needed backbone and perseverance (note the show's Venus–Neptune opposition is part of a T-square, with Mars–Saturn in Virgo as the apex). A downside to the Venus pop factory of cover songs and watered-down pop (orchestrated nowadays by two Venusian Simons: Libran Simon Cowell and Taurean Simon Fuller) is not being taken seriously in the music industry. Fortunately, Easton fought to reinvent herself and was tenacious (having her own Mars–Saturn aspect – an opposition from Cancer to Capricorn) and able to move away from her pop package (natal Venus conjuncts her MC). Cheryl Baker, *Eurovision Song Contest* winner with Bucks Fizz, also has Venus on the MC.

The pop career of Michelle McManus (Venus opposite Neptune), winner of *Pop Idol 2*, sank without trace soon after her victory in December 2003. Steve Brookstein (Sun conjunct Neptune, Venus square Pluto) and Leon Jackson (Sun conjunct Neptune, both square Moon) had similar fates. True to the 'letting go' aspect of Neptune, record labels drop these artists at the first sign of their fame waning. *Fame Academy* winner David Sneddon (Sun square Neptune–MC) rejected his pop status (he won the competition when transiting Pluto hit his MC), went underground and returned as an Indie singer-songwriter. (Jupiter in the 6th is often an indication of a brief flash of fame – popular for a season before returning to a more mundane position in or out of the industry.)

Will Young, the first *Pop Idol* winner (Venus conjunct Neptune), appears to be an exception to the rule. With a Moon–Pluto conjunction which is square to Mercury, he has carved out a career and his own fan-base. *The X Factor* winner Shayne Ward (Mercury conjunct Pluto) is working hard to avoid the one-hit wonder curse of reality TV, and Darius Danesh has been another to escape the stereotype, despite having been in two high-profile TV talent competitions.

TV will continue to churn out ready-made celebrity and instant pop stars, and the manufactured celebrities will work hard to extend their minutes of fame under the public glare. Jupiter–Chiron–Neptune is unlikely to herald the end of our fixation with celebrity but it will act as a signpost for a new series of fashions reflected by the ingresses of Uranus in Aries and Neptune in Pisces.

Jupiter, Chiron and Neptune's interplay from May 2009 to February 2010 (during which they conjunct one another at various times at 21°, 24° and 26° Aquarius) is explored by Melanie Reinhart on her website, www.melaniereinhart.com. She writes: 'Chiron's placing in Aquarius concerns our vulnerability to "group think" and its potential to mislead and even wound us.' And certainly with this triple conjunction, there's a temptation to sleepwalk through the constant wave of suffering (and manipulation) around us, to adopt a detached numbness to avoid relevant social issues, and believe what we're told/sold – until, that is, Uranus in Aries awakens the Ram and we start refusing to follow the herd. Melanie has observed that the founding of the United Nations took place during the last triple conjunction (which occurred in Libra) and warns us: 'We have been living in a field of socially sanctioned addiction to various kinds of distractions, so we need to "go against the prevailing view" [and] begin to cultivate the capacity to "stay with" our experience… There is less resistance, and therefore this is a time to stay focused.' The current period is an ideal time to renegotiate the people's rights, to examine our dreams and visions, and emerge with a new, workable social commitment to one another; a 'rekindling of faith and hope', as Melanie puts it. It is our first opportunity to envision the years of Neptune in Pisces that lie ahead, and to make a very personal decision: to either escape by default (to go AWOL) or to make a commitment to transcend what so many people are settling for.

Starting at Zero: Setting the Scene for Neptune in Pisces

It's been my experience that when an outer planet moves through the final few degrees of a sign, we let go of (or 'say goodbye' to) certain aspects, ideas and even iconic figures that have been at the very heart of that ingress. For example, Neptune's exit from Aquarius (which brought the fashion of a digital age of aesthetic 'cool' for all) coincided with the death and canonization of ruthless Apple co-founder Steve Jobs (Neptune was at 28° Aquarius). *The Telegraph* (6 October 2011) wrote that Jobs convinced consumers that 'purchasing Apple products somehow conferred membership of an exclusive and visionary club' (the shadow 'Leo-side' to everyman Aquarius).

The previous changeover saw the deaths of Princess Diana and Mother Teresa when Neptune was at 27° Capricorn in August–September 1997. Both passings impacted the world: some people were part of a wave of grief (Neptune) while others exhibited head-shaking incredulity at the extreme set of emotions that were provoked. At the time of their deaths, neither figure had been enjoying the Neptunian fog of blind admiration she once had, although both had embodied Neptune in many ways: the fairytale media princess reaching out in Angola and the nun devoted to ministering to the poor and sick in India. (TR Uranus was conjunct Diana's Jupiter in Aquarius for much of 1997 – this fits in well with the symbolism of her work to publicize landmines, is mirrored by her need to 'blow the lid' on aspects of the Royal Family, and is reflected in her sudden, violent death in a foreign country before she could do so.)

I was intrigued to read about the deaths of two high-profile 'queens' in August 2007, a time when Saturn was leaving the sign of Leo. New York high society socialite Brooke Astor died on the 13th (Saturn at 27° Leo) and Leona Helmsley, the imperious New York 'hotelier from hell', passed away exactly a week later (Saturn at 28° Leo). Both donated millions to their city: Astor was a noted philanthropist who said, 'Money is like manure; it should be spread around', while Helmsley, on the other hand, was branded the 'Queen of Mean' who apparently said, 'Only the little people pay taxes.'

Outer planets spend much time creeping towards the end of the sign or in retrograde motion over its final degrees. But in highlighting the key 'letting go' period before the ingress, I would consider whether the planet has already traversed to the final degree of that sign and is now journeying back to that degree. And I would look at the amount of time a planet has left in the sign before the ingress.

For example, Neptune had travelled all the way to 29°57' by April 1997 and, at the time of Diana's and Mother Teresa's deaths that autumn, it was retrograde but only five months away from its first entry into Aquarius. In the example of the New York doyennes, Saturn moved into Virgo on 2 September 2007, just a few weeks after the deaths of Astor and Helmsley.

But what of the first degree of a sign? The recent entry of Neptune into Pisces has surprised and taught me how significant it is when it comes to deaths and endings, too. But whereas the final few degrees are the 'last stand' (the end of an era), endings occurring while the planet has *just entered the new sign* seem to be harbingers of events to come and signposts of the mood of the new transit. Deaths or events when outer planets are at 0° set the scene for the years ahead. Derrick Bird's shocking killing spree occurred just days after Uranus moved into Aries. It could be said that, on one level, Bird acted out our own collective frustration with the helplessness and apathy of Uranus's seven years in Pisces, and took a very violent course of action to express himself (Uranus in Aries). Certainly the impact of Uranus in Aries (e.g. civil unrest and fighting collectively for individual rights and freedom) is being felt and heard in the news: from the thuggery and civil disobedience in London, the sudden violence in Norway, revolution in Egypt and collected protests in Wall Street to violence linked to youth (Aries), such as the shooting of three kindergarteners with a gun brought to school by a six-year old, and the very publicized and shocking spectacles of two leaders killed by shots to the face or head (Aries): Osama Bin Laden and Muammar Gaddafi. Remember the gung-ho and self-righteous, self-congratulatory Aries 'winner' energy of both murders?

In April 2011, when Neptune was at 0° Pisces, France became the first European country to ban the niqab and burqa (suggesting an increasingly uneasy alliance between country and religion as Neptune travels through Pisces for the next 14 years). But perhaps more apt was that this happened when Uranus (which represents freedom of speech as well as censorship and bans) was at 0° Aries (a sign that rules the face, and a sign concerned with *firsts*). On 1 May, China (infamous for its censorship of political ideology on the Internet) outlawed smoking in public places (I've often seen transits or directions involving Mars/Aries and Uranus – *extinguishing the flame* – when people give up 'lighting up'), and on 1 July 2011, books by sci-fi writer and Scientology founder L Ron Hubbard were banned in Russia as 'extremist' (Uranus). Bans 'in the name of freedom' seem to be the order of Uranus in Aries!

Other Planetary Activity
Before considering Neptune's brief entry into Pisces in 2011, I think it is important not to forget that during this time:

- Pluto was in Capricorn square Uranus in Aries

- Saturn was in Libra

- Jupiter moved from the latter half of Aries to the end of the first decan of Taurus

Saturn in Libra appears to be reflected in the equal rights actions legalizing civil partnerships/gay marriage in some American states, as well as the announcement (26 April) that the first Gay Pride rally in Moscow would take place. During Saturn in Libra, the Presbyterian Church has approved the ordination of people in same sex relationships, and on 23 May 2011 the Church of Scotland announced that it would soon allow gays to become ministers. The lesson of Saturn in Libra must surely be to learn diplomacy, negotiation and compromise – and this seems to be reflected in the number of coalitions set up around the time of its entry in late 2009 and once again in mid-2010. Its arrival (and station) at 29° Libra (late January to early March 2012) is the true test of such coalitions.

Neptune in Pisces
Neptune in Pisces will not only bring Piscean themes to the fore (from issues of religious devotion and gurus to 'telepathic' forms of everyday communication to changes in drug laws and an array of new addictions), it will also have a direct link to Virgo areas of life (from the disappearance of a retirement age, to diseases, viruses and plagues, and to the scandal/uncertainty/evaporation of charities, pensions and health care provisions).

First off, here's some data from Neil F. Michelsen and Rique Pottenger's *American Ephemeris for the 21st Century* (ACS Publications, 2010):

4 April 2011, 13:52 GMT
    Neptune enters Pisces

3 June 2011, 07:29 GMT
    Neptune goes retrograde at 0°55' Pisces

5 August 2011, 02:55 GMT
    Neptune retrogrades back into Aquarius

3 February 2012, 19:04 GMT
    Neptune enters Pisces

30 March 2025, 12:01 GMT
    Neptune enters Aries

22 October 2025, 09:49 GMT
    Neptune retrogrades back into Pisces

26 January 2026, 17:38 GMT
    Neptune enters Aries

So, what happened in the four months (4 April to 5 August 2011) during which Neptune travelled through Pisces? And how does this act as an omen for the years to come, starting in February 2012?

I went online and looked up the news on Wikipedia for each one of those days, and here are some of the highlights, particularly those from the very start of the ingress. Bearing in mind that the other outer planets will 'create' their own 'headlines' in the news, I have attempted to focus on those that have a strong Neptunian feel.

The Promises of Politicians
4 April: Neptunian US President (of Hope) Barack Obama announces he will fight another election just hours after the ingress.

4 April: Controversial former musician, Michel 'Sweet Micky' Martelly, wins the Haitian Presidential Election; he is known for his use of profanity and homophobic slurs on stage.

4 April: As part of the British Government's package of welfare reforms, the 1.5 million claiming incapacity benefit (Neptune) will now be required to attend work capability assessments (Virgo–Pisces polarity).

4 April: A boat carrying asylum seekers and migrants (Neptune) from Libya to Italy sets off today. Two days later it capsizes and more than two hundred people drown. *During Neptune in Pisces, will we see more migrations of 'nomadic' communities without a fixed abode?*

Hacking, Invasions and Injunctions, Oh My!
I used to wonder whether the age of Neptune in Pisces would bring greater awareness of psychic phenomena and planet-visiting aliens, but it appears that we are experiencing invasions and abductions of a very different kind – most notably,

the invasion of privacy and abduction of personal data. (Viruses – computer and otherwise – also fall under this umbrella.) Cyber warfare – politically motivated hacking, espionage and sabotage – is the new global world war of the 21st century.

Is nothing sacred? Privacy laws and invasions appear to be key themes. With Twitter postings, computer hackings and the super-injunctions scandal, we are becoming aware that no one can stop leaks or get away with cover-ups for long. There's an obsession with exposing high-ranking subterfuge (Uranus in Aries square Pluto in Capricorn) and the emergence of Julian Assange's WikiLeaks online (Neptune) has guaranteed an instant, global awareness of the merest whiff of scandal (Neptune). The law appears to be powerless at stopping such infiltrations and leaks – and consensus suggests this is a 'good thing' when applied to large corporations and public figures (News International, philandering footballers) but a 'bad thing' on a personal level (Milly Dowler and other victims of crime). Some of the biggest battles of Neptune in Pisces will revolve around the processing and containment of information (mutable), and we are already aware that major power lies in the collection, sale and distribution of personal data (the Mercury-ruled sign Virgo).

6 April: Silvio Berlusconi, beleaguered and scandal-soaked Prime Minister of Italy, stands trial (yet again). This time, the charge is for having sex with an underage prostitute.

8 April: News International announces it will admit liability in some of the breach of privacy cases being brought in relation to phone hacking by *The News of the World.*

Employees of *The News of the World* tabloid had been accused of engaging in police bribery and hacking into the phones of celebrities, politicians and royalty. But discoveries were made in April proving that the phones of murdered schoolgirl Milly Dowler, the relatives of deceased soldiers, and victims of the 7/7 London bombings were also hacked. Ironically on 7 July itself – following a public outcry, various resignations and concern over publisher Rupert Murdoch's stranglehold over the media in the UK – *The News of the World* was closed (the final edition was printed on 10 July, ending 168 years of publication). Murdoch has a very fishy chart, with Sun–Mercury in Pisces and Neptune elevated on the MC – he is

everywhere and has infiltrated most areas of media. Neptune's move into Pisces appears to have signalled a change in his fortunes – for the time being. (In spring 2011, by Solar Arc, Mercury had just squared his Neptune and, if his birth time is accurate, TR Neptune was squaring his Solar Arc MC at 0° Sagittarius.)

21 April: US Congressman Ed Markey sends Steve Jobs a letter asking him to explain the purpose of a file embedded on iPhones/iPads that keeps a detailed log of the device's location. Some governments announce intentions to investigate any violation of privacy laws.

25 April: WikiLeaks (founded 4 October 2006 with Jupiter in Scorpio square Neptune in Aquarius) releases classified cables detailing the interrogations and victimization of the elderly and mentally ill (Neptune) carried out by the US in Guantanamo Bay detention camp. The people were later released without charge.

26 April: Sony's PlayStation Network remains offline after a worldwide security breach obtains the personal information of 77 million users, making this the largest breach of personal info in history. (On 3 August, McAfee uncovers one of the largest series of cyber attacks against the IOC, the United Nations, the Indian government and major businesses.)

9 May: Super-injunctions are big news due to anonymous writers on Twitter deciding to 'name and shame' a list of celebrities who had issued gagging orders (most, in fact, were not 'super-injunctions'). 'Super-injunctions' ensure that facts/allegations are not allowed by law to be reported – and the injunction itself is said not to legally exist (Neptune).

9 May: American billionaire Louis Bacon wins a judgment in the UK against Wikipedia, *The Denver Post* and WordPress, allowing him to obtain information about the identities of those who have allegedly defamed him.

29 April: Prince William and Catherine Middleton marry, starting perhaps another fairytale worthy of Neptune (a stellium in Aries suggests new beginnings for the British royals).

10 May: Max Mosley loses his European Court of Human Rights bid to force newspapers to warn people before exposing aspects of their private lives.

4 July: Hackers break into Fox News' Twitter account on Independence Day to post a story that Obama has been killed.

Deaths of Neptunian Figures

When deaths occur at the beginning of a planet's sojourn through a sign, what is this telling us? Consider the deaths of three significant Neptunian people while Neptune was at 0° Pisces: Osama Bin Laden, Amy Winehouse and Sai Baba. Bin Laden's death could signal the start of a search for another guru or saviour for those who believe in his cause (Neptune/Pisces). And while martyred Amy Winehouse – the first music industry victim of the Neptune in Pisces era – may have joined the 'Club of 27', her passing may be the first of a new wave of drug-related deaths in the years to come. Or her predictable but pointless passing (ditto Whitney Houston on 11 February 2012, with Neptune back at 0° Pisces) could actually signal a change in the perception (or in the law) of drugs and act as a wake-up call to the current Neptune in Capricorn generation intent on having it all (Capricorn) but throwing it away (Neptune).

Sai Baba

In *The Daily Telegraph* (5 August 2011), the subheading ran: 'The death of an Indian guru who built up a worldwide following of up to 50 million people has triggered an unholy scramble for control of his £5.5 billion empire.' This, of course, begs the question: how does a man of God in poverty-stricken India accumulate that sort of fortune? And, in the age of Neptune in Pisces, who will India seek out now their beloved guru has left the earthly plane some years earlier than he predicted?

With his trademark saffron robes and Afro hair, Sathya Sai Baba (who died on 24 April 2011) stood at 5ft 2in but was truly a towering, influential Neptunian guru to millions of followers. Like most Neptunian figures there are numerous believers and detractors. Sai Baba's devotees hold on to his wise teachings (which on the whole can't be faulted), his education centres, philanthropic work and ability to work miracles (creating objects out of thin air) as proof of his benevolent sincerity and divinity. His critics cite the persistent allegations of sexual abuse with boys, the role he may have played in the murder of four followers, and the 'trickery' in manifesting holy ash and trinkets of a clever magician who held his gullible followers and Indian's elite in his hands. (When seeing these manifestations on film, the sleight of hand trickery of a magician appears to be at work, but, with Neptune, one never knows…)

There is also the accumulation of 'facts' about his birth. There's a belief that he was the reincarnation of an earlier saint of the same name (Sai Baba of Shirdi) and that he was born on 23 November 1926 in Puttaparthi, around the time of the original Baba's prediction of his reincarnation. Yet some cite a later birth date (4 October 1929). The arguments and responses can be found at: http://saibabaexposed.blogspot.com/2006/10/sai-babas-school-records-new-light.html and www.saisathyasai.com/baba/Ex-Baba.com/ssb-school.html

Does Sai Baba's death, when Neptune was at 0° Pisces, leave the door open for new spiritual philosophers (or opportunists) to rush forward and assume the position he has left vacant? Or will a country that is polluted by corruption and, to some extent, spiritually bankrupt be lost without a guru to guide it?

A Few Additional Thoughts

We can expect breakthroughs in Neptune-related illnesses such as myalgic encephalomyelitis (ME) and viruses, and health issues such as euthanasia. On 15 May 2011, the people of Zurich voted to reject a ban on assisted suicide in Switzerland, and also rejected the restricting of assisted suicide to Zurich residents only. On 31 May, the World Health Organization classified cell phone radiation as a 'carcinogenic hazard' and a 'possible carcinogenic to humans' (i.e. linked to causing cancer). On 7 July, Jerusalem scientists identified the molecular basis for the breakage of DNA (which results in the development of cancer). On 1 July, the Danish drug company Lundbeck restricted use of its Nembutal drug to stop it being used in lethal injections in some US states. And on 29 July, Johnson & Johnson announced that it would lower the maximum daily dosage of its Extra Strength Tylenol to reduce the risk of liver damage.

Films released during this time include Neptune-tinged stories such as *Insidious* (a movie about a boy who enters a comatose state and becomes a vessel for ghosts in the astral dimension) and *Source Code* (a tale in which a time-loop program allows a man, whose brain is being kept alive, to return to the past in someone else's body and re-enact the last part of the life to alter future events). As always, film will lead the way and give us a glimpse of Neptune's return to its own sign.

Labours of Love

I hope this book has been an educational and entertaining exploration of some of my perspectives on chart delineation. For me, it has been a labour of love.

Chart interpretation begins with an understanding and scrutiny of the various parts of the astrological jigsaw. We then work to coordinate these into a coherent whole – blending both contradictory and complementary themes.

The placements and aspects in our charts are dynamic energies that search for experiences; in doing so, they create life tasks and scripts. Like antennae picking up familiar signals that are pertinent to our journey of self-discovery, the components of our horoscopes strive to seek some form of expression (hopefully consciously!) to manifest in our life.

As astrologers, we need a method – to play detective, see the patterns that form in the horoscope and to follow the trails, spot the overtones and signatures. The initial stage is Mercurial inasmuch as we observe, interpret and then articulate these symbols in a language the client understands. Yet our job is to transcend the technique, to explore the significance and find the meaning (Jupiter) in these symbols; to *discover* the narrative that has formed as a result of these patterns – and to embark on this journey *with* the client.

Vivian Robson reminds us that the natal chart refers to a person – it's not a set of disconnected planetary influences – and he advises us to take into account the person's mental, moral or spiritual development. We must remember that natal astrology calls for fluid skills and an understanding of human nature; we must ask what the client needs from us and remember that the client is always greater than the sum of their horoscope's parts.

Let us engage in dialogue to discover how these astrological patterns play out specifically in our client's life. Context is vital to our assessment of any horoscope. As Richard Idemon once said, 'There is no way of looking at the chart of a human being without that human *being* there to give you feedback.' Interpretation is context-driven, but it is a joint endeavour – we are part of that process and the very act of our interpretation and articulation impacts the astrologer–client dynamic.

At times we must help to undo what Melanie Reinhart calls 'astrological preconditioning': 'A form of mental indigestion (chronic or acute) brought about by taking in too much astrological junk-food from various sources.' These are the sorts of notions and prejudices that clients have about particular chart placements. Melanie calls them 'awful, archaic, pre-psychological stuff, condemnatory in tone and totally without subtlety or compassion, having no sense of "life process". In short, no wisdom and no heart.' ('Astrological Pre-conditioning', Melanie Reinhart, written in March 2010.)

Following Our Bliss

Ultimately the true *heart* of the chart is the Sun, the source of vitality of our inner and outer lives. Following the message of our Sun (its placement and aspects) reminds us of the need to be authentic, to follow our hearts, to have *purpose*. What are we *really* here to do? More than anything, the Sun rise reminds us to say 'yes' to life each morning, to recognize cycles and seasons, to make an *individual contribution to the whole*. As others have pointed out, if death is the 'opposite' of birth, there's no opposite of life, so we must engage in the process of living, to 'follow our bliss', as Joseph Campbell advised, and experience being alive.

To engage in the activity of our Sun is to truly feel alive, to re-link to a source of power that is not only greater than us but also a significant part *of* us. Our job as astrologers is to help clients reconnect with their life force – this warm light at the heart centre of their universe – to strive to be whatever they must be. In truth, the *whole* chart can be used to help fulfil the ultimate message written in the Sun's position. In enabling clients to understand their natal Sun placement – to encourage them to engage in all parts of its meaning – we have the opportunity to help them manifest the most personal and compelling of journeys: their vocation.

Perhaps the reason Sun Sign astrology books have been so popular in the past 50 years is because they speak to the very heart of what *we know we must become* in order to feel fulfilled and serve a purpose. Sun Sign columns put us in the centre of the universe, under the spotlight for a moment – at best, they give us a brief, digestible glimpse of our calling.

The birth chart is a map – *one* map – that can help us become aware of our nature and our birthright. I'd like to end by quoting two eloquent astrologers, Howard Sasportas and Dennis Elwell, on the processes of self-realization and self-actualization: the need to fulfil our destiny by becoming who we were born to be.

In *The Twelve Houses* (Flare, 2007), Sasportas writes:

> Eastern philosophy applies the term *dharma* to denote the intrinsic identity and latent life-pattern present from birth in all of us… Each of these patterns has its own kind of truth and dignity… All of us possess certain intrinsic potentials and capabilities. What's more, somewhere deep within us there is a primordial knowledge or preconscious perception of our true nature, our destiny, our abilities, and our 'calling' in life. Not only do we have a particular path to follow, but on some instinctive level, we know what that is.

In an interview conducted in 1999 by Garry Phillipson, Dennis Elwell reminds us:

> At our birth the cosmos will have been working in a certain direction, towards the specific ends which were symbolized in the current state of the solar system, and all creatures and things born at that time were intended to contribute towards the further realization of those ends, according to their capacity as a vehicle. You might say that our human mission is to tune the microcosm to the macrocosm, both as individuals and collectively…

One of our tasks is to establish ourselves as a creative centre. We are not automatically at the centre of our life activity, and it is something to be worked at, to be achieved by stages. This function relates to the embodied Sun. But not everybody is living creatively. I don't mean we should all be painting watercolours, or doing embroidery, and such like. It is a matter of being creative in the life-situations that come our way, through the conscious exercise of spiritual intelligence. We can leave the stamp of our own personality on the opportunities and trials we encounter, or we can react robot-like according to our immediate feelings of pleasure or hurt. Such feelings are lunar; they arise as a sort of conditioned reflex, and come laden with the experiences of the past. The Sun on the other hand declares: Behold, I make all things new!

The Moon is our satellite – a comforter on our journey, a backpack filled with basic foodstuffs for survival as well as baggage that can sometimes weigh us down. But it is our journey around the Sun – seeing it and the backdrop of zodiac signs from a continuously different perspective every day of the year – that is a true source of bliss and re-creation. Yet on this voyage, we soon realize it is not a 'destination': our aim is not to reach the Sun, but to allow it to be our guiding light in our daily, annual and lifetime journey – and to participate in the seasons it brings.

Putting it All Together: The Worksheet

	Cardinal	Fixed	Mutable
Fire			
Earth			
Air			
Water			

Chart Ruler

Sun Dispositor

SUN   MOON   ASC

Four Angles and Links

Major Aspects

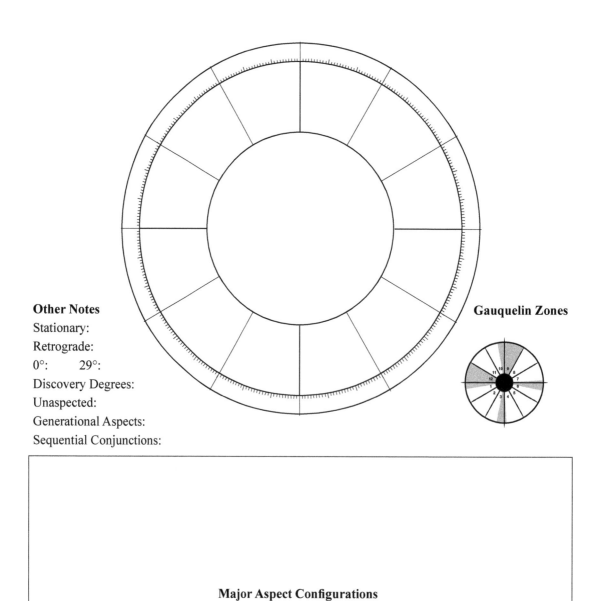

Other Notes
Stationary:
Retrograde:
0°:   29°:
Discovery Degrees:
Unaspected:
Generational Aspects:
Sequential Conjunctions:

Gauquelin Zones

Major Aspect Configurations

Putting it All Together: _____

1. The Distribution of Planets

2. The Set of Signs on the Four Angles

3. The Sun–Moon–Ascendant Trio

4. Elemental and Modal Balances/Imbalances

5. Major Aspects

6. Major Aspect Configurations

7. Spotting Overtones

Putting it All Together: The Worksheet

	Cardinal	Fixed	Mutable
Fire			
Earth			
Air			
Water			

Chart Ruler

Sun Dispositor

SUN   MOON   ASC

Four Angles and Links

Major Aspects

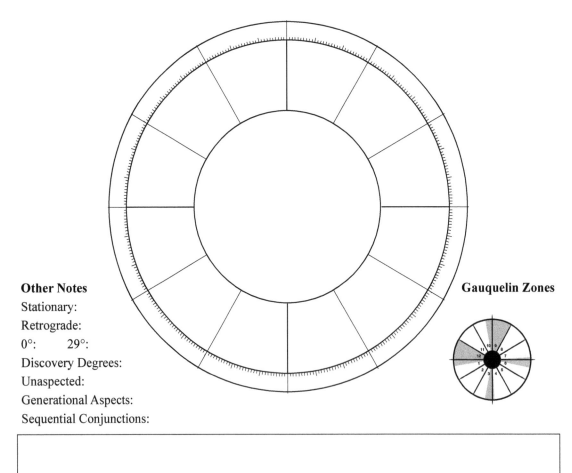

Other Notes
Stationary:
Retrograde:
0°:   29°:
Discovery Degrees:
Unaspected:
Generational Aspects:
Sequential Conjunctions:

Gauquelin Zones

Major Aspect Configurations

Putting it All Together: _____

1. The Distribution of Planets

2. The Set of Signs on the Four Angles

3. The Sun–Moon–Ascendant Trio

4. Elemental and Modal Balances/Imbalances

5. Major Aspects

6. Major Aspect Configurations

7. Spotting Overtones

Being Frank – An Interview

In conversation with editor John Green. This interview first appeared in the November/December 2008 of *The Astrological Journal*. Reprinted with the permission of John Green.

I caught up with Frank at the AA Conference in September 2008, where we discussed his background, his views on various aspects of astrology, and his plans to create an astrology centre in London.

JG: What first got you interested in astrology?

FC: My mother used to visit various psychics and fortune tellers; she was very interested in that side of things and I would be fascinated hearing of her encounters. At age 16, in August '89, I went to see the astrologer Tad Mann, who had been recommended by a psychic my Mum and I had been to see. He, and writers such as Linda Goodman, opened the door to astrology for me.

I was fascinated by a chart's symbols and possible meanings. That afternoon, I sat down, looked at my own chart and began to learn the symbols, to work out what a trine was, etc., and gradually pieced it together myself. It was a good signpost for what was to come: having to do things myself and being the young kid on the block, too!

JG: What about palmistry?

FC: Palmistry came a year later, thanks to my Dad. My father never really 'believed' in astrology, although he was a great worshipper of the Sun and the Moon. He was an atheist from the age of 9, grew up in dire poverty, and was sent into the Workhouse as a child. Uranus was the handle to his bucket chart, which was very Martian and Plutonic, and he was an agitator and activist who died on the day of his Uranus Return six years ago. He would listen to me talk astrology and respected my intelligence enough to realise that I thought there was something 'in' the subject. Well, he was full of surprises: he went off to see a palmist quite unexpectedly, and came home and told us about it. He found it quite remarkable, so we followed him – my mother went and then I visited.

Later, I saw another palmist, an eccentric who made some horrendous predictions that never

happened: she told me I would marry at 21 and my partner would die, which worried me no end at the age of 17! So I thought I should learn this subject – surely there must be a better and more responsible way of practising it? And as a headstrong Aries, I wasn't about to be told a statement so cut-and-dried about my future. I often say to palmistry students, 'If it's all mapped out, then what are we doing here?' Life may be about rediscovering who we were born to be, but surely whatever 'free will' we have is linked to that creative journey of discovery?

As palmists, we're not required to have the qualifications or professional codes which astrology demands of us, and this can leave room for abuse and unethical predictions such as hers. Well, her prediction certainly wiped out my desire to be married at 21.

JG: That was so irresponsible.

FC: Yes it was, but there are people still doing it, trying to be powerful. I see it as the Jupiter syndrome, the need to be guru and all-knowing. In truth, I think what initially attracted me to palmistry more than astrology was that I thought it could reveal somebody's future more clearly. That interested me, but then listening to the palmist's prediction kicked that out of me!

JG: Do you link the two?

FC: I always do both in consultations, sometimes more astrology than palmistry. They back each other up very well. In one of my palmistry books [*Palmistry 4 Today*], I liken the hand to an aerial view of a road map. We're in the driver's seat and the palm is like the SatNav (forgive me for these modern references!); we can see the road ahead and the key parts of that journey because we've decided to drive in that direction; we can see a certain amount of the road in front of us, but we might decide to go a different way. Palmistry gives an overview of the journey and the possible avenues ahead.

I liken astrology again to driving a car, but this time it's more akin to looking out the windscreen – we're able to hear the noise of cars, chatter and other activity; we can see more detail, colour, texture. So to me, astrology gives a tremendous amount of detail in the here and now, where palmistry gives us a very good overview of how past actions and reactions have brought us to our current location. By definition, the birth chart doesn't change throughout our life, but the hand is constantly changing to reflect the decisions we are making: that's why they call it 'the living hand'.

So I see them both as different tools, but the birth chart gives me more detailed information. I do a print of the hand when the client arrives. I have the chart prepared, transits, Solar Arc directions (no progressions), and the consultation chart, which I could use on its own without anything else.

JG: Why Solar Arc and not progressions?

FC: I joke that it was surely an Aries who said, 'Lord give me patience, but hurry!' The other joke is that I thought I had discovered Solar Arc all by myself. I started to look at degrees between planets and angles and was amazed at the link with corresponding life events. I've got Jupiter about 9 degrees away from my Midheaven and that is when I went to the most amazing Hindu school as my secondary school. I went early at the age of nine. Jupiter in Aquarius coming up to the Midheaven in Aquarius exposed me to a completely different way of thinking as a child.

As an astrologer, I suddenly realised other people were using this method of prediction and that it was called Solar Arc. Solar Arc is just simple, straightforward, very Arian, and great to teach. Maybe I'm being more than flippant here, but when people say that progressions are more subtle and connected to inner cycles, I joke that it's an excuse because they don't work well enough, that they can't be seen to be working!

With Solar Arc you can see it all manifest in the interior *and* exterior life. I had a client recently whose Moon was 9 degrees away from Neptune in the 4th House and she spoke of the bewilderment of losing her mother at age 9. The symbolism is often as simple and literal as that. Solar Arc is like the markings on the hand: instant and immediate.

JG: You started your own publishing company. Why?

FC: Gosh, I don't know. Perhaps it's the same audacity that I had when I started learning palmistry. I went to university shortly after I started reading hands and was soon teaching it at the university in an evening class. I guess there's an audacious quality to Aries with Mars on the Midheaven! With my book on entertainers [*British Entertainers: The Astrological Profiles*], I suppose I didn't think that mainstream publishers would be so interested in the data collection, so I went ahead and published it myself.

JG: Did you start the data collection from when you first got interested?

FC: I was always interested in celebrity charts, not because there's a desperate thespian waiting to come out, but I think it's that with celebrities there's so much access to biography. I have hundreds of biographies, five thousand odd clippings, which were once in alphabetical order but... I like to hear people speaking their charts and you get that in biographies. Also teaching, I got tired of seeing the same old charts: Freud, Jung, Princess Diana, now Camilla.

JG: I think any royal's chart.

FC: Well, when I do Solar Arc lectures and seminars I use Prince Harry because he had no transits when his mother died but Neptune was one minute from the Ascendant by Solar Arc. He also had a number of heavy directions to the MC/IC complex at that time. So that's one of the most immediate examples of Solar Arc in action. But I always apologise in advance for using a royal chart, as I feel they're so overused, and more often than not are quite unremarkable charts.

I built up my data collection and got in touch with Lois Rodden in '93 and we corresponded and worked closely on different projects for ten years. I offered to help edit her *Profiles of Women* revision, provided hundreds of dated events and checked the data and the biographies she had written. It was such an important volume and I was proud to work on it.

There are data collectors out there who just collect and I always wanted to go further than that. Evangelism, alcoholism – anything that might be seen in the chart is what I want to research. What makes someone follow that path? Do people with certain shared experiences also have common links in their horoscope? You don't always find the answers, of course, but every chart gives you a further perspective or angle and it enriches your astrology.

JG: What's your favourite chart at the moment?

FC: My own – as always! At present [2008], everyone's looking at Amy Winehouse's chart, but because she's a bit of a train wreck right now, it upsets me and I want people to leave her alone! When you study astrology, I think you have the opportunity to see the humanity that's common to us all. I thought of interviewing Myra Hindley for my first palmistry book but my publishers advised against it. They thought it would cause outrage or upset, and it probably would have done, so I left well alone. Yet in spite of the terrible things she did, her hand would have had some of the personality traits that we all possess. The public don't want to know that, they want to demonise certain people, and that's understandable, particularly to those families' lives she wrecked. But if an act has been carried out by a human, it's also potentially capable of being performed by us all. Astrology and palmistry can reveal what we all have in common underneath, plus so many other aspects; it's the particular delicate balance of all these aspects that makes us unique. But such a sensitive issue as Hindley and her atrocities would not have been a place to start arguing this point.

JG: What about your school, the London School of Astrology?

FC: Sue offered to sell it to me in 2003. It was a challenge and the perfect opportunity to teach and to keep learning. I saw the LSA as a sort of maverick in terms of schools, not bound by politics or handcuffed by committee, and I loved the freedom to be able to invite astrologers from all over the world to visit and teach; those whom I admire and whose work I respect. It's given me a great opportunity to meet astrologers and students. It's hard work, and I joke that I run it as a benevolent dictator. I'm probably the most non-committee person in the world. I try to run it well and give the students an eclectic mix of people teaching them, a solid foundation in astrology and a thorough introduction to various types of astrology.

JG: So what's next?

FC: I'm committed to running the school. I've got books I want to write on astrology and palmistry. I've been wanting to write my book on the Midheaven for years but then the LSA came along. I feel I need to write it now. I set myself a test: I listened to what others had to say on the Midheaven and thought that if they have the same take on it and similar ideas (or if they do it better than I ever could!), then I wouldn't bother writing it. But I still think I have something new to say on the subject, so I'll continue researching for the time being!

The next new project is to get an astrology centre up and running; I'm working on that at the moment. I'll give people news on it when I have it. I really want a building that has a library, a study centre, consulting rooms, etc. Imagine a place where astrology students from any school or group can drop in, catch a talk, research, and mingle with other students. I think my Mars–Jupiter on the MC in Aquarius needs to do this, and I feel this is something I would like to create for the community. It has to be run as a business; I'll need people's help in different ways to keep it going. My feeling, though, is that it needs to be spearheaded by one person to get it moving. But it doesn't need a figurehead; it simply needs a positive ethos that is inclusive rather than exclusive.

JG: Is there anything you would change about your own chart?

FC: I'd rather think about changing the less attractive aspects of my character, rather than my chart. What I would change astrologically is how astrologers are prone to judging the native rather than the birth chart. I briefly knew a consultant astrologer who took delight in listing the zodiac signs she hated! A magical aspect of being a consultant is to discover how the client is using the tools of their birth chart, rather than us bombarding them with a series of fixed personality traits. Ideally, I would want to encourage more observation and dialogue, rather than pigeonholing or judgement.

Old books are full of personality pronouncements that are truly damaging to the student astrologer. I often encounter this with students who have read about Mercury retrograde in the natal chart and then label themselves 'stupid' or unable to learn the subject. Isn't it a twisted irony that we can put students off our subject with descriptions of their own charts, instead of helping them explore the various layers of their horoscopes? Who can forget the wonder of seeing and exploring our own chart for the first time? What a missed opportunity if that discovery is tainted by a lack of care on our part as writers or astrologers.

And another irony is that people do remarkable things with planets that are so quickly labelled 'weak' or 'afflicted'. I tell students about Martina Navratilova, born with her Chart Ruler Mars in Pisces in the 12th, yet as a supreme athlete she's an outstanding example of Mars in action. That example, and many others, is one of the reasons I continue to pay attention to some aspects of the Gauquelin work. And I've never seen a square in a horoscope without the potential or tools to do something outstanding with it. Why else would it be put there?

JG: What about the future for astrology?

FC: Who knows where astrology will go? But I love the anticipation and knowing that many of the students I teach at the LSA will be a part of it. But if I knew what would be 'the next big thing', I'd be writing and editing it now!

I think our astrology reflects the society we're in. Before Uranus moved into Pisces we started to hear regularly about political spin. With Uranus now [2008] in Pisces, many of us in Britain have felt so 'spun' that we're giddy, cynical, and have retreated into our own lives, dealing with the smaller picture. A million people can go on a march against going to war in Iraq and yet they have no say in the matter. Many of us feel jaded, fatalistic or simply unmotivated to make change. To me, the general ethos is to pass the buck or avoid investing in the future: if you make a mess, get the hell out of there before someone blames you; if something breaks, throw it away and buy a new one. In consequence, many feel that there's no point trying. In recent years, we've lacked a clear target that will help us instigate change.

When Uranus goes into Aries I think there will be a fresh sense of direction, in some ways similar to the '80s perhaps, when people had a cause to fight for and a common 'enemy'. I hope there'll be a new direction both politically and astrologically. I love the rich array of astrologies, even if the proliferation of techniques can sometimes leave me feeling punch-drunk, and the overly technical approach helps to remind me that we're dealing with fellow humans, not using a clinical system to crack another system.

I'm not interested in One True Astrology, although I feel that a great number of our ideas and tools need testing and retesting, and we need the courage to get it wrong and try it again. But surely if the way we see and experience life affects the way we view charts, then we all have our own, equally important approach? We're a community of mavericks used to being on the outside. That's both our strength and Achilles' heel. We've been hit by a number of Dawkins-type critics (ironically coming from a purely irrational angle), yet the biggest threat is within the ranks: our community, as it is with other areas, has been rife with politics and ego, jostling for position and all sorts of personal and professional attacks on each other. When I hear or experience this, I pray that we don't treat our clients or loved ones the way we treat our colleagues! At best, Uranus in Aries might enable us to rediscover the tools to represent, defend and move this remarkable subject forward in the world, and hopefully give us all a clearer sense of where we're going together as talented, individualistic members of a special community.

Recommended Reading

The following are recommended books for the student and professional astrologer. Each has enriched my understanding of astrology (particularly the ones I wrote myself!).

Textbooks/General Chart Delineation

The Contemporary Astrologer's Handbook	Sue Tompkins
The Knot of Time	Lindsay River and Sally Gillespie
Horoscope Symbols	Robert Hand
Key Words for Astrology	Hajo Banzhaf and Anna Haebler
Astrology in Action	Paul Wright
How to Read Your Astrological Chart	Donna Cunningham
Astrology for the Light Side of the Brain	Kim Rogers-Gallagher
Making the Gods Work for You	Caroline W. Casey

Aspects/Planet Combinations/Houses

Aspects in Astrology	Sue Tompkins
The Twelve Houses	Howard Sasportas
The Combination of Stellar Influences	Reinhold Ebertin
The Houses: Temples of the Sky	Deborah Houlding
Planetary Aspects: From Conflict to Cooperation	Tracy Marks
The Midheaven: Spotlight on Success	Frank C. Clifford

Psychological Astrology

Astrology, Karma & Transformation	Stephen Arroyo
New Insights in Modern Astrology	Stephen Arroyo and Liz Greene
The Astrology of Fate	Liz Greene
Images of the Psyche	Christine Valentine
The Soul's Code	James Hillman
Chiron and the Healing Journey	Melanie Reinhart

Forecasting/Cycles

The Gods of Change	Howard Sasportas
Predictive Astrology	Bernadette Brady
Planets in Transit	Robert Hand
Modern Transits	Lois M. Rodden
Solar Arc Directions	Frank C. Clifford

Consultations/Professional

Between Astrologers & Clients	Bob Mulligan
Astrology: Transformation & Empowerment	Adrian Duncan
Dialogues	Frank C. Clifford & Mark Jones
Doing Time on Planet Earth	Adrian Duncan
The Consulting Astrologer's Guidebook	Donna Cunningham
Using Astrology to Create a Vocational Profile	Faye Cossar
Money: How to Find It with Astrology	Lois M. Rodden

History/Philosophy/Astrology Today

Cosmic Loom	Dennis Elwell
The Moment of Astrology	Geoffrey Cornelius
The Passion of the Western Mind	Richard Tarnas
True as the Stars Above	Neil Spencer
Astrology in the Year Zero	Garry Phillipson
A History of Western Astrology (vols 1 and 2)	Nicholas Campion
The Future of Astrology	Edited by A.T. Mann; various authors
Astrology: The New Generation	Edited by Frank C. Clifford; various authors

Reference Books/Data Collections

The American Ephemeris for the 21st Century (2001 to 2050) at Midnight	Neil F. Michelsen
The Book of World Horoscopes	Nicholas Campion
Tables of Planetary Phenomena	Neil F. Michelsen
Astro-Data vols I–V	Lois M. Rodden
The Astrologer's Book of Charts	Frank C. Clifford
British Entertainers: The Astrological Profiles	Frank C. Clifford
A Multitude of Lives	Paul Wright
A Chronology of American Charts	Ronald Howland

Techniques

Mundane Astrology	Michael Baigent, Nicholas Campion and Charles Harvey
Working with Astrology	Michael Harding and Charles Harvey

Notes and References

In my office, I have three filing cabinets dedicated to astrological research with over one thousand files of news clippings of people in the public eye! I've referred to these (and numerous biographies) for the various biographies and snapshots in this book. Many of the book's quotes have come from online sources such as www.thinkexist.com and www.brainyquote.com, or from articles, interviews and books in my library.

1. Robert Hand, *Horoscope Symbols,* Whitford Press, 1981, p. 42.

2. Linda Reid, *Astrology Step By Step,* Canopus, 2001, p. 113.

3. These ideas were stimulated by my discussions with Lois Rodden, who had written about it in *Money: How to Find It with Astrology,* Data News Press, 1994.

4. For a complete exploration of retrogradation, see Erin Sullivan's insightful volume, *Retrograde Planets: Traversing the Inner Landscape,* Arkana, 1992.

5. Noel Tyl, *Synthesis & Counseling in Astrology: The Professional Manual,* Llewellyn, 1994, p. 39.

6. Squares: The actor James Earl Jones wrote eloquently of his lifelong stammer and self-imposed silences as a child (he was virtually mute from 6 to 14). Jones himself has Mercury (on the Ascendant in Capricorn) square Uranus (in Aries) – a planetary combination associated with stuttering, as well as mental agility. The following excerpt from his autobiography *Voices and Silences* (Prentice Hall, 1993) aptly conveys the energy of the square aspect: 'A stutterer ends up with a greater need to express himself... the desire to speak builds and builds until it becomes part of your energy, your life force.' Appropriately for the square's demand for mastery, as an adult Jones's resonant baritone has been a key to his acting fortunes, and he is best remembered for lending his voice to CNN and the character Darth Vader in *Star Wars.*

7. All quotes are from *Jeffrey Archer: Stranger than Fiction* by Michael Crick, Hamish Hamilton, 1995.

8. For an interpretation of Nixon's chart, see *From Symbol to Substance* by Richard Swatton, Flare, 2012.

9. http://www.nelsonearthday.net/nelson/index.htm

10. For an astrological biography on Newman, check out Alex Trenoweth's article in the January/February 2009 issue of *The Astrological Journal.*

11. Penny Junor, *Margaret Thatcher: Wife, Mother, Politician,* Sidgwick & Jackson, 1983.

12. Joan Bakewell, as quoted in *The Mail on Sunday* (London), 29 October 2000.

13. Meryle Secrest, *Stephen Sondheim: A Life,* Bloomsbury, 1999.

14. *Conversations with Maya Angelou,* ed. Jeffrey Elliot, Virago, 1989.

15. All quotes are from *Marilyn Monroe: Private and Undisclosed* by Michelle Morgan, Constable, 2007.

16. All quotes are from *The Story of Anne Frank* by Mirjam Pressler, Macmillan, 1999.

17. In 2009, the BBC's miniseries *The Diary of Anne Frank* aired. Actress Ellie Kendrick, who gave a moving, insightful portrayal of Anne, was born with the Sun at 15° Gemini, Venus at 8° Taurus and Mars at 4° Aries, linking strongly to Anne's chart.

18. The authenticity of his birth certificate posted online by his supporters (to quash rumours that he was not born in the USA) has been questioned because it does not contain every vital statistic. It is, in fact, an official short-form computerized copy requested after birth that omits information such as parental and medical signatures. In the light of continued scepticism, newspapers published in Hawaii in 1961 announcing his birth are the best evidence of his American birth.

19. All quotes, unless otherwise stated, have been taken from *Obama From Promise to Power* by David Mendell, Amistad, 2007.

20. The 10th House cusp calculated in Equal houses. Whereas the MC/IC is a psychological axis, speaking of the parental inheritance and family 'messages' we hear early and are encouraged to pursue, the EQHS 10th is the area that governs our work structure and choices and our public role. Early in life, it speaks of parental work choices that affect us. Transits/directions to this cusp coincide with landmark work/career developments (much the same as when a planet ingresses into a new sign in Whole Signs, except that with the EQHS 10th cusp it bears a direct relationship to our personal horizons/relationship dynamics by squaring the ASC–DSC degree).

21. This is descriptive of the conjunction of Solar Arc Mercury with the Sun by Solar Arc at age 10 (they are ten degrees apart in Obama's chart).

22. His Pluto–Ascendant line runs directly through the rural village of Kogelo, Kenya (0°s01', 34°e21'), where his father's family originated.

23. This transit was in effect during his mother's year-long battle with ovarian cancer and her death that 7 November.

24. There are many parallels in their horoscopes: Alex Haley (11 August 1921, 04:55 EDT, Ithaca, NY, from birth record) was born with a Sun–Neptune aspect (a conjunction at 18° and 13° Leo respectively) and the Moon at 27° Scorpio (near Obama's MC). Both writers have embodied Neptune in their work: Haley was accused of plagiarizing and fictionalizing

much of *Roots*; Obama's frank and idealistic account includes fictional characters and personal revelations of drug and alcohol use – this took potentially damaging revelations out of the hands of the media.

25. Obama lost his father on 24 November 1982, as SA Neptune crossed his MC in Scorpio (progressed Moon opposed natal Pluto one month earlier).

26. See the work of Liz Greene; an introduction is given in *Astrology for Lovers* (Weiser, 1989), originally written in 1980. Much of the Leo myth can be seen in the modern day tale of Disney's *The Lion King*.

27. This sense of purpose was reinforced astrologically by a solar eclipse, which occurred seven days after Obama's birth at 18° Leo, his Descendant degree.

28. Fittingly with Mercury–Neptune, his half-sister Maya went on to teach multicultural education, education philosophy and global dance.

29. With reference to Saturn, 17°–18° Aquarius appears to be important in America's political and racial history. The March on Washington (28 August 1963) occurred with Saturn at 18° AQ, Kennedy was assassinated as it reached 17° AQ, and a full Saturn cycle later (29 April 1992), Rodney King's racist attackers were acquitted, prompting the LA riots.

30. It is this Leo–Aquarius axis that has been hit most by transits. His keynote address on 27 July 2004 occurred with Mars just past his Descendant. One month after the final exact Neptune–Ascendant transit, Obama announced his candidacy for President (10 February 2007). The Sun at 20° Aquarius had just passed Neptune and was approaching an exact opposition to Saturn at 21° Leo. Super Tuesday (5 February 2008) arrived and brought Mercury retrograde at 19° Aquarius. Obama became the Democratic Nominee on 3 June 2008 with Mars at 13° Leo.

31. At the time of his election win, Obama's progressed ACG map shows the Saturn–Ascendant line running through Washington, DC.

32. Reverend Wright has Venus at 8° Scorpio conjunct Obama's Neptune. Although Obama was originally inspired by him, he nevertheless distanced himself from some of Wright's more controversial statements in an address known as 'A More Perfect Union' (Venus–Neptune) on 18 March 2008 (a day when TR Mercury and Venus opposed Obama's natal Pluto in the 7th).

33. In the chart of Clinton's second-term inauguration on 20 January 1997, Saturn in Aries in the 11th opposes Mars in Libra in the 5th (which is conjunct natal Mars–Neptune Rising). This is descriptive of a moral witch hunt aggressively pursued by preacher's son Kenneth Starr to impeach Clinton for impropriety (Saturn) and sexual dalliances (Mars in the 5th).

34. A highly recommended exploration of the astrology of contemporary America.

35. There's always a temptation to employ more techniques! Bernard Eccles introduced me to the concept of Midpoint Transits. Two further Midpoint Transits at the time of his election win: Neptune/Pluto was at 25° Capricorn (conjunct his Saturn) and Jupiter/Uranus at 18° Aquarius (on his Ascendant).

36. For example, the USA's Pluto is at the midpoint of Obama's pivotal Jupiter–Saturn conjunction, the Moon is on his South Node and opposing Uranus, and Venus placements are conjunct.

37. *Time* magazine, 27 October 2008.

38. Carter Smith, *Presidents: Every Question Answered*, Hylas, 2004, p.12.

39. *Ministry of Greed* by Larry Martz with Ginny Carroll (Weidenfeld & Nicolson, 1988).

40. Talk show hosts – especially those who thrive on 'confessional TV' – have prominent Jupiters and often an emphasis on the 9th. Jupiter and Neptune (and their signs) appear particularly strong in the charts of those who have taken advantage of the medium of television to promote their causes (Jupiter) and sell salvation to a wide range of people (Neptune).

41. *Tammy: Telling It My Way* by Tammy Faye Messner, Villard, 1996.

42. D. Shewey, *Rolling Stone Review*, Blandford, 1985.

Additional Profile References

Tammy Faye Bakker

- Jim Bakker with Ken Abraham, *I Was Wrong*, Thomas Nelson, 1996.
- *The Eyes of Tammy Faye* (film, 1999).
- *Fall from Grace* (film, 1990). Starring Kevin Spacey (Sun in Leo conjunct Jim's Pluto; Mars–Pluto in Virgo conjunct Jim's Descendant) and Bernadette Peters (Sun in Pisces, Moon in Scorpio).

Irene Cara

- Jeff Guinn and Douglas Perry, *The Sixteenth Minute*, Tarcher/Penguin, 2005.
- Unpublished, autobiographical manuscript by Cara.

Mary Tyler Moore

- Mary Tyler Moore, *After All*, Putnam, 1995.
- Rebecca Stefoff, *Mary Tyler Moore: The Woman Behind the Smile*, Signet, 1986.

Martina Navratilova

- Martina Navratilova with George Vecsey, *Martina*, Ballantine, 1985.
- Johnette Howard, *The Rivals*, Broadway, 2005.
- Adrianne Blue, *Martina Unauthorized*, Gollancz/Witherby, 1994.
- Sandra Faulkner with Judy Nelson, *Love Match*, Birch Lane, 1993.

Data – *list compiled by Sy Scholfield*

I owe a great many thanks to Sy Scholfield for supervising and compiling the following list of data used in the book. Always sceptical of quotes and unverified sources – and the various errors that have crept into online astrological databanks – Sy was able to double-check much of the data using new sources, and in many cases I had the original document on file. Together, I hope we've been able to provide the very latest and credible information. Sy can be contacted via his website www.syscholfield.com and I would recommend him to those looking to have data researched, verified and compiled for projects, books or articles. His other websites are at www.aussie-stars.com and www.astroqueer.com

Academy Awards (first ever ceremony): 16 May 1929, 20:00 PST (+8), Hollywood, California, USA (34n06, 118w20). Source: Sy Scholfield quotes *Inside Oscar* edited by Gail MacColl (Ballantine, 1993), p.8, copy on file. RR: B.

John Addey: 15 June 1920, 08:15 GDT (-1), Barnsley, England (53n34, 1w28). Source: From him to Lois Rodden in 1979. RR: A.

Muhammad Ali: 17 January 1942, 18:35 CST (+6), Louisville, Kentucky, USA (38n15, 85w46). Source: Birth certificate from Ed Steinbrecher, copy on file. RR: AA.

Debbie Allen: 16 January 1950, 21:45 CST (+6), Houston, Texas, USA (29n45, 95w21). Source: Birth certificate obtained by Frank Clifford, copy on file. RR: AA.

Don Ameche: 31 May 1908, 19:00 CST (+6), Kenosha, Wisconsin, USA (42n35, 87w49). Source: Birth certificate obtained by Edwin Steinbrecher, copy on file. RR: AA.

Maya Angelou: 4 April 1928, 14:10 CST (+6), Saint Louis, Missouri, USA (38n38, 90w12). Source: Birth certificate quoted in *Contemporary American Horoscopes* by Janice McKay and Jessica Saunders (Astrolabe, 1990). RR: AA.

Benigno Aquino: 27 November 1932, 00:01 AWST (-8), Concepcion, Tarlac, Philippines (15n19, 120e39). Source: From biography and his family, as quoted by Serafin Lanot. RR: C.

Corazon Aquino: 25 January 1933, 04:00 AWST (-8), Malate, Manila, Philippines (14n35, 121e00). Source: From birth certificate, as quoted by Sy Scholfield. RR: AA.

Jeffrey Archer: 15 April 1940, 11:45 GDT (-1), London, England (51n30, 0w10). Source: From him to Marjorie Orr (place confirmed at birth registry by FCC). RR: A.

Joan Baez: 9 January 1941, 10:45 EST (+5), Staten Island, New York, USA (40n35, 74w09). Source: Birth certificate obtained by Ed Steinbrecher, copy on file. RR: AA.

Cheryl Baker: 8 March 1954, 13:00 GMT (+0), Bethnal Green, London, England (51n32, 0w03). Source: From her to an astrologer on BBC1's *The Eleventh Hour* (November 1996). RR: A.

Joan Bakewell: 16 April 1933, 22:30 GDT (-1), Stockport, England (53n25, 2w10). Source: Frank Clifford quotes a reliable private source for data from her. RR: A.

Jim Bakker: 2 January 1940, 11:00 EST (+5), Muskegon Heights, Michigan, USA (43n12, 86w15). Source: Birth record obtained by Genevieve Edwards, copy on file. RR: AA.

Tammy Faye Bakker: 7 March 1942, 03:27 CWT (+5), International Falls, Minnesota, USA (48n36, 93w25). Source: Note from birth registry obtained by Edwin Steinbrecher. RR: AA.

Florence Ballard: 30 June 1943, 05:45 EWT (+4), Detroit, Michigan, USA (42n20, 83w03). Source: Birth certificate obtained by Frank Clifford, copy on file. RR: AA.

Brigitte Bardot: 28 September 1934, 13:15 GDT (-1), Paris, France (48n52, 2e20). Source: Birth certificate details obtained by Michel and Françoise Gauquelin. RR: AA.

Kathy Bates: 28 June 1948, 11:12 CST (+6), Memphis, Tennessee, USA (35n08, 90w02). Source: Note from birth registry obtained by Frank Clifford, copy on file. RR: AA.

Jennifer Beals: 19 December 1963, Chicago, Illinois, USA (41n51, 87w39). Source: Various online biographies. RR: X.

Alexander Graham Bell: 3 March 1847, 07:00 LMT (+0:12:52), Edinburgh, Scotland (55n57, 3w13). Source: Birth certificate obtained by Chrys Craswell. RR: AA.

Pete Bennett: 22 March 1982, 05:30 GMT (+0), East Dulwich, London, England (51n27, 0w05). Source: From his mother to Robert Currey. RR: A.

Derek Bentley: 30 June 1933, 23:50 GDT (-1), Blackfriars, London, England (51n31, 0w07). Source: Astro-Databank quotes the biography *My Son's Execution* by William George Bentley (W. H. Allen, 1957): 'born just before midnight'. RR: B.

David Berkowitz: 1 June 1953, 16:52 EDT (+4), Brooklyn, New York, USA (40n38, 73w56). Source: Copy of hospital records obtained by Victoria Shaw, quoted in Lois Rodden's Astro-Databank. RR: AA.

Silvio Berlusconi: 29 September 1936, 06:30 MET (-1), Milan, Italy (45n28, 9e12). Source: Birth certificate obtained by Grazia Bordoni. Bordoni also quotes Berlusconi's lawyer for a time of 05:40 from Berlusconi himself, and Zucchi, a colleague, for 6:00 AM. RR: AA.

Justin Bieber: 1 March 1994, 00:56 EST (+5), London, Ontario, Canada (42n59, 81w14). Source: Frank Clifford quotes *Justin Bieber: The Unauthorized Biography* by Chas Newkey-Burden (Michael O'Mara, 2010), p.15. RR: B.

The Big Time (TV series): 2 July 1980, 20:10 GDT (-1), London, England (51n30, 0w10). Source: Frank Clifford quotes newspaper sources on date for Sheena Easton's episode; Sy Scholfield quotes Broadcasting Guide, *The Times*, 2 July 1980, p.27. RR: B. (The series began on 28 October 1976, 21:25 GMT (+0), London, England (51n30, 0w10). Source: Sy Scholfield quotes *The Times*, 28 October 1976, p.31. RR: B.)

Bin Laden Murdered: 2 May 2011, 00:40 (-5), Abbottabad, Pakistan (34n09, 73e13). Source: FCC quotes newspapers on date. Wikipedia has 'after 1 a.m.'. RR: B.

Shirley Temple Black: 23 April 1928, 21:00 PST (+8), Santa Monica, California, USA (34n01, 118w29). Source: Birth certificate obtained by Tom and Thelma Wilson, copy on file. RR: AA.

Tony Blair: 6 May 1953, 06:10 GDT (-1), Edinburgh, Scotland (55n57, 3w13). Source: Birth certificate quoted by Caroline Gerard. RR: AA.

Robert Bloch: 5 April 1917, 21:20 CST (+6), Chicago, Illinois, USA (41n51, 87w39). Source: From him by letter to Edwin Steinbrecher. RR: A.

Boy George: 14 June 1961, 02:50 GDT (-1), Bexley, Kent, England (51n26, 0e10). Source: Sy Scholfield quotes George on Twitter, stating that he'd found his baby book. (Previously, a time of 02:30 originated from George to Laura Boomer.) RR: AA.

Susan Boyle: 1 April 1961, 09:50 GDT (-1), Blackburn, West Lothian, Scotland (55n52, 3w34). Source: Birth certificate quoted by Caroline Gerard (Susan Magdalen Boyle). RR: AA.

Ian Brady: 2 January 1938, 12:40 GMT (+0), Glasgow, Scotland (55n53, 4w15). Source: Birth certificate obtained by Victoria Shaw, copy on file; same in *A Multitude of Lives* by Paul Wright (Parlando, 2009). RR: AA.

Christian Brando: 11 May 1958, 19:36 PDT (+7), Los Angeles, California, USA (34n03, 118w15). Source: Birth certificate obtained by Frank Clifford, copy on file. RR: AA.

Marlon Brando: 3 April 1924, 23:00 CST (+6), Omaha, Nebraska, USA (41n15, 95w56). Source: Birth certificate details quoted in *The Gauquelin Book of American Charts* by Michel and Françoise Gauquelin (ACS, 1982). RR: AA.

British Broadcasting Corporation (BBC): 1 January 1927, 00:00 GMT (+0), London, England (51n30, 0w10). Source: Sy Scholfield quotes 'New Statutes', *The Times*, 1 January 1927, p.6. RR: B.

Steve Brookstein: 10 November 1968, Dulwich, London, England (51n26, 0w05). Source: From various online sites including his own, www.stevebrookstein. com. RR: X.

Bobby Brown: 5 February 1969, 05:21 EST (+5), Boston, Massachusetts, USA (42n21, 71w03). Source: Birth certificate obtained by Frank Clifford, copy on file. RR: AA.

Rita Mae Brown: 28 November 1944, 04:45 EWT (+4), Hanover, Pennsylvania, USA (39n48, 76w59). Source: From her to Lee Lehman. RR: A.

Anita Bryant: 25 March 1940, 15:10 CST (+6), Barnsdall, Oklahoma, USA (36n34, 96w10). Source: Birth certificate quoted in *Contemporary American Horoscopes* by Janice McKay and Jessica Saunders (Astrolabe, 1990). RR: AA.

Jeff Buckley: 17 November 1966, 22:49 PST (+8), Anaheim, California (33n50, 117w55). Source: Sy Scholfield quotes the biography *Dream Brother: The Lives and Music of Jeff and Tim Buckley* by David Browne (HarperEntertainment, 2001), p.58. RR: B.

Ted Bundy: 24 November 1946, 22:35 EST (+5), Burlington, Vermont, USA (44n29, 73w12). Source: Birth certificate obtained by T. Pat Davis. RR: AA.

Angelo Buono, Jr: 5 October 1934, 04:09 EST (+5), Rochester, New York, USA (43n10, 77w37). Source: Birth record obtained by Victoria Shaw, copy on file. RR: AA.

George W. Bush: 6 July 1946, 07:26 EDT (+4), New Haven, Connecticut, USA (41n18, 72w55). Source: Karen Castilla quotes hospital records; same on birth certificate. RR: AA.

Lord Byron: 22 January 1788, 14:00 LMT (+0:00:40), London, England (51n30, 0w10). Source: Birth record ('a letter preserved in the British Museum') quoted in *A Thousand and One Notable Nativities* by Alan Leo. RR: AA.

Marti Caine: 26 January 1945, 15:15 GDT (-1), Sheffield, England (53n23, 1w30). Source: From her by letter to David Fisher. RR: A.

David Cameron: 9 October 1966, 06:00 GDT (-1), London, England (51n30, 0w10). Source: From him to astrologer Annabel Herriott in 2005. RR: A.

James Cameron: 16 August 1954, Kapuskasing, Ontario, Canada (49n25, 82w26). Source: Biography *The Futurist: The Life and Films of James Cameron* by Rebecca Keegan (Random House, 2009), p.3. RR: X.

Joseph Campbell: 26 March 1904, 19:25 EST (+5), White Plains, New York, USA (41n02, 73w46). Source:

From his mother to Erin Cameron in 1981; place of birth from his website www.jcf.org. RR: A.

Irene Cara: 18 March (birth year withheld for reasons of confidentiality), 10:41 EST (+5), Bronx, New York, USA (40n51, 73w54). Source: Birth certificate quoted by Cara to Lynn Rodden. RR: AA.

Karen Carpenter: 2 March 1950, 11:45 EST (+5), New Haven, Connecticut, USA (41n18, 72w54). Source: Note from birth registry obtained by Edwin Steinbrecher, copy on file. RR: AA.

Johnny Carson: 23 October 1925, 07:15 CST (+6), Corning, Iowa, USA (40n59, 94w44). Source: Birth certificate quoted in *Contemporary Sidereal Horoscopes* (Sidereal Research Publications, 1976). RR: AA.

Barbara Cartland: 9 July 1901, 23:40 GMT (+0), Edgbaston, Birmingham, England (52n28, 1w57). Source: Mother's diary quoted in a letter to Marc Penfield, copy on file. RR: AA.

Jason Castro: 25 March 1987, Dallas, Texas, USA (32n47, 96w48). Source: His official website, 'Quick Facts', www.jasoncastromusic.com/bio. RR: X.

Charles, Prince of Wales: 14 November 1948, 21:14 GMT (+0), London, England (51n30, 0w10). Source: Buckingham Palace records. RR: A.

Nicolas-Jacques Charrier: 11 January 1960, 02:10 MET (-1), Paris, France (48n52, 2e20). Source: News report quoted in *DATAsophia* No. 4 (1997). RR: B.

Cher: 20 May 1946, 07:25 PST (+8), El Centro, California, USA (32n48, 115w34). Source: Birth certificate quoted in *Contemporary American Horoscopes* by Janice McKay and Jessica Saunders (Astrolabe, 1990). RR: AA.

Deepak Chopra: 22 October 1946, 15:45 IST (-5:30), New Delhi, India (28n36, 77e12). Source: From him to Linda Clark. The Chopra Centre sent a Vedic chart to subscribers with a time of 15:51. RR: A.

Winston Churchill: 30 November 1874, 01:30 GMT (+0), Woodstock, England (51n52, 1w21). Source: Father's letter ('safely born at 1:30 this morning after about 8 hrs labour') quoted by son Randolph in biography *Winston S. Churchill: Youth, 1874-1900* (Houghton Mifflin, 1966). RR: AA.

Bill Clinton: 19 August 1946, 08:51 CST (+6), Hope, Arkansas, USA (33n40, 93w35). Source: Note from his mother to Shelley Ackerman, copy on file. RR: AA.

Hillary Clinton: 26 October 1947, 08:02 CST (+6), Chicago, Illinois, USA (41n51, 87w39). Source: Alice Mason reported in 2003 that she had talked to the Clinton Democratic Office in NY and was told by a helpful associate that Hillary was born at a recorded 8:02 a.m. Previously, Eileen Applegate quoted an article from the *Chicago Sun Times* stating, 'Her mother went into Edgewater Hospital after midnight and Hillary was born early on the morning of October 26th.' Frances McEvoy wrote that Hillary's mother states in an article to the *Chicago Sun Times* in 1992 that Hillary was 'born in time for breakfast'. Celeste Longacre quotes Hillary for 8 p.m., as does Kt Boehrer through a mutual friend. Frank Clifford has a letter from Mrs Clinton's office at the White House (while her husband was President) refusing to give out her birth time. RR: DD.

Leonard Cohen: 21 September 1934, approx. 06:45 EDT (+4), Montreal, Canada (45n31, 73w34). Source: His mother quoted for 'daybreak' by Cohen to Linda Clark. RR: A.

Stephanie Cole: 5 October 1941, 12:00 GDT (-1), Solihull, England (52n25, 1w45). Source: From her to Frank Clifford, from her mother's memory: 'twelve noon or very close to'. RR: A.

Pauline Collins: 3 September 1940, 19:40 GDT (-1), Exmouth, England (50n37, 3w25). Source: From her to Frank Clifford quoting her 'mother's excellent memory'. RR: A.

Francis Ford Coppola: 7 April 1939, 01:38 EST (+5), Detroit, Michigan, USA (42n20, 83w03). Source: Birth certificate details quoted in *The Gauquelin Book of American Charts* by Michel and Françoise Gauquelin (ACS, 1982). RR: AA.

Simon Cowell: 7 October 1959, Lambeth, London, England (51n25, 0w08). Source: From various online sites. RR: X.

Wes Craven: 2 August 1939, 16:54 EST (+5), Cleveland, Ohio, USA (41n29, 81w41). Source: Birth certificate obtained by Frank Clifford, copy on file. RR: AA.

Michael Crawford: 19 January 1942, 04:00 GDT (-1), Salisbury, England (51n05, 1w48). Source: His autobiography, *Parcel Arrived Safely* (Century, 1999), recounts a telegram announcing his birth. RR: AA.

Michael Crick: 21 May 1958, Northampton, England (52n14, 0w54). Source: From various online sites. RR: X.

Quentin Crisp: 25 December 1908, 13:00 GMT (+0), Carshalton, England (51n22, 0w10). Source: David Fisher quotes Zerda Barlow, from Crisp by letter, 'at about one in the daytime'. Richard Geyman quotes him for 'between noon and 1 p.m.'. RR: A.

Tony Curtis: 3 June 1925, 09:00 EDT (+4), New York, New York, USA (40n43, 74w00). Source: Family records quoted by his daughter Jamie Lee Curtis to Marc Singer. RR: AA.

Jeffrey Dahmer: 21 May 1960, 16:34 CDT (+5), Milwaukee, Wisconsin, USA (43n02, 87w54). Source: Birth certificate information obtained by Stephen Przybylowski. RR: AA.

Dalai Lama XIV: 6 July 1935, approx. 05:00 USZ6 (-7), Hongya (Tibetan: Takster), Qinghai, China (36n23,

101e52). Source: Various information indicates a birth time of around sunrise. In the biography *Dalai Lama, My Son* (Viking Arkana, 2000) his mother is quoted as saying he 'was born early in the morning, before sunrise'; the biography and the film *Kundun* give dawn; and David Fisher quotes Valerie Matthews of Scotland for a letter from Pema Dorjee at the office of his Holiness that gave 'between 5:30 and 6:30 in the morning'. RR: C.

Darius Danesh: 19 August 1980, 14:34 GDT (-1), Glasgow, Scotland (55n53, 4w15). Source: Birth certificate quoted by Caroline Gerard (Navid Darius Danesh-Zad). RR: AA.

Sammy Davis Jr.: 8 December 1925, New York, New York, USA (40n43, 74w00). Source: From various internet sites. RR: X.

Doris Day: 3 April 1922, 16:30 CST (+6), Cincinnati, Ohio, USA (39n10, 84w27). Source: Birth certificate obtained by Frank Clifford, copy on file. RR: AA.

James Dean: 8 February 1931, 02:00 or 09:00 CST (+6), Marion, Indiana, USA (40n33, 85w39). Source: Birth certificate quoted by Steven Przybylowski for 09:00. Sy Scholfield cites the biography, *James Dean* by George Perry (DK ADULT, 2005; 'Authorised by the James Dean Estate') for a reproduction of Dean's baby card: 'Feb. 8th 9 a.m.' (p.21), yet with regard to the time of birth Perry states that 'the birth certificate says it was at 2 a.m., rather than the more civilized 9 a.m. that was given on the announcement card' (p.20). Friend Elizabeth Taylor is quoted as saying they were both born at 2 a.m. RR: DD.

John DeLorean: 6 January 1925, 12:00 EST (+5), Detroit, Michigan, USA (42n20, 83w03). Source: Birth certificate details quoted in *The Gauquelin Book of American Charts* by Michel and Françoise Gauquelin (ACS, 1982). RR: AA.

Diana, Princess of Wales: 1 July 1961, 19:45 GDT (-1), Sandringham, England (52n50, 00e30). Source: From Diana to her astrologer-friend Debbie Frank, and from Diana's mother to Charles Harvey. (Birth times and anecdotes given later by Diana appear to have been 'red herrings'.) RR: A.

Leonardo DiCaprio: 11 November 1974, 02:47 PST (+8), Los Angeles, California, USA (34n03, 118w15). Source: Birth certificate obtained by Frank Clifford, copy on file. RR: AA.

Rudolf Diels: 16 December 1900, 06:00 MET (-1), Berghausen, Germany (51n07, 6e55). Source: Note from birth registry obtained by Edwin Steinbrecher. RR: AA.

Richard Dimbleby: 25 May 1913, 12:00 GMT (+0), Richmond-upon-Thames, London, England (51n27, 0w20). Source: From the biography *Richard Dimbleby* (Hodder & Stoughton, 1975) by his son Jonathan Dimbleby, 'midday'. RR: B.

Celine Dion: 30 March 1968, between 12:00 and 13:00 EST (+5), Charlemagne, Canada (45n43, 73w29). Source: From her to Paddy de Jabrun ('born at Noon'); James Elliot quotes her on the radio for 12:30; John McKay-Clements quotes a family member (via her production company) for 'between 12:30 and 1:00 pm'. RR: A.

Walt Disney: 5 December 1901, 00:35 CST (+6), Hermosa, Chicago, Illinois, USA (41n55, 87w43). Source: Marion March quotes the Disney Studio office. Sy Scholfield quotes *The Animated Man* by Michael Barrier (University of California Press, 2008), p.332, for verification of birth date and place of Hermosa from Saint Paul Congregational Church (Chicago) records. RR: A.

Benjamin Disraeli: 21 December 1804, 05:30 LMT (+0:00:40), London, England (51n30, 0w10). Source: Sy Scholfield quotes the biography *The Life of Benjamin Disraeli, Earl of Beaconsfield* by William Flavelle Monypenny and George Earle Buckle (Russell & Russell, 1968), p.22. RR: B.

Divine: 19 October 1945, 07:28 EST (+5), Baltimore, Maryland, USA (39n17, 76w37). Source: Biography *Not Simply Divine* by his manager Bernard Jay (Virgin, 1993), copy on file. RR: B.

Robert Downey, Jr: 4 April 1965, 13:10 EST (+5), Manhattan, New York, USA (40n46, 73w59). Source: From him to a colleague, quoted by Marion March. RR: A.

Ann Dunham: 29 November 1942, 08:34 CWT (+5), Sedgwick, Kansas, USA (37n55, 97w25). Source: Online copy of birth certificate obtained by Steven Stuckey. RR: AA.

Marc Dutroux: 6 November 1956, 07:35 MET (-1), Ixelles, Belgium (50n50, 4e22). Source: Birth certificate obtained by Michael Mandl, quoted by Grazia Bordoni. RR: AA.

Bob Dylan: 24 May 1941, 21:05 CST (+6), Duluth, Minnesota, USA (46n47, 92w06). Source: Birth certificate obtained by Edwin Steinbrecher, copy on file. RR: AA.

Dynasty (TV series): 12 January 1981, 20:00 MST (+7), Denver, Colorado, USA (39n44, 104w59). Source: Sy Scholfield quotes *The New York Times*, 12 January 1981, p.C19: ABC network. RR: B.

Matthew Eappen: 24 May 1996, 08:35 EDT (+4), Boston, Massachusetts, USA (42n21, 71w03). Source: Birth certificate quoted by Frances McEvoy. RR: AA.

Earth Day: 22 April 1970, 12:00 EST (+5), New York, New York, USA (40n43, 74w00). Source: Sy Scholfield quotes *The New York Times* for traffic closure on Fifth Avenue from noon to 2 p.m. for the parade, and the Earth Day special televised from noon. While the Earth Day event occurred across the USA, New York City had the largest attendance. RR: B.

Sheena Easton: 27 April 1959, 15:40 GDT (-1), Bellshill, Glasgow, Scotland (55n49, 4w01). Source: Birth certificate, copy on file (Sheena Shirley Orr). RR: AA.

Clint Eastwood: 31 May 1930, 17:35 PST (+8), San Francisco, California, USA (37n47, 122w26). Source: Birth certificate details quoted in *The Gauquelin Book of American Charts* by Michel and Françoise Gauquelin (ACS, 1982), copy on file. RR: AA.

Queen Elizabeth II: 21 April 1926, 02:40 GDT (-1), Mayfair, London, England (51n31, 0w09). Source: Official announcement from the Home Office obtained by Cyril Fagan. RR: AA.

Queen Elizabeth II's Coronation: 2 June 1953, 12:34 GDT (-1), Westminster, London, England (51n30, 0w09). Source: www.westminster-abbey.org/our-history/royals/coronations/elizabeth-ii RR: B.

Robert Englund: 6 June 1947, 04:26 PST (+8), Glendale, California, USA (34n08, 118w15). Source: Birth certificate obtained by Frank Clifford, copy on file. RR: AA.

Chris Evert: 21 December 1954, 04:30 EST (+5), Fort Lauderdale, Florida, USA (26n07, 80w09). Source: Birth certificate obtained by Robert Jansky. (Chris Evert gave 04:00 to Frank Clifford.) RR: AA.

Douglas Fanueil: 28 August 1975, 02:14 EDT (+4), Boston, Massachusetts, USA (42n21, 71w03). Source: Birth certificate obtained by Francis McEvoy. RR: AA.

Roger Federer: 8 August 1981, 08:40 MEDT (-2), Basel, Switzerland (47n33, 7e35). Source: From his website www.rogerfederer.com/en/rogers/profile/index.cfm; the birth time was later removed. RR: A.

Sarah Ferguson: 15 October 1959, 09:03 GMT (+0), London, England (51n30, 0w10). Source: Buckingham Palace records; same from her to her astrologer Penny Thornton. RR: A.

Jane Fonda: 21 December 1937, 09:14 EST (+5), Manhattan, New York, USA (40n46, 73w59). Source: Birth certificate given to Lois Rodden, copy on file. RR: AA.

Kathy Ford: 11 February 1940, 05:30 EST (+5), Belding, Michigan, USA (43n06, 85w14). Source: From her to Penny Thornton as quoted in *Suns and Lovers* by Penny Thornton (Thorsons, 1986). RR: A.

Steven Forrest: 6 January 1949, 03:30 EST (+5), Mt. Vernon, New York, USA (40n55, 73w50). Source: Birth certificate quoted by Forrest to Lois Rodden. Rectified by him to 03:21. RR: AA.

Anne Frank: 12 June 1929, 07:30 MET (-1), Frankfurt am Main, Germany (50n07, 8e40). Source: Baby book at the Anne Frank Museum and Archives in Amsterdam, quoted by Betty Altschuler. RR: AA.

Viktor Frankl: 26 March 1905, afternoon to evening, Vienna, Austria (48n13, 16e20). Source: Sy Scholfield quotes Frankl's autobiography *Recollections* (Basic, 2000), p.19, which states that his mother 'felt the first labor pains' in the afternoon. Same detail in the biography *Viktor Frankl* by Anna Redsand (Houghton Mifflin Harcourt, 2006), p.7-8, which adds that his birth occurred 'later that day'. RR: C.

Anna Freud: 3 December 1895, 15:15 MET (-1), Vienna, Austria (48n13, 16e20). Source: Grazia Bordoni quotes Sigmund Freud's letter. RR: A.

Sigmund Freud: 6 May 1856, 18:30 LMT (-0:57:44), Freiberg, Moravia (now Príbor, Czech Republic) (49n38, 18e09). Source: Father's diary (written in Hebrew and German). RR: AA.

Janie Fricke: 19 December 1947, 06:03 CST (+6), South Whitley, Indiana, USA (41n05, 85w38). Source: Date and place from various reference books and interviews; time from her to Frank Clifford. RR: A.

Friends Reunited (Incorporation): 24 February 2000, 00:00 GMT (+0), Cardiff, Wales (51n29, 3w13). Source: wck2.companieshouse.gov.uk/ RR: AA.

Caril Ann Fugate: 30 July 1943, 12:55 CWT (+5), Lincoln, Nebraska, USA (40n49, 96w41). Source: Birth certificate obtained by T. Pat Davis, copy on file. RR: AA.

Simon Fuller: 17 May 1960, Hastings, England (50n51, 0e36). Source: From various online sites. RR: X.

John Wayne Gacy: 17 March 1942, 00:29 CWT (+5), Chicago, Illinois, USA (41n51, 87w39). Source: Hospital records obtained by Edith Custer. RR: AA.

Clemens von Galen: 16 March 1878, 21:30 LMT (-0:32:28), Dinklage, Germany (52n40, 8e07). Source: Note from birth registry obtained by Edwin Steinbrecher. RR: AA.

Charlene Gallego: 19 October 1956, 14:50 PST (+8), Stockton, California, USA (37n58, 121w17). Source: Note from birth registry obtained by Edwin Steinbrecher. RR: AA.

Gerald Gallego: 17 July 1946, 09:00 PST (+8), Sacramento, California, USA (38n35, 121w29). Source: Biography *A Venom in the Blood* by Eric van Hoffmann (Zebra/Kensington, 1990), p.63. RR: B.

Indira Gandhi: 19 November 1917, 23:11 IST (-5:30), Allahabad, India (25n27, 81e51). Source: From her private secretary to Robert Jansky. RR: A.

Mohandas Gandhi: 2 October 1869, approx. 07:25 LMT (-4:38:24), Porbandar, India (21n38, 69e36). Source: Various astrologers give birth times around one hour after sunrise, including 07:08 by Cyril Fagan, 07:09 in *Notable Nativities* by Alan Leo, 07:33 in *Sabian Symbols*, and 07:45 in *Notable Horoscopes* by B.V. Raman. RR: C.

Judy Garland: 10 June 1922, 06:00 CST (+6), Grand Rapids, Minnesota, USA (47n14, 93w31). Source: Note from birth registry obtained by Edwin Steinbrecher, copy on file. RR: AA.

Samantha Geimer: 31 March 1963, York, Pennsylvania, USA (39n58, 76w44). Source: Online adoption registry http://registry.adoption.com/records/168558.html RR: X.

Ed Gein: 27 August 1906, 23:30 CST (+6), North La Crosse, Wisconsin, USA (43n51, 91w15). Source: Birth certificate obtained by G. S. MacEwan, quoted by Lois Rodden. RR: AA.

Linda Goodman: 9 April 1925, 06:05 EST (+5), Morgantown, West Virginia, USA (39n38, 79w57). Source: Birth certificate obtained by Frank Clifford, copy on file (same from Goodman to Bibi DeAngelo). RR: AA.

Jade Goody: 5 June 1981, Bermondsey, London, England (51n30, 0w05). Source: From various online sites. RR: X.

Berry Gordy: 28 November 1929, Harper Hospital, Detroit, Michigan, USA (42n20, 83w03). Source: Various biographies, including his autobiography, which states that he has no idea of his birth time. RR: X.

Marjoe Gortner: 14 January 1944, 18:49 PWT (+7), Long Beach, California, USA (33n46, 118w11). Source: Birth certificate quoted in *Contemporary American Horoscopes* by Janice McKay and Jessica Saunders (Astrolabe, 1990). RR: AA.

Steffi Graf: 14 June 1969, 04:40 MET (-1), Mannheim, Germany (49n29, 8e29). Source: Hans Taeger quotes Graf's birth record from a German data collector. RR: AA.

Billy Graham: 7 November 1918, 15:30 EST (+5), Charlotte, North Carolina, USA (35n14, 80w51). Source: Birth certificate details quoted in *The Gauquelin Book of American Charts* by Michel and Françoise Gauquelin (ACS, 1982). RR: AA.

Cary Grant: 18 January 1904, 01:07 GMT (+0), Bristol, England (51n27, 2w35). Source: Lois Rodden quotes the biography, *Conversations with Cary Grant*, p.1. Sy Scholfield and Frank Clifford quote Grant in *Evenings with Cary Grant* by Nancy Nelson (W. Morrow, 1991), p.27: 'I first saw the light of day – or rather the dark of night – around 1:00 a.m. on a cold January morning.' RR: A.

Linda Gray: 12 September 1940, 07:27 PST (+8), Santa Monica, California, USA (34n01, 118w29). Source: Birth certificate obtained by Frank Clifford, copy on file. RR: AA.

Germaine Greer: 29 January 1939, 06:00 AEST (-10), Melbourne, Victoria, Australia (37s49, 144e58). Source: From her to Tiffany Holmes. RR: A.

Tanni Grey-Thompson: 26 July 1969, 01:25 GDT (-1), Cardiff, Wales (51n29, 3w13). Source: Frank Clifford quotes her autobiography *Seize the Day* (Coronet, 2002), p.2. RR: B.

Guyana (Independence): 26 May 1966, 00:00 GYT (+3:45), Georgetown, Guyana (6n48, 58w10). Source: *The Book of World Horoscopes* by Nicholas Campion quotes *Keesing's Contemporary Archives*, p.21428, same in 'The Times', 26 May 1966. RR: B.

Jessica Hahn: 7 July 1959, 16:55 EDT (+4), Brooklyn, New York, USA (40n38, 73w56). Source: From her to Howard Sheldon in August 1988 ('four-fifty-something'). NB: Other references state her birth place as Massapequa, New York. RR: A.

David Hamblin: 8 August 1935, 21:50 GDT (-1), Manchester, England (53n30, 2w15). Source: His mother's diary quoted on his official website www.davidhamblin.net/autobiography.html RR: B.

Thomas Hamilton: 10 May 1952, 08:50 GDT (-1), Glasgow, Scotland (55n53, 4w15). Source: Birth certificate quoted by Caroline Gerard. RR: AA.

Mata Hari: 7 August 1876, 13:00 LMT (-0:23:04), Leeuwarden, Netherlands (53n12, 5e46). Source: Note from birth registry obtained by Edwin Steinbrecher, copy on file. RR: AA.

Wolf von Harnack: 15 July 1888, 17:15 LMT (-0:35:04), Marburg, Germany (50n49, 8e46). Source: Note from birth registry obtained by Edwin Steinbrecher. RR: AA.

Tom Hayden: 11 December 1939, 02:00 or 14:00 EST (+5), Detroit, Michigan, USA (42n20, 83w03). Source: From him to Edwin Steinbrecher, '2:00 a.m. or 2:00 p.m.'. RR: C.

Patty Hearst: 20 February 1954, 18:01 PST (+8), San Francisco, California, USA (37n47, 122w25). Source: Birth certificate quoted in *Contemporary American Horoscopes* by Janice McKay and Jessica Saunders (Astrolabe, 1990). RR: AA.

Edward Heath: 9 July 1916, 'night' GDT (-1), Broadstairs, England (51n22, 1e26). Source: Sy Scholfield quotes the biography *Edward Heath* by George Hutchinson (Longmans, 1970), p.3: 'on the summer Sunday night'. RR: C.

Harry Helmsley: 4 March 1909, Manhattan, New York, USA (40n46, 73w59). Source: Birth certificate obtained by Frank Clifford, copy on file, no time. RR: X.

Leona Helmsley: 4 July 1920, 06:00 EDT (+4), High Falls, Marbletown, New York, USA (41n50, 74w08). Source: Birth certificate quoted in the biography *Palace Coup* by Michael Moss (Doubleday, 1989), p.33, copy of book on file. RR: AA.

Jimi Hendrix: 27 November 1942, 10:15 PWT (+7), Seattle, Washington, USA (47n36, 122w20). Source: Birth certificate obtained by Janice MacKay, copy on file. RR: AA.

Audrey Hepburn: 4 May 1929, 03:00 GDT (-1), Ixelles, Belgium (50n50, 4e22). Source: Birth certificate obtained by Luc DeMarre. RR: AA.

Katharine Hepburn: 12 May 1907, 17:47 or 19:11 EST (+5), Hartford, Connecticut, USA (41n46, 72w41). Source: Birth certificate quoted by Howard Hammitt and Ralph Kraum. Frank Clifford quotes a telegram announcing Hepburn's birth among her personal effects auctioned by Sotheby's, 'Catherine Houghton Hepbourn, second, came at seven elevin [sic] tonight, Eight half pounds, all well.' Copy on file from Sy Scholfield. RR: AA?

Hermann Hesse: 2 July 1877, 18:30 LMT (-0:34:56), Calw, Germany (48n43, 8e44). Source: Sy Scholfield quotes Hesse's mother's diary, transcribed in *Sei du Selbst* by Hesse (Braun G. Buchverlag, 2002). RR: AA.

Myra Hindley: 23 July 1942, 02:45 GDWT (-2), Crumpsall, Lancashire, England (53n31, 2w15). Source: David Fisher quotes the biography *Inside the Mind of a Murderess* by Jean Ritchie (Angus and Robertson, 1988): "between 2.30 and 3 a.m." RR: B.

Alfred Hitchcock: 13 August 1899, Leytonstone, London, England (51n34, 0e01). Source: Online birth certificate obtained by Sy Scholfield, copy on file. RR: X.

Adolf Hitler: 20 April 1889, 18:30 LMT (-0:52:08), Braunau am Inn, Austria (48n15, 13e02). Source: Church baptismal record obtained by Heinz Noesselt. RR: AA.

Dustin Hoffman: 8 August 1937, 17:07 PST (+8), Los Angeles, California, USA (34n03, 118w15). Source: Birth certificate quoted in *The Gauquelin Book of American Charts* by Michel and Françoise Gauquelin (ACS, 1982), and *Contemporary American Horoscopes* by Janice McKay and Jessica Saunders (Astrolabe, 1990). RR: AA.

Billie Holiday: 7 April 1915, 02:30 EST (+5), Philadelphia, Pennsylvania, USA (39n57, 75w10). Source: Birth certificate, as quoted in biography 'Billie Holiday' by Stuart Nicholson (Victor Gollancz, 1995), p.18. RR: AA.

Anthony Hopkins: 31 December 1937, 09:15 GMT (+0), Margam, Wales (51n34, 3w44). Source: From him to Dave Hayward in 1991. (Hopkins gave 10:30 to Joan Abel in 1978.) RR: A.

Whitney Houston: 9 August 1963, 20:55 EDT (+4), Newark, New Jersey, USA (40n44, 74w10). Source: Birth certificate obtained by Kathryn Farmer, copy on file. RR: AA.

L. Ron Hubbard: 13 March 1911, 02:01 CST (+6), Tilden, Nebraska, USA (42n03, 97w50). Source: From him to Doris Chase Doane quoted in *Progressions in Action*. RR: A.

India (Independence): 15 August 1947, 00:00 IST (-5:30), Delhi, India (28n40, 77e13). Source: *The Book of World Horoscopes* by Nicholas Campion quotes *The Times*, 15 August 1947, p.4. RR: B.

Goran Ivanisevic: 13 September 1971, 01:00 MET (-1), Split, Yugoslavia (now Croatia) (43n31, 16e27). Source: Frank Clifford quotes him, September 1999. RR: A.

Leon Jackson: 30 December 1988, 18:33 GMT (+0), Bellshill, Glasgow, Scotland, (55n49, 4w01). Source: Birth certificate quoted by Caroline Gerard. RR: AA.

Steve Jobs: 24 February 1955, 19:15 PST (+8), San Francisco, California, USA (37n46, 122w25). Source: Birth certificate quoted by Pat Taglilatelo. RR: AA.

Holly Johnson: 9 February 1960, 16:30 GMT (+0), Wavertree, Liverpool, England (53n24, 2W56). Source: In 1997, Johnson gave Frank Clifford a birth time of 'before 12 noon'. In an email to Frank Clifford (1 July 2002), Johnson stated, 'After a conversation with my father I now believe "about half past four in the afternoon" to be correct.' He gave the same data to Sy Scholfield. RR: A.

James Earl Jones: 17 January 1931, 06:05 CST (+6), Arkabutla, Mississippi, USA (34n42, 90w07). Source: Frank Clifford quotes Jones's autobiography *Voices and Silences* by Penelope Niven (Scribner, 1993). RR: B.

Jim Jones: 13 May 1931, 22:00 CST (+6), Crete, Indiana, USA (40n03, 84w52). Source: Date and time from birth registrar to Frank Clifford by telephone. RR: AA.

Janis Joplin: 19 January 1943, 09:45 CWT (+5), Port Arthur, Texas, USA (29n54, 93w56). Source: Birth certificate obtained by Frank Clifford, copy on file. (Her birth announcement states 09:30.) RR: AA.

Christina Kay: 11 June 1878, 04:55 GMT, Edinburgh, Scotland (55n57, 3w13). Source: Birth certificate quoted in *A Multitude of Lives* by Paul Wright (Parlando, 2009). RR: AA.

Christine Keeler: 22 February 1942, 11:15 GDT (-1), Uxbridge, London, England (51n33, 0w29). Source: Cyrus Abayakoon, in 'Astrological Quarterly', December 1963, vouches for the accuracy of the data. RR: A.

Kitty Kelley: 4 April 1942, 17:00 PWT (+7), Spokane, Washington, USA (47n40, 117w26). Source: From her in an interview in the *Spokane Spokesman Review*. RR: A.

Ellie Kendrick: 6 June 1990, London, England (51n30, 0w10). Source: Wikipedia. RR: X.

Joan Kennedy: 5 September 1935, 06:10 EDT (+4), New York, New York, USA (40n43, 74w00). Source: Birth certificate quoted by Dana Holliday. NB: In her book, *The Joy of Classical Music* (Doubleday, 1992), Kennedy writes, 'I was born on September 2, 1936, the oldest of two daughters.' Sy Scholfield notes that

Kennedy's parents, Virginia Joan Stead and Harry Wiggin Bennett Jr., were married on 8 June 1935 (*The New York Times*, 9 June 1935, p.N5); no notice of Kennedy's birth on any date in *The New York Times*. In his book, *Jackie, Ethel, Joan: Women of Camelot* (Warner, 2000), J. Randy Taraborrelli writes, 'Virginia Joan Bennett was born in the early-morning hours of September 2, 1936, at Mother Cabrini Hospital in Riverdale, New York.' RR: AA.

John F. Kennedy: 29 May 1917, 15:00 EST (+5), Brookline, Massachusetts, USA (42n20, 71w07). Source: From his mother to Garth Allen. RR: A.

Ted Kennedy: 22 February 1932, 03:58 EST (+5), Dorchester, Massachusetts, USA (42n18, 71w05). Source: Hospital records obtained by Ruth Dewey. RR: AA.

Billie Jean King: 22 November 1943, 11:45 PWT (+7), Long Beach, California, USA (33n47, 118w11). Source: Birth certificate obtained by Doris Chase Doane in *Progressions in Action*. RR: AA.

Coretta Scott King: 27 April 1927, 16:00 CST (+6), Marion, Alabama, USA (32n38, 87w19). Source: Birth certificate quoted in *Contemporary American Horoscopes* by Janice McKay and Jessica Saunders (Astrolabe, 1990). RR: AA.

Martin Luther King, Jr: 15 January 1929, 12:00 CST (+6), Atlanta, Georgia, USA (33n45, 84w23). Source: From his mother to Ruth Dewey, 'high noon'. RR: A.

Rodney King: 2 April 1965, 07:00 PST (+8), Sacramento, California, USA (38n34, 121w29). Source: Birth certificate given to Lois Rodden, copy on file. RR: AA.

Stephen King: 21 September 1947, 01:30 EDT (+4), Portland, Maine, USA (43n39, 70w15). Source: From him to D. Jo and M. J. Wagner, quoted in 'Mercury Hour', 1981. RR: A.

Evel Knievel: 17 October 1938, 14:40 MST (+7), Butte, Montana, USA (46n00, 112w32). Source: Birth certificate details quoted in *The Gauquelin Book of American Charts* by Michel and Françoise Gauquelin (ACS, 1982). RR: AA.

Reggie Kray: 24 October 1933, 20:00 GMT (+0), Hoxton, London, England (51n32, 0e04). Source: Online birth certificate, copy on file. RR: AA.

Ronnie Kray: 24 October 1933, 20:10 GMT (+0), Hoxton, London, England (51n32, 0e04). Source: Online birth certificate, copy on file. RR: AA.

Peter Kurten: 26 May 1883, 03:30 LMT (-0:28:04), Mulheim, Cologne, Germany (50n58, 7e01). Source: Note from birth registry obtained by Edwin Steinbrecher. RR: AA.

Angela Lansbury: 16 October 1925, 00:45 GMT (+0), London, England (51n30, 0w10). Source: From her to Karen Christino. RR: A.

Peter Lawford: 7 September 1923, 08:00 GDT (-1), London, England (51n30, 0w10). Source: From Lawford to Betty Collins, data from his mother. (Another reference, *The Man who Kept the Secrets* by James Spada, states the birth took place in the late afternoon, possibly giving Sagittarius Rising.) RR: A.

Christopher Lee: 27 May 1922, 14:45 GDT (-1), London, England (51n30, 0w10). Source: Autobiography *Tall, Dark and Gruesome* (W. H. Allen, 1977), p.12. RR: B.

Vivien Leigh: 5 November 1913, 17:30 LMT (-5.53), Darjeeling, India (27n02, 88e16). Source: From the biography, *The Oliviers*, by Felix Barker (Hamish Hamilton, 1953), p.77: 'not long after the sun had disappeared' (sunset calculated as 17.16). RR: B.

John Lennon: 9 October 1940, 18:30 GDT (-1), Liverpool, England (53n25, 2w55). Source: Lennon's aunt 'who was present at the birth' quoted by his step-mother, astrologer Pauline Stone. RR: A.

Monica Lewinsky: 23 July 1973, 12:21 PDT (+7), San Francisco, California, USA (37n47, 122w25). Source: Birth certificate obtained by Jack Fertig. RR: AA.

Denise Lewis: 27 August 1972, 04:25 GDT (-1), West Bromwich, England (52n31, 2w00). Source: Frank Clifford quotes her autobiography *Personal Best* (Century, 2001), p.11. RR: B.

Liberace: 16 May 1919, 23:15 CWT (+5), West Allis, Wisconsin, USA (43n01, 88w00). Source: Note from birth registry obtained by Edwin Steinbrecher, copy on file. RR: AA.

Nancy Lieberman: 1 July 1958, Brooklyn, New York, USA (40n42, 73w59). Source: Various biographies. RR: X.

Lorna Luft: 21 November 1952, 15:53 PST (+8), Santa Monica, California, USA (34n01, 118w29). Source: Birth certificate quoted in *Contemporary American Horoscopes* by Janice McKay and Jessica Saunders (Astrolabe, 1990), copy on file. RR: AA.

John Major: 29 March 1943, 'between 02:00 and 04:30' GDT (-1), Carshalton, London, England (51n22, 0w10). Source: Frank Clifford quotes birth certificate for date and place. Time from Major to Russell Grant. RR: C.

Nelson Mandela: 18 July 1918, afternoon, Umtata, South Africa (31s35, 28e47). Source: Frances McEvoy quotes her son and daughter-in-law for a time of 'afternoon' from Mandela's entourage. RR: C.

Charles Manson: 12 November 1934, 16:40 EST (+5), Cincinnati, Ohio, USA (39n10, 84w27). Source: Birth certificate obtained by Frank Clifford, copy on file. Same data quoted in *Contemporary American Horoscopes* by Janice McKay and Jessica Saunders (Astrolabe, 1990). RR: AA.

Ferdinand Marcos: 11 September 1917, 07:00 AWST (-8), Sarrat, Philippines (18n10, 120e39). Source: Sy

Scholfield quotes the biography *The Young Marcos* by Victor G. Nituda (Foresight International, 1979), p.47, for data from his mother: 'Born at 7 a.m. on September 11, 1917 in the town of Sarrat, Ilocos Norte.' RR: A.

Imelda Marcos: 2 July 1929, 05:30 AWST (-8), San Juan de Dios Hospital, Pasay, Manila, Philippines (14n33, 121e00). Sources: Birth certificate, obtained by Sy Scholfield, copy on file. The biography *The Untold Story of Imelda Marcos* by Carmen Navarro Pedrosa (Tandem, 1969), p.10, gives 'born at dawn' at San Juan de Dios Hospital, which is located in Pasay, Manila; same details in the biography *Imelda Marcos* by Pedrosa (1987). RR: AA.

Marcos Flight: 25 February 1986, 21:00 AWST (-8), Manila, Philippines (14n35, 121e00). Source: From various online accounts, including http://choosethecross.com/?m=20080225, that state 9 p.m. or shortly after. RR: B.

Princess Margaret: 21 August 1930, 21:22 GDT (-1), Glamis Castle, Scotland (56n36, 3w00). Source: Birth registry quoted by Joanne Clancy. Sy Scholfield quotes 'The Duchess of York: Doctors' Good Report', *The Times*, 23 August 1930, p.10: 'Whitehall, 22nd August, 1930. Yesterday evening at 22 minutes after 9 o'clock, her Royal Highness, The Duchess of York, was safely delivered of a Princess at Glamis Castle.' RR: AA.

Princess Margaret's Announcement: 31 October 1955, 19:21 GMT (+0), Clarence House, London, England (51n30, 0w10). Source: From *Daily Mail*, 1 November 1955, p.1, copy on file. RR: B.

Dean Martin: 7 June 1917, 23:55 CST (+6), Steubenville, Ohio, USA (40n22, 80w38). Source: Birth certificate obtained by Frank Clifford, copy on file (17 June has been given in error). RR: AA.

Ricky Martin: 24 December 1971, 17:00 AST (+4), Hato Rey, Puerto Rico, USA (18n25, 66w03). Source: Birth certificate quoted in *Ricky Martin: An Unauthorized Biography* by Kristen Sparks (Berkley Boulevard Books, 1999), p.13, copy on file. RR: AA.

Paul McCartney: 18 June 1942, 14:00 D-GDT (-2), Liverpool, England (53n25, 2w55). Source: From Linda McCartney to Tom Hopke. RR: A.

John McEnroe: 16 February 1959, 22:30 MET (-1), Wiesbaden, Germany (50n05, 8e14). Source: Biography *McEnroe: A Rage for Perfection* by Richard Evans (Simon and Schuster, 1982); Marc Penfield quotes a letter from McEnroe's mother for 22:20 (not confirmed). RR: B.

Gillian McKeith: 28 September 1959, 21:05 GDT (-1), Perth, Scotland (56n24, 3w28). Source: Birth certificate quoted by Caroline Gerard (corrected from the 29 September date listed in the first edition of this book). RR: AA.

Ed McMahon: 6 March 1923, 14:23 EST (+5), Detroit, Michigan, USA (42n20, 83w03). Source: Time of birth from family Bible quoted in the autobiography *Here's*

Ed by him and Caroll Caroll (Putnam, 1976), p.40. *Contemporary American Horoscopes* by Janice McKay and Jessica Saunders (Astrolabe, 1990) quotes birth certificate for date and place, and time of 15:00. RR: AA.

Michelle McManus: 8 May 1980, 21:00 GDT (-1), Glasgow, Scotland (55n53, 4w15). Source: Birth certificate quoted by Caroline Gerard. RR: AA.

Richard Carleton Meeker, Jr.: 3 July 1956, 10:10 PDT (+7), Los Angeles, California, USA (34n03, 118w15). Source: From his mother's autobiography *After All* by Mary Tyler Moore, copy on file. Sy Scholfield confirms date and place from the California Births Index online. RR: B.

Russ Meyer: 21 March 1922, 09:35 PST (+8), Oakland, California, USA (37n48, 122w16). Source: Birth certificate obtained by Frank Clifford, copy on file. RR: AA.

George Michael: 25 June 1963, 06:00 GDT (-1), Finchley, England (51n36, 0w10). Source: Birth certificate obtained by Frank Clifford, copy on file for date and place. Janey Stubbs quotes his office for his birth time. RR: A.

Bette Midler: 1 December 1945, 14:19 HST (+10), Honolulu, Hawaii, USA (21n18, 157w51). Source: Birth certificate details quoted in *The Gauquelin Book of American Charts* by Michel and Françoise Gauquelin (ACS, 1982), and *Contemporary American Horoscopes* by Janice McKay and Jessica Saunders (Astrolabe, 1990). RR: AA.

Mina: 25 March 1940, 15:00 MET (-1), Busto Arsizio, Italy (45n37, 8e51). Source: Birth certificate quoted by Grazia Bordoni. RR: AA.

Liza Minnelli: 12 March 1946, 07:58 PST (+8), Los Angeles, California, USA (34n03, 118w15). Source: Birth certificate obtained by Robert Paige, copy on file. RR: AA.

Marilyn Monroe: 1 June 1926, 09:30 PST (+8), Los Angeles, California, USA (34n03, 118w15). Source: Birth certificate obtained by Bob Garner, copy on file. RR: AA.

Mary Tyler Moore: 29 December 1936, 10:45 EST (+5), Brooklyn, New York, USA (40n38, 73w56). Source: Birth certificate obtained by Thelma and Tom Wilson, copy on file. RR: AA.

Giorgio Moroder: 26 April 1940, 02:45 MET (-1), Ortisei, Italy (46n34, 11e40). Source: Note from birth registry obtained by Grazia Bordoni, copy on file. RR: AA.

Jim Morrison: 8 December 1943, 11:55 EWT (+4), Melbourne, Florida, USA (28n04, 80w36). Source: Birth registration card obtained by Bob Garner, copy on file. RR: AA.

Rupert Murdoch: 11 March 1931, 23:59 AEST (-10), Melbourne, Australia (37s49, 144e58). Source: Gwen Stoney quotes a newspaper announcement given in *A Paper Prince* for 'midnight ending the day'. (Sy Scholfield quotes the birth notice in *The Argus* [Melbourne], 13 March 1931, p.1: On the 11th March, at midnight). RR: B.

Benito Mussolini: 29 July 1883, 14:00 LMT (-0:49:56), Dovia di Predappio, Italy (44n06, 11e58). Source: Birth certificate obtained by Michel and Françoise Gauquelin, copy on file. RR: AA.

Rafael Nadal: 3 June 1986, 18:20 MEDT (-2), Manacor, Spain (39n34, 3e12). Source: Birth certificate quoted in the Spanish newsletter, *Cyklos* (December 2010). Previously Patrick de Jabrun quoted an unspecified biography for a time of 19:15. RR: AA.

Martina Navratilova: 18 October 1956, 16:40 MET (-1), Prague, Czechoslovakia (50n05, 14e26). Source: From her to Frank Clifford, 1995 ('16:40 give or take a few minutes'). RR: A.

Jawaharlal Nehru: 14 November 1889, 23:30 LMT (-5:21), Allahabad, India (25n27, 81e51). Source: From his secretary by letter in June 1962, obtained by Bangalore Raman. RR: A.

Judy Nelson: 17 September 1945, Fort Worth, Texas, USA (32n44, 97w19). Source: The biography *Love Match* by Sandra Faulkner (Carol, 1993), copy in hand. RR: X.

Paul Newman: 26 January 1925, 06:30 EST (+5), Cleveland, Ohio, USA (41n30, 81w42). Source: Birth certificate obtained by Frank Clifford, copy on file. RR: AA.

Jack Nicholson: 22 April 1937, 11:00 EST (+5), Neptune, New Jersey, USA (40n13, 74w01). Source: From him to Mark Johnson. Fredrick Davies in *Signs of the Stars* quotes Nicholson for 11:20 AM. Birth certificate, obtained by Frank Clifford, filed in May 1954 has no time of birth, copy on file. RR: A.

Dennis Nilsen: 23 November 1945, 04:00 GMT (+0), Fraserburgh, Scotland (57n42, 2w00). Source: Birth certificate quoted in *A Multitude of Lives* by Paul Wright (Parlando, 2009). RR: AA.

Richard Nixon: 9 January 1913, 21:35 PST (+8), Yorba Linda, California, USA (33n53, 117w49). Source: Birth record from the attending nurse (time and date of birth) obtained by Frank Clifford, copy on file. RR: AA.

Barack Obama: 4 August 1961, 19:24 AHST (+10), Honolulu, Hawaii, USA (21n18, 157w52). Source: Birth certificate published online, copy on file (supported by birth announcements in Hawaii). RR: AA.

Laurence Olivier: 22 May 1907, 05:00 GMT (+0), Dorking, England (51n14, 0w20). Source: From his autobiography *Confessions of an Actor* (Weidenfeld and Nicolson, 1982), copy on file. RR: B.

Jacqueline Kennedy Onassis: 28 July 1929, 14:30 EDT (+4), Southampton, New York, USA (40n53, 72w23). Source: From her to mutual friends of Frances McEvoy. RR: A.

Lee Harvey Oswald: 18 October 1939, 21:55 CST (+6), New Orleans, Louisiana, USA (29n57, 90w05). Source: From his mother to T. Pat Davis. RR: A.

Panorama (BBC TV series) Interview with Princess Diana: 20 November 1995, 21:40 GMT (+0), London, England (51n30, 0w10). Source: Sy Scholfield quotes *The Times*, 20 November 1995, p.43. RR: B.

Alan Parker: 14 February 1944, Islington, London, England (51n33, 0w06). Source: Various online biographies (Alan William Parker). RR: X.

H. Ross Perot: 27 June 1930, 05:34 CST (+6), Texarkana, Texas, USA (33n26, 94w03). Source: Birth certificate details quoted in *The Gauquelin Book of American Charts* by Michel and Françoise Gauquelin (ACS, 1982). RR: AA.

Anne Perry (Juliet Hulme): 28 October 1938, 22:15 GMT, Blackheath, London, England (51n28, 0w00). Birth certificate obtained by Frank Clifford, copy on file for date and place. Dana Holliday quotes Perry personally for her birth time. RR: A.

Bernadette Peters: 28 February 1948, 22:45 EST (+5), Ozone Park, New York, USA (40n41, 73w51). Source: Birth certificate obtained by Tom and Thelma Wilson, copy in hand. RR: AA.

Marcel Petiot: 17 January 1897, 03:00 (Paris Time, -0:09:20), Auxerre, France (47n48, 3e34). Source: Birth certificate obtained by Sy Scholfield, copy on file. Same on a note obtained by Edwin Steinbrecher from birth registry. RR: AA.

Philippines (Independence): 4 July 1946, 09:15 AWST (-8), Manila, Philippines (14n35, 121e00). Source: *The Book of World Horoscopes* by Nicholas Campion quotes a letter from the National Historical Institute to Serafin Lanot, confirmed by local newspaper reports of 5 July 1946. RR: A.

Roman Polanski: 18 August 1933, 10:30 GDT (-1), Paris, France (48n52, 2e20). Source: Birth record obtained by Luc de Marre, quoted in the Taeger *Horoscope Lexikon*. RR: AA.

Enoch Powell: 16 June 1912, 21:50 GMT (+0), Stetchford, Birmingham, England (52n29, 01w54). Source: From him to the Astrological Association's Data Section. RR: A.

Elvis Presley: 8 January 1935, 04:35 CST (+6), Tupelo, Mississippi, USA (34n15, 88w42). Source: Birth certificate obtained by Eugene Moore, copy on file. RR: AA.

Joan Quigley: 10 April 1927, 16:17 CST (+6), Kansas City, Missouri, USA (39n06, 94w35). Source: From her to E. Rowland, quoted by Doris Chase Doane. RR: A.

Ricardo Ramirez: 28 February 1960, 02:07 MST (+7), El Paso, Texas, USA (31n45, 106w29). Source: Birth certificate obtained by Victoria Shaw, quoted by Lois Rodden. RR: AA.

John Bennett Ramsey: 7 December 1943, 00:45 CWT (+5), Omaha, Nebraska, USA (41n15, 95w56). Source: Birth certificate quoted by Stephen Przybylowski. RR: AA.

JonBenét Ramsey: 6 August 1990, 01:36 EDT (+4), Atlanta, Georgia, USA (33n45, 84w23). Source: Frank Clifford quotes birth announcement, as seen on 'Larry King Live' (12/11/02); same details in *The Death of Innocence* by John Ramsey, Patsy Ramsey and Patricia Ann Ramsey (Thomas Nelson, 2000). RR: AA.

Nancy Reagan: 6 July 1921, 13:18 EDT (+4), Manhattan, New York, USA (40n46, 73w59). Source: Birth certificate (without time) printed in *Nancy Reagan: the Unauthorized Biography* by Kitty Kelley (Simon & Schuster, 1991); time from *Fly Away Home* by John Weld, p.187 (his mother Deborah Lewis cast a horoscope for a 17-year-old Nancy Davis); copies of both on file. RR: B.

Ronald Reagan: 6 February 1911, rectified to 03:43 CST (+6), Tampico, Illinois, USA (41n37, 89w47). Source: Various information suggests a birth in the early morning before sunrise. The biography *Dutch* by Edmund Morris (Random House, 1999) gives 04:16 though the footnoted source is ambiguous (it is likely to be a rectification, as astrologer and expert rectifier Vivia Jayne is quoted on the same page). Joan Quigley, Nancy Reagan's astrologer, rectified the time to 03:43 from family information that he was born 'early morning'. Doris Chase Doane in *Dell Horoscope* gave 02:00, a birth time she said that she and Carroll Righter had been using for 40 years. *American Astrology*, March 1976, states that it has a questionnaire returned from Reagan giving 'early morning'. RR: DD.

Robert Redford: 18 August 1936, 20:02 PST (+8), Santa Monica, California, USA (34n01, 118w29). Source: Birth certificate obtained by Tom and Thelma Wilson, copy on file. RR: AA.

Vanessa Redgrave: 30 January 1937, 18:00 GMT (+0), Blackheath, London, England (51n28, 0w00). Source: Her autobiography *Vanessa Redgrave* (Hutchinson, 1991), p.3, copy on file. RR: B.

Robert Ressler: 15 February 1937, Chicago, Illinois, USA (41n51, 87w39). Source: Wikipedia. RR: X.

'Rivers of Blood' Speech: 20 April 1968, 14.30 GDT (-1), Birmingham, England (52n28, 1w54). Source: '1968 in British Television', Wikipedia. RR: B.

Oral Roberts: 24 January 1918, 11:30 CST (+6), Ada, Oklahoma, USA (34n46, 96w41). Source: Roberts' publication, *Abundant Life*, quoted by Howard Hammitt. RR: B.

Anthony Robbins: 29 February 1960, 20:10 PST (+8), Los Angeles, California, USA (34n03, 118w15).

Source: Birth certificate obtained by Frank Clifford, copy on file. RR: AA.

Diana Ross: 26 March 1944, 23:46 EWT (+4), Detroit, Michigan, USA (42n20, 83w03). Source: Birth certificate quoted in *Contemporary American Horoscopes* by Janice McKay and Jessica Saunders (Astrolabe, 1990), and *The Gauquelin Book of American Charts* by Michel and Françoise Gauquelin (ACS, 1982). RR: AA.

Salman Rushdie: 19 June 1947, 02:30 IST (-5:30), Bombay (now Mumbai), India (18n58, 72e50). Source: From Rushdie to Penny Allen (former wife of novelist Ian McEwan), who told astrologer Catriona Mundle; copy of Mundle's letter to Sally Davis on file. RR: A.

Marquis de Sade: 2 June 1740, 17:00 LAT (-0:11:50), Paris, France (48n52, 2e20). Source: Birth record quoted by Richard Rongier (LAT not LMT was in operation). RR: AA.

Peter Sellers: 8 September 1925, 06:00 GDT (-1), Southsea, Portsmouth, England (50n46, 1w05). Source: From him to Edwin Steinbrecher. RR: A.

Aimee Semple McPherson: 9 October 1890, about 01:00 or about 17:00 LMT (+5:23:32), Salford, Canada (43n00, 80w50). Source: Sy Scholfield quotes the biography, *Everybody's Sister* by Edith Waldvogel Blumhofer (William. B. Eerdmans, 1993), pp. 42–3, 'It was evening on Wednesday, October 8, [on a farm just west of Salford, p. 24] when... [a] neighbour... drove off to get Mrs Gibbs, the local midwife. While she tended to Minnie upstairs, Herb and James Kennedy whiled away the time in the kitchen. A few hours later, early on the morning of the ninth, Mrs Gibbs came downstairs carrying a blanket-wrapped baby.' Blumhofer adds that the handwritten birth and marriage registers list Aimee's given name as 'Annie' (Annie Kennedy). However, Jim Eshelman quotes P.A. (July 1926), '4:00 to 6:00 p.m. from mother's statement'. RR: DD.

Robert Shapiro: 2 September 1942, 07:47 EWT (+4), Plainfield, New Jersey, USA (40n38, 74w24). Source: Birth certificate quoted by Lois Rodden, copy on file. RR: AA.

Cybill Shepherd: 18 February 1950, 19:52 CST (+6), Memphis, Tennessee, USA (35n09, 90w03). Source: Birth certificate quoted by Roscoe Hope in *American Astrology*, November 1986. RR: AA.

Brooke Shields: 31 May 1965, 13:45 EDT (+4), Manhattan, New York, USA (40n46, 73w59). Source: Tracy Marks quotes her autobiography *The Brooke Book* (Pocket Books, 1978). RR: B.

Harold Shipman: 14 January 1946, Nottingham, England (52n58, 1w10). Source: Sy Scholfield quotes the obituary, 'The Killer Doctor', online BBC News, 13 January 2004. RR: X.

Nina Simone: 21 February 1933, 06:00 EST (+5), Tryon, North Carolina, USA (35n12, 82w14). Source:

Birth certificate details quoted in *The Gauquelin Book of American Charts* by Michel and Françoise Gauquelin (ACS, 1982). RR: AA.

Don Simpson: 29 October 1943, 10:53 PWT (+7), Seattle, Washington, USA (47n36, 122w20). Source: Birth certificate obtained by Frank Clifford, copy on file. RR: AA.

O. J. Simpson: 9 July 1947, 08:08 PST (+8), San Francisco, California, USA (37n47, 122w25). Source: Birth certificate quoted in *Contemporary American Horoscopes* by Janice McKay and Jessica Saunders (Astrolabe, 1990). RR: AA.

Frank Sinatra: 12 December 1915, 03:00 EST (+5), Hoboken, New Jersey, USA (40n45, 74w02). Source: From Sinatra's father to Lynn Palmer. RR: A.

Maggie Smith: 28 December 1934, Ilford, Essex, England (51n33, 0e05). Source: Biography *The Maggie Smith Handbook* by Michelle Hutchins (Emereo, 2010). RR: X.

Patti Smith: 30 December 1946, 06:01 CST (+6), Chicago, Illinois, USA (41n51, 87w39). Source: From her to Debbi Kempton-Smith. RR: A.

David Sneddon: 15 September 1978, 18:46 GDT (-1), Maternity Hospital, Paisley, Scotland (55n51, 4w25). Source: Birth certificate quoted by Caroline Gerard. RR: AA.

Stephen Sondheim: 22 March 1930, 21:00 EST (+5), New York, New York, USA (40n43, 74w00). Source: Deb McBride quotes Sondheim for data from his father, who stated that the previous time of 03:30 given by Stephen's mother was incorrect. RR: A.

Sissy Spacek: 25 December 1949, 00:03 CST (+6), Tyler, Texas, USA (32n21, 95w18). Source: Note from birth registry obtained by Edwin Steinbrecher, copy on file. RR: AA.

Kevin Spacey: 26 July 1959, South Orange, New Jersey, USA (40n45, 74w15). Source: Various online biographies. NB: In the 2001 film *K-PAX* Spacey's character must return to his home planet at precisely 5.51 a.m. on 27 July. RR: X.

Jimmy Swaggart: 15 March 1935, 01:35 CST (+6), Ferriday, Louisiana, USA (31n37, 91w33). Source: Birth certificate quoted by Jeannine Pace. RR: AA.

Muriel Spark: 1 February 1918, 03:00 GMT (+0), Edinburgh, Scotland (55n57, 3w13). Source: Birth certificate quoted in *A Multitude of Lives* by Paul Wright (Parlando, 2009). RR: AA.

Aaron Spelling: 22 April 1923, 12:30 CST (+6), Dallas, Texas, USA (32n47, 96w48). Source: Birth certificate obtained by Frank Clifford, copy on file. RR: AA.

Steven Spielberg: 18 December 1946, 18:16 EST (+5), Cincinnati, Ohio, USA (39n10, 84w27). Source: Birth certificate from L. Lineauveuer, copy on file. Same in

Contemporary American Horoscopes by Janice McKay and Jessica Saunders (Astrolabe, 1990). RR: AA.

Jerry Springer: 13 February 1944, 23:45 GWT (-1), Highgate, London, England (51n34, 0w10). Source: From him to Frank Clifford. RR: A.

Jacqueline Stallone: 30 November 1921, 02:52 EST (+5), Washington, D.C., USA (38n54, 77w02). Source: From her to a colleague of Ed Dearborn. RR: A.

Sylvester Stallone: 6 July 1946, 19:20 EDT (+4), Manhattan, New York, USA (40n46, 73w59). Source: From his astrologer-mother Jacqueline Stallone, quoted by Jany Bessiere. RR: A.

Charles Starkweather: 24 November 1938, 20:10 CST (+6), Lincoln, Nebraska, USA (40n49, 96w40). Source: Birth certificate obtained by Victoria Shaw. RR: AA.

Kenneth Starr: 21 July 1946, 18:45 CST (+6), Vernon, Texas, USA (34n09, 99w15). Source: Birth certificate given to Lois Rodden. RR: AA.

Martha Stewart: 3 August 1941, 13:33 EDT (+4), Jersey City, New Jersey, USA (40n44, 74w05). Source: Birth certificate quoted by Lois Rodden, copy on file. RR: AA.

Barbra Streisand: 24 April 1942, 05:04 EWT (+4), Brooklyn, New York, USA (40n38, 73w56). Source: Birth announcement, as printed in a biography. Edwin Steinbrecher quotes Streisand to a mutual friend for 05:08 as being from her birth certificate. RR: AA.

Donna Summer: 31 December 1948, 21:00 EST (+5), Boston, Massachusetts, USA (42n21, 71w03). Source: Birth certificate obtained by Frank Clifford, copy on file. RR: AA.

Peter Sutcliffe: 2 June 1946, 20:30 GDT (-1), Bingley, England (53n51, 1w50). Source: Victoria Shaw quotes the biography *Somebody's Husband, Somebody's Son* by Gordon Burn (Heinemann, 1984), p.12. RR: B.

Sharon Tate: 24 January 1943, 17:47 CWT (+5), Dallas, Texas, USA (32n47, 96w49). Source: Birth certificate quoted in *The Gauquelin Book of American Charts* by Michel and Françoise Gauquelin (ACS, 1982), and *Contemporary American Horoscopes* by Janice McKay and Jessica Saunders (Astrolabe, 1990). RR: AA.

Elizabeth Taylor: 27 February 1932, 02:30 GMT (+0), Golders Green, London, England (51n34, 00w12). Source: Birth report, obtained by Sy Scholfield, copy on file. (Taylor gave 02:00 to Bob Prince; same from her mother in her autobiography.) RR: B.

Denis Thatcher: 10 May 1915, Lewisham, London, England (51n27, 0w01). Source: Biography, *Below the Parapet* by his daughter, Carol Thatcher (Chivers, 1997), p.30. (Dennis Thatcher). RR: X.

Margaret Thatcher: 13 October 1925, 09:00 GMT (+0), Grantham, England (52n55, 00w39). Source: From her private secretary to Charles Harvey. RR: A.

Thatcher Assisi Quote: 4 May 1979, 16:09 GDT (-1), Westminster, England (51n30, 0w09). Source: From The Margaret Thatcher Archive, www.margaretthatcher. org/document/104078 Time given as '1608'. The quote was spoken one minute into the interview. RR: A.

Grant Tinker: 11 January 1926, Stamford, Connecticut, USA (41n03, 73w32). Source: Sy Scholfield quotes media profile 'Tinker Known for Giving Producers a Free Hand', *The New York Times*, 1 July 1981, p.C23, but notes that other references give 17 January or 1925. RR: X.

Linda Tripp: 24 November 1949, 08:00 CST (+5), Jersey City, New Jersey, USA (40n43, 74w04). Source: Birth certificate given to Lois Rodden. RR: AA.

Donald Trump: 14 June 1946, 10:54 EDT (+4), Queens, New York, USA (40n43, 73w52). Source: Birth certificate, released by Trump to the media in 2011; same on his hospital card, copies on file. RR: AA.

Ted Turner: 19 November 1938, 08:50 EST (+5), Cincinnati, Ohio, USA (39n10, 84w27). Source: Birth certificate obtained by Frank Clifford, copy on file. RR: AA.

Tina Turner: 26 November 1939, 22:10 CST (+6), Nutbush, Tennessee, USA (35n42, 89w24). Source: Note from birth registry obtained by Frank Clifford, copy on file. RR: AA.

US Presidential Inauguration (First): 30 April 1789, around 12:45 LMT (+4:56:04), Wall Street, New York, USA (40n42, 74w01). Source: *The Book of World Horoscopes* by Nicholas Campion quotes *New York Daily Gazette* and *New York Daily Advertiser*, both 1 May 1789. RR: B.

Roger Vadim: 26 January 1928, 21:00 GMT (+0), Paris, France (48n52, 2e20). Source: Birth certificate obtained by Didier Geslain. Vadim's autobiography *Memoirs of the Devil* (Harcourt Brace Jovanovich, 1977), p.6, gives 'ten o'clock in the evening'. RR: AA.

Dick Van Dyke: 13 December 1925, West Plains, Missouri, USA (36n44, 91w51). Source: Various biographies. RR: X.

Neale Donald Walsch: 10 September 1943, 04:19 CWT (+5), Milwaukee, Wisconsin, USA (43n02, 87w54). Source: Birth certificate information obtained by Stephen Przybylowski. RR: AA.

Shayne Ward: 16 October 1984, 21:34 GDT (-1), Tameside, Ashton-under-Lyne, England (53n29, 2w06). Source: Birth certificate obtained by Frank Clifford, copy on file (a twin). RR: AA.

Andy Warhol: 6 August 1928, 06:30 EDT (+4), Pittsburgh, Pennsylvania, USA (40n26, 80w00). Source: The book, *Famous For Fifteen Minutes: My Years with Andy Warhol*, by Ultraviolet (Isabelle Dufresne) (Avon, 1990), includes a photo of the birth certificate (Andrew Warhola, filed in 1945, no time), and the unsourced claim, p. 38, 'little Andy is born at

6:30 a.m., as the day takes over from the night'. RR: B.

Diane Warren: 7 September 1956, 08:24 PDT (+7), Encino, California, USA (34n10, 118w30). Source: Birth certificate obtained by Frank Clifford, copy on file. RR: AA.

Dionne Warwick: 12 December 1940, 15:08 EST (+5), Orange, New Jersey, USA (40n46, 74w13). Source: Birth certificate details quoted in *The Gauquelin Book of American Charts* by Michel and Françoise Gauquelin (ACS, 1982). RR: AA.

Jeanne Weber: 7 October 1874, 11:00 LMT (+0:11), Kerity (Saint-Brieuc), France (48n31, 2w45). Source: Birth certificate obtained by Sy Scholfield, copy on file. Same in *Murderers and Psychotics* by Michel Gauquelin (Laboratoire d'Etude des Relations entre Rythmes Cosmiques et Psychophysiologiques, 1981). RR: AA.

Dr Ruth Westheimer: 4 June 1928, 04:00 MET (-1), Frankfurt am Main, Germany (50n07, 8e40). Source: From her to Evelyn Herbertz in 1985. RR: A.

Barry White: 12 September 1944, 16:42 CWT (+5), Galveston, Texas, USA (29n18, 94w48). Source: Birth certificate obtained by Frank Clifford, copy on file. RR: AA.

Oscar Wilde: 16 October 1854, 03:00 LMT (+0:25:00), Dublin, Ireland (53n20, 6w15). Source: Baptismal certificate quoted by Cyril Fagan. RR: AA.

Mary Wilson: 6 March 1944, 10:11 CWT (+5), Greenville, Mississippi, USA (33n25, 91w04). Source: Birth certificate quoted by Wilson to Lois Rodden in 1971. RR: AA.

Amy Winehouse: 14 September 1983, 22:25 GDT (-1), Enfield, London, England (51n40, 0w05). Source: From Winehouse's mother to a mutual friend of Margaret Zelinski. RR: A.

Louise Woodward: 24 February 1978, 03:00 GMT (+0), Elton, England (53n16, 2w49). Source: Monica Dimino quotes Louise's French teacher who had the data from Louise, time from her mother. RR: A.

Louise Woodward Verdict: 30 October 1997, 21:39 EST (+5), Cambridge, Massachusetts, USA (42n22, 71w06). Source: *Daily Mail*, 31 October 1997, p.1, copy on file. RR: A.

Tammy Wynette: 5 May 1942, 01:20 CWT (+5), on a farm in Itawamba County, north of Tremont, Mississippi, USA (34n14, 88w16). Source: Birth certificate information (which lists nearby Red Bay, a town in Alabama) obtained by Stephen Przybylowski, copy on file. (Chart has been calculated using Tremont's L&L.) RR: AA.

Will Young: 20 January 1979, 21:55 GMT (+0), Reading, England (51n28, 0w59). Source: Birth certificate obtained by Frank Clifford, copy on file (a twin). RR: AA.

Palmistry 4 Today

This acclaimed, fully illustrated textbook offers immediate access to the mysteries of the hand. In 4 easy-to-follow-steps, this innovative, fully revised and expanded edition presents: The Palm Detective; Timing Techniques; Love, Health and Career; and Palmistry in Action.

'An excellent book, well written and well illustrated, guaranteed to get the beginner hooked on palmistry from page 1; the practitioner could learn a lot from it too. Thoroughly recommended.' – *Prediction* magazine

'It's easy to read, packed with interesting information, beautifully presented and very well illustrated. It's honest and open, too, which I love the most… It's very modern and there are lots of really nice concepts here and much to learn.' – Lori Reid, leading palmist

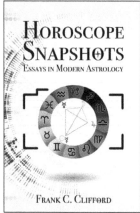

Horoscope Snapshots: Essays in Modern Astrology

In 18 engaging essays, discover: the deeper sides to your Sun sign; how your Sun, Moon and Ascendant differ; the real nature of Jupiter; parental significators; vocational indicators; and the role of Pluto in America.

'Entertaining as well as educational… Fascinating and fun to read.' – *Dell Horoscope*

'An informative, wide-ranging set of essays… The author is a very clear writer; his ability to create an immediate rapport with the reader draws one into reflective engagement right from the opening page.' – Anne Whitaker, *The Mountain Astrologer*

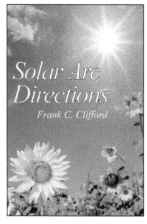

Solar Arc Directions

All you'll ever need to know about Solar Arc directions is packed inside this informative and popular manual, presented clearly and concisely. There are numerous examples and an introduction to Frank's work on Shadow Transits, an indispensable new method that connects directions to transits.
(Mini-book)

The Midheaven: Spotlight on Success

The Midheaven (MC) is associated with success, achievement and recognition. It has much to say about our reputation and public image, as well as early parental messages and ambitions. This absorbing volume offers many original insights from the author's years of research.
(Mini-book)

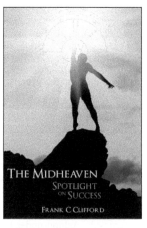

'Good things come in small packages… Clear and accessible for even newcomers to this method of forecasting.'

– Donna Van Toen, *NCGR Newsletter*

'This excellent punchy guide to the Midheaven cannot be bettered… A delicious concentrate of accessible astrology.'

– Victor Olliver, *The Astrological Journal*

www.frankclifford.co.uk

Two international astrologers examine (in four new essays): potential traps for the counselling astrologer; Mercury in consultation; the transformational potential of astrology; and the tools to use when preparing for a chart analysis.
(Mini-book)

This sparkling and entertaining guide on your Mars and Venus signs – written by two top media astrologers – is packed with practical advice and astrological insights into your relationship needs, passions, turn-ons and turn-offs.
(Mini-book)

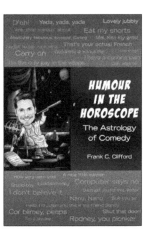

Which signs and planets link with which types of humour? With the help of numerous horoscopes, Frank Clifford has put together a unique volume of charts, observations and wicked one-liners that well and truly hit the astrological funny bone.
(Mini-book)

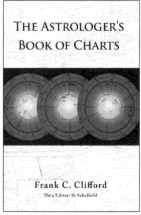

From Dolly to Dali, Nixon to Manson, George Galloway to Greta Garbo, Christine Keeler to Monica Lewinsky. 150 accurately timed and sourced horoscopes and worksheets. Includes new data. Charts presented in both Placidus and Equal.

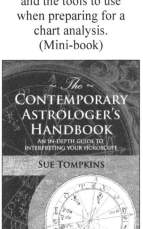

The author of *Aspects in Astrology* presents an authoritative guide to chart interpretation with an in-depth exploration of the planets, zodiac signs, houses and aspects. Included are biographies and step-by-step instructions for synthesizing the main horoscope factors.

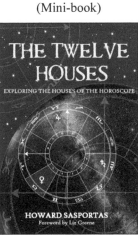

From an award-winning psychological astrologer comes the definitive book on the astrological houses. This edition of the best-selling handbook remains a firm favourite among students and professionals. With a new foreword by Dr. Liz Greene and tribute essays from astrologers.

Faye Blake (formerly Faye Cossar) shows how to create a vocational profile, which enables you and your clients to: identify talents, blocks and style; create a CV, website and logo; define goals and awaken life purpose and passion.

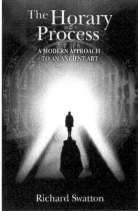

A clear guide to learning the craft of horary astrology and preparing for judgment. Sections include: horary as a magical art; the divinatory attitude; signification and rulership; the art of timing; and how to use horary methods on natal charts.

About Frank Clifford • www.frankclifford.co.uk

Data Collector: An astrologer and palmist since 1989, Frank Clifford began data collecting with Lois Rodden, contributing to and editing her magazine *Data News* and book *Profiles of Women* (1995). Frank's first book, *British Entertainers: The Astrological Profiles*, was published in 1997 and updated in 2003. Frank's database of celebrity data is on the Solar Fire program as *The Clifford Data Compendium* (1997, 2000) and on Astro-Databank, which he named. In 2009, he produced *The Astrologer's Book of Charts*, an eclectic collection of 150 horoscopes and worksheets of the famous for students and astrologers.

Publisher: Back in 1996 Frank founded Flare Publications, and since then he has edited/published two dozen books on astrology and palmistry, including *Astrology in the Year Zero*, *The Contemporary Astrologer's Handbook*, a revised edition of *The Twelve Houses* and many of his own titles (including *Horoscope Snapshots: Essays in Modern Astrology*). In 2010, Flare went into partnership with Faber to release its ebooks. Flare has also been instrumental in bringing astrology books and authors to the Chinese market.

Media Astrologer: Over the years, Frank's media work has ranged from the sublime to the ridiculous – from being interviewed for documentaries about the BBC comedy *Little Britain* and Danny Boyle's feature film *Sunshine*, guesting on Radio 4's *The Inconstant Moon* with Jeanette Winterson, and working with the Oxford University Press and Universal Studios... to being asked by *The Sun* to locate a then-missing Saddam Hussein! Frank has also combined his work as a consultant astrologer with that of Sun sign columnist for magazines such as *Marie Claire* (UK), *Quick and Simple* (Hearst, US), the celebrity weekly *Reveal* (UK) for three years, and the family monthly *Candis* for twelve years (UK). He has also been profiled in various broadsheets and tabloids, and has been featured regularly on TV and radio. For many years, Frank wrote columns in *The Astrological Journal* and the *ISAR Journal*, and continues to write for *The Mountain Astrologer*. In 2013, Frank became TMA's first guest editor and has since edited half a dozen issues (including issues on interpretation, forecasting and music).

Palmist: Frank is also a well known palmist and consultant (with *The Guardian* newspaper dubbing him the 'palm reader to the stars'), and his book *Palmistry 4 Today* (published in five languages) is considered *the* modern textbook on the subject. Frank's other book on palmistry, *Palm Reading* (Hamlyn, 2003, Flare new edition 2018), is a unique guide with profiles on love, work and personality for each part of the hand. Cards of these profiles were published in 2007. Most years Frank organizes the Palmistry Conference in London, which brings together some of the top hand analysts in the country.

Teacher: Back in 2004, Frank bought and began running the popular London School of Astrology (www. londonschoolofastrology.co.uk) and continues to organize certificate and diploma classes, seminars and residential courses in astrology and palmistry. Considered *the* students' choice for studying astrology in the UK, the LSA prides itself on hosting seminars and classes by some of the world's most accomplished astrologers. Frank has also set up an annual Astrology Student Conference (www.astroconference.com). He has given seminars and talks for many UK groups and schools (including the Centre for Psychological Astrology) and for NCGR groups in the US. Frank has also lectured in twelve countries (across Europe, Asia, Australia and the US), given keynote lectures at most international astrology conferences, and for some years was a regular guest tutor on a psychology course at the London Metropolitan University. He made his first trip to China in December 2012, where the press dubbed him 'the Dean of the Harry Potter School', and lectured at the Science Museum in Shenzhen. He returned in 2016 to speak for a bank as well as a business school at Guangzhou's prestigious university.

In 2012, Frank was honoured by his peers with The Charles Harvey Award for Exceptional Service to Astrology. In 2016, the ISAR membership voted his work on the power degrees of the zodiac 'Best Article 2014–2016' at their conference in Los Angeles. In recent years, Frank has written shorter volumes on specific astrological subjects: *Solar Arc Directions*, *The Midheaven: Spotlight on Success*, *Humour in the Horoscope: The Astrology of Comedy* and *Dialogues: Tools for the Working Astrologer*. The year 2018 sees the publication of a new textbook, *Birth Charts*, for students and teachers, new online courses with the LSA, and a lecture tour returning to Mexico, China and Australia.

The London School of Astrology

– the students' choice in contemporary astrological education –

• Accredited Foundation courses for beginners in central London
• Accredited Diploma courses for those with more experience
• Saturday seminars, summer school courses and other events
• Short courses in tarot and palmistry (modern hand analysis)
• A distance learning course in palmistry

• New online astrology courses for all levels

Learn astrology, palmistry and tarot in a fun, supportive environment
with the UK's most experienced astrologers/tutors

To find out more
Visit our website **www.londonschoolofastrology.co.uk**
Email: admin@londonschoolofastrology.co.uk

London School of Astrology
Postal address: BCM Planets, London WC1N 3XX

Telephone: 020 8402 7772

Self-knowledge, spiritual development, vocational training

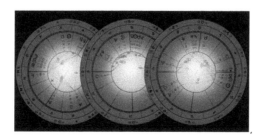

Lightning Source UK Ltd.
Milton Keynes UK
UKHW03f0815180618
324247UK00005B/232/P